Lighting Technology

A Guide for Television, Film and Theatre

Second Edition

Brian Fitt
and
Joe Thornley

Focal Press

OXFORD   AUCKLAND   BOSTON   JOHANNESBURG   MELBOURNE   NEW DELHI

Focal Press
An imprint of Butterworth-Heinemann
Linacre House, Jordan Hill, Oxford OX2 8DP
225 Wildwood Avenue, Woburn, MA 01801-2041
A division of Reed Educational and Professional Publishing Ltd

A member of the Reed Elsevier plc group

First published 1997
Reprinted 1998
Second edition published 2002
Transferred to digital printing 2004
© Brian Fitt and Joe Thornley 2002

British Library Cataloguing in Publication Data
A catalogue record for this book is available from the
British Library

Library of Congress Cataloguing in Publication Data
A catalogue record for this book is available from the
Library of Congress

ISBN 0 240 51651 6

For information on all Focal Press publications visit
our website at: www.focalpress.com

Contents

Acknowledgements

BBC
British Standards
Commission Internationale de L'Éclairage
DeSisti (UK) Ltd
Electronic Theatre Controls (Europe)
Fuji Photo Film Co. Ltd
GE Lighting
Health and Safety Commission
High End Systems
Minolta (UK) Ltd
Osram
Philips Lighting
Power Gems Limited
The Institution of Electrical Engineers

1
Introduction

Every year we all hope there will be a wonderful new light source but tungsten and discharge still dominate the lighting industry. To aid the production of a higher light output from luminaires, lamp manufacturers have made some progress by producing tungsten lamps with more compact filaments and discharge lamps with shorter arcs. This allows the concentration of the light output by utilising the optics more efficiently. There are hints of important progress in the production of light from Light Emitting Diodes with suggested outputs of around 100 lumens/W. One tremendous advantage of LEDs is that the majority of their output is in the visible spectrum, thus avoiding the generation of ultraviolet (UV) and infrared. At this stage, it is difficult to envisage devices such as these being used in conventional luminaires.

Since the previous edition, the most significant advances have been in the motorised light sector. To overcome the restricted range of projected patterns and colours, the manufacturers of moving lights are looking to computer generated images coupled with digital projection. This enables real time programming of the luminaire output with an almost unlimited pattern and colour range. The main problem is obtaining a high enough light output to blend with existing lighting arrangements. At present, most digital projection is aimed at audio-visual presentations and cinema projection, where the screen brightness is of a fairly low order.

Fluorescent lighting, which was introduced on a fairly large scale as an aid to producing more efficient lighting, has now settled down as a soft source. It is now generally used with small tungsten and discharge sources in hybrid studios, such as news and talking head areas, to create comfortable working conditions.

New dimmers have been introduced which have moved away from thyristor technology to provide a sine wave output (almost)! This enables a controlled switching of the output waveform, thus avoiding the use of chokes to smooth the output, which has the advantage of reducing some of the problems with mains borne interference and lamp sing but most significantly, lowers the weight of the dimmer. Manufacturers are now integrating dimmers into the suspension system, with control by DMX loops.

Control systems have become increasingly sophisticated due to the need to control large numbers of moving lights. DMX512 appears to have been adopted as the standard form of control signal.

As a result of more stringent budgets, particularly in television (TV), equipment is not being replaced as frequently as it used to be. Most of the impetus for change is either caused by a safety problem or the need to introduce the latest 'gizmo'.

We hope you will find the new streamlined edition as informative as the old one.

2
Lighting the subject

From the time when the Savoy Theatre, London, was first lit by electricity in 1881, the instruments used for artificial lighting have developed from very crude flood sources to the sophisticated moving light sources of today.

Early light sources were generally floodlights with little or no finesse. As taste became more refined, so did the lighting. The majority of lighting is placed at a reasonable height above the acting area. The reasons for this are quite simply that we do not wish the acting area to be full of equipment. This holds true for most lighting equipment, but in a TV or film studio the floor is also cluttered with cameras and booms, etc. As members of the human race we are conditioned that light is above us and at an average of about 45° to any standing object on earth. This fact lays down the most important ground rule for the artificial lighting of any scene. Artists throughout the ages have appreciated the light sources available to them. The sun provides a wonderful key light with warm rich colours and the blue sky provides a softlight of cool brilliance.

The subject may be either a performer or a static object and the lights have to be positioned and controlled to give the desired effect. Sometimes, compromise is necessary due to the position of scenery, cloths, and other objects which may give rise to unwanted shadows. The choice of luminaires for the lighting designer is extremely wide and varied, but all will have their particular favourites because they know that they can produce acceptable and repeatable results from some of the devices used in the past. Lighting designers these days can use lights from another branch of the industry to give some effects that were previously unobtainable.

To the untrained eye, lighting, either in the theatre, TV studio, on a film set or in a huge 'Pop rig' looks somewhat similar. However, closer inspection reveals that the luminaires used in the theatre are somewhat different to those used for film and TV and these days will probably have more in common with the 'Pop' industry. We find that stage lighting designers now use Parcans together with automated luminaires using tungsten and discharge sources. Many of the luminaires used on stage and for that matter in the pop world are now being used more and more in TV.

In our everyday lives as human beings, we go around in illumination that can vary from the minimum amount on a moonlight night to a maximum of an overhead sun in the Sahara desert. Other than a psychological difference, we are not disturbed by the differences between gloomy, grey overcast days and the intense blue skies of winter when the atmosphere is at its clearest. Visually, we are not worried by a lack of shadow detail, and on other occasions we see no problems with the intense black shadows created by sunlight. We do become disturbed however, by green light applied to the human skin, we also become rather unnerved by lighting when it comes from below subjects and not from above. In our everyday lives we are conditioned by the most basic form of lighting which consists of a reasonably well balanced mixture of sunlight and light from the blue sky.

In the absence of light from the sky, such as on the moon, we see extremely contrasting pictures due to one light source only, namely the sun. We feel much better when we are bathed in warm sunlight and not standing in the cool of a grey day. Some of this is caused by the generation of vitamins by sunlight, but mostly it is psychological. It is interesting to note that we also feel better on a sunny day in the middle of a cold winter. Red and yellow give us a cosy feeling, and this is probably occasioned by our mental stimulation with the association of the sun. It's a strange fact that as colour temperature increases towards the blue end of the spectrum, we do not necessarily feel warmer and we actually associate blue with cool conditions. Green has a refreshing quality, which is probably occasioned by the response of the eye which is at its peak with the green portion of the spectrum. We view black as a very sombre colour and associate it with the macabre. We generally associate white with coolness and a feeling of something that is quite unspoilt; it's interesting to note how disturbed we are by snow when it has become muddied, as the thaw sets in. From this short list of examples, it must become obvious that we can associate colours with a sense of stimulation of appreciation within the viewed scene, and many of the effects used in artificial lighting are based upon these feelings.

Light in its most basic form, daylight, consists of a mixture of sunlight and skylight. These can be analysed as the sun which provides extremely hard light that gives well defined shadows and a sense of depth; and the sky which gives very soft diffused lighting without any obvious shadows. The reasons that the light behaves in different ways is that the sun is a very small source in comparison to the subjects it illuminates, hence it produces the hard shadows, whereas the sky is an extremely large source in area and thus produces almost shadowless lighting. Note the term *almost* because *no* lighting is shadowless and if an object blocks some of the light rays it will produce a shadow, however diffuse!

'Soft' or 'hard' is a relative term. For instance, a softlight can give reasonably hard shadows, whereas a larger softlight positioned at the same distance, will produce a softer shadow. Conversely, a Fresnel lens luminaire with a brushed silk diffuser fitted can give quite a soft result when used close to the subject.

It must be remembered that both 'hard' and 'soft' light have the same physical properties. 'Hard' light consists of light rays going in straight lines from a very small source to the subject, whereas 'soft' light consists of the same light rays emerging from a larger source area going to the subject in straight lines from a variety of angles (see Chapter 6, Figure 6.18).

An important factor in the use of softlights, which is often forgotten, is that they have two planes of illumination, the horizontal and vertical. As the width of the softlight becomes greater, so the vertical shadows become more diffuse. When the height of the softlight is increased the horizontal shadows become more diffuse. Obviously, there is a finite size to softlights, but the most effective for many subjects are those that are reasonably wide in relation to their height.

We hear the term the 'quality of light' – all light is essentially the same, except for the colour. However, when we look at light from a carbon arc it appears to have a very hard, sharp, focused quality, whereas subjects lit by fluorescent lighting have a much softer look. The difference, on the surface, between a 150 A carbon arc with a Fresnel lens, and a 4 kW HMI with a Fresnel lens, is very slight. In practice the HMI appears to be a softer quality. These observations generally apply to hard light, whereas when we examine soft light, irrespective of the source, the results are always somewhat similar.

What constitutes good or bad lighting is very much the opinion of the observer, but there are certain ground rules which can define the quality of lighting as perceived by the viewer of the scene. A good example of bad lighting, when shooting film and TV material, is the incorrect colour of the light sources or choosing the wrong colour correction. The balance between modelling lights and fill lights has to be closely controlled or it may give problems with contrast and exposure and as well as creating 'grainy' or 'noisy' pictures. Highly saturated colours when used for TV give a very overpowering result due to the size of the screen image. Extremely steep lighting from above a person will give very distorted features on the face and for that matter if the lighting is from beneath (see Figure 2.1a and b). It is essential for film and TV to have a good contrast range within the scene to avoid a flat result. This is not to say that lighting has to obey a

(a)

(b)

Figure 2.1 (a) Underlit; (b) Steep lighting

fixed set of rather boring rules but the choice of light sources, colour and special effects has to be carefully thought out and balanced against what is stimulating and what is annoying. The very best lighting for film and TV will be largely unnoticed by the viewer and, if this is the case, the lighting designers' aims will have been achieved.

Most of the lighting conventions used in the film and TV industry emerged from the earlier days of film when all the material was shot in black and white. It was obviously extremely important to give a sense of depth to pictures and when one sees some of the original extremely old movies that were made without the use of enhanced artificial light, and shot purely by daylight, the results are somewhat flat and uninteresting. During the late 1920s and early 1930s increasing use was made of high powered light sources in the film industry and these enabled the lighting cameramen to achieve better results than previously. Hollywood discovered that a key light placed at the correct angle could enhance the artist greatly. Thus we had 'Paramount' lighting where a hard key light was fairly low and straight onto the face, which enhanced the beauty of ladies with high cheekbones, Marlene Deitrich being one supreme example. The film makers also learnt from portrait painters and noted that a more interesting result could be given when the key light was not straight to the face, but taken to the side and thus had a type of lighting known as 'Rembrandt' portraiture. Probably the pinnacle of black and white film lighting is that of *Citizen Kane*, with its highly dramatic portraiture and extremely imaginative use of shadows and highlights. The advent of colour film, with its lower contrast range meant that the lighting cameramen had to control the lights to a narrower band of illumination, using colour more imaginatively to obtain contrast.

Whereas the theatre and the concert arena have to be lit for the entire viewed scene, the film and TV industry is lit 'piecemeal'. Television studios will often record material using several cameras which will require the scene being lit as a whole. Traditionally, the film industry has shot scenes using one camera position at any one time, therefore the lighting is only adjusted for that camera position. When the camera position is moved, the lighting is re-adjusted to suit the new position. This has two distinct advantages, one of which – you only need one camera and secondly – not too many lights. This technique is also used in TV these days, particularly on location. A problem that exists with this technique is that continuity has to be watched very carefully, thus sunlight, if not accurately noted, could vary in its direction within a room. Obviously, this is much more applicable to drama than it would be to, say, musicals which would have to be lit in their entirety, irrespective of the varying camera positions. Close-ups in TV and film means that there is a need for better lighting on the artists and parts of the setting. The mere fact that the close-up can dwell on an area for quite considerable periods of time, necessitates a greater attention to detail.

2.1 Basic lighting

We have to remember that luminaires work in three dimensional space, they can move in two directions in the horizontal plane and be adjusted vertically. Additionally, we are concerned with the direction of light, the texture of light, the colour of light and the intensity of light.

Whereas lighting for the theatre and a pop concert relies upon the skill of a Lighting designer visually balancing the intensity of light and colour, in the film and TV industry there is a requirement to achieve certain light levels, and an understanding of the problems with the factors that have an influence on incident light, is useful subject matter for this book. The floodlighting fraternity use horizontal plane measurements for their lighting. In the film and TV industry, we are concerned with vertical planes such as actors and sets. In general, most people know that light falls off with the square of the distance, however, many people are unaware that the angle of the incident light falling on the subject also has an effect on the light level which consequently influences the reflected light which stimulates our eye, the film stock and the CCDs in the TV camera.

Light in the vertical plane

Most measurements assume that the light is directly on axis and that, at a set distance from the source, the incident light level will be I/d^2. In the examples that follow, it will be seen that the angle of incidence (Cosine law) also affects the light level.

Figure 2.2 Incident light

Figure 2.3 Lighting the subject: light in the vertical plane

Table 2.1

Horizontal distance (metres)	2.0	3.0	4.0	5.0
Throw in metres	2.97	3.72	4.57	5.46
$\cos \theta$	0.68	0.81	0.88	0.91
Uncorrected light level	2834	1806	1197	839
Corrected light level	1927	1462	1053	763

It will be noted that the differences in light level and incident angles are not very great except when close to the luminaire e.g. 2 and 3 m.

$$\text{Throw } (T) = \sqrt{[d^2 + (H - x \text{ or } y)^2]}$$

where: d is the horizontal distance in metres
　　　　H is the height of the luminaire above floor level
　　　　x or y is the subject height (1.3 m seated and 1.8 m standing)

$$\text{Cosine } \theta = \frac{d}{T}$$

Incident light level is given by:

$$\frac{I \text{ (candelas)}}{\text{Throw}^2 \ (T^2)} \times \frac{\text{distance } (d)}{\text{Throw } (T)} = \frac{Id}{T^3}$$

Basic lighting has very similar fundamental requirements, and the main forms of illumination used are as follows (see Figure 2.4).

Key light

Why is it called the key? The luminaire used provides the principal light on the scene and tends to be the key to the whole picture. It establishes the mood and character and generally is capable of producing acceptable results when used on its own. However, it makes no contribution towards the depth of the picture. Key lights for film and TV tend to be used at a vertical angle of 30° to the subject but can be within the range of 20°–45°, although the lower angle can produce disturbing glare to the actors. The key light can be used over a horizontal angle of incidence within 45° either side of the normal to the subject. As a general rule 30° vertical and 30° horizontal displacement gives extremely satisfactory results for visual close-ups.

Back light

A back light is needed so that separation and depth are enhanced. The positioning of back lights is extremely critical and they should not be placed too steeply in the vertical plane because they may spill over onto the subject's face and create rather disturbing effects. Back lights can be varied much more than a key light for their angle of incidence and in fact many good effects are produced by taking them to extremes. The back light is usually around half the power of the key light, but if increased gives a much more dramatic effect. Single back lights can be effective on the subject but quite often twin back lights are to be advocated for any subject with long hair.

Fill light

Why do we require fill light? When viewed with the eye, a subject lit with a key and back light will look perfectly all right, however, due to the restrictive contrast ranges used for film and TV, the results would look somewhat over-contrasted when viewed either on the cinema screen or the TV screen; therefore fill light is used to reduce the contrast by diminishing the shadow areas. As a guide, the lighting level of the fill light is about 50% of that of the key. One point that should be noted is that having made a shadow with one light, there is no way that the shadow can be

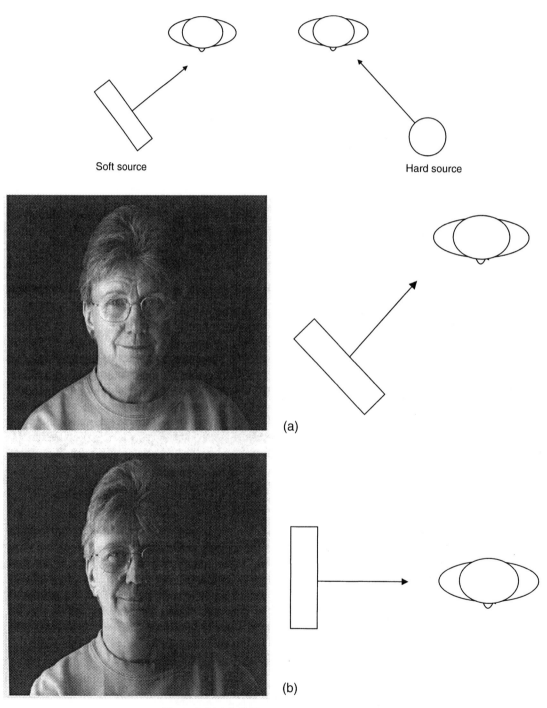

Figure 2.4 (a) Soft fill at 45°; (b) Soft fill from side

(c)

(d)

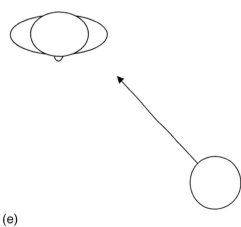

(e)

Figure 2.4 *Continued* (c) Hard fill from side; (d) Twin back lights; (e) Keylight only

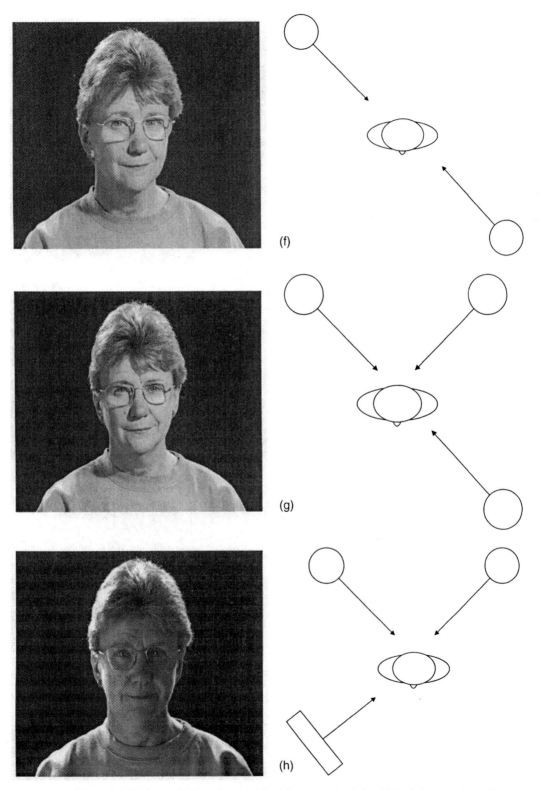

Figure 2.4 *Continued* (f) Cross keys; (g) Back lights and keylight; (h) Back lights and soft fill

Figure 2.4 *Continued* (i) Final lighting

removed or diminished to any great degree by the addition of more and more fill light. Fill light is often a soft source because we are used to the sky being our fill light. However, if we use hard light in a controlled manner, which is a technique used by lighting designers, then we can still achieve a pleasing result. Whereas, in the theatre and at a concert, double shadows might not be quite so apparent on the human face, they are extremely apparent in close-up in the film and TV media.

2.2   Choice of light sources and luminaires

Due to the merging of techniques throughout the lighting industry, it is very difficult to decide what type of source would be used in any one particular branch of the industry. However, we can generalise and say that in the film and TV industries, Fresnel lens luminaires using both tungsten and discharge sources predominate. High efficiency PAR discharge sources are being used in both the TV and film industries. Television studios favour tungsten as the predominant source, as it is easy to control and produces extremely good lighting effects; whereas film and outside broadcasts are very big users of discharge lighting. More recently 'low energy' lighting has been introduced into smaller studios, in the form of fluorescent lighting. Although not giving such strong subject modelling, as the more focused sources would, it does allow control of output light level by dimmers with consistently good colour and with less heat.

All lighting requires to be fairly accurately positioned to give the correct effect that the lighting designer desires. The height of the lights is important in relation to the horizontal distance to the subject. In film and TV, flexibility in height and in the xy axis, along and across the studio, is given by the various types of suspension systems on offer. With fixed suspension systems such as a TV studio grid, or truss members in a rig, movement is generally achieved by pan and tilt, horizontal and vertical movement being very restricted. It is of course possible to provide local flexible suspension such as pantographs, which allow adjustment in the vertical plane. In TV and film, the size of the luminaires prevents close proximity working and the type of suspension systems often do not allow precise positioning in the horizontal plane. This is often circumvented by using cross bars, enabling lights to be positioned in a more precise way but often with a penalty of tying up two suspension points.

If we look in lighting manufacturers' catalogues, we will see a variety of soft sources on offer, and these go from fairly large to small luminaires. Therefore, it would appear that the larger ones are softer than the smaller ones, and this of course is true if they are set from the subject at the same distance. However, the small soft near to the subject may provide a softer result than the larger one, at say, twice the distance. This is due to the apparent area of soft light at the distance, due to perspective, and of course, the same effect applies to hard sources. It should always be remembered that a softlight looked at full on, presents a large area source, but when viewed from the side, presents a very small source and this has often been the undoing of many a lighting designer in the TV industry. It's a wonderful way of producing unwanted microphone boom shadows!

In TV and film, because of the need for broad lighting techniques, luminaires with much softer edges are employed, therefore the Fresnel spotlight becomes more useful with its soft edge to the light beam which allows an integration of light sources for a much smoother result. In the film studio, a 2 kW Fresnel is a relatively low powered luminaire, 5 kW and 10 kW tungsten luminaires are more the norm. The need of the film industry for extremely high light levels, particularly when colour was introduced with the old Technicolor process, etc. necessitated high intensity carbon arc sources, culminating in huge things like the 'Brute' with a power of 225 A. The arcs were often used on location to balance the shadow areas in scenes lit by sunlight. The carbon arc was superseded by discharge luminaires using HMI and MSR lamps and there is much to commend these lighting sources, they provide a very high quality light output which is about four times greater than their tungsten counterparts. Unfortunately, they can only be dimmed to 50%, and thus do not allow for complex lighting effects changes.

In TV and film studios, the workhorse of the lighting director is the focusing Fresnel spot, whereas the same Lighting Director (LD) working outside on an OB or interview situation, will often use open faced luminaires. Normally, an LD who is given the choice will choose to work with the Fresnel spot because it offers many advantages over the open faced luminaire with a focal range from a 10° beam angle at spot to a 60° beam angle at full flood and a light output range of about 8:1. The light is very evenly distributed without striations in the beam and the barndoors provide a good soft edge cut off. The Fresnel luminaire, however, is most inefficient as a source with an efficiency of around 8% in spot and 26% in flood. When used in studios the lighting level from tungsten sources is quite acceptable because the cameras can be set to work at a much lower lighting level than is often possible on location where work is carried out in daylight and requires the artificial lighting to blend in with the high level of the ambient daylight and to match the same colour temperature. Interior shots on locations may be lit with either tungsten or discharge lighting and it may be necessary to work with daylight coming through the windows. When using tungsten, this problem can be solved by either placing an orange filter on the windows and balance for 3200 K, or balance for 5600 K and use a blue daylight correction filter in front of the luminaire which unfortunately reduces the light output to about 27% at the very time that a high output is required to try to match the daylight intensity. Another solution is to use discharge lighting which offers a high light level, blends exceptionally well with daylight and is cooler in operation, but is more expensive than tungsten and requires a control ballast.

The focusing open-faced luminaire, such as a 2 kW Blonde, has a much better efficiency than the Fresnel with up to five times more light in the spot mode; and nearly twice as much when in 'flood' compared to a 2 kW Fresnel. This variation in efficiency is due to the fact that in the 'spot' mode the lamp is relatively close to the reflector and the stray light is much reduced compared to the flood position. Redheads and Blondes are small, light and relatively inexpensive but the trade-off is a hard shadow produced from the direct light of the lamps' filament, with a second shadow produced from the reflector which is superimposed over the first shadow, giving harsh shadows. Light spill can be a problem and the barndoors are not very effective. The typical focusing range for a Blonde is from a beam angle of 23° in spot to a beam angle of 70° in flood with a light output range of 8:1. The Redhead goes from 42° in spot to 86° in flood with an output range of 6:1.

The profile spotlight enables precise control of the beam, the size of which is controlled by an iris diaphragm. Profile spots are also fitted with metal shutters for producing hard flat edges to the beam, and special shapes can be introduced into the projector gate of a profile spot. The edge of the light beam can be made either fairly soft or very hard by adjusting the lens. Many modern profile spots in use have zoom optics which allow a great deal of flexibility when rigging and lighting in the areas concerned. The Parcan has a beam width dictated by the type of lamp used. With the correct choice of lamp and subsequently rotating the position of the lamp, it is possible to vary the beam shape quite successfully. It may also be advantageous to use a brushed silk filter in the luminaire to further modify the beam spread. Although the Parcan does not have the same flexibility as, say, a Fresnel spotlight or a profile spot, they do have advantages – they are cheap to purchase, fairly easy to maintain and allow a multiplicity of effects at not too high a cost.

Lighting in the film industry generally tends to be from the floor upwards. Because of the rehearse/shoot techniques of the film industry, a production is generally filmed shot by shot. To make more effective use of either studios or locations several scenes may be shot at the same time, but not necessarily in the order of the script and final print, and put together in the editing room. To make the lighting as flexible as possible, it is useful to have the luminaires mounted on adjustable stands which can be moved to new positions very quickly by the electricians on the set, rather than having the lights suspended from the ceiling which tends to be rather fixed and time consuming when changes are required. For the suspension of lighting units in film studios, the simplest form is to have a block and tackle with the capability of running along a steel RSJ mounted at roof level. Thus a single point suspension can be used which could be pulled across or along the studio. One drawback to this system is that to introduce any new light at any position often requires shifting other lights which causes further rigging problems. Another technique is to suspend long platforms with handrails either side, called 'boats', where several luminaires can be rigged on the rails and manipulated by electricians manually. Although access to the luminaires is obviously better, changing the position of the boats in the studio is a time consuming process, and probably only pays dividends when luminaires are set up for quite considerable periods of time on a major production.

Film lighting does not rely upon dimmers to balance the lights. Lighting intensity is adjusted by spotting and flooding luminaires, by the careful selection of the power output of luminaires and, if necessary, scrims and neutral density filters can be used to achieve technical balance. The main reason for this technique being used is that film stock is generally balanced for 3200 K or for 5600 K daylight. Although the film stock concerned will have some small latitude of colour response to the lights concerned, the film industry has always gone along with the fact that the lights should be relatively fixed in relation to the 3200 K or 5600 K standards. When filming, it is necessary that the majority of the luminaires will be either tungsten or discharge sources; if not, there will be a requirement to colour correct some of the various light sources. For many years, tungsten was the main source of most illumination in the film studios, with carbon arcs being used when higher power was required. Nowadays, discharge lighting is normally used, due to its greater efficiency and cooler operation.

2.3 Lighting systems

Television lighting, which evolved from film lighting, relied on the tried and tested methods used by the film makers for many years, and many of the original TV studios were, in fact, converted film studios. As TV became more and more sophisticated and the need for a greater productivity arose, the studios had to become more efficient with their output being raised so that the need for additional studios was avoided. During the 1960s it was possible that a day's filming would yield 2 minutes of finished material, whereas in TV the need was to produce 30 minutes from each day of production. The basic luminaires used in TV, after the Second World War, were the Fresnel spotlights in 1 kW, 2 kW, 5 kW and 10 kW versions together with a miscellany of softlights such as Scoops, Tenlites, Hewitt Banks, etc.

In Europe during the 1950s, tremendous strides were made in modernising TV studios; the greatest of these was the adoption of motorised rigging systems, such as the monopole and motorised barrel winch. This enabled a small team of electricians to service a studio rapidly and effectively and most important of all – safely. Subsequently the monopole system was generally employed where fairly accurate rigging was required, but not used on a saturated basis, working on the principle that lights could be moved to suit during the rigging periods. The solution reached by the BBC for monochrome TV during the 1960s, was to equip all its main production studios with motorised barrel winches utilising 2 kW Fresnel luminaires and Tenlites for soft sources.

The advent of colour saw a different technique evolve at the BBC. The single Fresnels and softlights were replaced with the multi-purpose luminaire which is a combination of a softlight and a hard light. This tends to be somewhat of a compromise as a soft source because of its small physical size and compact reflectors, but it was a fairly good Fresnel spotlight. By having the complete area covered with the multi-purpose units, a saturated lighting system was evolved where the need to rig and de-rig luminaires was avoided, and the BBC achieved extremely high productivity in its studios, based at that time on multi-camera shooting techniques. The multi-purpose luminaires were generally fitted with a twin 2.5 kW lamp in the Fresnel half and four 1250 W linear lamps in the soft half. This allowed the luminaires to be either in a 2.5 kW mode, or a 5 kW mode and enabled the operators to control the light level and colour temperature over various distances of 'throw' within the studio. A later development provided one filament at 1.25 kW with the other at 2.5 kW, thus enabling a range of one third, two thirds or full power, giving a much better control of light intensity within the limits of colour temperature, with the soft end of the luminaire fitted with 4 × 625 W lamps capable of being switched between 1.25 kW and 2.5 kW only.

With the spread of colour TV in the United Kindom experiments took place to ascertain the parameters that could be used to maintain good colour balance for the pictures, but allowing some form of control on the lighting itself, and it was found that a tolerance of 200 K either side of 3000 K was reasonable; thus the cameras were lined up for this colour of incident light. The light level requirement was given by the sensitivity of the colour cameras working between f2.8 and f4.0. The dimmers used in TV studios normally have a square law light output, which means that the square of the fader setting from 1 to 10 gives the percentage light output, i.e. level 6 = 36%. It is normal when commencing operations in the studio to align the channel controllers to position '7' which means that the dimmer would supply current to operate the lamp at 49% of its light output; its colour temperature at this point is approximately 3000 K. As we have an acceptable variation of ±200 K, it allows the fader lever to go down to '5' with a 25% light output and when faded up to 'full', to have 100% light output; thus we have 2 stops (4:1) variation in the light level. This system allows a wide variation in the intensity of light and allows a great deal of control so that we may balance the light sources. However, it requires that all luminaires are fed from dimmers; thus there is a need for large dimmer installations.

When using discharge lighting at 5600 K the tolerance is generally accepted to be ±400 K.

In both the film and TV industries, if the key light is between 30° and 45° in the vertical angle to the subject, the luminaires height above the studio floor will be dictated by the power output of any luminaire used and the intensity of light required on the subject; e.g. a low powered luminaire will be positioned closer to the subject and consequently will be lower in height to maintain the same incident angle. In TV this approximates to around 4 m above floor level. In the film studio it may be that the height above the floor is increased by using higher powered luminaires. In all branches of entertainment lighting the luminaire positions are greatly affected by their relationship to the scenery. On some occasions it will be impossible to get the preferred light source high enough and it may be necessary to use a smaller luminaire closer to the subject. On other occasions large pieces of scenery, as found on the opera stage or the double storey building on the film set, may force the luminaires to be unnaturally high, creating a requirement for much more powerful luminaires. Due to the decrease in lighting levels required in TV studios, we have seen the introduction of 3 kW lamps to replace 5 kW lamps in 5 kW luminaires with a light output in the same ratio as the kilowatts i.e. 5:3.

Generally in TV studios, there is no problem with large variations in light levels as they are well controlled within the studio area. On outside broadcasts, it is a vastly different situation where the light level may vary from almost nothing to light levels as high as 120 000 lux. There are occasions, however, where the controlled conditions of the studio and variations in light level of the outside world have to come together, and these are usually in studios where windows are provided to give a natural backing. Although neutral density filters can be used on the windows it will also be necessary to raise the interior light level so that there is some approximation to the incoming daylight. However, this usually results in some form of discomfort glare to the artists and the generation of heat, caused by the high light levels. In these cases, of course, one invariably resorts to discharge lighting with its much more efficient light output. An important factor when designing for studios such as this, is the direction of the light through the windows. It's rather unfortunate if you are facing south west in the northern hemisphere and getting the rays of the dying sun. One method that was used at the BBC to control the incident light from the outside world was to use Polaroid sheet applied to the windows, with a rotating Polaroid filter in front of the studio camera. The rotational Polaroid only caused a 50% reduction in the reflected light from the subject to camera. However, the combination of the rotating and fixed Polaroid allowed the windows to be controlled from 50% transmission down to virtually 0% transmission. With the addition of an electronic exposure sensing circuit it was possible to have the rotating Polaroid filter automatically adjust according to the incident daylight. This method is only useful if the window has small areas of glass, as Polaroid sheet is only obtainable in fairly small sizes. Incidentally, the luminaire employed as the frontal key was a 1.2 kW Fresnel spot discharge source in 'flood'.

Temporary TV studios overlooking sporting events may require several levels of lighting being used to match the daylight, and it may be that the daylight keylights are 4 kW Fresnel discharge sources in full spot to give sufficient light level, whereas the night time lighting may be down to quite small discharge sources such as the 575 W in full flood. The natural light will vary in relation to the artificial light; but by using a selection of luminaires with various power outputs and switching between them it is possible to balance for the incident daylight. Of course, it is possible to balance for the maximum incident light level and just let the background slowly diminish over a period of time but with presenters using prompters and the danger of a high glare factor it is preferable to adjust the lighting to create more comfortable conditions. As the natural light diminishes changes are made between the various sources and it is hoped that these go relatively unnoticed by the viewer.

When filming for slow motion, the camera has to operate at a high shutter speed so that when played back at normal speed it produces a slow motion replay. By increasing the frames per second rate means that every time the frame rate is doubled from normal, i.e. from 50 frames to 100, we would have to double the light level to produce the same exposure effect. High speed video and filming is required in industrial research applications. Frame rates may be anything from 1000 to 10 000 fps. When filming at rates of 1000 and 2000 frames, light levels of 120 000 lux are necessary and to put this in perspective normal sunlight level is around 130 000 lux. It is obviously possible to produce high light levels using many tungsten sources but this has a heating effect which does not help with experiments. The most efficient way of producing the very high light levels required is to use discharge lighting. Due to the fact that discharge lighting is approximately four times more efficient than tungsten, a 1 kW HMI unit will be 4 times brighter than a 1 kW tungsten unit. It is possible to increase the light output of a double ended HMI lamp by doubling the current through the lamp for a very short period of time, therefore a 4 kW HMI lamp can be boosted to 8 kW for periods up to 20 seconds, more than enough for usual high speed video cameras. The ballasts have to be flicker free to provide a steady light output at high shutter speeds.

Light sources and luminaires come in a variety of shapes and sizes and whether tungsten, discharge, fluorescent or any other type of lighting is used, the final result will depend upon the intensity, colour, quality of light and incident angle to the subject. Lights are only a means to an end and even the most modern lighting devices will not correct for bad lighting practices.

To put the whole subject in perspective a famous British lighting director once said of one of his colleagues 'that man could obtain good pictures using candles mounted in milk bottles '.

3
Theory of light

3.1 Electromagnetic spectrum

The narrow band of electromagnetic radiation which lies between UV and infrared with wavelengths from 0.0004 mm (400 nm) to 0.0007 mm (700 nm) is detectable by the human eye and is known as light (see Figure 3.1).

When an object is heated it radiates energy in the form of electromagnetic waves. These waves go from the radio wave end of the electromagnetic spectrum through the infrared, the visible, the UV, X-ray and gamma ray. Ultraviolet is invisible to human beings, but unfortunately, in significant amounts is extremely harmful. Infrared is also invisible and produces a sensation of heat, but fortunately with no adverse side effects. For most of the hot objects that we encounter on the planet earth the energy lies mainly in the infrared region. A cooker hot plate may show no visible signs of heat, but when a hand is held over it, it feels warm; we are experiencing infrared at about 500 K. When the hot plate is turned up and reaches 1000 K we see a slight glow coming from the element which is the onset of visible radiation. The plate also becomes noticeably hotter, showing

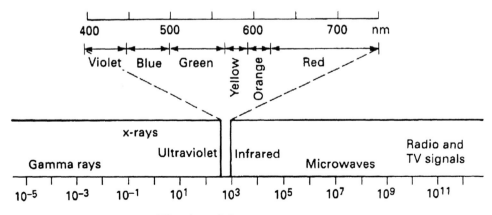

Wavelength in nanometres

Figure 3.1 Electromagnetic spectrum

that there is an increase in the amount of radiated energy. A good example of infrared radiation is that from the black luminaires that are used in the entertainment industry. There is no visible sign of heat from the body of the luminaire, although we get a nasty burn if we touch it.

The tungsten filament lamps radiate a white light around 3000 K. To produce UV radiation in significant amounts, temperatures of 3500 K and higher are required and most solid objects on earth melt by the time they reach this temperature. We generally produce temperatures around the 6000 K mark by mercury vapour lamps, such as fluorescents, xenons and HMI lamps and they all emit large amounts of UV radiation. When using discharge light sources, we have to be very much aware of the dangers connected with this type of illumination.

UV radiation

Description	Wavelength
UV – A	315–380 nm
UV – B	280–315 nm
UV – C	100–280 nm

Ultraviolet radiation covers the range 4–400 nm and it begins at the short wavelength limit of visibility (violet) and extends to X-rays. It is divided into near (400–300 nm), far (300–200 nm) and extreme (below 200 nm). The near UV energy is known generally as blacklight and often is used to excite fluorescent pigments used in dyes, paints and materials to produce effects for advertising and more importantly to us, in the theatre and sometimes on TV. The UV radiation in sunlight on the surface of the earth extends from about 320 nm to 390 nm and is generally our source of getting a suntan, with very long exposures causing cancer of the skin. Radiation between 300 nm and 390 nm is little absorbed by our bodies and therefore is not so active on human cells. Below 300 nm, UV becomes exceedingly dangerous to the human being. The radiation between 300 nm and 200 nm is well absorbed by the body, produces damage to cells and the effect is nearly always permanent. This is the reason we have to be so careful with discharge sources such as HMI and MSR.

For the purposes of this book, we are mainly concerned with the visible part of the spectrum and to a large extent the infrared. The visible gives us the light by which we can illuminate for the purposes of entertainment, the infrared gives us problems with heating and subsequently ventilation, which will be discussed later in the book.

3.2   F-number (f-stop)

The 'f-number' is the measurement of the *theoretical* amount of light that can pass through a lens. It is also colloquially known as the 'stop'. To obtain the f-number of a lens, the focal length is divided by the diameter of the aperture. Thus, a 50-mm lens which has an aperture 25 mm wide, will be an f2 lens. The following are typical f-stops found on lenses: f1, f1.4, f2, f2.8, f4, f5.6, f8, f11, f16, f22, f32.

Each of the above divisions is 'one stop'. The reciprocal of the square of the f-number, it gives the amount of light passing through the lens i.e. $1/stop^2$.

f-no	f-no^2	$\dfrac{1}{\text{f-no}^2}$	Transmission %
1	1	1	100.0
1.4	2	1/2	50.0
2	4	1/4	25.0
2.8	8	1/8	12.5
4	16	1/16	6.25
5.6	32	1/32	3.13
8	64	1/64	1.56
11	122	1/122	0.78
16	256	1/256	0.39
22	484	1/484	0.20
32	1024	1/1024	0.10
45	2048	1/2048	0.05

Note: The transmissions given are for perfect lenses and do not include optical loss.

3.3   The eye

A major problem with the human eye is that it can be fooled; it is not an absolute measuring instrument such as a colour meter, but relies mainly on comparative measurements to assess information (see Figure 3.2). If we show a human being, in a darkened room, a succession of similarly coloured lights with intervals of darkness between, the subject is totally unaware of a change over quite a wide range, e.g. from pale blue to a mid blue. However, two colours when shown side by side have only to vary by a small amount and the difference is noticeable. As we can process much visual information using our superior intelligence, the human eye does not have to be as good as that of many birds and animals.

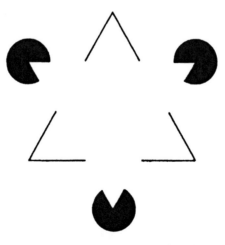

Figure 3.2 The figure has many possible triangles although no triangles have been drawn. The V shaped figures can be 'closed' by your brain to form one large triangle, or 'closed' opposite the apex to form three. The eye can use the portion of the V triangle 'undermeath' the large white one to close off three smaller white triangles with an apex in each circle. You can also see a six pointed star by combining the large white triangle and the one formed by the Vs. These illusory triangles are called *Kanizsa triangles* after Professor Gaetano Kanizsa of the University of Trieste who first introduced them (Kanizsa, 1976)

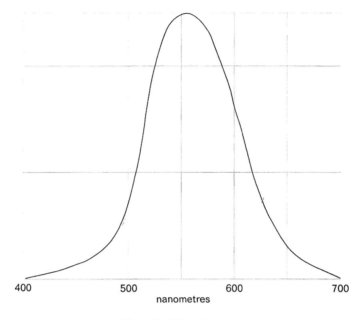

400   500   600   700
nanometres

Figure 3.3 Photopic curve

When light enters the lens of the eye, it is received by the retina which consists of millions of photoreceptors, packed into an area about $1.5\,cm^2$. Human beings have two types of receptors called 'rods' and 'cones', because we live in two distinct worlds – night and day. The cones which number approximately 7 million, are for the detailed full colour examination of objects in bright light; the rods, which number approximately 130 million, are for the examination of objects in low light conditions. Rods and cones are not dissimilar in their individual sensitivity; but to achieve a higher sensitivity several rods are coupled together, and this accounts for the eyes' loss of sharpness at night. Due to the cones' lower sensitivity, we all feel better doing fine work in high light levels when the cones are working efficiently.

The most important aspect of the eye is photopic vision which is used at normal levels of illumination. Not every individual has the same sensitivity, therefore the Commission International de l'Eclairage (CIE) adopted an internationally agreed response, which is called the CIE standard observer. This gives the standard sensitivity for the eye for wavelengths from 380 nm to 760 nm. The peak sensitivity is at 555 nm, whereas the sensitivity at 400 nm is about 1/1000th of the highest level (see Figure 3.3). In practice, this means that a Watt of radiation in the green part of the spectrum has an effect 1000 times greater than one Watt of radiation at the blue end of the spectrum.

A point worth making here, as it is relevant, is that the photo receptors can only respond by changing their voltage which gives no absolute information as to the colour of the stimulus that caused the change. For the eye to assess accurately the colour and pass the information to the brain, nerve cells from differing colour receptors must be stimulated so that the relative amounts of colour energy in the viewed scene can be assessed.

Thus a stimulation of a *red receptor* and a *green receptor* will give a result between pale yellow and deep orange, depending upon the balance of the two receptors.

As we go about our daily lives, the world is viewed under many different sources of illumination. The colour of noon daylight is much bluer than the incandescent light used in our homes. Fluorescent lighting, as well as street lighting does not always provide good colour rendering. However, an apple held in our hand when we stand in any of these light sources appears to be

Figure 3.4 Sensitivity of eye receptors

the same colour *irrespective* of the light source. It is as though our brain is programmed to recognise the object, allowing for the colour differences, therefore our colour vision may not be totally dependent upon the visual input to the brain (see Figure 3.4).

Finally, our two eyes give us depth and the three-dimensional image of objects. We can however, be tricked by perspective so we need additional information. Generally this is produced by shading, for example, old silent movies illuminated largely in flat lighting, do not have the depth that the later monochrome studio films had in the 1940s and 1950s. The use of stronger keylights and backlights, copied from the film industry, enabled black and white TV to have some illusion of depth. Although the use of colour gives areas of contrast there is still a need for punchy lighting.

Adaptation and glare

The light sensitivity of the eye usually adapts itself to the illumination we are observing. A good example of this is coming from a fairly dark room into very bright sunlight and it doesn't take very long for us to adjust to the new conditions, although the light levels are incredibly different.

Adaptation requires a period of time to work and in fact requires a long time to get used to dark after light, more than 30 minutes, but on the other hand it does not take long to be accustomed to light after dark. There are limits to adaptation and this can be when luminance is so great that glare can occur. We have all had the problem of reading from white paper in a full summer sun, where the luminance value may be as high as 25 000 candela/m^2, and although it may be possible to read under these circumstances it is very uncomfortable. Why do we suffer from this problem? It is caused because the eye is not a perfect optical instrument and can be affected by the scattering of the light rays which causes a high intensity source to be seen as if it were surrounded by haze. Where part of the retina is suddenly illuminated, the whole retina drops very rapidly in sensitivity (within 0.1 of a second). A good example of this is looking at a window which occupies part of the viewed scene which causes the eye to decrease in sensitivity and although the window may be reasonably clear, the remainder of the environment has become rather dark. Both of the above effects are very well known to the average motorist, either driving during the day when the road surface may reflect very bright areas, or indeed at night, the headlights of the oncoming vehicles. Unfortunately, as we all know, it takes some time for our eyes to readjust to normal after we have received sources which give us glare problems. There are two forms of glare; the first which impairs the visual performance is called 'disability glare' and the second, which can cause visual discomfort, is called 'discomfort glare'.

Disability glare is caused by a bright source in the field of view, whereas discomfort glare is caused by excessively bright areas in the field of view and is usually caused by too high a difference between the dark areas and the bright areas being viewed. Generally, the luminance differences in the field of vision should not exceed 10 to 1.

We have tried to show in this section that although the eye is a marvellous instrument, it is not perfect. There is much that we do not know about its operation although the evidence so far shows that there is much in common between the eye, TV cameras and film cameras. In fact, it has been suggested that the coding system for passing colour information in the human brain is very similar to that used in the vision chain of any TV station.

3.4 Colour perception

The early philosophers, such as Pythagoras and Euclid, debated the nature of light and how the eye responded to a viewed scene. Theories went from a projected image from the viewed object which entered the eye, to the possibility that sensing rays went from the eye to the subject, rather like radar and that these rays would pass information back to the eye. We now know that most objects do not radiate any light waves whatsoever, and only convert the incident light on them into the shape, colour and appearance that we see. The two sensations we are most concerned with are the brightness and colour of an object. It was probably very fortunate for most scholars of today that Isaac Newton left Trinity College Cambridge when the university closed because of the plague and spent the next two years at the family farm. It was during this period of time that he focused his attention on the nature of light and subsequently produced his classic book 'Opticks'.

Newton's experiments with colour were conducted by allowing sunlight to pass through a small hole in a darkened window. This beam of white light was passed through a glass prism and the emerging light spread out in a 'spectrum' of colours. The colours were red, orange, yellow, green, blue, indigo and violet. History tends to give Newton the credit for discovering the prism for this effect but this was not the case; it had been observed by scholars for many years. What Newton did was to take the original idea of splitting light via a prism and then use this to examine the colours coming through. By selecting one colour from the first prism and passing that colour through a second prism, he discovered that the second prism had no effect at all on the colour of the original light. He therefore concluded that colours were not the result of the prism changing the light but the fact that all normal white light contained the observed colours and the prism only acted to separate the colours. Having separated the colours out, Newton thought he should be able to return them back to the original white light source and by using an inverted prism after the first prism, he was able to re-create a white beam of light. Newton had experimented with coloured objects under the various sources of illumination and from these experiments discovered most of the concepts that enabled modern colour theory to evolve. For instance, he found that a red object would efficiently reflect red light but would appear very dark and nearly black when illuminated by lights of other colours. It was apparent to Newton that objects have colour because they reflect certain colours while absorbing the remainder of the spectrum. If we view the spectrum as split by a prism, as Newton did, we will notice that it does not contain all of the colours that we encounter in our everyday lives such as magenta or black and white.

Newton's theories caused a great stir in the world at large and one of the reasons for this was the fact the most human beings first learn about colour by painting. The lessons learnt from mixing the colours of paint are somewhat different to those for mixing the colours of light. It has to be realised that light is the source of all colour but pigments in paint are simply reflectors or absorbers of parts of the light that illuminates them. If a beam of red light and a beam of green light are superimposed the result is yellow. On the other hand, if we mix red and green paint we get rather a nasty looking 'brown black' colour. When using light, all spectral colours can be created by adding various component parts of the red, green and blue light and the system used is called 'addition', ultimately creating white. Pigments derive their colours by subtracting parts of the spectrum, therefore the system with pigments is called 'subtraction' and ultimately creates black (see Figure 3.5a and b).

The light from the sun and incandescent sources is generally white by nature and contains all the colours of the spectrum, however, as we will discover in other sections of the book various sources produce light by exciting portions of the visible spectrum to gain a response from the eye; but because they do not contain all the colours of the spectrum some distortion of colour can take place.

If we ring a colleague in Australia from England and we describe a red dress, they will have some idea of what we're talking about, a problem arises when we require our colleague to reproduce exactly the colour of the dress. How can we specify colour and its brightness accurately. One of the first attempts to define colour precisely was by an American called Albert Munsell in 1915, and his three-dimensional colour system is still in use today. The Munsell system enables three qualities to be quantified and these are:

1 *hue*   Describes the basic colour such as red or blue;
2 *value* (*or brightness*)   Refers to how light or dark the colour appears (it is a measure of the amount of reflected light);
3 *chroma* (*or saturation*)   Refers to the intensity of colour; as a colour moves away from white it becomes more and more saturated.

However the Munsell system is only as good as the illumination it is viewed in. We have all come across the problem of the piece of material that we're buying in the shop or the suit that we have selected which looks much better when we go to the doorway of the shop and examine it under daylight. We are also aware of how bad our skin looks under sodium street lighting. Coloured objects reflect light, the problem is that they don't reflect the entire spectrum of the light that falls on them or the light that falls on them is deficient in some way. The effect that the source of light

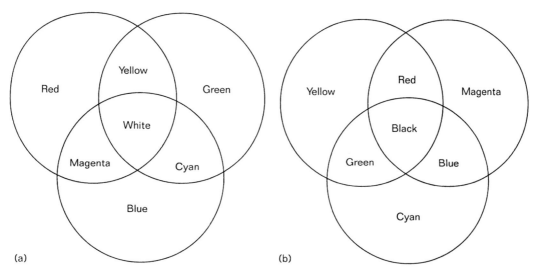

(a)   (b)

Figure 3.5 (a) Additive colour mixing; (b) Subtractive colour mixing has on any object is known as the colour rendering. In general, under normal illumination such as daylight, incandescent light, etc., there will be no problems, however discharge lighting (which may be fluorescent, street lighting or the type that we would use in studios or on location) will cause colour distortion by not having continuous spectral outputs. For instance, a green sample of cloth will only look green if there is green energy in the incident light. When we look in the manufacturers' data on lamps, we will invariably find in the sections on fluorescent, discharge etc., reference to the colour rendering index.

Two approaches have been used to describe colour, the first uses standard colour samples such as the Munsell system against which materials can be compared. A second system is to analyse the light reflected from a surface and then assign a set of values which specify the colour. As we are now looking at reflected light we can use the primary colours of red, blue and green, giving a 'tri-stimulus' to the eye. The first system to try to define the colour by its spectral components was that of Newton, but Newton used seven basic primaries derived from his prism observations where from any mix of the seven it was possible to produce a range of colours towards white. One of the problems with the Newtonian system was that it didn't contain the entire range of colours, for instance lacking any reference to purple.

To be able to compile a very accurate system of colour specification, it was necessary to have a deeper knowledge of colour mixing, which unfortunately Newton did not have. He was also incapable of measuring light with the great accuracies that are required for modern colour measurement.

In 1931 it was decided by the CIE to develop a more accurate colorimetric system. To comprehend the system that the CIE adopted, we have to understand how metamerism works. The spectral difference between sources can be quite considerable as shown in Figure 3.6 where a stimulus consisting of continuous power throughout the visible spectrum is matched by three narrow bands of energy in the red, green and blue only. If we choose three primary sources of light which are derived from standard white light filtered by a red, a green and a blue filter, we can use these as standard sources for colour mixing. The CIE system is based upon using a standard observer who is seated in front of a white screen. On one half of the screen is projected some arbitrary light source, on the other half of the screen is projected a combination of our three

Figure 3.6 Spectral distribution

primaries. The observer has to adjust the intensity of the three primaries until both sides of the screen match exactly in colour and brightness. Although the two halves of the screen now look the same, they do not necessarily have the same spectral composition. The amounts of the red, blue and green sources specify the colour that we are viewing but not the light itself. Those three numbers are unique to the colour observed.

The theory of colour matching is quite complex and the CIE set out to create a system that was relatively easy to use and understand. Figure 3.7 shows the three primaries chosen by the CIE and these are called $\bar{x}$, $\bar{y}$ and $\bar{z}$; where $\bar{x}$ corresponds to the red primary, $\bar{y}$ to the green primary and $\bar{z}$ to the blue primary. The green primary curve ($\bar{y}$) shows the sensitivity of the human eye to light of different wavelengths and, as can be seen, the eyes' sensitivity is at a maximum of around 550 nm but very poor towards the blue and red ends of the spectrum. By using the 'photopic curve', as it is known, as a 'multiplier' for any spectrum which is being analysed, we can calculate the apparent brightness. In other words, the source has much more energy than we are able to absorb.

The X, Y and Z values are called the tri-stimulus values of the spectrum and the relative amounts of each give the colour and brightness of the viewed scene. To find X, we have to multiply the spectrum as measured, by the curve and the result gives the energy required for the stimulus. We would also have to do the same for the Y and Z values. The values of X, Y and Z are able to specify the colour accurately. The trouble is, it's very difficult when given these values to imagine what the colour actually looks like. We need a method by which we have an instant reference to the colour itself. The easiest way of looking anything up is to have a visual presentation, and in this case it is the CIE chromaticity diagram (see Figure 3.8). The diagram is another version of Newton's colour wheel system, thus as we did with the Newton system we can use the chromaticity diagram to analyse colours. Newton's original colour circle didn't include purple which is of course a combination of red and blue, but as can be seen we do have a purple line (see Figure 3.9). What has happened is we have plotted the spectrum locus

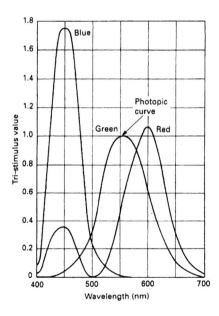

Figure 3.7 CIE primary functions

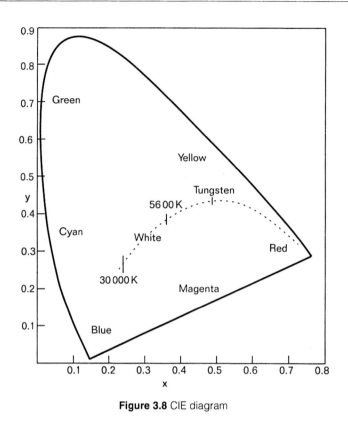

Figure 3.8 CIE diagram

on a graph which has an x axis and a y axis. The colour co-ordinates are derived from the following formula:

$$x = \frac{X}{X + Y + Z}$$

$$y = \frac{Y}{X + Y + Z}$$

$$z = \frac{Z}{X + Y + Z}$$

As the sum of $x + y + z$ will always equal 1, we only need two variables as the third can be determined from the other two. By convention, we use the co-ordinates x and y to describe the colour. It must be noted however, that those co-ordinates only specify the hue and the saturation of the colour but *not* its brightness. To ascertain the brightness, we have to use the value of Y, the green tri-stimulus value (photopic curve). As we move from the periphery of the colour locus towards the centre of our diagram, saturation of colours diminishes until we reach white. The centre of the colour locus which is positioned at the co-ordinates x = 0.33, y = 0.33, where the saturation has become zero. This point is known as *equal energy white* or reference white (colour temperature 9600 K).

In the laboratory we can do a spectral analysis of a source and then by using the CIE values compute the amount of X, Y, Z to give the tri-stimulus values. However, this method is not possible in practice, and conveniently for us hand held tri-stimulus meters have been developed which measure the values of the three primaries, do the computations for us and present the figures for the co-ordinates and brightness very neatly on a digital display.

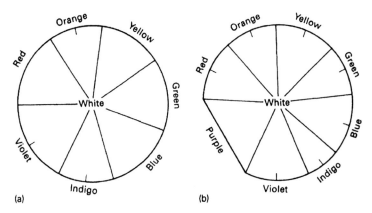

Figure 3.9 (a) Newton wheel; (b) Modified by Harris

The CIE method enables us to do two things:

1   to analyse the colour of a surface, and
2   to analyse the spectrum of a light source coming to a surface.

Most of our use of a colour meter is to measure the colour of the light source, be it normal or modified by filters, etc. If we are examining the colour of a surface, then we need to know the colour of the reference source to reduce the variables to manageable proportions. The CIE adopted three standard light sources and these are:

1   *Source A*:   This is a source typical of an incandescent lamp operated at a colour tempera-
                  ture of 2856 K.
2   *Source B*:   This source is typical of noon sunlight and has a colour temperature of about
                  4870 K.
3   *Source C*:   This represents an overcast sky or average daylight and has a colour tempera-
                  ture of about 6700 K.

In 1965, the CIE introduced a system to regulate the colour rendering index (Ra). The system measures eight colour samples taken from the Munsell system, illuminated with a test source and this is compared with a reference illumination. The reference source has a value of 100, and due to the deficiencies in spectral output, the test source can at best equal or generally be less than the reference source and thus the Ra can never be greater than 100, and in most cases will be 90 or less (see Table 3.1).

Blackbody radiation

The scientists studying blackbody radiation discovered the following facts:

1   The spectrum is continuous, just like the sun's and includes all the visible colours together
    with the infrared and UV spectra.
2   When a graph is plotted of intensity versus wavelength, there is always a maximum intensity
    at only one wavelength.
3   As the object becomes hotter, the wavelengths of maximum radiation become shorter.
4   The hotter the object becomes the greater the total amount of radiation from a given area.

Table 3.1

CIE general colour rendering index (Ra)	Typical application
Greater than 90	Where accurate colour matching is required, e.g. colour print inspection.
80 to 90	Where accurate colour judgements are necessary and/or good colour rendering is required for reasons of appearance, e.g. shops and other commercial premises.
60 to 80	Where moderate colour rendering is required.
40 to 60	Where colour rendering is of little significance but marked distortion of colour is unacceptable.
20 to 40	Where colour rendering is of no importance and marked distortion of colour is acceptable.

Note: For film or TV use we would need an Ra index of at least 80.

Lacking the knowledge of today's scientists, their predecessors postulated the theory of a body absorbing all the radiation falling on it and to do that effectively, it would have to be black and hence the world was introduced to the term 'blackbody'. What the scientists didn't know was that the blackbody was capable of radiation and although not commonly realised, every object radiates some light. The chair we sit on appears quite cool but in a room at 20°C, it is still 293° above zero Kelvin and according to the known laws of physics will radiate energy. Many modern surveillance systems actually look for radiated energy of low intensity. One good thing about blackbody radiation is that it starts in the very deep reds and goes to the very deep blues, passing through white in the process which, as human beings we happily accept. When we depart from the blackbody curve and approach green or magenta we are psychologically disturbed.

Figure 3.10 shows blackbodies at 2000 K, 3200 K, 5600 K and 6500 K. In addition to the visible spectrum, many other wavelengths are also radiated; the more the temperature is raised, the more energy and subsequently light is radiated. The curves also show a shift towards the blue end of the spectrum as the energy becomes greater. Modern incandescent lamps are very close to the blackbody radiation curve and in general are given a colour temperature to signify the colour of their light output. Incandescent lamps that we deal with have a colour temperature around the 3000 K mark. The sun is around 5000 K and light from the blue sky is generally from about 6000 K upwards.

If we wish to measure purely colour temperature, we measure the relative amounts of red and blue of the blackbody curve of the source in question. When the source deviates from the blackbody curve we would have to use a tri-stimulus meter so we can measure the green component.

Why is it that the discharge source is so different from that of the incandescent? Probably at some time in our lives, we have thrown an object into a fire and then been amazed at the magnificent colours produced when it burns. The colours are unique to the substance. In 1752 a Scotsman, Thomas Melvill, studied the light from a flame through a prism and discovered that the spectrum was not continuous. Some parts of the observed spectrum were bright and other parts were dark. When Melvill experimented with different chemicals burning in the flame, he found the locations of the bright and dark areas changed. From the early nineteenth century onwards the spectroscope was developed to enable researchers to examine the various colours generated within light sources. Each chemical element has a unique set of wavelengths and thus bright lines within its spectrum, and these can be used just like 'fingerprints'. With the advent of electricity research was carried out on the effect of voltage when applied to gasses. During the latter part of the nineteenth century many different gasses were studied and their element lines were plotted, and it was discovered that some gases have thousands of lines and some have

Figure 3.10 Continuous spectrum emitted by four typical blackbodies

very few. Sodium in particular has only two lines in the yellow part of the spectrum, so close together they appear as one and this is the characteristic of many street lights that are in use today. Neon on the other hand, has very strong lines in the red and orange.

Observing these bright line spectra was one thing, but to actually understand their generation was another. Ernest Rutherford, of atomic energy fame, was the first to postulate the theory of the planetary atomic structure. This theory suggests that the atom is mostly empty space, rather like our solar system and that the individual parts of an atom orbit a nucleus. The scientific theory of the time however, did not explain the existence of bright line spectra. In 1913, Niels Bohr a Danish physicist, set out to explain how the bright line spectra evolved. His theory was that the electrons occupied defined orbits around the nucleus; these orbits were governed by the amount of energy an electron had as it orbited the nucleus. If the electron was given additional energy by some means, the electron could be made to move to one of the higher levels within the atom. As well as moving, the excited electron had also become unstable. To regain stability, the excited electron would have to fall back to the lower level from whence it came and in the process lose the energy again, in the form of light.

Each element has a unique atomic structure and also has its own bright-line spectrum. When we view sources made up of several lines of energy we do not see the individual lines because our eyes integrate all the energy and tend to mix the colours together. However, it may be that the energy is not in the visible spectrum at all and is produced in the UV region. This energy while not directly visible is able to produce visible light by exciting certain chemicals and a good example of this is the fluorescent light.

Fluorescence occurs when a fluorescent molecule absorbs energy and emits light. Fluorescent lamps are a glass tube coated internally with a phosphor, which is a chemical substance with an energy structure that produces bands of colours rather than individual line spectrum. An electric current flows through the vaporised mercury in the fluorescent tube and in so doing excites the electrons. When the electrons fall back to the lower levels they release energy. Some of the energy generated is in the visible region of the spectrum but mostly it is in the UV and it is this UV energy that causes the phosphors to glow. It should be noted that higher energy sources can excite phosphors but lower energy sources are incapable, thus UV will cause the production of light but infrared energy cannot. Fluorescent tubes tend to have much energy at the blue end of the spectrum as well as nasty spikes in the green, and to balance their colour, combinations of phosphors are used so that the integrated light output approaches that of normal incandescent lamps. Thus we hear terms like 'daylight', 'warm white' etc. which are descriptions of their inherent colour, but not always of their colour rendering properties.

Tri-phosphor fluorescent tubes have coatings which produce narrow band energy in the red, green and blue regions and work by stimulating the red, green and blue receptors. By concentrating the energy into narrow bands it is possible to have tubes with a high light output. By adjusting the red, green and blue balance of the phosphors, various correlated colour temperatures can be produced. These tubes have been adopted for specialist use in TV and film luminaires as they have good quality colour coupled with low heat dissipation and a good lumens per Watt output.

The modern discharge sources such as the *HMI* and *MSR*, operate from the principles discussed, usually with an electric arc exciting mercury vapour and rare earth gases in various forms to give blends of colour. If we observe from its cold state a discharge lamp slowly warming up to its final operating temperature, we will see the discreet bands of energy joining in at various levels to form the colours that make up the composite output.

3.5 Spectral output of sources

Although the graphs in Figure 3.11 are apparently very different to each other, the various light sources all produce a sensation of white in the human eye. When a light source produces light at every wavelength in the visible spectrum it is considered a continuous source. Although these sources appear white as far as we are concerned, when objects are viewed under the various types of illumination, we get different responses. As a yardstick, it would be nice to have a source that gave a perfect white, and such a source wouldn't show any imbalance towards the red, the blue or the green of the spectrum, and would contain equal amounts of each. This source is called an 'equal energy source' and has been discussed in reference to the CIE system.

All blackbody sources are continuous radiation sources and although biased heavily either to the red or the blue according to the temperature of the radiator, the colour distortion is at a minimum. The interesting thing about continuous sources is the fact that nature has provided sources of this type from time immemorial and all the light derived from hot objects, such as candles, oil lamp, wood and coal fires, obeys the laws of the blackbody radiator. It is only in recent times that sources of a different type have been developed for use by mankind; the reason being more light for the power consumed and is usually a consumer led development by lamp manufacturers. Probably the most well known of these is the fluorescent tube. One advantage of using mercury discharge sources was that they provided high efficiencies of light output. In the earlier days of discharge lamps however, quantity was put very much before quality. In the basic mercury discharge lamp, radiation is mainly found in the blue, green and yellow sections in very narrow band spikes and obviously does not give a good colour response. Typical examples of basic discharge lamps are those used in street lighting and some forms of crude floodlighting, which tend to be either rather blue or predominantly yellow. To improve the colour of the light source, it is necessary to introduce elements such as tin, indium, sodium, lithium and scandium. One of the problems with using some of these elements is the fact that they could react with the silica envelope and rapidly destroy the lamp. In practice, by using

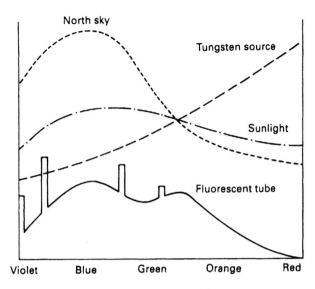

North sky

Tungsten source

Sunlight

Fluorescent tube

| Violet | Blue | Green | Orange | Red |

Figure 3.11 Spectral distribution curves of four common sources

metals in the form of their halide salts (hence the name metal halide lamps) most of the problem is overcome. The table below gives examples of the radiation that can be produced with the various elements:

Tin	orange/red radiation
Scandium	blue and green radiation
Sodium	yellow radiation
Thallium	green radiation
Lithium	red radiation

By selecting the various metals and metal halides that can be used, we can introduce more spectral spikes into the characteristic and eventually end up with colour rendering of a very high order, such as those in HMI and MSR lamps.

3.6 Filters

We will discuss in other sections the need for the almost apparent perfection of the white light that we use either for daylight matching or for incandescent source matching. In this section we shall talk mainly about distorting the colour of light.

The choice of colour to create the required effect or mood in theatre was established from very early days by placing a coloured glass or silk in front of the light source. In 1858 Covent Garden introduced overhead gas battens running the width of the stage, and providing colour change by stitching together two foot wide lengths of gauze coloured red, green and blue which could be pulled around the gas batten to produce the required colour. Alternative materials were silk, calico or tammy. A high price was paid for early experiments with lighting and the attempts to provide colour. Theatres caught fire and many people died, it is therefore no wonder that the Fire Officers of today insist that all materials used as colour filter must pass the appropriate safety tests.

Early colour filter material was made of gelatine dyed to the required colour. This offered an enormous range, but suffered the problem of handling. As it dried out, it would become very brittle and virtually shatter and fall to pieces and of course, presented a fire hazard. However, the use of gelatine filter persisted into the 1960s. The advent of electric lamps in the late 1890s provided another possibility for colouring the light by dipping the lamps into coloured lacquer. This provided an excellent choice of colours but, of course, it could not be changed once the lamp had been coated. With the introduction of the incandescent tungsten filament lamp in the early 1900s, the heat was to prove too much for the lacquer coating for anything other than low wattage sources. This led in the early 1930s, to the introduction of a new colour material made from cellulose acetate by a complicated method of shaving thin sheets from a large block of the dyed material and polishing the sheet until it became a transparent colour filter. This type of filter persisted for many years but has been replaced by plastic materials that can be coated with the appropriate colours on a continuous production method of manufacture.

The two main colour filters in use today are polyester and polycarbonate. Both are suitable for tungsten halogen luminaires and both have their attractions. Polyester is normally cheaper but does not last so long, and the polycarbonate tends to justify its price by the reduction in replacement costs and the time involved. Both materials are available in over 100 colours and hues and can even be used by adding colours in the same luminaire to create your own special shade for the LD who can't find the one he wants in the swatch book.

Glass filters have always been used and are still in use today. However, after the initial euphoria over the fact that the glass filter does not fade or burn out, one soon finds that they are so restrictive that they are not a very practical solution. The colour restriction is caused by the glass manufacturer requiring the lighting filter stockist to order what is known in the glass industry as a 'melt' which could be about one tonne, but of course, it is all one colour which will supply his customers for years. Unfortunately, any one particular melt cannot be guaranteed to match the next melt, therefore some permanent applications such as cyclorama backings that were thought to be ideal for glass filters, were faced with changing all of the filters when replacements were required, because the new colours stood out from the rest. An additional problem with the glass filter is that they can shatter if they are unevenly heated, causing a safety problem when used in overhead luminaires.

In general, the filters used for TV, film and stage are essentially types of plastic with dyes in them. Other specialist filters can be produced and these are dichroic layers on sheets of glass. Dichroic filters work by having a very thin layer of a chemical deposited on a piece of glass. The thickness of the surface coating will be one quarter of the wavelength of the light concerned and is obviously extremely thin. The filter works by reflecting selected wavelengths within the spectrum and if a blue dichroic filter, such as the type used with small luminaires, is examined, it will be found that one surface reflects yellow in large amounts. Dichroic filters rely upon the light being perpendicular to the surface of the glass due to the need to keep a precise quarter wavelength for the selection of the colour to be reflected. Light incident from other angles will be affected in different ways, thus it is possible in practice to see a slight variation in colour over the width of a light beam when using dichroic filters. This problem could be solved by curving the filter surface so that all rays are normal to it.

Manufacturers of dichroic filters are able to tailor the surface coatings very precisely to select portions of the electromagnetic spectrum, particularly with infrared and UV where the division between the visible light and the harmful rays is very narrow. A good example of dichroics are the infrared reflectors used on cold lamp sources in projector systems and in many of the low voltage sources used in shop displays and architectural lighting (see Figure 3.12).

In the past, specialist dichroic filters were produced mainly for luminaires such as the Redhead and Blonde for 'tungsten to daylight' conversion. The heat resisting glass on which the dichroic coating was deposited, had to be carefully selected, to take account of the heat differential from

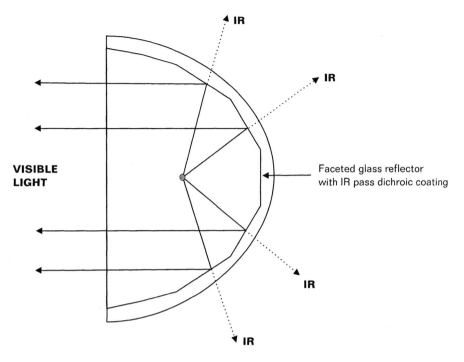

Figure 3.12 Cool light reflector

the edge of the glass to the centre of the glass. This means that the co-efficient of expansion of the glass chosen has to be very small. The glass substrate is approximately 3 mm (0.125″) thick. One problem with manufacturing dichroic filters, is that the evaporation chambers can limit the physical size of the area of the filter, and the Blonde dichroic was probably one of the largest made. The dichroic coating has to be absolutely uniform to prevent colour changes over its surface. One advantage of dichroic filters is that their colour lasts much longer in use; therefore they are ideal for low maintenance installations. The colour range at the present time is limited to around 20 colours, but in the future, this will no doubt be expanded. It is, of course, possible to use a combination of filters to produce a fairly wide range of colours but for each filter there will be an insertion loss in the optical chain so the overall result might be quite inefficient. Dichroic filters can be used for ellipsoidal spotlights, PAR units and smaller spots such as the MR16s. They come in a range of standard frame sizes to suit various applications and are as follows:

Filter size	
Millimetres	Inches
254 × 254	10 × 10
190 × 190	$7^1/_2 \times 7^1/_2$
86 × 86	$3^3/_8 \times 3^3/_8$
50 *round*	2 *round*

One of the problems for manufacturers of dichroic filters is to match the very wide range of polyester filter materials available on the market. Whereas in the past 1 and 2 kW sources were often used for profile spots, with the more efficient lamps and luminaires in use today, the heat from the lamp has been considerably reduced and is approximately 25–33% of the old type. This means that plastic filters will last much longer in use. The cost of dichroic filters is also generally higher than the equivalent plastic ones which means that unless there are strong reasons for using the dichroic type, plastic filters will predominate for a long time to come. Dichroic filters are used in vast numbers in the moving light industry to produce a wide range of colour effects. In this case they are chosen mainly for their long life.

Many books have been written on the subject of the use of colour to create the right mood and setting from joy to sadness, from shock to restful security. However tempting it is to pursue this course, we must confine our studies to producing the colours for the LD to use and the simple physics involved to achieve the desired effect. The LD has two variables to consider:

1   the colour of the light, and
2   the colour of the subject.

He has total control of the first variable but the second is completely beyond his control and must be determined at an early stage of planning if he is to achieve the desired artistic effect. The correct colour of costumes and scenery must be used during the rehearsals when the colour filters are being chosen or disaster will result.

As human beings we tend to associate reds and yellows with bright and breezy situations and blue with much more sombre occasions, red is also associated with daylight and blue with night.

Originally very few filters were produced for effects purposes, but over the years manufacturers have come to produce vast ranges of subtle colour filters. Most of these, we suggest, are required by the individual foibles of the lighting practitioners and not necessarily by the requirements of the viewer. It is our experience that most practitioners of the art of lighting tend to do things on a trial and error basis when selecting filters.

Other types of filter required in the lighting industry are the kind that either change the colour of the light source itself, or change the colour of the viewed image as seen by TV, film or photographic cameras. It must be said at this time that any filter which changes the nature of the light cannot necessarily be designated as a particular colour filter, a colour temperature changing filter or any other type. A filter essentially changes the colour of a light source and therefore could be used for any purpose where the resultant colour may be required. What is extremely important, for the purposes of this book, is how do we achieve good filtering, and at the same time keep a high transmission level so we do not waste large amounts of light. It also has to be remembered that a filter called 'Bright Rose' looks decidedly not 'Bright Rose' when put in front of a predominantly blue source.

A good filter should only be interested in the visual energy, i.e. that from 400 to 700 nm. A perfect filter would only remove that portion of energy in which we are interested in a very precise way. However filters cannot be made to this sort of tolerance and generally have some form of overlap and thus remove other bits of energy from the light beam. When light falls on any material, three things occur, some light will be reflected, if the material is translucent enough some light will pass through the material and some of the light will be absorbed within the material. The absorbed light will be converted to heat energy. When the majority of the light is either reflected or transmitted or a combination of the two effects, the smaller quantity will be the heating effect. To illustrate this effect, white and other pale coloured materials usually reflect most of the incident light. For example most people will wear lightly coloured clothing in the summer which reflects most of the energy in the sunlight but we generally wear dark coloured clothing in the winter to keep us warm. The black telephone sitting in the sunlight on our desks has an extremely low reflectance and it also transmits little or no light. Consequently the telephone gets rather hot, which may be good news for the telephone company's replacement programme, but is not so good for the user.

When we wish to change the colour of a light source for effect or colour correction, we will invariably put some form of coloured filter in the light path. We cannot introduce a colour that is not present in the source. The colour of the emerging light from the filter depends upon the spectrum of the incident light striking the filter and on the characteristics of transmission of the filter itself. As well as the *colour* of the emergent light from a filter we will also be very much concerned with the *quantity of light* the filter lets through, otherwise known as the *transmission*. A filter works by subtracting selected portions of the spectrum away from the light source. If we start with the same amounts of red, green and blue light in the light source, and our filter takes away the green component, we are left with the red and blue, which when mixed together gives *magenta*. Thus our magenta filter can also be called a *minus green* filter. A yellow filter would allow the red and green portions of the spectrum through, taking away the blue, thus it can be called a yellow filter or a *minus blue*. A cyan filter allows the blue and green light through and stops the red portion of the spectrum, therefore a *cyan* filter is also a *minus red*.

So far, we have looked at removing one colour, if we remove two colours we can then produce our three primary *additive* mixing colours used for lighting, i.e. if we remove the red and blue components we are left with *green*. The removal of red and green gives *blue*; finally if we take away the blue and green we are left with *red*.

As will be realised, the filters we have just given as examples have the ability to subtract light *away from a portion of the visible spectrum*, it will also be obvious that we are looking at a *subtractive* light process. The amount of light transmitted by any of these filters will be determined by the density of colour of the filters which is determined by the thickness of the colour layer. By using combinations of the basic magenta, yellow and cyan filters, which are often used in photographic processes, in various thicknesses, almost any colour can be produced (see Figure 3.13).

The alternatives given in Table 3.2 for red, green and blue show the two methods of achieving the same result.

A fine example of the two principles of additive and subtractive colour was demonstrated by Adrian Samoiloff in the 1920s when he had a stage act of illusions created with coloured light and selectively coloured subjects; one of which was to make the actor up in red cosmetics and wearing a coat of black and blue/green stripes. The actor would first be illuminated using a red filter when he would appear to be a white man in a black coat, and then illuminated with a blue/

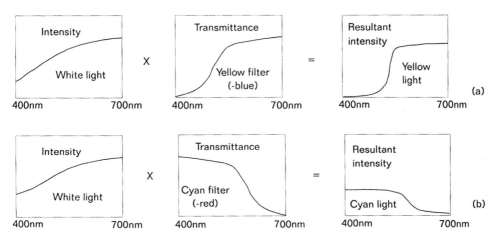

Figure 3.13 Subtractive filters: (a) Yellow; (b) Cyan

Table 3.2

Desired effect	Filters required
White	None
Black	*Yellow, cyan, magenta
Red	Yellow, magenta or (-blue, -green)
Green	Yellow, cyan or (-blue, -red)
Blue	Cyan, magenta or (-red, -green)

Note: * In other words removing all the light from the source.

green filter, he appeared to be a black man in a striped coat. This effect can be very interesting by design but quite a disaster if created by accident.

When we use two filters to produce a result, what has happened is that the original incident light has been modified by the characteristics of the first filter and consequently the emergent light from the filter is modified by the characteristics of the second filter. The transmission has also been affected and working this out is relatively simple, because if half the light was removed by the first filter and half of this light passed through the second filter, we would have ended up with a quarter of the original light. By this simple example it can be seen that the transmission can be down to quite low percentages on some colours; particularly when we are using primary transmission colours. Colour filters for light sources are usually produced with specified colours in various densities to meet the needs of the LDs. Some luminaires used for colour effects, which have a single light source, have to use combinations of yellow, magenta and cyan filters to achieve their results. A close examination of some manufacturers' filters particularly in the yellow range, will reveal that a medium yellow filter could be made up from two or more sheets of less dense yellow filters. Other than the need to remove portions of the visible spectrum for effects purposes, there is on occasions need to remove the UV and infrared energy from the spectrum. For example, when filming in museums, special precautions have to be taken to remove much of the infrared and UV portions of the spectrum from the light sources to avoid contaminating the colours on valuable paintings and objets d'art.

Colour temperature correction filters are those that change the balance between the red and blue portions of the spectrum only. To change a source from 3200 K to 5600 K means that the red end of the spectrum has to be diminished; therefore there is a higher balance of blue to red in the filter. To change a 5600 K source to 3200 K, an orange correction filter removes part of the blue from the light beam to achieve a correct red/blue balance.

We need to use coloured filters to correct the output of light sources in one of two ways. It may be that we have a 3200 K source that requires to be raised to 5600 K to be used with daylight sources. It could be that we are using a source of 5600 K and this requires correction down to 3200 K. A problem that exists with filters is the fact that they cause a definite change and are dependent upon the light source for the resultant colour output. A blue filter placed in front of a 3200 K lamp would create much less change than if it were used to filter a discharge source. As this is the case, we can hardly label a filter as a 2000 K correction filter. Luckily for us, there is a way around the problem and we do this by using 'micro reciprocal degrees'. Suffice to say that a filter will cause a constant shift in the reciprocal value of the colour temperature of the source. To make the maths easier, the reciprocal value is multiplied by 1 million, and thus *mired* stands for 'MIcro REciprocal Degrees'. Thus a colour temperature of 2000 K is equivalent to 500 mireds and 4000 K equates to 250 mireds. A filter which changed the light from the source from 2000 K to 4000 K would thus produce a change of −250 mireds. This filter can be designed so that it always produces the change of −250 mireds, irrespective of the original source. Note that filters which decrease the colour temperature of sources have positive values, but filters which increase the colour temperature have minus mired shifts.

If we look at some examples, they give a good idea how this system can be used in practice.

		Mireds
1	5600 K Source	178
	Filter value	+72
	Final mired value	250

Therefore Colour temperature $= \dfrac{1 \times 10^6}{250} = \textbf{4000 K}$

2	3200 K Source	312
	Filter value	−72
	Final mired value	240

Therefore Colour temperature $= \dfrac{1 \times 10^6}{240} = \textbf{4167 K}$

3	4000 K Source	250
	Filter value	−72
	Final mired value	178

Therefore Colour temperature $= \dfrac{1 \times 10^6}{178} = \textbf{5600 K}$

Note that although the same filter has been used in examples (2) and (3), the Colour Temperature change in (2) is **967 K** and in (3) **1600 K**.

One type of filter that we require which would fail in its task if it changed the colour of the light in any way, is the neutral density filter. Its very name indicates its purpose, it has to be absolutely neutral and diminishes only the quantity of light and not the colour of light. It generally has two purposes, one of which is to diminish the amount of light entering the camera lens or it can be used to filter the light coming through windows and other apertures to allow a balance between a mixture of natural light and artificial light on any scene.

All the foregoing comments have been made with regard to light that was basically white in content on entering the filter. If the light entering a filter was essentially magenta in colour and filtered by a green filter, the result would be no light, as the green light has already been removed and the green filter would just remove the red and blue components of the magenta. This is obviously an extreme case but can serve to illustrate the need to be careful when filtering light sources.

3.7   Conversion of light in film and TV cameras

One only has to go to various TV viewers' homes and see the adjustments made to individual receivers to realise that opinions on what constitutes good colour vary quite considerably, therefore before we progress any further, perhaps it would be wise to declare the main objective in the reproduction of colour in any system of image transference. This objective must be that if we were able to look at the reproduced scene, side by side with the original, there would be very little difference between the two.

Whether light is a wave or a particle, there is no escaping the fact that light is a form of energy, similar to heat, electrical, mechanical and nuclear. In nature energy changes from one form to another. The energy conversion we are most interested in is the conversion of light, either into chemical energy, such as in the eye or in the process of filming, or by the photons that are guided by a lens to the electronic receptors in our TV cameras.

Modern 35 mm film emulsion can withstand enormous exposure latitudes and to some extent colour distortion. We as professionals in the entertainment field, must have standards to adhere to and as boring as it may seem, these usually involve a scientific measurement or some form of discipline in operational procedures. Whether we are going to produce negative film or reversal film the basic system is the exposure of three layers of emulsion to red, green and blue light. Those layers are inherently superimposed within the emulsion itself. It is of course possible to individually process the red, green and blue light arriving at the film by using three separate film stocks, and this was the basis of the old Technicolor system used from 1932 to 1955. One of the problems with using three different stocks for the red, green and blue components is that although it is easy to separate the constituent colours, the superimposition of the three images to reproduce the final image is somewhat difficult and requires a high degree of precision. Even with the Technicolor process, the final copy of film sent to the cinemas for projection was multi-layer film stock. Although cameras have an iris exactly the same as the eye, we can only reduce the amount of light hitting the film, we cannot increase the light level above the largest opening in the iris of the lens. If we wish to have greater sensitivity, we have to change to a different type of film. As a general rule, the more sensitive film becomes, the greater is the granular structure. The reason for using larger grains in the film is that they stand a higher chance of being struck by the photons. This use of a larger grain structure is similar to the grouping of the rods in the human eye. In the case of the eye, and in the film, the sharpness of the image reduces with the need for greater sensitivity.

The exposure of film to light causes the photons to strike the silver halide crystals in the film emulsion and these will change according to the intensity of the light. Photographic emulsion is naturally sensitive to the blue part of the spectrum; to increase the sensitivity to the green and red layers sensitising dyes have to be added to the emulsion. If we use the basic emulsion as the top layer in our system, it will be sensitive to the blue part of the spectrum and because of this fact we need no filter for the blue input from the lens. Because of the sensitivity of the other two layers to the blue, we reduce the blue going through the film by having a yellow filter immediately beneath the top layer. If the bottom layer is made sensitive only to red light we will not need a red filter. Between the yellow filter and the red emulsion is the green emulsion. As the blue light has been prevented from reaching this emulsion, which is sensitive only to the green part of the spectrum, we do not need a green filter. By constructing the film this way, we have effectively had three single exposures for the red, green and blue but all taken at the same time and in perfect register. Also by allowing the longest wavelengths to travel the furthest through the layers, we reduce the tendency to scatter, which causes lack of resolution.

The film is now processed so that cyan, magenta and yellow images are formed in the three layers. This is typical of negative film stock. To produce the positive from this stock, it is basically only necessary to photograph it with a similar type of negative, although in practice very sophisticated films can be used for the reversal process. Films can be balanced for artificial light or daylight and this is accomplished by the balance between the red and blue emulsion sensitivity. Figure 3.14 shows the difference between negative film for daylight and negative film for artificial light.

As can be seen, this film is composed of three emulsion layers being sensitive to red, green and blue light along with a protective layer, a yellow filter layer, an anti-halation layer and other layers, all coated on a clear safety base. The other side of the base is coated with a black resin backing to provide such properties as anti-scratch and anti-static. It also provides for lubrication

Figure 3.14 Film comparison (courtesy of Fuji Film Co. Ltd)

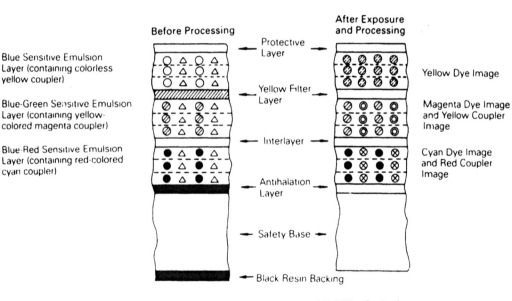

Figure 3.15 Negative film layers (courtesy of Fuji Film Co. Ltd)

so that its passage through the mechanical system is made easier. Different couplers are incorporated in the various emulsion layers and through post exposure processing, colour dyes and mask images are formed in the emulsion (see Figure 3.15). The film contains an orange coloured mask which allows for correct colour rendition when prints are made through this negative material on a positive film.

Television cameras have to analyse the light from a scene and the method is somewhat different to that used with film. The charge coupled devices (CCD) used in cameras have the

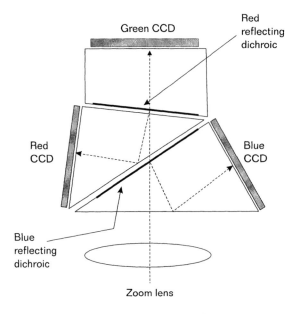

Green CCD

Red
reflecting
dichroic

Red
CCD

Blue
CCD

Blue
reflecting
dichroic

Zoom lens

Figure 3.16 CCD splitter block

same colour sensitivity, and are therefore not adjusted for the individual red, green and blue components of the light. Secondly, there are no commercially available sensors capable of producing the red, green and blue signals in a single device as required for the process of high quality broadcast colour TV. A fundamental requirement for broadcast TV standards is that three individual sensors have to be used together with colour filtering systems. Thus, the use of the three colour sensors and the consequent splitting of light that has to occur makes the colour camera optically very complex. Light falling on the three sensors must have a common entrance, i.e. each sensor must see exactly the same scene in order to avoid optical distortion. When processing the light through the optical system this has to be done with minimum loss, avoiding either excessive lighting levels in the studio, or producing noisy pictures by not having sufficient light to satisfy the sensitivity of the camera sensors. Most of the optical requirements with the systems for colour cameras can be met by using zoom lenses to create a single path from the viewed scene to the camera electronics. The diagram shows a typical beam splitting system to derive the red, green and blue components (see Figure 3.16).

What is a CCD? A charge coupled device is a solid state chip covered in several hundred thousand photosensitive cells, all of this built onto a device roughly a centimetre square. Each photosensitive cell represents one piece of picture information (pixel). Like camera tubes, CCDs have the same colour sensitivity, therefore three devices and filters for the red, green and blue components have to be used. As the CCDs are built to an absolute, almost perfect matrix, there is a lack of geometric distortion in pictures. The three chips have to be positioned extremely accurately so that the individual elements are aligned to an error of about half a pixel. If a registration accuracy of 0.05% is required, this means the alignment must be accurate to two thousandths of a millimetre which can only be accomplished by the camera manufacturer. If we are aligning the chips on the prism block to this degree, it is not difficult to imagine that heat can pose a problem. Temperature differences within the optical block will obviously cause misregistration, due to different coefficients of thermal expansion. One advantage of this system is that having been aligned in the factory, the system will not drift out of tolerance. A further tremendous advantage of CCDs is that they have a superb colour response although a problem is that the peak sensitivity is in the infrared region. This has to be corrected, otherwise we would have problems with the reds in the system, and an infrared 'cut off filter' is fitted to the optical path to do just this. A major advantage of CCD systems is that they are more sensitive (around 250 ASA) than tube systems (about 64 ASA) and this has allowed the incident light level in studios to be reduced from 1600 lux to between 300 and 800 lux, dependent upon the type of production.

4
Light measurements

4.1 Units, terminology and calculations

To measure and record light a unit was required that could be understood and repeated experimentally. This was the candle – but not any old candle. It had to be well defined so that it was repeatable (well, almost repeatable). It is quite laughable today to think of a world wide standard measurement of light being dependent on the repeatability of a burning candle, but it is a fact and the specification for the standard candle defined the type of wick and the tallow mixture to be used and the dimensions were an $\frac{1}{8}$ inch wick and a candle with a diameter of $1\frac{1}{8}$ inches.

Owing to the unreliability of a wax candle, it was replaced by a lamp burning vaporised pentane with an intensity equal to about 10 of the original candles. Eventually, even this was considered inaccurate and in 1909 a filament lamp was adopted as the standard, which continued until 1948. To enable very accurate measurements to be made, it was decided, at this time, to create a standard based upon the light emitted from a platinum radiator at 1773°C contained within a special vessel. The unit of luminous intensity, the candela, is defined as 'the luminous intensity, in the perpendicular direction, of a surface of 1/600 000 square metres of a blackbody, at the temperature of freezing platinum, under standard atmospheric pressure'.

The radiant flux is the amount of light energy that is given off by an object each second and is measured in 'joules per second' (the physical unit of measurement is known as a watt). A 100 W lamp therefore, radiates a total of 100 J of light energy each second. However, a 100 W tungsten lamp only radiates approximately 6 W of visible light, the remainder being radiated as non-visible infrared. The more we compress the energy from the light source into the visible spectrum, so we raise the amount of useful watts of light output. Low pressure sodium lamps emit practically all their light at around 590 nm, as this is very close to the peak sensitivity of the eye, it is highly efficient in terms of the number of lumens per watt. Thus, by concentrating the energy into narrow bands, it may be possible to produce light sources with outputs as high as 160 lumens/W and, in fact, it is this type of light generation that is employed in modern high energy light sources such as the HMI, MSR lamps.

As the eye varies in sensitivity with the wavelength of light, it is impractical to use the watt as a measure of the light output, we therefore use the following photometric units which take into account the response of the eye.

Luminous flux measures the total light output of a source and its unit of measurement is the *lumen*. However, in film and TV we are interested in luminaires that focus the light in a specific

Table 4.1 Luminance values

Source	Luminance (in cd/m^2)
Sun	1600×10^6
Crater of Carbon arc	200×10^6
Tungsten lamp (100 W clear)	6.5×10^6
Tungsten lamp (100 W pearl)	8×10^4
High pressure Mercury lamp (400 W clear)	120×10^4
Fluorescent lamp (80 W)	0.9×10^4
Low pressure Sodium lamp (140 W clear)	8×10^4
Clear blue sky	0.4×10^4
White paper (reflection factor 80%) illumination 400 lux	100
Grey paper (reflection factor 40%) illumination 400 lux	50
Black paper (reflection factor 4%) illumination 400 lux	5

direction and light emitted in a specific direction is measured in candelas, and is called the *luminous intensity.*

The incident light striking a unit area is called the illuminance and is measured in lumensm^2 (lux). As well as incident light, we are very much concerned with reflected light. The light emitted from a unit area in a specific direction is called luminance and is measured in candelasm^2, which indicates how bright an object actually appears, and this may be an illuminated area or the area of a source of light. The luminance of a surface determines how bright that surface actually appears.

1 nit = 1 cdm^2

1 footlambert = 3.426 cdm^2

1 apostilb = 0.3183 cdm^2

Table 4.1 gives the values of luminance for typical sources.

As an example of how we may apply the photometric units in practice, let us consider the light being emitted with a luminous intensity of one candela. The light is assumed to be distributed evenly in all directions, and the two areas shown are representing parts of the inner wall of two spheres, one at one foot from the source and the other at one metre from the source.

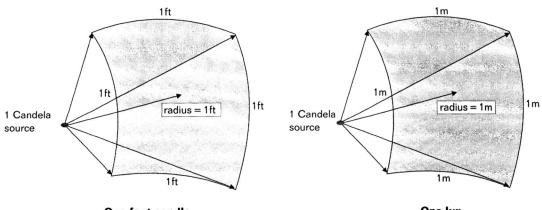

One foot candle　　　　　　　　　　**One lux**

Figure 4.1 Candela/lux/foot candle relationship

$1 \ m^2 \approx 1,000,000 \ mm^2$
$1 \ ft^2 = 92,903 \ mm^2$

$\therefore$ The conversion factor is $\dfrac{1,000,000}{92,903} = 10.76$

$$\boxed{\dfrac{lux}{10.76} = fc} \quad \text{or} \quad \boxed{fc \times 10.76 = lux}$$

Figure 4.2 Relationship of lux to foot candles

By definition, one foot candle is the amount of light falling on an area of one square foot at a distance of one foot from a source of one candela. The principle is the same for one lux being defined as the amount of light falling on an area of one square metre at a distance of one metre from a source of one candela.

To find the relationship between foot candles and lux, it is necessary to relate the areas being illuminated (see Figure 4.1). By converting the area of one square foot to square millimetres, we have 92 903 mm² and of course, one square metre is 1 000 000 mm². If we now divide the larger area by the smaller area we get a factor of 10.76 which is the conversion factor to use when relating foot candles to lux in Figure 4.2.

4.2   Laws – inverse square and cosine

Although there are many ways of reducing the light output of a luminaire, there is not one way of increasing it, therefore our only interest is the reduction of light and the laws that it obeys.

If a diffusion filter or wire gauze is placed in front of a light source, one would expect it to reduce the light output and it is equally obvious that if the material restricts half of the light, then the level will fall by 50% (Figure 4.3). It would appear by similar rationale, that the light from a luminaire would fall off with distance and a common misunderstanding is that at double the distance one would expect to get half the light. This is not so. The light is governed by a simple formula called the 'Inverse square law' which states that the light is falling off as the distance

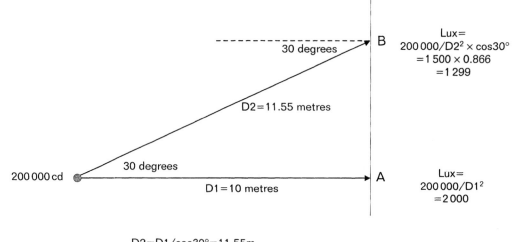

D2=D1/cos30°=11.55m

Figure 4.3 Light output

squared. Therefore if the distance from the light is doubled, the light will fall to one quarter. It must be said at this point that normal point light sources conform to the inverse square law when calculating illuminance. However, if we look at a larger source area, such as a fluorescent fitting, this needs to be dealt with in a different way. In situations such as this, the inverse square law can be used only if the distance of the light source from the subject is five times the maximum dimension of the source itself. For example, if the source is half a metre across, the inverse square law will only be accurate from a minimum distance of 2.5 m upwards.

$$\text{Lux} = \frac{\text{Source cd}}{\text{D}^2 (\text{metres})} \qquad \text{Foot candles} = \frac{\text{Source cd}}{\text{D}^2 (\text{feet})}$$

If a light reading is taken at a given distance, say 10 m and has a value of 1000 lux, we can determine the light intensity from the luminaire by simply multiplying the lux reading by the distance squared, i.e. 1000 lux $\times 10^2 = 1\,00\,000$ candelas. We now have a constant value for the intensity of the luminaire and it is expressed in candelas. As we arrived at the candela value by multiplying a lux reading by the distance squared, it is equally true that we can divide the candela value by any distance squared and obtain the lux reading at the new distance.

When the incident light falling on a cosine corrected light cell is normal (at 90°) to the plane of the cell, the cell will correctly measure the incident light. If however, the light reaches the cell at any angle other than normal, the amount of light to be measured will change. This variation in light is in direct relation to the angle the light enters the cell, and the light diminishes as the cosine of the angle to the normal and this is known as 'Lamberts cosine law'. Thus, in theory, light that enters the cell from the side, in other words 90° to the normal would be 'zero' on a cosine corrected meter. This variation comes about by the fact that the light has to cover a greater area when striking from any angle other than normal (see Figure 4.4).

Clearly (b) is longer, therefore the hatched area is larger,

e.g.   original area $= a^2 = 4 \times 4 = 16$

New area $= a \times b = 4 \times 5 = 20$

Also $1620 = 0.8 = \cos \theta$

The best example of the spread of light is to consider the follow spot used in a theatre. When normal to a surface it produces a round beam of light. When pointed at an angle to the stage, to cover the artist, the beam is now spread in an elongated shape. The amount of light in the beam

Figure 4.4 Cosine variation

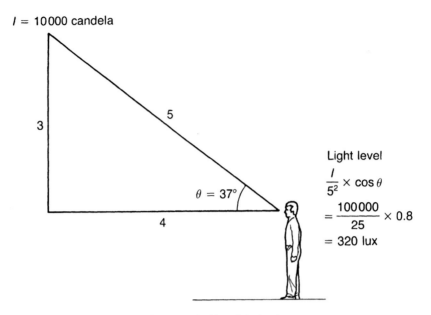

I = 10000 candela

5

3

θ = 37°

4

Light level

$$\frac{I}{5^2} \times \cos\theta$$

$$= \frac{100\,000}{25} \times 0.8$$

$$= 320 \text{ lux}$$

Figure 4.5 Incident light level

has not changed, but the area covered has increased; thus the illumination per unit area has diminished. Obviously, if the beam is elongated more and more as the light approaches from the side, the area covered by the light beam becomes infinite. Thus the amount of light per unit area becomes less and less and approaches zero (Figure 4.5).

With very shallow angles to normal, the variations are not significant, but as the angles become greater and approach anything from 45° to 90° quite large variations in light level can occur. This is particularly so when considering outside broadcast lighting and the floodlighting industry have had problems with this phenomenon for many years. Just to give an example, the cosine of 30° = 0.866, the cosine of 45° = 0.77, the cosine of 60° = 0.5, the cosine of 75° = 0.259, the cosine of 90° = zero.

As well as changing in one plane, the light can change in two planes at the same time. The light in the horizontal plane can come in at an angle as well as from the vertical plane, so both our x and y co-ordinates can vary. If this is the case, we have variations of the cosine law from two directions and this is normally called the 'cosine cubed law'.

4.3   Polar diagrams and their interpretation

We can determine two main important facts about the light output of a luminaire from its polar plot – the intensity of the light and its coverage. All lighting manufacturers use the same system to produce their catalogue information, so it is worth investigating the method of the test to help to understand the results. Whilst light meters are used to read the light arriving at the subject and so provide us with the actual information to work with, it is quite impossible to assess a luminaire against the manufacturer's catalogue information in the same way, because of the variables that must be catered for before a light output comparison can be made.

The supply voltage must be stabilised at the design voltage of the lamp, a 5% reduction at 230 V will result in an approximate light loss of 15%. The lamp used for the test will have been calibrated by the manufacturer, who also supply a laboratory report, showing the exact voltage to

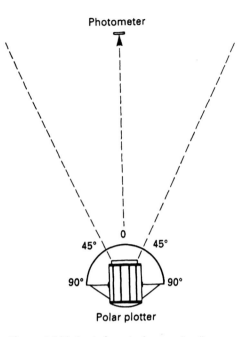

Figure 4.6 Method of producing a polar diagram

run the lamp at to achieve the stated wattage and colour temperature. This sample lamp is kept by the luminaire manufacturer as his standard for all tests (see Figure 4.6).

When assessing a polar diagram, determine if the manufacturers' light readings were taken with a wire guard in place; because a 25-mm wire guard will reduce the total light by about 8% – a ploy often used to enhance a products' specification. When making a polar curve, the luminaire must be checked to see that the reflector is centralised and that the lamp filament is in line with the centre of the reflector. Assuming that lenses and reflectors are clean, then a meaningful test can be made. With the light cell set at the same height as the centre of the luminaire, two methods of test are available to us; a polar test or a flat wall test.

A flat wall test is made by moving a light meter with a cosine corrected cell across a screen at a set distance from the light and readings recorded at regular intervals, keeping the cell parallel to the surface. The most used method is a polar test, where the light is rotated and the cell remains stationary. Then, if flat wall information is required, it can be produced mathematically by applying the Cosine and the inverse square laws. Any tests must be conducted in a darkened room and care must be taken to see that no reflected light from walls or ceiling reach the light cell. The readings can be taken at any distance, however, a very short distance will require very accurate measurements to be made, because any error in the distance will be magnified by the effect of the inverse square law, so that a slight change in distance can produce a large change in the light level.

Typically, luminaires up to 1 kW are measured at 5 m, 1 kW–5 kW at 8 m and 10 kW at 10 m, but this is only a guide because the test can be made at any chosen distance. The polar plotter is made up of a stand or platform that will allow the luminaire to rotate. A semicircular scale is placed under the luminaire, equally divided in degrees, and this scale is locked off to the luminaire, so that it rotates with it. A pointer is fixed to the bottom of the support structure so that it remains static. The test can now be made by aligning the centre of the scale with the pointer, and positioning the centre of the light output beam onto the cell. This setting up procedure is usually easier to achieve by first setting the focus to the spot position. The luminaire

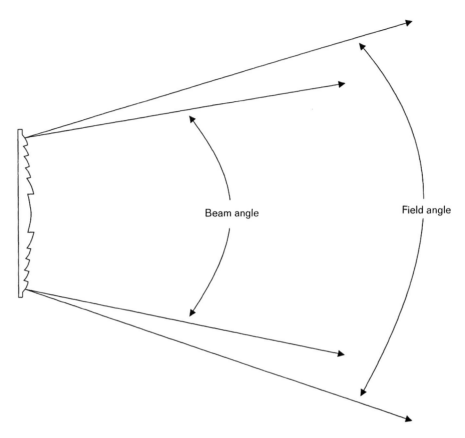

Figure 4.7 Beam and field angles

can now be rotated and readings taken at regular intervals. A typical method is to take readings at every degree for the spot position, and every 2.5° for the full flood position. The centre reading starts at zero degrees and the readings are taken left and right of centre. Having taken the readings and plotted them on a graph, similar to the one illustrated by the Fresnel polar diagram (see Figure 4.8), it is normal to place a mark at the point on the curve that corresponds to 50% of the centre brightness and another mark at 10%. These are known as the 'beam angle' and the 'field angle' respectively (see Figure 4.7).

The significance of the 50% beam angle is that if two lights are required to overlap and provide an even reading across the two distributions they must overlap at the 50% mark to produce 100% to match the centre reading. The 10% mark is normally considered to be the total angle of the light, in view of the fact that any light outside of this reading is of little use.

The readings are taken in lux at a given distance, but are normally quoted in candelas. This is arrived at by multiplying the lux reading by the distance squared from the light to the cell. It is more useful to display the information in candelas because the light level in lux at any distance can be easily calculated by dividing the candela reading by the required distance squared. In this way the manufacturer makes up the typical light output readings in lux at various distances that are used in the catalogue data sheets. Then with a little trigonometry, the diameter can be predicted, given the output angle of the light and the distance. The shape of the flood position in the Fresnel distribution illustrated will produce an even reading across a line 90° to the source. Because the readings are higher either side of the centre this will compensate for the greater distance that the light is projected to reach that part of the distribution.

Figure 4.8 Fresnel polar distribution

4.4 The measurement of colour temperature

William Thomson (later to become Lord Kelvin) was an eminent physicist of his day (1824–1907), and was responsible for establishing the Kelvin scale used for colour temperature measurement. Kelvin was faced, when experimenting, with two scales on which temperature could be measured – the Fahrenheit system and the Celsius or, as it is more commonly called – the Centigrade system.

The Fahrenheit system was developed by Daniel Gabriel Fahrenheit (1686–1736), a German physicist who worked in The Netherlands and also invented the alcohol and mercury thermo-meters. The Fahrenheit scale is based on 32° which represents the freezing point of water and 212° which is the boiling point of water, the interval between these two points being divided into 180 parts or degrees.

The Centigrade system was developed by Anders Celsius (1701–1744), a Swedish professor of astronomy who proposed a temperature scale of 0 to 100 degrees be adopted with 0° *as the boiling point* of water and 100° *as the freezing point.*

It was not until after the death of Celsius that Carolus Linnaeus (1707–1778), a Professor of Medicine in Sweden reversed the scale to make the 0° the freezing point and 100° the boiling point. The conversion between the two systems being $F = 95 \times C° + 32$.

Both of these systems were in use for standard temperature readings and both suffered the same problem, namely that the scale did not start at the lowest point of a temperature range and produced negative values.

In their time the scales might have seemed adequate and to represent the Centigrade scale starting at zero, this being the freezing point of water, seemed a good idea. Unfortunately, water freezes at different temperatures at different altitudes and various degrees of purity and quite frankly, has no relevance at all, it could just as easily have been any other substance.

Kelvin decided that both temperature scales were unsuitable for scientific measurements. He had no argument with the Centigrade scale, it was its starting point that caused the problem. Being not only a prominent physicist but a brilliant mathematician, he calculated the theoretical point of absolute zero as being −273° on the Centigrade scale. At this point no material can be further lowered in temperature. This then was his starting point – to set zero on the Kelvin scale at −273° Centigrade, thus from zero upwards getting only positive values.

Since the Kelvin scale is a Centigrade scale displaced from its zero by 273°, a tungsten filament which is glowing and radiating a colour that is 3000 K is burning at a temperature of 2727 °C.

The Kelvin colour temperature scale can only be used when measuring a source that emits energy in a continuous spectrum and approximates to a blackbody radiator such as a tungsten filament, or the ultimate in light sources, the sun.

What this means is that a lamp with a 2700 K colour temperature produces approximately the same spectrum of light as a blackbody at 2700 K. (Most hot objects do not follow Planck's blackbody radiation law: only perfectly black objects do). If we examine the visible spectrum portion of the blackbody curves given it will be seen that the curves are continuous over the visible wavelengths. As the object becomes hotter, it is noticeable that the amounts of red energy and blue energy are varying in relation to each other. If we could have a meter which measured the ratio of the red/blue balance, we would then have a reasonably close approximation to blackbody temperatures. In fact, the older style of colour temperature meters made throughout the world generally worked on the fact that they employed a red and blue filter to measure the relative amounts of each and thus find the corresponding colour temperature.

The colour of light emitted from a discharge lamp cannot be expressed in Kelvins because the spectral output in the lamp is not continuous but dependent on the gases and rare earths used in its manufacture to introduce the required additional colours which help to create the colour of the source (see Figure 4.9), and the compounds used emit colours in only comparatively narrow bands. In photographic and TV cameras the film stock and the colour receptors are responsive to the amounts of red, green and blue in the light, but unfortunately due to the spiky nature of the colour distribution from a discharge lamp a standard colour meter that measures only the

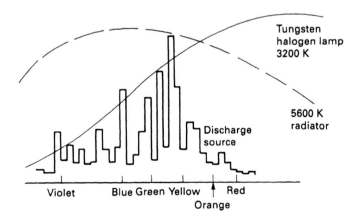

Figure 4.9 Comparison of discharge and incandescent sources

red/blue balance of a source will give erroneous readings because it is not measuring the total spectral output.

4.5   Types of meter

Luminance (reflected) light meters

Photographic meters, either the built in type as with most modern 35-mm cameras, or a hand held meter, measure the reflected light from the scene which is going to reach the film. As the film has a certain sensitivity, either the stop and/or the speed of the shutter have to be adjusted so that the correct quantity of light reaches the emulsion, so that well exposed pictures are produced. Of course, nowadays, most cameras do everything automatically. The basis of reflected light measurements is an 18% reflectance value which produces an average brightness standard of measurements for film and TV cameras. At this point it must be stated that we are only measuring the amount of light, not the colour of the source, as long as the meter responds faithfully to all visible wavelengths. If we have a red card that reflects 18% of the light striking it or we have a green card with the same reflectance, they will appear to be the equivalent as far as a camera is concerned because we haven't taken any account of the colour involved. We have all been caught out by taking pictures of snow scenes or pictures in very dark areas when the average brightness cannot equate the scenic values very accurately to the 18% reflectance.

Luminance meters are used for the measurement of a light source or surface brightness. Two of the most important factors with a luminance meter is the angle of acceptance so it can cover very small areas at a distance and secondly, is to ensure that there is no light entering the cell outside the angle of acceptance, which would give false readings. For average use, an acceptance angle of one degree is acceptable, however for very accurate luminous measurements on small areas one third of a degree is possible in some meters. A normal luminance meter will be calibrated in candelas per metre squared and alternatively foot lamberts. Photographic luminance meters will have systems where film speed and other parameters can be entered so that an exposure value can be obtained from the meter readings. In addition to a standard luminance meter, it is now possible to obtain meters where the measurements of the colour tri-stimulus values are made in addition to the candela per metre squared units or foot lamberts. These meters would be used where the light sources are too small to be measured with standard colorimeters, for example, LEDs and small lamps. They are also useful to measure light sources when they are operating and obviously very hot. Further use is for inaccessible or distant light sources, and some meters allow accurate measurements of areas as small as 1.3 mm in diameter.

Illuminance (incident) light meters

A better way of measuring the amount of light is by taking incident light readings which are not influenced by the subject matter itself. If we measure incident light, it is then up to the operator to adjust the equipment being used to give a balanced exposure on the scene itself. A good modern incident light meter should be capable of measuring the luminance in either lux or foot candles. In addition, it's much better if the meter has a digital readout so the figures are accurately displayed. The spectral response must match within fairly close limits the CIE photopic luminosity curve which gives the correct assessment of colour balance for incident light readings (see Figure 4.10).

In our measurement of incident light, it is essential that we use a cosine corrected cell which gives readings which are correct and take into account the angle of the light incident on the

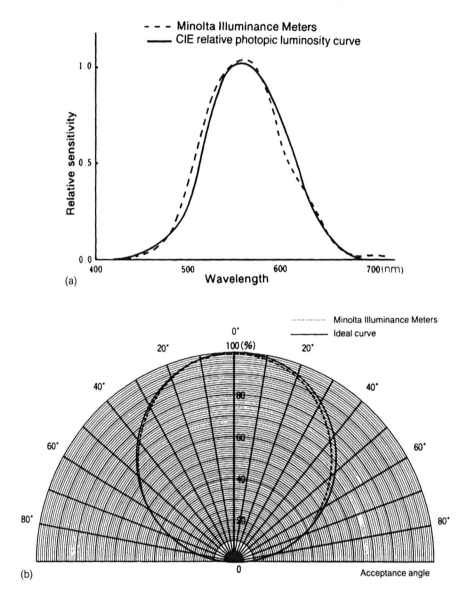

Figure 4.10 (a) Incident light meter – spectral response; (b) Incident light meter – acceptance angle characteristics (courtesy of Minolta (UK) Ltd)

meter. It is also important that the meter would be facing the direction of the most interest visually, i.e. along the path that the camera would look at the scene. When taking measurements on vertical or horizontal surfaces, the meter should be parallel to the surface.

Tri-stimulus colour meter

In film and TV we need accurate measurements of incident light onto subjects. We also need an accurate measure of colour temperature if we are using sources that approximate to the blackbody curve and there is also a need to measure colour accurately so that errors are avoided when operating discharge sources in either film or TV. A tri-stimulus meter is really a clever little hand held computer. It contains three photo cells which are filtered to detect the primary stimulus values of blue, green and red light under a special opal diffuser. This diffuser is specially made to take account of the direction of light and therefore inherently calculates the cosine angle of incident light. The incident light level can be derived from the output of the green photo cell as this relates to the photopic curve. It would appear that only the blue and red photo cells would be required to give a colour temperature reading; however meters of this type will compute a point on the spectrum locus from an analysis of the red, blue and green receptors. A big advantage of using meters such as this, is that colour shifts can be accurately measured by using the x and y co-ordinates on a CIE spectral diagram. Readings can be assigned a 'K' output reading signifying colour temperature, but it may be that the meter is measuring a discharge source. This can be given a correlated colour temperature. The correlated colour temperature is the nearest point on the blackbody locus which matches the source. The measurements always have to be referred back to the x y co-ordinates to get an accurate representation from the CIE diagram. Meters such as this although relatively expensive compared with a basic incident light meter, are invaluable and in fact, indispensable to the assessment of any lighting.

5
Light sources

Light can be produced from electricity in several ways and the most important are:

- *Incandescence* Light and infrared energy are produced by raising the temperature of a substance (e.g. tungsten) until it is incandescent.
- *Electrical discharge* Light is produced by electricity passing through a gas or vapour, agitating or exciting the atoms of the filling to produce light, UV energy and infrared energy.
- *Fluorescence and phosphorescence* The process by which UV energy is converted into visible light by phosphors.

Source	Lumens per watt
100 W household lamp	13
3200 K tungsten halogen lamp	26
HF fluorescent lamp	80
HID lamp 6000 K	95

Table 5.1 Output as a percentage of input power

3200 K Incandescent lamp	
Losses	12%
Infrared	77.5%
Ultraviolet	0.5%
Visible light	10%
Fluorescent lamp (HF operation)	
Losses	28.5%
Infrared	0.5%
Ultraviolet *(for phosphor conversion)*	40%
Visible light	31%
Metal Halide discharge lamps	
Losses	18%
Infrared	34%
Ultraviolet	11%
Visible light	37%

5.1   Incandescent sources

The original lamps were very expensive. From 1883 to 1900 the price was 25p while an engineer's salary was £1.50 per week, so in today's terms, 16% of an engineer's weekly salary would seem extortionate for a common household lamp. In 1840 Joseph Wilson Swan showed an experiment of burning a thin filament made of carbon in the open air. It lasted a few seconds and was the first of his experiments. The development of the incandescent filament lamp was long and tedious, Swan finally completed his design and was able to demonstrate it in Newcastle in 1879. At the same time Thomas Edison was working along the same lines in America and was astute enough to take out a British patent for a carbon filament burning in a vacuum. The following 4 years were largely taken up by a legal battle between Edison and Swan over the rights to the idea with the only winners being the Patent lawyers, for in 1883 they called off the fight and joined forces, registering the Edison and Swan United Electric Light Company. The manufacture of the carbon filament, which incidentally has the reverse characteristic to tungsten inasmuch as its resistance decreases as it heats, was manufactured until 1906 when the tungsten filament was first produced for domestic sales. This enabled the bulb manufacturers to greatly increase the light output from the filament by lacing it around supports and coiling it back upon itself to maintain a high temperature by the close proximity of the filament coils to each other. The filament could also run at comparatively high colour temperatures in view of the fact that the melting point of tungsten is 3410°C.

A common household 240 V 100 W bulb has 1147 mm of wire in the filament. Therefore the next development was the coiled coil filament where the wire is returned and coiled again on itself; this was a great advance in reducing the size of the source. Various improvements were introduced in the following years, one of which was the use of nitrogen and argon in the lamp to retard evaporation of the filament and thereby prolong its life.

The next significant development in lamps occurred during the late 1950s and when it became commercially available in 1960 was known as the Quartz Iodine lamp, later to be renamed Tungsten Halogen with its benefit of the tungsten halogen cycle. Other advances were made by including internal reflectors inside the envelope of the lamp and in some instances a dichroic coating which not only reflected the light forwards but permitted the infrared end of the spectrum to pass through the reflector, thereby reducing the heat in the beam.

Tungsten halogen lamps can be divided into two groups of manufacture – synthetic silica quartz and hard glass. In the case of the synthetic silica quartz, the walls are extremely strong and have a high melting point thus allowing a small envelope which permits a comparatively high internal pressure. This has the effect of doubling the life in comparison with hard glass. Therefore the hard glass envelope is thinner and much larger but still maintains the tungsten halogen cycle. At half the life one is not disappointed to find that it is approximately half the price, thus the cost per hour of life is approximately the same. Therefore the choice is purely a high initial capital investment with the synthetic silica quartz lamps with reduced maintenance replacements against the low initial cost of the hard glass.

The electric lamp is a heat generator from which we can get a little light. This would appear to be an odd statement until one compares the efficiency. The conversion of total electrical energy in a 3200 K lamp produces 10% light and 90% waste. The light energy is transmitted through the air which is also absorbing heat from the beam and the remainder of the heat is absorbed by the subject being illuminated – a very important fact when considering ventilation requirements for a building (see Figure 5.1).

The temperature of the lamp is one of the manufacturers' main design considerations, with the need to operate at relatively high temperatures, bearing in mind the melting point of tungsten which is 3410°C. The high efficiency 3400 K (3127°C) lamps are obviously burning very near their

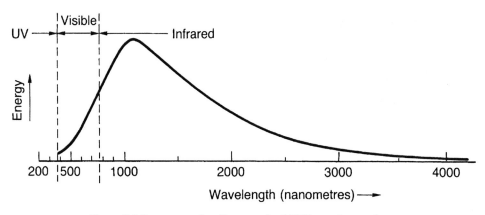

Figure 5.1 Energy–wavelength curve of a 500W incandescent lamp

melting point and therefore only give approximately 20 hours life. The lamp designer has to concern himself not only with the correct temperatures to keep the tungsten halogen cycle working, but also the filament design to achieve the exact colour temperatures required (Figure 5.2). He also has the problem of maintaining the lamp's seal temperature within the manufacturer's stated maximum. This is because the 'lead out' of the filament through the silicon quartz envelope is made by a thin foil of molybdenum. The expansion of molybdenum and quartz are not quite the same, therefore as the temperature increases the difference increases and at very high temperatures the seal between them would become porous and the molybdenum would oxidise.

Typically, the maximum temperature of molybdenum seals fall into three categories:

1 Long life lamps with a maximum temperature of 350°C,
2 Short life lamps 400°C, and
3 Special lamps designed to work with a maximum seal temperature of 500°C.

However, caution should be taken with the high temperature seal lamps because some of them have a shorter light centre length than the standard lamps and cannot be interchanged, because of misalignment within the optical system, however when used in a purpose designed luminaire, the higher seal temperature lamps permit the manufacturer to design much smaller lamp housings. When lamps are used in a design with inadequate ventilation, the end of life can be seal failure rather than filament failure. At the other end of the scale, if the source is force cooled by a fan, reducing its wall temperature to 250°C the tungsten halogen cycle is affected.

Filament vibration can sometimes cause an acoustic problem. With a sinusoidal voltage applied to the lamp, the current produces a shock on the filament every half cycle. The lamp manufacturers tried to reduce this effect by calculating the spacing of the supports and clamping the filament supports onto the filament using non-magnetic wires to try to dampen the vibration. With thyristor dimmers the situation is worse and this is because the current is rapidly switched on every half cycle and does not increase slowly as it would in a sinusoidal waveform. The worse position for vibration is at half power when the dimmer is firing at a 90° angle. Manufacturers of high quality dimmers use a choke in the output to dampen this effect. It is an interesting experiment to observe the filament movement with various firing angles by taking a standard lens and positioning it at its focal length from the filament projecting the image onto a screen, the filament can be focused and the movement observed.

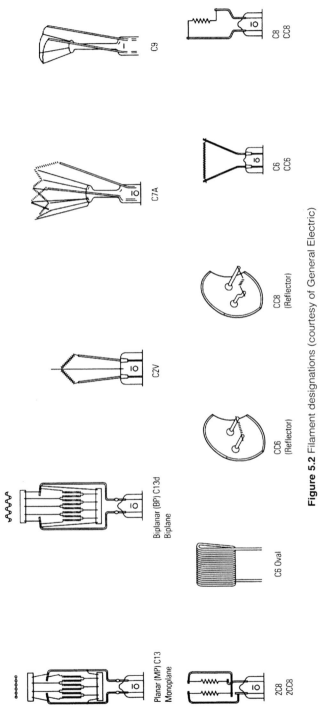

Figure 5.2 Filament designations (courtesy of General Electric)

C9

C8
CC8

C7A

C6
CC6

CC8
(Reflector)

C2V

CC6
(Reflector)

Biplanar (BP) C13d
Biplane

C6 Oval

Planar (MP) C13
Monoplane

2C8
2CC8

Figure 5.3 (a) A typical high wattage studio lamp; (b) A typical 4-pin twin filament studio lamp; (c) A typical low wattage theatre class tungsten halogen lamp; (d) End section of a typical quartz linear tungsten halogen lamp (courtesy of General Electric)

    The cause of the inrush current on the initial switch on of a cold filament is that tungsten has a comparatively low resistance in its cold state. The current initially reaches a very high value but as soon as the filament heats, its resistance increases and the current soon falls. To generalise, the inrush current can be from 10 to 17 times the normal running current, depending on the filament size and the impedance of the circuit, but only lasts for approximately 0.2 to 0.8 seconds. This can become a problem in determining the type of fuse for a circuit and the current rating of miniature circuit breakers (see Dimmer section – circuit protection).

All lamps are designed for one specific voltage, the manufacturer decides the following criteria: operating voltage, colour temperature, life, current and the wattage which is a product of the current and voltage. The performance of a light source is tested in an integrating sphere, where the total luminous efficacy is measured and then expressed in the manufacturer's data as 'lumens per watt'. The higher the lumens per watt, the higher the lamp temperature and consequently the colour temperature.

If any parameters are changed, all the other values must change because they are all inter-related. The easiest way to understand that is to take the case of varying the voltage to the lamp. If the voltage is reduced, the flow of current will reduce, and as the wattage is a function of volts × amps, the wattage will reduce. Because the filament is now burning at a lower tempera-ture, the colour of the light will change and will move towards the red end of the spectrum and the good news is that the life will be extended.

It is apparent by now that it is very difficult to calculate the outcome of a voltage change because all of the values that could be used for a formula are variables with no constant to latch onto. Even the resistance of the filaments increases when it is heated, therefore, when we reduce the voltage and thus the heat of the filament, the resistance will decrease.

It is however, possible by the use of the graph in Figure 5.4 to read off all the changes that take place with varying voltage by starting with a complete set of known values. Fortunately, every lamp manufacturer provides the relevant information which is peculiar to his product so it is necessary to first determine the make and type number of the lamp. A typical example would be type: CP-40 (ANSI code FKJ) 240 V, 1000 W, 3200 K, 26 lumens/W, thus giving a total of 26 000 lumens and a life of 200 hours.

It will be seen that the horizontal scale of Figure 5.4 refers to percentage change of the applied voltage and the vertical scale shows the resultant change by percentage of the manufacturer's stated values.

Do remember to convert any value into a percentage of the manufacturer's stated value. For example, taking the CP-40 1000-W lamp quoted earlier, we have a rated voltage of 240. If the voltage is reduced, to say 205 V, a reduction of 35 in 240 equals 14.6% (say 15%). Referring to the horizontal scale of the graph, percentage change of the applied voltage, a reduction of 15% gives a value of 85% voltage. Move vertically up the 85% line and read off the following values:

Light output	60% of 26 000 lumens	= 15 600 lumens
Watts	77% of 1000 W	= 770 W
Current (A)	92% of 4.17 A	= 3.84 A
Colour temperature	94% of 3200 K	= 3008 K
Life (est.)	300% of 200 hours	= 600 hours

In the case of life, it was necessary to project the life curve above the graph and estimate that it would meet the vertical line at approximately 300%. When the life value is changed consider-ably, it cannot be estimated with great accuracy, however the principle gives a good indication of the life that one would expect. The example quoted is in fact the result of running the lamp at position 7.5 on the lighting control console, if it has a square law fader characteristic (refer to Chapter 8).

The electrical supply system in the United Kingdom is normally very good. However, the supply authorities are very generous with themselves in allowing a maximum variation of +10%

Figure 5.4 Characteristics of tungsten halogen lamps

and −6% about 400 V for three-phase supplies and +10% and −6% for 230 V supplies which represents 253 V to 216.2 V. Referring to the graph, 253 V equals 106% voltage for a 240 V lamp which would result in a life of 50%, so don't always blame the lamp manufacturer for poor life performance – it might not be his fault.

As a matter of interest, the change to a stated value of 230 V for the mains supply (for European harmonisation) has not caused too many problems in practice as most systems in the United Kingdom still operate at about 240 V and therefore most lamps will be supplied as 240 V versions for the United Kingdom.

When a tungsten filament is burning at a comparatively high temperature, tungsten atoms leave the filament and normally attach themselves to the inside surface of the lamp envelope. This is most noticeable in the household bulb, which becomes quite black by the end of its life. Theatre and studio lamps, before tungsten halogen designs became available, had the same problem resulting in the reduction of both light and colour temperature throughout their life. The chemical principle of including a halogen gas in the lamp to reduce blackening was well known for many years before it became practical to produce a lamp to accommodate it.

The first lamps to appear on the market in the early 1960s used a quartz envelope and an iodine filling. This had the desired effect but unfortunately the iodine had a slight pink colour when hot and changed the colour of the light. The new development was called *quartz iodine* but in fact most of the halogen gases would work in the same way. Unfortunately, most of these gases radiate a colour when heated or were quite obnoxious towards the tungsten filament, eating it away before it reached old age. Some halogens would even attack the filament when it was on the shelf, resulting in a very short life instead of an extended one. In general, the more reactive the halide, the more effective is the halogen cycle. So in theory, fluorine, the most reactive, should be the best but it is so reactive that it even attacks the glass or quartz. Therefore iodine, bromine and chlorine are the only ones in use for halogen lamps. Over the next 5 years, the manufacturing techniques improved, enabling the lamp manufacturers to use bromine in place of iodine and a synthetic hard glass in place of pure quartz.

Although this was a great technological breakthrough because bromine did not add an obvious colour to the light, and the new material for the envelope was cheaper than pure quartz, it produced havoc with the lamp manufacturers' marketing departments that had spent years promoting quartz iodine only to have the name changed because the product no longer used quartz or iodine. The safe way out was apparent, because all lamps would use a tungsten filament and a halogen gas filling, therefore the name *tungsten halogen* was adopted.

The tungsten halogen cycle is simple in principle. Tungsten atoms 'boil off' and leave the filament; as they cool below 1400°C they combine with the halogen atoms and circulate within the lamp envelope. If the temperature fell below 250°C they would separate. However, by moving the envelope closer to the filament, thus maintaining a higher temperature, the compound will not separate. So the tungsten and halogen atoms circulate, in a convection effect, until they find a temperature above 1400°C, (the filament) when the compound separates and deposits the tungsten atoms back onto the filament (Figure 5.5).

Thus, it implies that the life of the lamp is infinite but, in practice, there are minuscule variations of thickness in the filament and the tungsten atoms are redeposited unevenly. Eventually, therefore, weak areas develop on the filament and ultimately cause lamp failure.

It would appear that a problem might occur when a tungsten halogen lamp is dimmed to a very low level, due to the fact it becomes cooler. However, in practice the evaporation from the filament is substantially reduced and the small amount that does deposit on the envelope is removed when the lamp temperature is restored to full.

The advantages of tungsten halogen lamps are:

1   An extended life by using halogens and higher filling pressures with quartz envelopes.
2   A constant light output throughout life.
3   A constant colour temperature throughout life.
4   A smaller quartz envelope means that compact luminaires can be designed.
5   Reduced maintenance costs in time spent replacing lamps.
6   In general, a higher light output is achieved (higher lumens/watt).

Enlarged cross-section

Figure 5.5 Simplified mechanism of the tungsten halogen cycle

R7s

G6.35
GY6.35
GZ6.35

G5.3

GY5.3
(Flat pins)

GX5.3
(Round pins)

2 button

GY9.5
GZ9.5

G7.9 (std. volts)
GX7.9 (Low volts)

Ferrule Contact

E12/15

BA15d

BA15s

P30s
P30d

P40s

Large Indexing Ring
(Ring is flat opposite pin)

Small Indexing Ring
(Ring is a full circle)

E26

P28/25

E39

Double Contact
Medium Ring

G17q
GX17q

G22

Figure 5.6 Some photographic lamps with their IED codes and normal names or common abbreviations. Note that the illustrations are not to scale (courtesy of General Electric)

One aspect of tungsten halogen sources that has to be considered is UV radiation. Synthetic quartz will pass UV rays and can cause a slight sunburn. For instance, if the skin is exposed continuously for 4–5 hours with a light level of 2000 lux, a slight reddening of the skin will take place with a 3200 K lamp. At half this level, 1000 lux, the time would be double. The problem applies particularly to lamps running in open reflector luminaires. If however, the lamps are operating behind a lens which is normally manufactured from borosilicate glass, the problem does not exist because borosilicate glass is a good UV filter.

Lamps for entertainment, in the main, have compact filaments to produce the smallest size source for the optical systems employed, with the exception of floods and softlights, where an elongated filament is a distinct advantage when trying to evenly illuminate a large reflector.

5.2 Discharge sources

If we accept that the sun was the first light source with a nuclear fusion reaction in its core, which is approximately 14 000 000 K and an outer surface temperature of 5800 K, then an electrical discharge was certainly the second.

Benjamin Franklin, the American statesman and scientist, who helped in the forming of the American Constitution, demonstrated how to electrocute oneself by flying a kite in a thunderstorm. That part of the experiment did not work, however, the real object of the experiment did. Franklin was so convinced that lightning was caused by an electrical discharge that he submitted himself to the risk of electrocution by pointing his finger at a metal ring attached to the end of a silk line that was holding the kite and demonstrated that a spark jumped from the metal ring to his finger. This experiment proved that light was generated from an electrical discharge and that Benjamin Franklin became the inventor of the lightning rod (which was a side product of the experiment).

We now know that the electrical discharge in the form of lightning is caused when the changing temperature within a cloud produces raindrops, hail and ice particles, which collide causing friction that produces a negative charge in the falling particles whilst the smaller rising particles within the cloud gain a positive charge. In this way, charges of up to 1 million volts can be produced in the clouds and cause sheet lightning if the discharge takes place between clouds, and fork lightning if the discharge is conducted to earth with a power estimated to be between 20 000 and 40 000 A.

Sir Humphrey Davey (the inventor of the miners' safety lamp), demonstrated an electrical arc between two rods of carbon in 1810. To maintain an arc the two rods were continuously adjusted at the same rate as they were being burnt away. A hot, dirty job, bearing in mind that carbon vaporises at 3382°C. These experiments employed Alessandro Volta's type of battery that used alternate plates of zinc and silver. This demonstration took place at the Royal Institution in London and required 2000 battery cells to provide the voltage and current required to maintain the arc. Battery operated carbon arc lights first appeared for entertainment when they were used at the Paris Opera. They were also used for floodlighting in the Place de la Concorde in 1830 and later at the Royal Exchange in London.

The early work by Humphrey Davey in his experiments with carbon arcs laid the ground for the film industry to develop a succession of arc lights from 1900 through to 1965. In the early 1900s the film industry blossomed in Hollywood and the studios all had their own generators to run the lighting. Because carbons arcs require a direct current (d.c.) to maintain an arc and a voltage in the range 40 V–85 V between the carbons, the generators were made to produce 115 V d.c. so that a resistance ballast could be conveniently connected in series with the supply to limit the current flow and maintain the arc volts.

The size of the luminaires were rated by the current that was drawn by the carbons, e.g. 40 A, 60 A, 150 A, 225 A and 300 A. For comparison, today's discharge lamps have a range which includes 125 W, 200 W, 270 W, 400 W, 575 W, 1.2 kW, 2.5 kW, 4 kW, 6 kW, 12 kW and 18 kW.

The 'Brute', an extremely powerful 225-A Fresnel spotlight, was developed in 1950 with geared drive to feed the carbons as they burnt away and to rotate the positive carbon at the same time. The 'Brutes', which were regarded with great affection, have today been replaced by discharge sources but comparisons are still being made between the old and the new. The light readings published by Mole Richardson (England) when they introduced the 'Brute' in 1953 make interesting reading:

At full flood, over a throw of 35 ft (10.67 m) the light level was 1000 foot-candles (10 760 lux) with a beam width of 25 ft (7.62 m).
or
At full flood over the longer distance of 60 ft (18.29 m) the light level was 340 foot-candles (3661 lux) with a beam width of 43 ft (13.1 m).

The first practical discharge lamps were the cold cathode carbon dioxide 'Moore' tubes of 1895. Light is produced by the activity caused when fast moving electrons collide with molecules of gas. In order to accelerate electrons in the early lamps, the applied voltage was in the order of 2000–10 000 V at high frequency. Cold cathode tubes contain gas at low pressure, about 1/100 of an atmosphere. The colour of the light is dependent on the gases used. Carbon dioxide emits a very white light of very low intensity. Neon, first isolated in 1898, produces a red light and was used extensively in advertising displays from 1922.

The hot cathode lamp was a much better commercial proposition because it could operate at mains voltage. This was made possible by using metallic substances such as 'thoriated tungsten', which when heated to incandescence, produces a high level of electronic activity in the tube. By 1932 the hot cathode lamp led to the development of the high pressure sodium and mercury lamps with their much higher efficiency and these lamps are still in use in today's street lighting.

In all types of discharge lamps an arc is struck between two electrodes in an envelope containing an inert gas or vapour (Figure 5.7). A choke or electronic ballast is used in the a.c. supply to limit the flow of current after the arc has been established. Striking the arc is usually achieved by applying a high voltage across the electrodes to break down the resistance between them so that the gases or vapours inside the lamp may start conducting. Typical starting voltages are between 2000 V and 10 000 V. At this point, the ballast takes over and regulates the flow of current. This starting up procedure normally takes from 1–2 minutes until the heat in the lamp vaporises the metallic elements which emit their characteristic colours, but if the lamp is switched off it will require to cool down before it can be restruck. The cooling time can take from 2–5 minutes to allow the internal pressure of the lamp to reduce to a level where conduction can occur. Alternatively, lamps are designed to be 'hot restrike' in which case a voltage between 20 000 and 70 000 is applied to overcome the high internal pressure and provide instantaneous starting when the lamp is hot. Discharge lamps are made using mercury, halides, rare earths and gases; often containing a mixture of many types of chemicals. There are some 40 metal halides to choose from and each manufacturer has his own 'brew'. Iodides of sodium produce mainly

(a)

Figure 5.7 (a) MSI discharge lamps (courtesy Philips Lighting)

(b)

(c)

Figure 5.7 *Continued* (b) MSR discharge lamps; (c) MSR SA discharge lamps (courtesy Philips Lighting)

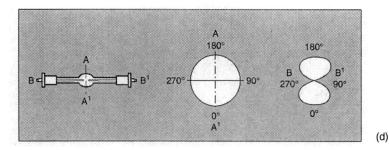

(d)

Figure 5.7 *Continued* (d) The axial and perpendicular polar light intensity distribution diagrams of a MEDIUM SOURCE lamp (courtesy Philips Lighting)

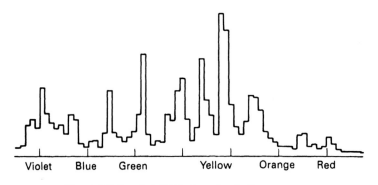

Violet   Blue   Green   Yellow   Orange   Red

Figure 5.8 Spectral distribution of a discharge source

yellow light, mercury emits blue/green light in the visible parts of the spectrum and a great quantity of invisible radiation in the UV wavelengths. Thallium is used because it emits mainly green light (see Figure 5.8).

There are many types of discharge lamps, each with its own reference code, although many have similar characteristics (Table 5.2). We will only consider here the lamps that will be useful in entertainment, being those that approximate to daylight or have a correlated colour temperature approaching 3400 K. As the lamp manufacturing companies develop a new design of lamp, they register the reference as a trade name so other manufacturers are obliged to make up their reference for a similar development.

Although lamp manufacturers quote a colour temperature of the light in Kelvins this is only an approximation to the nearest point on the blackbody curve.

The total output from a lamp is made up of many separate colours from any number of the halides and gases employed to achieve the correct colour balance in the red, green and blue parts of the spectrum to match the response requirements for colour films and TV cameras.

Discharge lamps are generally made of a synthetic quartz material which permits very high operating pressures within the lamp when it is hot, therefore caution must be taken when relamping to ensure that the lamp has cooled down before the luminaire is opened. The operator must avoid handling the envelope even when the lamp is cool to prevent grease from the skin contaminating the quartz envelope. Care has to be taken when inserting a lamp into its holder because exerting pressure on the envelope can cause a fracture at its joint to the base.

The discharge lamp emits large quantities of radiation in the UV wavelengths which pass straight through the quartz envelope; it is therefore most dangerous to be directly exposed to the lamp. It must always be housed or have a lens or protective glass in front of it. It is fortunate that

Table 5.2 Lamp types

Sources require an a.c. supply	
HMI	Hydrargyrum (Latin for mercury). Medium arc. Iodides
	95 lumens/W, 6000 K
	Made by Osram
HMI/SE	Single Ended version of the HMI
	95 lumens/W, 6000 K
	Made by Osram
MSR/HR	Medium Source Rare earth, single ended
	95 lumens/W, 6000 K
	Made by Philips
CID	Compact Iodide Daylight
	70–80 lumens/W, 5500 K
	Made by GE Lighting
CSI	Compact Source Iodide
	90 lumens/W, 4000 K
	Made by GE Lighting
DAYMAX	Mercury Halide source
	95 lumens/W, 5600 K
	Made by ILC, USA
BRITE ARC	Mercury halide source
	95 lumens/W, 5600 K
	Made by Sylvania, USA
Sources are fed from d.c. supplies	
EMI	Xenon
	40 lumens/W, 6000 K
	Made by GE Lighting
XBO	Xenon
	40 lumens/W, 6000 K
	Made by Osram

all standard borosilicate Fresnel lenses have the characteristic of absorbing UV but if the luminaire is open faced the safety glass provided must also be capable of absorbing the UV radiation. Because of the UV radiation, safety standards require that a switch is fitted to the lens door or safety glass to automatically extinguish the lamp to prevent hazards to the operators and artists by opening the luminaire while the lamp is on. Alternatively the lens door or glass must be securely fastened by fixing screws or bolts.

The end of life of an incandescent lamp is very obvious, however this is not the case with a discharge lamp. Normally the end of life will be caused by the electrodes burning back during their life, creating a larger gap, the effect of this is a poor starting characteristic requiring many attempts to get the lamp to run continuously after the initial high voltage spark is applied. Therefore inconsistent starting is an indication of the end of life.

Discharge lamps provide a comparatively small light source. This is certainly welcomed by luminaire manufacturers enabling them to make efficient optical systems. Another bonus is that the total light output of a discharge lamp is comparatively constant throughout its life. However, many lamps suffer devitrification of the quartz during life which is not visible to the eye but has the effect when the lamp is running hot of diffusing the inside surface making the apparent source size that of its envelope. This is most noticeable in ellipsoidal spotlights and follow spots where the initial light output can be *double* that of the light performance halfway through the lamps life. The effect of the apparently enlarged source size due to devitrification does not significantly affect focusing Fresnels.

Most of the modern developments in daylight balanced lamps have an efficacy of about 95 lumens/W. It is useful at this point to make comparisons with the studio incandescent tungsten halogen lamp of 3200 K that has an efficacy of 26 lumens/W. This means that the discharge lamp has approximately four times the light output of the tungsten halogen lamp for the same wattage or, an alternative comparison is, that for the same light output the discharge lamp is running at 25% of the tungsten halogen 'lamp watts' – an important fact when considering the heating effect in the luminaire and the air conditioning installation in a studio.

We make the point of saying 'lamp watts' because the current drawn from the mains may be much higher than would be expected. This is because the current and voltage are not always in phase and can have a 'power factor' as low as 0.5 when a choke ballast is used.

A typical example is a 2.5 kW discharge lamp compared with a 2.5 kW incandescent lamp. From a 240 V supply, the tungsten halogen lamp would draw 10.42 A, in the case of a discharge lamp supplied from an inductive ballast with a power factor of 0.6, the current drawn from the supply is 17.36 A, (W = VI cos ϕ, where cos ϕ is the cosine of the angle of lead or lag of the current). This is obviously an important consideration in supply requirements. The current apparently lost between the resistive load and the inductive load is known as the 'wattless' current. Manufacturers usually add components to the ballast circuit to improve the power factor so that it approaches 'unity'.

Light flicker is caused by the light following the mains frequency from zero to a maximum value and back down to zero again. This causes a flicker at twice mains frequency when the source is current regulated by a choke and a film camera set to certain shutter speeds or shutter angles will 'see' this fluctuation and produce reduced exposure frames at repetitive intervals. This effect will render conventional ballast equipment useless at high shutter speeds. However, the problems can be overcome by the use of an electronic square wave ballast. By using very fast switching times between the positive and negative half cycles the current 'OFF' period is

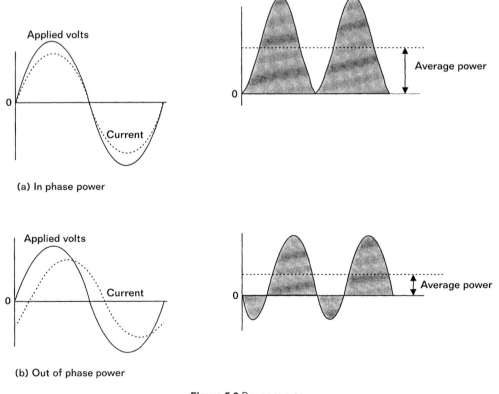

(a) In phase power

(b) Out of phase power

Figure 5.9 Power curves

very small compared with the current 'ON' period; consequently the light output appears to be constant, and the user does not have to worry about any synchronisation for the various shutter angles of film cameras and the time-bases of TV systems (Figure 5.9).

Gas discharge lamps generate light from an electrical discharge with a fixed characteristic voltage which may be 70 V for low wattage lamps rising to 225 V for high wattage lamps. The resistance of the lamp falls rapidly above this voltage to a very low value and any attempt to simply connect a lamp to the supply would result in an uncontrolled power output and the bulb would simply explode. The gas behaves as a resistor to the current but has a negative characteristic, therefore to prevent the current increasing to very high levels and possible destroying the lamp we must control the flow of current.

5.3 Control of discharge sources

With a.c. operated devices, there are three ways in which we can control the flow of current:

1 a resistor,
2 a capacitor, or
3 an inductor.

The main disadvantage of using a resistor is the high losses (I^2R) which results in very low efficiency and the generation of a lot of heat. A capacitor has the lowest inherent losses but unfortunately the waveform produced can damage lamp electrodes. Thus, these disadvantages of the resistor and capacitor has led to the inductor being the most commonly used type of ballast for discharge sources.

These ballasts are composed of copper coils wound around an iron core, in order to limit the losses in the ballast and to ensure that the lamp current is stabilised for various conditions, it is important to have the correct combination of the sizes of wire used, the type of magnetic core and the air gap. Due to an inductance being used in circuit, the power factor ($\cos\phi$) of the system is very low and a typical value is 0.5. To conform to the requirements of the supply authorities means that the power factor has to be raised to certain minimum value. This is usually accomplished by placing a capacitor across the mains input in front of the ballast. The inductance is chosen to have the right level of reactance to be able to support the difference between the lamp voltage and supply voltage at the rated current.

A complication is the tendency of the higher wattage lamps to have high operating voltages, say 225 V, and therefore only a small difference from the normal single phase supply voltage. The answer to this is not simply to use a smaller choke to support the voltage difference because after ignition a cold lamp will run at a voltage of only 30 or 40 V. If a small choke were used the starting current would be very large and would damage the lamp. The result is that many ballast chokes of 4 kW and above have a boost transformer connected to the input to ensure that the supply is always high enough above the lamp voltage. All this makes the choke very heavy and almost always fitted with wheels.

Electronic ballasts overcome the weight problems associated with conventional ballasts by using switching regulators to control the output current feeding the lamp circuit, thus avoiding the need for a current limiting choke. The switching regulators will be running at a set frequency in the range 20 kHz–50 kHz according to the manufacturer's circuit design.

The essential components of an electronic ballast are:

1 A rectifier to convert the input supply to d.c.
2 A reservoir capacitor to convert the raw d.c. to smooth d.c.

3   A switching current regulator to limit the output current.
4   A d.c. to a.c. converter circuit to produce the actual square wave.

Discharge lamps, in practice, vary slightly in their operating performance due to the manual manufacturing methods which are generally employed. Even from the same manufacturer there are slight variations in the arc voltage and if on the low side this means that the lamp output will be lower in wattage than the stated output. Some may, of course, have high voltage and this means that the power is above the stated value of the lamp, thus overheating the arc and causing short life in the lamp. The lamp voltage is also variable with age. Other than the variations of voltage from a manufactured batch, there are also reasonable voltage differences between similar lamps produced by various manufacturers. To get around this problem, it is preferable that the electronic flicker free ballast system can sense the volts and the current and automatically adjust one to the other to give 'power control' so that the wattage output of the lamp is kept consistent with the manufacturers' stated values. The frequencies of the square waves used with flicker free ballasts are between 40 Hz and 400 Hz.

It is essential that the output of the switching regulator is filtered so that high frequency components between 25 kHz and 50 kHz are not superimposed on the square wave output.

One of the foremost electronic ballast suppliers, Power Gems of Manchester, England use a 100 Hz square wave output with a switching frequency for the current regulator of 25.6 kHz. The units they produce are equipped with *active power factor correction circuits* (see Figure 5.10) giving a power factor close to 'unity' and also have a microprocessor management system to

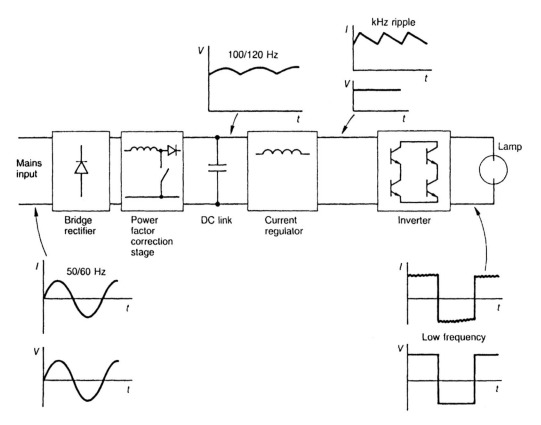

Figure 5.10 Electronic ballast (power factor corrected)

give messages on a LCD display for system status and information on any fault condition. Typical fault conditions may be 'over or under voltage', 'output over current', 'over temperature', etc. In all these conditions the output will shut down, a message will be displayed and a fault code stored in the internal logging system.

Many of the electronic ballasts of today have various outputs which can be selected according to the mode required e.g. 'flicker free', 'silent' 50 Hz, 'silent' 60 Hz, etc. When used in the modes other than 'flicker free' the appropriate square wave output has the square edges of its waveform 'rounded off' by circuits in the ballast unit, so that it approximates to a sinusoidal waveform.

An advantage of the electronic ballast is that it is possible with the correct selection of the discharge lamp to obtain a degree of dimming. However, dimming can only be performed over a comparatively small range typically 50% of the light output before the arc becomes unstable. One major problem that can exist during dimming is a colour shift so it is wise therefore to do tests before relying on dimming a discharge lamp.

Ignition system

To enable a discharge lamp to ignite, high voltage peaks have to be applied to the lamp, and the peaks are proportional to the gas pressure in the lamp envelope. Thus there is a difference between the ignition of a cold lamp which is at relatively low pressure and of a hot lamp which is at high pressure. The ignition voltage will be generally at least 2000 V and anywhere up to 10 kV with cold lamps. Some special discharge lamps which have a higher filling pressure in the cold state require higher voltages. When the lamp is hot, the pressure has increased by at least 10 times and to re-ignite lamps when hot voltages of between 20 and 70 kV are required depending upon the type of lamp.

Figure 5.11 shows three types of igniters used with discharge sources. In order to keep the igniter unit to a small size requires that the components are small and consequently this means that to avoid abusing the circuit the starting time must remain for very short periods (0.5–3 seconds). There is also a requirement to limit the number of starts per minute and this is generally specified by the lamp manufacturer. On the other hand, the lamp requires a minimum period of energisation to ensure that it starts reliably and again these times are given by the lamp manufacturer. Control of the ignition period is usually accomplished by means of an electronic time switch placed in the power supply or the lamphead.

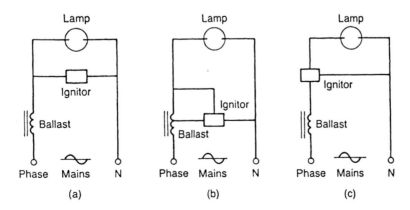

Figure 5.11 Three different types of igniter: (a) Parallel igniter; (b) Igniter on ballast tap; (c) Series igniter

Problems in practice

If a magnetic ballast is used to regulate the current to the lamp and the unit does not have a good power factor the only problem that ensues is that the voltage and current are out of phase to some degree but their waveforms are essentially sinusoidal in shape. If an electronic ballast is used with a poor power factor there will be a substantial distortion of the electrical supply waveform, due to the nature of the circuits employed. This distortion, caused by a high harmonic content can give problems with a generator. The generator may become confused as to what are the correct circuit volts, and the Automatic Voltage Regulator (AVR) will take corrective action, usually raising the voltage which results in the connected equipment being over-volted.

With a balanced load on each leg of a three-phase supply there is virtually no neutral current when using loads with a high power factor; but balanced loads with high harmonic content will produce very high neutral currents due to the addition of triplet harmonics (Figure 5.12). In practice this means that the neutral conductor has to be rated much higher than would normally be expected.

In the case of both magnetic and electronic ballasts a poor power factor means that some energy is wasted, only the 'in phase' current and voltage components of the supply qualify as watts! The wattless component means that losses in the generator will be higher, thus to supply the useful and wasted electrical energy the generator will have to be larger than would appear at

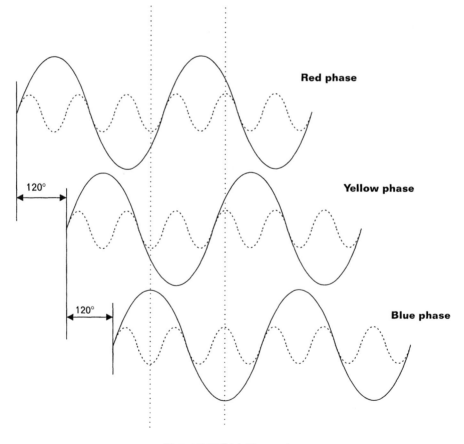

Figure 5.12 Triplet harmonics

face value. Power factors of around 0.7 will mean that a generator needs to be about 30% higher in output. This reflects in the cost of generation and the overheating in the system will result in increased maintenance.

The lamp envelope surrounding the arc acts rather like a miniature sound chamber and its shape affects the acoustic output of the arc. Although not usually a problem when using magnetic ballasts with a sine wave output; a square wave presented to the electrodes can induce an audible noise in the arc as well as in the ballast. Additionally, if there is too much ripple on the square wave supply there can also be quite high frequency noise coming from the lamp. These high frequency components are often the cause of lamp instability.

A very important factor with regard to the operation of solid state ballast units is the ambient temperature in which they will operate so that the solid state devices within the units do not overheat and fail. It is possible to fan cool all the devices within the unit but this has to be carefully engineered as the units may be used in all types of conditions where there could be an ingress of either dust or water vapour. In the Arizona desert, just to make things worse, there is a high proportion of copper dust – which is a good recipe for a high voltage flash-over.

The noise from the fans and the electronics in the ballast unit, although very low can be troublesome when the units are close to the acting area. Whilst the noise in the ballast can be isolated by running it in a remote position, care should be taken when positioning luminaires to determine if any noise is being directed towards any microphones in use. The noise from the luminaires is more of a problem when using the smaller sources from 200 W to 1.2 kW. Above these wattages the lights are generally working further away and the problem becomes less.

Other types of interference can be present in an electronic ballast. The output from the ballast can produce:

(a)   Voltage spikes which can be sent back down the supply line and hence onto the mains, which in turn can affect other electronic equipment connected to the same supply.
(b)   Radio interference transmitted down the supply cable to the luminaire which is picked up by microphone cables in close proximity, causing audible hum on the sound output.

The introduction of the EMC Directive requires that these problems are reduced significantly by the manufacturers; probably by the addition of high quality filters in the ballast unit.

5.4   Xenon discharge lamp

The xenon discharge lamp is very similar in appearance to other discharge lamps and has the same type of quartz envelope that should not be handled without gloves, because if oil from the fingers is left on the envelope, it will cause devitrification of the quartz when it is heated and produce a grey mark on the envelope that will overheat and can cause the quartz to blister. If a lamp has been handled it should be cleaned with alcohol before it is used.

The lamp also requires a very high voltage of approximately 40 000 V to restrike it when it is hot and it produces large quantities of UV radiation, but here the similarity with other discharge lamps ends. Xenon's have been used for many years in film projectors and follow spots with great success, mainly due to the following advantages:

(a)   D.C. operation means that the arc does not flicker.
(b)   The lamps have a very good daylight colour rendering 5600–6000 K correlated colour temperature, with a colour rendering index approaching 95.
(c)   A small source size with all of the useful light concentrated at the point on the cathode known as the 'cathode spot' which is near to the negative electrode. This means that the

source can be positioned very accurately in a mirror optical system to redirect most of the light to the first lens in the system.

(d)   When the lamp is switched on there is instant constant light with no warm up time required. The lamps can be switched on and off without the problem of waiting for them to cool before being restruck.

(e)   A wide range of lamps is available from 75 W through to 10 kW.

With so many advantages over other discharge lamps, why hasn't the xenon lamp been more widely used in TV and film studios? Mainly, because the disadvantages and problems encountered with xenon lamps outweighs the advantages.

A typical example is a 2 kW xenon lamp, where the arc characteristics are 2000 W at 25 V d.c., drawing 80 A and producing 80 000 lumens, which is 40 lumens/W, approximately half the value of other discharge lamps, with a typical life of 2000 hours. The lamp is supplied with d.c. from an a.c. supply using a transformer/rectifier unit, which because of the high current, low voltage requirements of the lamp, is very large and heavy. The main problem here is the high lamp current of 80 A which implies a cable of considerable cross sectional area to carry the current from the transformer/rectifier unit to the luminaire. Recent developments have solved the ballast problem by using similar technology to that used for HMI ballasts. The units are very small and weigh around 12 kg.

Finally, the main problem is one of safety, because of the extremely high internal pressure of the xenon lamp's filling, which can be from 6 to 8 atmospheres when cold and 15–20 atmospheres when hot. This means that special precautions must be taken to prevent access to the housing for a considerable period after switch off to allow the internal pressure to drop and when cold the manufacturers recommend that protective gloves and goggles are worn when handling the xenon lamp and special precautions are taken when transporting it. So it would appear that the use of xenon lamps will be restricted to follow spots for some time to come.

5.5   Fluorescent lamps

A fluorescent lamp produces light by the effect of phosphorescence (Figure 5.13). The arc discharges through low pressure mercury vapour and generates UV with a small amount of blue light. The phosphor coating on the inner surface of the glass tube converts this UV energy into visible light; the colour from the fluorescent tube we perceive depends upon the type of

Figure 5.13 Low pressure mercury vapour fluorescent lamp

phosphors used in the coating. When light sources which use phosphorescence are switched off, there is a short 'afterglow', therefore, the use of phosphors smoothes out some of the variations in the light output.

The light output is affected by the temperature of the lamp, due to varying the internal vapour pressure of the gas in the tube. Lamps are usually designed to operate in an ambient temperature of around 20°C and if the lamp runs hot, or indeed cold, a lower light output results.

Fluorescents normally run from 50 Hz or 60 Hz supplies, but there are great advantages in increasing the frequency of operation. The efficacy (lumens per Watt) of fluorescent lamps is increased by about 10% if we change the frequency from the normal mains to between 20 kHz and anything up to 100 kHz. However, the increase in efficacy is less at frequencies in excess of 30 kHz, therefore this is the normal region for high frequency operation. A benefit of using frequencies between 30 and 45 kHz gives the advantage that it is outside the audible range and below frequencies at which losses in the electronic ballast system would become noticeable.

Figure 5.14 (a) Standard fluorescent tubes; (b) tri-phosphor tubes

Due to a reduced power consumption in a high frequency system, the temperature in luminaires will be lower than those at normal mains frequencies. By using high frequency electronic ballasts it is possible to reduce the amount of flicker which is normally noticeable in mains operated ballasts. This has the advantage of overcoming the stroboscopic problems with moving machinery or fast moving subjects, and obviously can be a great advantage when using film or TV cameras. Originally, fluorescent lamps were approximately 25 mm in diameter and about 1.5 m long, eventually the diameter of tubes decreased and the lamps have been moulded into various shapes, such as a circle and U-tube. Nowadays, a whole range of compact fluorescent lamps is produced, with each lamp folded in half, with the ends connected to a single lamp cap. Various phosphors are used to give good colour rendering with a choice of colours (see Figure 5.14). By using high frequency ballasts, it is possible to achieve very high efficacies.
Typical efficacies are as follows:

40 W tubular range	100 lumens/W
55 W compact bi-axial	85 lumens/W
36 W compact bi-axial	80 lumens/W
26 W compact quad	70 lumens/W

5.6   Light emitting diodes (LED)

We are all familiar with LEDs being used as indicator lights and displays on all types of electronic equipment. By using new LED materials, and improving the production process, much brighter LEDs in a wide range of colours have been produced. One advantage of LEDs for converting electrical energy into light, is that most of the energy radiates in the visible spectrum, unlike incandescent and other types of lamps where energy is radiated in the non-visible spectrum such as UV and IR. The energy emitted from LEDs is in very narrow wavelengths. This means that the light output at that wavelength is highly efficient, although due to the low wattage of LEDs the light output is relatively low when compared with other light sources. The luminous intensity of LEDs is usually expressed in milli candelas at a defined current level. The following Table 5.3 gives some idea of the values reached at the present time for modern LEDs.

LEDs are made from Gallium based crystals with additional materials added to produce the distinctive colours, i.e. phosphorus, nitrogen, etc.

To produce white light from LEDs we have to use combinations of the primary colours, i.e. red, green and blue and this can be done by using layers on the surface of the LED chip. The

Table 5.3 Light output of LEDs

LED colour	Standard brightness				High brightness			
	Chip material	Wave-length (nm)	Light output (mc)	Viewing angle	Chip material	Wave-length (nm)	Light output (mc)	Viewing angle
Red	GaAsP/GaP	635	120	35	AS AllnGaP	635	900	30
Orange	GaAsP/GaP	605	90	30	AS AllnGaP	609	1300	30
Amber	GaAsP/GaP	583	100	35	AS AllnGaP	592	1300	30
Yellow	GaP	570	160	30	–	–	–	–
Green	GaP	565	140	24	GaN	520	1200	45
Turquoise	–	–	–	–	GaN	495	2000	30
Blue	–	–	–	–	GaN	465	325	45

nm = nanometre; mc = milli candela.

luminous intensity is approximately proportioned to the amount of current supplied to the LED; in other words, the greater the current, the higher the intensity. At the present time, there are design limits because LEDs are designed to operate at around 20 mA. By using LEDs in clusters, it is obviously able to produce more light but unfortunately, a side effect may be that, due to heat, the current in each LED has to be reduced. Due to the fact that LEDs are solid state devices, particularly bearing in mind they don't have filaments, etc., they have an incredibly long life and lives of upwards of 1 00 000 hours at 25°C are quoted. A typical LED will go to half its original intensity after 1 00 000 hours, although the LED will continue to operate. It has to be borne in mind that LEDs are current driven devices, and the light output is directly related to the current, but if we exceed the maximum current rating, this will produce excessive heat and the result generally is a reduced light output and a reduction in the operating life. Some small luminaires have been produced for architectural colour washes with a unit producing a 24 bit colour range, giving 16.7 million colours. The sources used are variable intensity coloured LEDs. A unit capable of producing 1000 candela is fitted with 278 LEDs comprising 108 red, 85 green and 85 blue to give the colour mixing required. The correlated colour temperature is 12 700 K. The power requirement for the unit is 1.3 A at 24 V d.c., consuming 33 W. The unit weighs 1.8 kg and is approximately 300 × 150 mm. More development is going on in the world of LEDs and several large international companies have combined to pool research and development and it is suggested that ultimately, power outputs of 100 lumens/W could be possible from LEDs.

6
Luminaires

6.1 Optical design theory

The Fresnel and plano-convex lenses

In 1748 George Louis Leclerc de Buffon originated the idea of dividing a plano-convex lens into separate concentric rings in order to significantly reduce the weight. In 1820 the idea was adopted by Augustin Jean Fresnel (pronounced 'Frenel') to overcome a real problem in lighthouses. Before this date the only way of controlling the light distribution from a lighthouse was with mirrors.

Fresnel adapted de Buffon's idea to make a one piece moulding of the separate concentric rings which could be pressed in a mould of large diameter but maintaining a thin cross section to reduce its weight. In this way, very short focal length lenses could be produced which would normally require a very thick cross section. Therefore, a Fresnel lens can be considered to be equivalent to a standard plano-convex lens of the same focal length.

In Figure 6.1 the plano-convex lens is superimposed on the equivalent Fresnel lens showing that the same curvature of the plano-convex lens can be achieved by moving sections of the surface down to the same plane. The sketch is an over-simplification of a Fresnel lens design, but it is sufficient to show the principle.

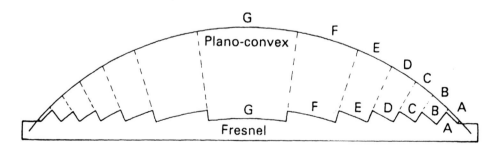

Figure 6.1 Fresnel/plano-convex lens comparison

The focal length of either lens is the point behind the lens where an object in front of the lens will be focused. The focal point can be found by focusing a bright object such as the sun onto a surface and measuring the distance from the lens to the image when it is in sharp focus, in the same way that all young boys ignite a piece of paper by focusing the sun's rays onto it with a lens.

If a light source is placed at the focal point of a lens, the reverse procedure would be expected, thereby producing an image of the filament when it is projected onto a screen. This is the position of the source when a Fresnel or plano-convex luminaire is focused to the full spot position. The sharpness of the filament image is smeared over by adding a slight diffusion to the rear surface of the lens. As the source is moved forward the beam will increase in angle and achieve full flood in its most forward position. The two luminaires that employ the above lenses are obviously the Fresnel and the plano-convex. Other luminaires that employ the plano-convex lens are the profile projector (ellipsoidal as it is known in the USA) follow spots and effects projectors.

6.2   Reflection and refraction

We are so accustomed to the reflection of light that we would not normally stop to consider that our very existence depends upon it. For every item that we see is reflecting light to our eyes so that we can form an image of it. When we think of a reflector, we visualise a bright shiny surface, however, every solid that is exposed to light is a reflector, otherwise we could not see it. The laws of reflection (Figure 6.2) are the same for all bright plane surfaces that is, if the surface is not diffused, which would have the effect of scattering the light.

If we consider a bright, shiny surface with a light ray falling onto it we can see that the ray is reflected off the surface at the same angle as it approaches it. That is, if the angle is measured from a line drawn at a tangent to that part of the reflector (Figure 6.3). This rule remains true for any shape of reflector and as the angle of reflection becomes less as the ray approaches 90° to the surface, (at which point the angle onto the reflector is the same as the angle off the surface) so that the light ray is returned to its place of origin, which explains why a flash from a camera will overexpose any part of the subject that is exactly 90° to the camera. A simple simile can be applied to estimate where the reflected light will be directed, because it behaves in the same manner as a billiard ball striking a cushion where the angle off the cushion is the same as the approach angle.

Figure 6.2 Reflection

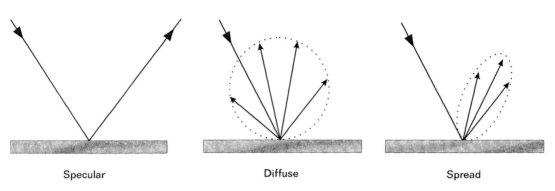

Specular   Diffuse   Spread

Figure 6.3 Types of reflection

The most obvious demonstration of refraction is shown in Figure 6.4 where a stick is placed into the water at an angle. If this is viewed from the side the stick appears to change direction. This displacement of the image accounts for the difficulty in trying to pinpoint the position of an object under water, such as a fish. We can therefore say that refraction causes a light beam to change direction when striking or leaving a surface of a transparent material.

Figure 6.5 shows a piece of glass with a light ray entering from the left-hand side. At the point of entry, the ray is refracted down towards the norm, this being a line at 90° to the surface. The ray does not change direction through the glass, no matter how thick it might be, but it does change direction on leaving the surface of the glass on the right-hand side, adopting the same angle of refraction as it had when approaching the other side, but now it is displaced.

Figure 6.5 also shows an overlay of the refraction in the sheet of glass with a front surface of a lens superimposed onto it. The dotted line shows the original refraction of the light ray, which

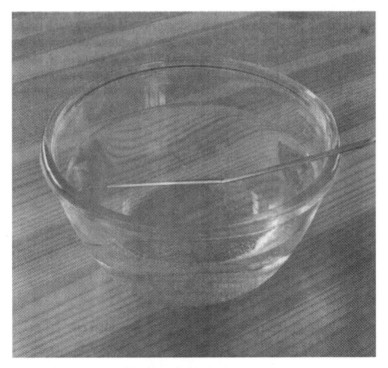

Figure 6.4 Refraction in water

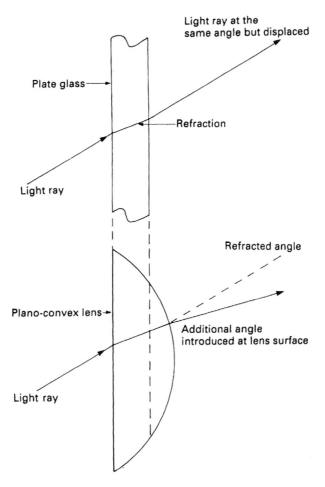

Figure 6.5 Refraction in glass

is now also influenced by the curvature of the lens. So, it can be stated that the direction of a light beam passing through a plano-convex lens is changed, firstly by the refraction and secondly, by the angle of the surface at the point of departure. The reason for refraction occurring in the first place comes about by the difference in optical density of the two substances; in this case that of air and glass. Each has assigned a refractive index which relates to the speed with which light can pass through it. The refractive index of a vacuum is 1.0 at which light travels at 300 000 km/second, so all other transparent substances have a refractive index greater than 1.0. Glass is typically 1.5 to 1.9, showing its higher optical density, with the resultant lowering of the speed of light through it, and a refractive index of 2.0 would halve the speed of light.

Air is so near to the value of a vacuum that we can ignore the difference and treat air as having a refractive index of 1.0. Given the wavelength of the ray of light, the refractive index of the glass, and the angle of approach, the resultant displacement of the light ray can be calculated.

6.3   Reflector designs

Figure 6.6 shows a simple solid cone which is responsible for all the reflector shapes that would be required for any type of luminaire. It can be seen that by cutting through the cone, along the

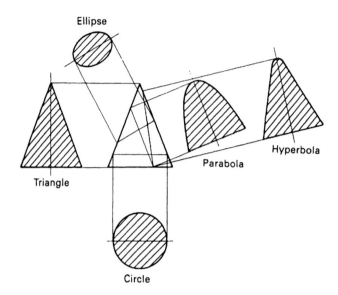

Figure 6.6 Sections of a cone

lines indicated, that five basic shapes are generated. We will employ some of them in the following reflector designs.

The circular true radius reflector is used extensively in luminaires such as Fresnels and PCs and in fact, any design that requires a single small source of light. It can be seen from Figure 6.7a that all light falling onto the reflector is returned to its place of origin where it joins the rest of the light. Although this reflector provides the single source requirement, it is very inefficient because it is quite useless to extend the reflector to collect more light if the resultant redirected rays cannot be directed onto the lens, particularly when rays from a filament are not a point source (see 6.7b). The reflector is therefore designed with the source in the full flood position which is nearest to the lens by drawing the two outer extremes of collection from the lens through the source and then projecting them to determine the maximum diameter that is required for the reflector. Any true radius reflector with its centre at the source will suit the design so the resultant size and radius can be determined by the luminaire size and the cooling requirements. Figure 6.7c shows the inefficiency of this type of reflector which does not collect all the light. This system is even more wasteful in the spot position which is rather ironic because most lighting men think that the high intensity spot is the more efficient position of focus, but it is obvious from the figure that a lot more light goes through the lens in the flood position. A good point to remember when using colour filters where the most arduous position for the filter is when the luminaire is in full flood with the added heat of the lamp being very close to the lens and therefore close to the filter.

Figure 6.8 shows an elliptical reflector in its most common application in a profile projector. With the source placed at F_1 the reflected light is directed to F_2. This reflector system is comparatively efficient compared with the true radius reflector but it still suffers the losses shown. It is pointless making the reflector larger to collect more light if the resultant increase in collection cannot be directed onto the first lens at an angle that can be redirected by the lens. Some designers have used an annular reflector to redirect the wasted light back through the gate, however the steep angle of collection and redirection normally provides only 15% more efficiency at a much higher cost. A much better refinement is to use condenser lenses placed between the gate and the light source, this has the effect of directing the diverging rays of light through the gate and is normally a standard high temperature plano-convex lens. The first design requirement must be the light output angles. Once these have been fixed, the correct lens

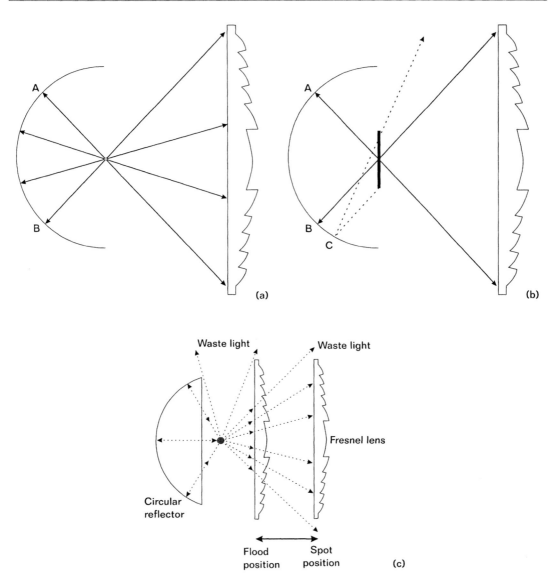

Figure 6.7 (a) Circular reflector; (b) Waste light; (c) Fresnel lens system

combinations can be determined and their relative positions drawn in. The gate diameter can now be positioned and the light ray lines drawn from the lenses to the reflector. Having satisfied these design requirements, any size of elliptical reflector can be used, with the choice varying from a long thin shape to one that appears to be almost a circle. They will all obey the same reflective law. This can be easily demonstrated with a piece of string and two drawing pins where the pins will be F_1 and F_2 and the string will represent the light ray. This form of design provides a wonderful range of ellipsoidal sizes to be considered but would no doubt cause great hilarity in the tool room where the finished reflector tool is made. We would therefore recommend the method of construction shown in Figure 6.9.

The parabolic reflector is normally used as the name implies, in applications where a near parallel beam of light is required. The searchlight is a good example where the discharge source

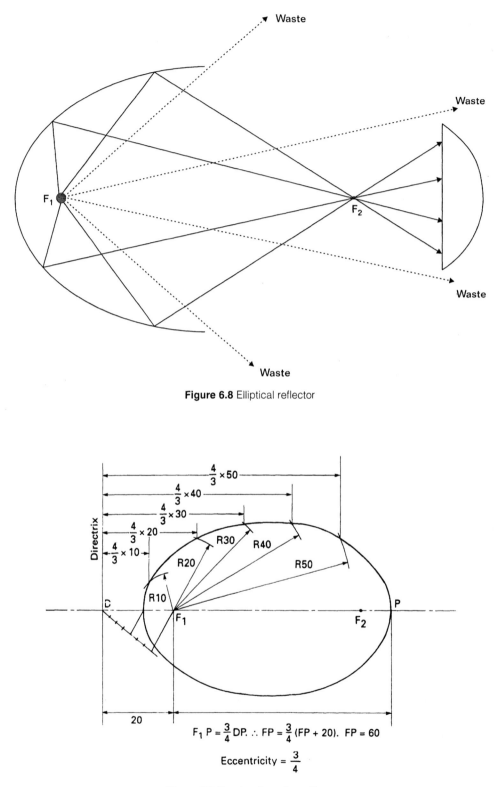

Figure 6.8 Elliptical reflector

$$F_1 P = \frac{3}{4} DP. \therefore FP = \frac{3}{4} (FP + 20). \quad FP = 60$$

$$\text{Eccentricity} = \frac{3}{4}$$

Figure 6.9 Construction of an ellipse

is mounted along the optical centre line facing the reflector. In this way a very efficient collection is achieved because all the light from the source is reflected in the output beam.

Figure 6.10 shows a typical design for a beam light where the forward light from the source is redirected back through the source by a true radius reflector which can be part of the lamp's envelope which has been silvered or a separate reflector mounted in front of the source. Greater efficiency can be gained by the use of low voltage lamps that provide higher lumens per watt and a small source size, typically 12/24/48 V lamps are used. The only problem is, of course, that the mains electricity must be reduced by some form of either transformer or power supply circuit.

The type of open faced luminaire shown in Figure 6.11, achieves a degree of focusing by moving the source along the optical centre line of the reflector. The direct light from the source will not change, but the reflected light can be superimposed onto the centre of the distribution, producing a higher lighting level. This reflector design is arrived at by tracing the required rays back to the reflector where a tangent can be drawn between the angle from the source and the required ray. In this way a series of tangents can be formed into an approximation of the required curve. A good example of this type of reflector is the 'Redhead'.

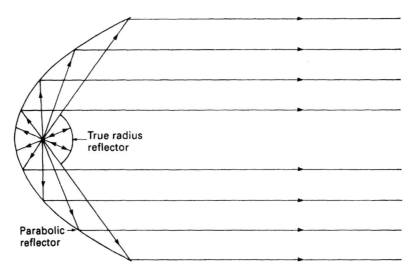

Figure 6.10 Parabolic reflector used in a beam light

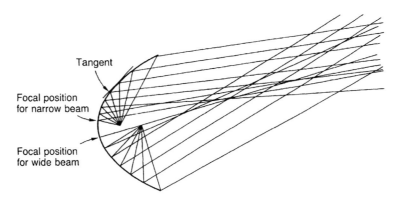

Figure 6.11 Focusing open-faced reflector

The softlight reflector shown in Figure 6.12 is constructed in the same manner as the open-faced reflector by ray tracing. However if the light output is to render a soft shadow the small source must be covered up so that it does not produce a conflicting shadow which would appear as a well defined hard shadow from the source, followed by a secondary soft shadow from the larger reflector. As the softness of shadow is a direct function of the size of the reflector and the distance of the luminaire from the subject, it is desirable to have the largest reflector surface area that can be achieved. Additionally, a light stippling of the reflector will help to diffuse the light. Sometimes matt white paint is used, however, this deteriorates with age and becomes yellow, resulting in a reduction in the colour temperature. The reflector placed in front of the source is normally a true radius reflector so that the light rays from it can be ignored because they will be incorporated with the other rays produced by the source.

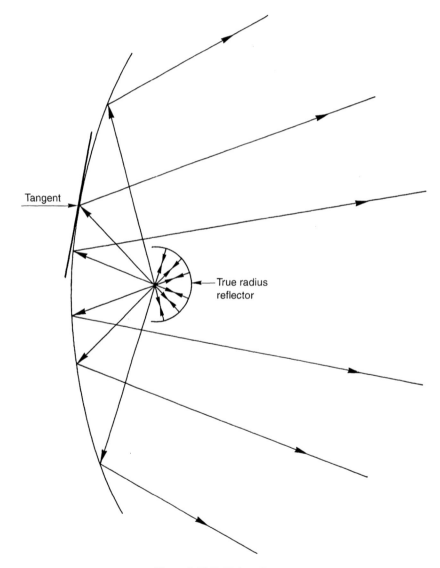

Tangent

True radius reflector

Figure 6.12 Softlight reflector

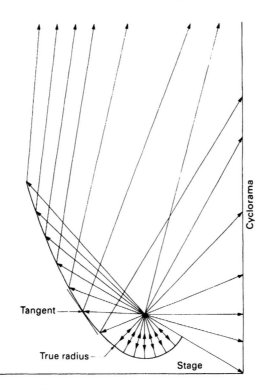

Figure 6.13 Cyclorama light reflector

The cyclorama reflector shown in Figure 6.13 is made by ray tracing in the same manner as the open faced reflector, but in this case an asymmetric distribution is required to provide as much light as possible to the top of the cyclorama. It is quite common with this design to make the bottom of the reflector a true radius drawn around to the point of cut off at the bottom of the cyclorama. In this way, the only light falling on the bottom of the cyclorama is the direct light from the source. The amount of reflected light is increased as the distribution extends up the cyclorama in an attempt to cancel out the fall off of the light through the inverse square law. It is not however practical to achieve a constant lux reading up the cyclorama because the light level at the bottom of the cyc will always be determined by the direct light from the source leaving insufficient reflected light available to match it, so the next best type of distribution is one that falls off evenly at a constant rate without dark or light bands which would draw attention to the change.

When lighting a large cyclorama from the top only; if an even distribution is required in the vertical plane, the cyc lights will need to be mounted 3 m or more from the cyc cloth and level with its top. A more common method is to use top and bottom mounted cyc lights to achieve this even distribution on the cloth. The reflector design is the same in principle for both top and bottom cyc units; a top unit is basically a 'bottom' unit turned upside down to achieve an asymmetric light distribution.

6.4   Luminaire types

The entertainment lighting industry should have its own dictionary of names and descriptions to guide the potential user through their catalogues. Every manufacturer has attributed to the proliferation of pet names for their products, so what is basically the same luminaire can have many names. Originally, no doubt, it was fun to build up a vocabulary that could only be understood by the lighting fraternity, thus adding mystique to the art.

The list is endless and not one of the names describes the use of the luminaire and each manufacturer uses a different name for a similar type. To expose the mystique we will place every luminaire in the entertainment business into only 11 groups, each group can be subdivided when reading a lighting catalogue into Wattage, Voltage, Beam Angle, Incandescent or Discharge Source, Manual or Pole Operated Controls followed by the finer points which separate one make from another. The 11 basic types are:

1 Fresnel
2 PC
3 Profile
4 Follow spots
5 Floodlight
6 Softlight
7 Focusing reflector light
8 Beam light
9 Sealed beam and PAR lights
10 Cyclorama/Backing light
11 Effects

We will now break down the 11 groups, describing their use and optical systems.

1 *Fresnel* This luminaire employs a Fresnel lens and circular reflector with the source placed at the centre of radius of the reflector (Figure 6.14). To focus the light the source and reflector are moved together. The spot position of focus is when the source is at the focal point of the lens and maximum flood is achieved when the source is nearest to the lens. The variable beam is typically 8°–60° and provides a soft edge keylight used as the main illumination on the artist or subject in TV, film and photography and for large area illumination in theatre. One disturbing fault with the Fresnel is that light is scattered from the top of the risers on each zone of the lens which can cause a problem of spill light.

2 *Plano-convex* The PC uses a plano-convex lens and circular reflector and is similar to the Fresnel in construction and performance (Figure 6.15). It is used mainly in theatre and has a beam appearance of an out of focus profile. In performing a similar role to the Fresnel the question is often asked 'Why do we require both types?' The main reason is that it has a well defined soft edge to the beam and does not produce spill light that would otherwise fall onto parts of the set or backing and cause problems. The disadvantages however are that the filament tends to image itself in full spot and any plano-convex lens has the problem of producing a dark hole in the centre of the beam between the full flood and the full spot positions. Some manufacturers provide a diffusion on the rear surface of the lens to reduce both problems.

3 *Profile (Ellipsoidal USA)* Europeans refer to this luminaire (Figure 6.16) as a profile describing its ability to project an outline of a cut-out image placed in the gate; whereas in the USA it is referred to as an 'ellipsoidal' which describes the type of reflector employed. The unit uses one or more plano-convex lenses and an ellipsoidal reflector, with the option of having condenser lenses to improve the light output. The light source is positioned at the first point of focus of the reflector. The beam size and focus of a zoom type can be varied by

Figure 6.14 (a) Discharge; (b) Tungsten (courtesy DeSisti (UK) Ltd)

moving the inter-relationship of the two lenses and the beam can be modified to provide a hot centre or an even field by fore and aft movement of the source in the reflector. Normally the most rear position of the source in the reflector provides the most even beam and produces the sharpest images of the gate, shutter blades and gobos. To obtain an efficient zoom, the beam angles are normally restricted to 2:1, i.e. 16° to 32° or thereabouts. One luminaire can be designed to cover all of the beam angles but it would be very inefficient in terms of light output and would be as long as the narrowest beam luminaire and as wide as the largest lens – thus very heavy – instead of a thoroughbred a 'luminaire camel'. On wide angle, the edge of

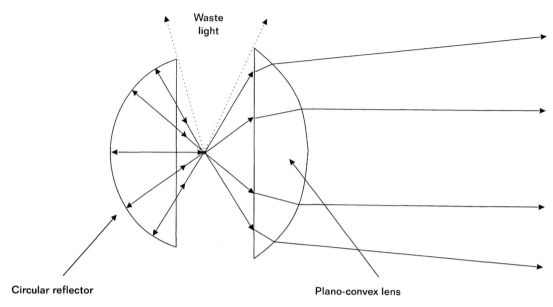

Figure 6.15 PC luminaire optics

the beam is often ringed in a halo of blue halation which can be removed by placing a reducing cut-out circle between the lenses at the expense of the luminance efficiency. Typical beam angles are 5° to 45°. The beam shape can be modified by four beam shaping shutters or an iris diaphragm which can be focused from a sharp definition to a soft edge. This luminaire is the workhorse of the theatre used mainly as a keylight for the artist, or as a silhouette projector. For TV and photography it is used as a gobo projector for backgrounds. The beam is a clear cut, well defined illumination that can be focused to provide a sharp image or the focus can be backed off to provide a soft edge without emitting spill light. The main disadvantage is that the housing is fairly long, particularly on narrow angle units and can prove a problem in restricted rigging space. In the past profile luminaires mainly used 1 kW and 2 kW lamps but in the past few years compact filament 575 W tungsten lamps have been used to give a high light output. Profile spots have now been developed using 150 W metal halide lamps with a 9000 hour lamp life. A light output of 612 lux can be achieved with an 18° beam angle at 10 m, with the advantage that all objects placed in the gate will remain relatively cool.

4 *Follow spots*   The optics for the follow spot are the same as the profile projector and the unit only varies from the above by the following characteristics. The gate area is much more elaborate than the profile, it omits the four beam shaping shutters and replaces them by two horizontal blades; one in the top of the gate and one underneath the gate. A single lever operates both blades in unison producing a variable parallel slot of light known as 'Chinese'. The blades can close the gate completely, giving a blackout known as a 'dowser'. In addition to the iris diaphragm for spot size and gobo projection, a dimmer iris is often provided by placing it in the light path but keeping it well out of focus. This has the effect of dimming the light without changing the colour temperature or the shape of the spot – a desirable feature for normal control and very useful when balancing the light on stage from two spots at different distances. A cruder, simple way of achieving this effect in profiles, as well as follow spots, is to put a barndoor from a Fresnel into the colour runners and move all four blades inwards to dim the output. Some follow spots provide a mechanical coupling between the two lenses to

(a)

(b)

Figure 6.16 (a) Fixed profile; (b) Zoom profile (courtesy of ETC Europe)

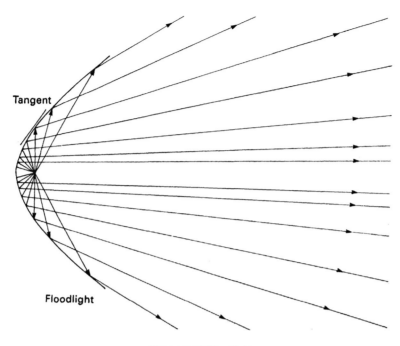

Tangent

Floodlight

Figure 6.17 Floodlight

produce a zoom effect of automatically maintaining focus when changing distance. The main advantage of a follow spot is the ability to focus constant attention onto a moving artist, however, the disadvantage of a low angle follow spot without other illumination is a complete lack of modelling and atmosphere for anything other than the 'sock it to them' approach.

5 *Floodlight* From Figure 6.17 it can be seen that the floodlight produces a very wide angle illumination which is unfortunately totally uncontrollable. The beam will not provide a cut off if a barndoor is used because of the large area of the source and reflected light, and therefore spills onto everything in front of it. It is hardly ever used in TV, except for house or working lights, and in the theatre it is limited in use to large areas of colour wash. Other disadvantages are the shadows cast from this type of luminaire give a confused rendering. The shadow from the filament is very hard in the vertical plane and softer in the horizontal if a linear lamp is used. Add to this the secondary shadow of the light from the reflector which appears softer than the shadow from the source and the resultant illumination is beyond control. The advantages are a very wide angle and high efficiency because most of the light is projected out of the housing. The units are usually low cost. The same principle of an open faced reflector is used in the portable 'Redhead', refined by moving the lamp to give spot and flood focusing. The disadvantages of poor barndoor control are tolerated in favour of the high light output, small size and weight.

6 *Softlight* The name Softlight refers to the shadow definition and implies that the edge of the shadow bleeds away without a defined edge to it. The ultimate softlight is the bounced light from the North sky which is so large in comparison to man that the light approaches from a very large angle so that we appear to have no shadow at all. There is therefore no such thing as a small softlight and the term is open to abuse. We do know, however, that the larger the reflector the softer the shadow so the design of a softlight is always a compromise between the largest that can be reasonably achieved and the size that can be tolerated. Softlights are

mainly used in photography and TV as a fill light to lift the shadow areas created by the key light to an acceptable level for the film stock or TV camera. It is desirable to achieve this without creating more shadows on the subject. The main disadvantage is light spilling onto backings or cycloramas – this can be partly controlled by an egg crate louvre placed in the front of the luminaire which restricts the light output to an angle of 90° vertical, 120° horizontal. The term 'soft' and 'hard' are comparative and do not define the shadow created by the light. Charles Neenan tackled the problem by defining the shadow and produced a test whereby a cross is placed in front of a backing and the light is measured in the shadow area and the lit area. The two are expressed as a ratio, known as 'the Neenan factor'. Whilst this method of test works, the industry has not adopted it, still preferring to put up a hand in front of a backing, and, after much consideration declaring the shadow to be good, bad or indifferent (see Figure 6.18).

7 *Focusing reflector light* There are many types and wattage of focusing reflector lights but the most famous is the 'Redhead'. The name describes the colour of the housing, but of course

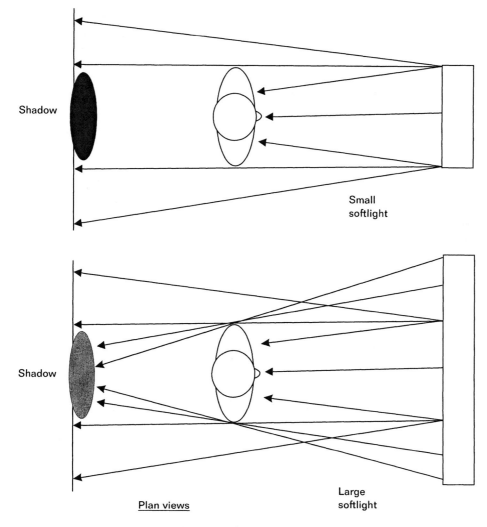

Figure 6.18 Softlight illustration

the French have their own way of expressing themselves and call it a 'Mandarin' referring to its segmented shape. The unit is mainly used in TV and photography and is particularly useful in interview situations because of its comparatively high light output from a small unit and the ability to focus the beam. This focusing is achieved by moving the lamp fore and aft in the reflector which provides two superimposed beams, one from the direct output of the source, and the other from the reflector. When the lamp is moved into the spot position the reflector provides the increased intensity in the centre of the beam while the overall total light output angle remains practically the same because of the direct illumination from the filament. Two problems with all open-faced lights are hard shadows and the need to provide a safety glass or mesh to catch the quartz from the envelope in the event of the lamp shattering. The standards require that particles of quartz 3 mm or more in size are arrested.

8 *Beam light*   This luminaire employs a parabolic reflector with the source placed at its centre of focus. With an ideal point source, the optical system would produce a parallel beam of light, the same diameter as that of the reflector. However, if a true radius reflector is placed in front of the source, it prevents the light from the source leaving the housing in a direct line, thus reflecting all the light that falls onto it back to the source and hence through the filament to the parabolic reflector. In real life, the size of the source has the effect of slightly spreading the beam and typical beam angles are 4° to 8°. A slight amount of focus can be achieved by moving the source fore and aft in the reflector and this will provide a few degrees change in the beam. This optical system has been used for many years in lighthouses and searchlights where in the old type of searchlight, a positive carbon was mounted along the centre axis of the reflector with its light emitting crater facing the reflector. The beam light was originally used by necessity in large opera houses and the big 'Germanic type' theatres, because of its high efficiency and narrow beam required when lights were positioned a long distance from the stage.

The main disadvantages of a beam light are that the beam angle cannot be increased to any great extent by focusing and that the most efficient luminaires will use a low voltage lamp to make use of its small source size and high light output (lumens per Watt) therefore requiring a transformer in the mains supply line. The main advantages are a very narrow beam for long throw applications, a high efficiency and very little spill light.

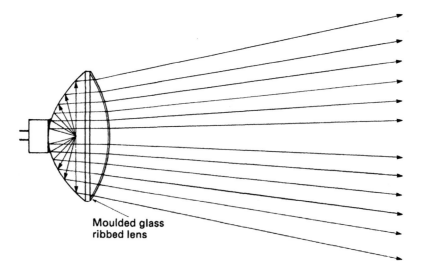

Moulded glass
ribbed lens

Figure 6.19 Sealed beam optics

9 *Sealed beam and PAR lights*   A sealed beam lamp (Figure 6.19) employs the same optics as the beam light but replaces the front reflector with a moulded lens which has the effect of controlling the beam to a predetermined angle. Because the lamp is completely sealed, it can be run at a high pressure and consequently provides a high efficiency. The lamp manufacturers offer a choice of five beam angles by lamp selection, each lamp has a different lens moulded onto the front in quite the same manner as the car headlamp. The most popular lamp in entertainment is the PAR 64 and as with all PAR lamps, the number is the diameter expressed in 1/8 of an inch, therefore a PAR 64 is eight inches in diameter or 204 mm. The beam is usually oval and typical beam angles are (9°H 12°W) (10°H 14°W) (11°H 24°W) (21°H 57°W) (70°H 70°W) for 240 V lamps. Beam angles and efficiency vary with voltage, particularly when comparing 240 V lamps with 120 V versions because of the small filament in the low voltage lamps. The most common application of this lamp is the Parcan generally used on 'pop' rigs for its high light output, small size, low cost and light weight. It is the only luminaire that comes to mind that costs less than the lamp that is used in it. Alternatively, manufacturers make a lamp with a plain glass front for use with a selection of separate lenses. Luminaires with parabolic reflectors and separate lamps are also manufactured, employing discharge sources and compact filament tungsten sources (see Figure 6.20).

10 *Cyclorama/Backing light*   From Figure 6.13 it can be seen that the lower part of the reflector is a true radius about the source. This has the effect of returning all of the light that falls onto it back to the filament and through the envelope to the main part of the reflector. The main part of the reflector is designed to direct as much light as it can towards the top of the distribution and to only light the bottom part of the cyclorama with direct light from the filament. With the inverse square law working against the designer, it is always a problem to get enough light to

Figure 6.20 (a) Discharge PAR features (courtesy of DeSisti (UK) Ltd)

Figure 6.20 *Continued* (b) PAR luminaire (courtesy of Electronic Theatre Controls (Europe))

the top of the cyclorama, so it is realised that a cyclorama or backing cannot be evenly lit from the top or bottom only when the units are placed relatively close (i.e. 1 m). It is necessary to light from both positions if an even effect is required. If only top or bottom lighting is used, then the fall off of the light should be designed to be a continuous reduction without any dark or bright bars. In this way, the change is not exaggerated.

The choice of linear tungsten halogen lamps is important because of the ring supports that hold the filament in the centre of the envelope. These cause shadows which will appear as five or six fanned out dark bars, projecting up the cyc, and can be overcome with the use of frosted lamps. When assessing the light distribution of cyclorama lights, it is not possible to get a true result by observing only one unit, because the lights are designed to have a wide horizontal angle of distribution, typically 45° each side of centre. It is necessary to use at least three units spaced at the recommended distance from the cyclorama and positioned at the correct distance apart; this being when the overlapping lighting gives an even horizontal coverage. Under these conditions it is possible to assess the vertical distribution on either side of the centre unit. Polar figures are not normally produced for cyc lights because they have no practical application, so it is normal for manufacturers to set up three lights as described above, and take readings progressively up the cyclorama and to show this information graphically. When setting cyc lights, it is a good guide to remember that it is the horizontal distance of the units from the cyclorama that determines the coverage, a small change in the horizontal distance will create a large change in light level opposite the luminaire and almost no change in the light level at the furthest point on the cyc because the length of throw in the vertical direction has hardly changed.

It is normal to place the groundrow 1 m from the cyc and have each recurring colour at 1.2 m centres (Figure 6.21). Top cyc units are rigged approximately 3 m away from the cyc at 2.5 m centres (see Figure 6.22).

Figure 6.21 Groundrow

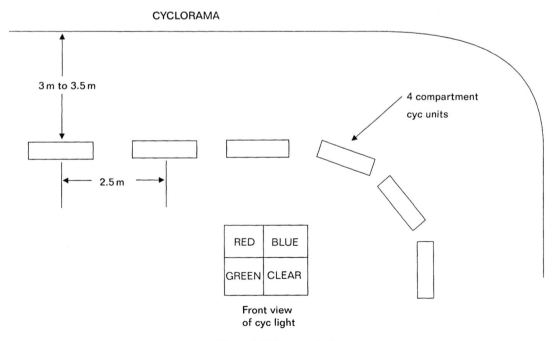

Figure 6.22 Top cyc lights

Cyclorama lights are made in the following configurations:

● Single, double and triple units,
● four lights in line with hinges between each compartment for bending around corners, and
● four-way unit mounted in domino formation.

All types of units allow for up to four colours before the first colour is repeated to provide colour mixing or four particular choices of colour, but don't forget to include a clear compartment if you are using a red/green/blue colour mix to desaturate the colours. Also remember that the dimmer setting is just as important as the colour that has been chosen.

The design of colour frame can have 'tiger teeth' along the edge to break up the shadows created by the linear lamp filament being in line with the inside edge of the colour frame. This can be important in TV when lighting the cyclorama from the top and allowing it to spill out onto the floor. The main disadvantages of cyclorama lighting systems is that they eat up dimmer circuits at an alarming rate, so it is necessary to investigate distribution systems that can be patched from acting area lights to the cyclorama when required, and the possibility of using a 9-way plug and socket system at 4×5 kW per circuit, the cyc lights can then be daisy-chained to work in parallel. The space taken by the luminaire is always difficult to find in operation, and the TV lighting barrel system presents a particular problem of trying to rig the lights on the side of the cyclorama that is presented with the ends of the barrels without tying up every barrel for this purpose – a point often overlooked when designing a studio lighting barrel system.

11 *Effects light*   Effects projectors normally employ a true radius reflector or an elliptical design similar to the reflector used in a profile projector. Figure 6.23 shows an elliptical reflector with its increased efficiency when compared with a true radius type. The first element is normally a heat absorbing glass that has the effect of reducing the heat passing through it by about 80%, with a light loss of approximately 20%. This special glass requires an airflow over its surface to dissipate the heat collected. An alternative heat filter is a glass with a dichroic coating which reflects the heat from the surface of the coating back into the luminaire. This type of filter is slightly more efficient than heat absorbing glass but care must be taken to ensure that the source is not overheated.

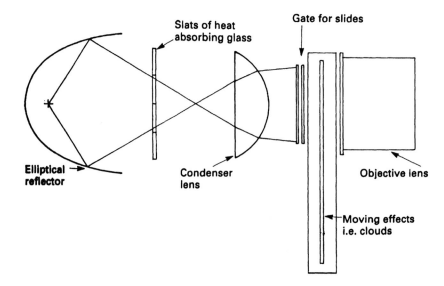

Figure 6.23 Effects optics

The condenser lens as the name implies helps to direct diverging rays of light through the gate and can be a conventional plano-convex lens or to provide a slightly diffused output and a weight saving, a Fresnel lens is often employed. The gate is designed to accept a conventional photographic slide or a large piece of glass with the scene to be projected painted onto it. It is therefore possible to make a photographic slide of the actual backing required from the correct position to give the correct perspective and then project it onto a white backing. In the same way, an effects projector can be used to project a scene onto a backing for the scenic artist to sketch in the outline with the correct perspective before painting it. An alternative accessory is a rotating disk positioned on the front of the projector with the appropriate effect painted onto the rotating glass i.e. rain, fire, snow, etc. In this way a moving effect can be created at variable speed. A choice of objective lenses is made available to give the coverage required at the appropriate distance. Disadvantages are the high cost of the projectors and high effects costs, comparatively low light output levels that cannot compete with high lighting levels on the TV and film set. A very steady mount is required, as any vibration will produce judder in the output beam and ruin the effect.

A modern development is an effects system which uses a small motor driven drop-in unit for the gate of modern low wattage luminaires. The unit consists of a motor driven roller and a take-up roller with a continuous belt of stainless steel or polyester with etched patterns. There are a large selection of off-the-shelf designs and it is also possible to create your own effects and these can be manufactured in either stainless steel or polyester loops. The units can be controlled via the mains or driven from DMX control systems.

6.5   Special designs

Multi-purpose luminaire

This is basically a focusing Fresnel mounted back to back with a Softlight and was developed for TV in 1961 (see Figure 6.24).

The reason for the development was a requirement to mount luminaires at regular intervals all over the studio at approximately 2 m centres, known as a saturated lighting system, where in this way a light can be found somewhere near the required place, pulled along its barrel and positioned. The luminaire is then rotated, offering the choice of Fresnel key light or Softlight. A switch is then selected to divert the electrical supply to the chosen light, and a second switch selected to provide a choice of power. This is achieved by using 4 tungsten halogen linear lamps in the soft end, and a twin filament, 4 pin lamp in the Fresnel end.

This arrangement is intended to cover 80% of the requirements of the LD, with the remainder being mounted for each show. The additions include 1 kW Fresnels, profiles or specials as required. To add more flexibility to the system, the multi-purpose luminaires are mounted onto pantographs to provide a degree of independent height adjustment. The BBC adopted this form of luminaire in all their major studios, claiming very fast turn round time, increasing the output from the studio. Leaving the lights permanently rigged, substantially reduced the damage normally caused when lights are continuously rigged and de-rigged.

6.6   Fluorescent lighting

Fluorescent light sources have been used in TV over quite a number of years but generally in situations where they were used more for effect rather than for their intrinsic lighting values. In

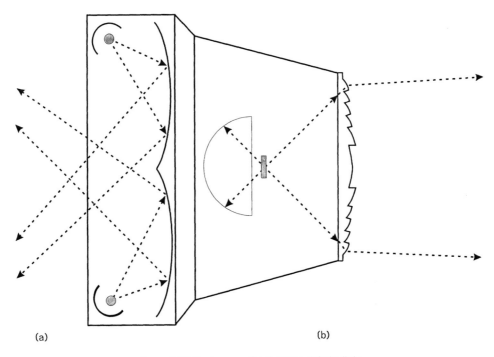

(a)   (b)

Figure 6.24 Dual source (a) Softlight; (b) Keylight

more recent times, with the advent of smaller fluorescent tubes and high frequency operation, it has been possible to design luminaires not too large in physical size for use in studios and on location. The claimed benefit of using fluorescent light sources is that they are much more efficient than tungsten with three to four times the efficacy (lumens per Watt). Although they have a high efficacy they do not lend themselves as a focusing source, and for example they have an efficiency (usable light divided by total light output) of around 40% which is comparable to the 49% of an open faced luminaire in flood and the fluorescent luminaires only gain by the tubes producing more visible light and less infrared than the equivalent tungsten source and therefore, per watt, have a light output which is about twice that of tungsten. The fluorescent luminaires tend to be a cooler source of light and they produce less glare to the artiste.

Fluorescent units designed for TV usually operate on frequencies between 28 kHz and 42 kHz giving an improved efficacy of output and virtually flicker free light. Modern phosphors allow for colour rendering indices of better than 70 and can be as high as 90 but this usually means a reduction in the efficacy of the fluorescent tube.

The fluorescent lamps selected for this type of lighting have the normal phosphor coating inside the tube together with a coating of various rare-earth high output phosphors, similar to those used for the production of TV colour cathode ray tubes, and are called tri-phosphor tubes. By varying the combination of the red, green and blue phosphors, different shades of white can be produced and these lamps are referred to as tri-phosphor lamps. This type of lamp can provide high light output with good colour rendering with a reduction of around 7–10% in input power compared with more conventional phosphor coated fluorescents.

Early applications for fluorescent lighting in TV were broad sources such as fill lights and for back lighting large diffuse panels used for Chroma Key. One special use was in the design of fittings used over snooker tables for tournaments which required a soft source which was also

Table 6.1 Light output comparison (at 3 m)

Luminaire type	Power rating (W)	Mode	Beam width	Light output (lux)
Vid-lite (fluorescent)	375	n/a	60°	830
Quasar (fluorescent)	416	n/a	76°	700
Mizar (tungsten)	500	Flood	46°	900
Pulsar (tungsten)	650	Flood	72°	920
Redhead (tungsten)	800	Flood	86°	720
Piccolo (discharge)	200	Flood	48°	1150
Piccolo (discharge)	575	Flood	46°	2000

Note: Manufacturers' published figures.

cool. The main use of fluorescent lighting is usually in News and Current Affairs studios where the set-ups are fairly static and it is reasonably easy to control the light.

Although there are small News areas that exclusively use fluorescent lighting, generally because of the comfort level due to the low heat produced, the general application of fluorescent lighting would appear to be in hybrid type studios where the keylights are small tungsten Fresnel sources, with the fill light produced by fluorescent sources. The overall aim is to keep the heat level in the area fairly low.

To obtain higher light levels from fluorescent fittings it is possible to fit intensifiers which are essentially reflectors fitted to the front, which instead of letting the light spill to the sides and top and bottom, reflects it back in the general direction of the main beam. As with all light sources, the introduction of louvres or controlled screens, invariably reduce the light by a small amount. Dimming of fluorescent units can be accomplished by a manual control using a potentiometer, a standard 0–10 V analogue control signal or DMX digital control signal.

One of the problems with fluorescent lighting for TV is that it is not focused light but tends to be a broad source of illumination and therefore only controlled by the use of louvres (control screens). Although the louvres can reduce the amount of light emanating from the side of the beam, the sources are very wide angle in application, thus their adoption into normal production TV studios would probably not be advantageous because of their physical size and control of light. Fluorescent fittings can now produce outputs of around 600 lux at a distance of 3 m from the subject with unit dimensions of 500 × 400 mm and in excess of 900 lux at 3 m from units approximately 700 mm across by 700 m high (Table 6.1). Although generally the lighting is acceptable for fairly static newsreaders, the lack of pronounced modelling does reduce the three dimensional effect on camera. The small amount of heat generated by fluorescent lighting means that these fittings are advantageous in situations where ventilation is poor.

Fluorescent luminaires for TV, film and photography, particularly digital imaging photography, come in power sizes from around 100 W to about 1000 W.

6.7 Battery hand lamps

These are mainly used for news gathering on outside locations, so they are completely self powered from their own battery. The most popular batteries for size to weight ratio are nickel–cadmium. A typical luminaire has an open-faced reflector, containing a tungsten halogen or discharge lamp. The largest tungsten halogen lamp is 250 W at 30 V and the range of daylight discharge lamps include 125 W, 200 W, 275 W and 400 W. The battery unit will also be complete with a high frequency converter for the discharge lamp. A degree of focusing is obtained by moving the lamp in the reflector.

General care of Ni–cad batteries

Ni–cad batteries retain their capacity better if the discharge cycle is completed to the point where the knee of the discharge curve is reached. To discharge batteries beyond this point may push some cells into deep discharge from which they may not recover, thus potentially rendering the battery useless. Overcharging a battery is not good practice and *if a battery has been left charged for some time or is partially discharged, it should not be recharged before it is discharged fully.*

Charging batteries

A typical charger of the fast type will charge a fully discharged 7 Ah battery in approximately 2 hours, or a 4 Ah battery in approximately one hour and then drop to a trickle charge state.

There is no common connector standard for many of the proprietary battery packs and belts used in the lighting industry; therefore, it is important to have the necessary adapter leads for the various items of equipment.

6.8   Assessment of luminaires

The LDs assessment of a luminaire is how well can he achieve his lighting requirements with this instrument, which is quite understandable from his point of view. The electrician that has to rig and set it has quite different criteria and the maintenance engineer has his own particular problems to keep it in good repair. The LDs assessment is quite straightforward and can be seen by demonstration, it is also well documented by the lighting manufacturer with polar figures for the light output.

We shall therefore turn our attention to the mechanical assessment that will affect the reliability and practical needs of the user. It is most interesting to watch the experienced practical user at any exhibition. He will walk up to a luminaire and in minutes run through a set routine of things to try, gained by years of disappointment and annoyance with things that can go wrong and just don't work in the way that they should. His checklist leaves the manufacturer in no doubt that he is demonstrating his product to a discerning user.

Luminaire checklist

Pan and tilt

Unlock the tilt lock knob and see if the unit is in the centre of gravity. Not only does the luminaire take charge and trap your fingers, if it is not in balance, but it will also put a pressure on the locking mechanism that can result in the luminaire drooping after it has been set; so the second test is to lock the tilt mechanism and try to force the luminaire downwards, making it slip in the yoke. If the unit is pole operated, try the tilt and pan for backplay in the drive mechanism. In the case of the tilt, an out of balance luminaire will result in a jerky movement in one direction and a heavy load in the opposite direction; this is caused by the load alternately taking charge and then being arrested by the gears. Backplay in the pan movement will result in a horizontal wandering movement after the light has been set. Check that the carcass rotates in the yoke assembly correctly, particularly with open barndoors. When pan and tilt pole operation is fitted, ensure that they can be over-ridden by manual adjustments.

Focus

Here we are looking for a smooth movement, best tested with the luminaire pointing 45° down from the horizontal. This will show up judder, if it exists, or sticking, followed by a sudden movement, both of which cause lamp failure due to the fact that the lamp must be lit to focus it when the vibration on the hot filament can cause it to rupture. Check for 'end stops' on lamp holder movement within the luminaire body.

Shutter blades

Profile shutters have always been a problem, mainly because they are in the hottest part of the beam and will normally run at a temperature that makes them glow red, so adequate insulation on the operating handle is essential. The most common complaint however, is the shutter blades that slide down in the guides when they get hot, so try it after the other tests have been done to make sure that you maintain a positive movement on the blade at high temperature (see Figure 6.25).

Profile edge focus

Most manufacturers demonstrate a profile projector in a sharp focus position, demonstrating its ability to project a well defined image. Adjust the lens movement to the minimum and maximum angles to determine if the edge is sharp over the whole range and at the same time observe the edge for colour fringing. It is most important with the profile that it can be soft focused, so determine there is sufficient lens movement at both ends of travel to achieve a soft edge.

Barndoors

The main points to observe are that the flaps stay put with sufficient friction to sustain the top flap when it is hot. A floppy barndoor flap is the lighting man's cross. Check that smooth rotation can be achieved by poking it with a pole (quite a common practice). Light leaks can be assessed by half closing the two small flaps and then bringing the large flaps in to touch them. A well defined 'letter box' shape should be produced at this point; observe any spill light that comes out of any slot between the sides of the short flap and the large flap. This is a good time to see if spill light comes out between the back of the barndoor and the front of the housing. One easy way to

Figure 6.25 Shutter blades

check for spill light is to pass your hand around the area of concern, which will soon pick up any unwanted light.

Safety requirements

The following items should be checked. Has the luminaire had a drop test done, and if so, was a certificate issued. If so this should be provided. Luminaires are also generally supplied with safety bonds or chains and these should come with certificates or specifications indicating their suitability for use with the item of equipment. Have adequate safety precautions been taken against an exploding lamp and the loss of minute pieces of glass? Secondly, have precautions been taken with regard to lens breakage and the possibility of large pieces of glass leaving the luminaire. Ensure that the most important bolts and screws which attach items that may become dislodged from the luminaires are adequate for the purpose intended. Are supplementary safety bonds or clips provided for any detachable accessories, such as colour frames, barndoors, etc. or how are the barndoors retained in normal practice? Check for any sharp edges or dangerous protrusions which in practice may give problems for the operators.

Burning angle

It is a requirement to state the permitted burning angle of the luminaire. This is normally found on the product label and will give the permitted angles above and below the horizontal. This limitation can be imposed by either the luminaires' cooling system or the lamp manufacturer.

Spares

Ask to see the spares list. Some manufacturers do not automatically provide one; this could save a lot of trouble identifying spare parts in the future. Check on the availability of spares and what components are used and where are they sourced.

Lamps

Determine if the type of lamp used is made by more than one manufacturer or if not, is it going to be readily available in your area. One common problem with lamps is arcing at the pins. Check the clamping arrangements for any lamps in use. In addition check for the ease of operation when fastening and unfastening lamps in their holders.

General

A general inspection should examine the ease of stacking for storage purposes. Where is the attached luminaire cable stored when not in use? Check for ease of handling when being carried and rigged.

6.9   Centre of gravity (C of G) considerations

Every luminaire is suspended by a yoke, stirrup or fork that will enable the luminaire to rotate (pan) and to tilt. It is the tilt movement that requires to be mounted at the C of G of the luminaire. Whilst every luminaire has a means of locking the tilt movement, or in the case of a pole operated unit, gears are provided to hold it steady in tilt, it is necessary to position the yoke at the C of G to prevent judder. In the case of pole operation, if the luminaire is out of balance it will be difficult to rotate the pole in one direction and judder will result in the other direction caused by the gears alternately releasing the load and stopping it again. In the case of the manually operated luminaire, an out of balance unit causes two main problems: one, when the tilt lock is released the out of balance weight takes charge and rotates the luminaire very quickly, normally trapping your fingers between the housing and the yoke. The annoyance caused by an out of balance luminaire is seen when rigging lights onto a bar which has already been fully rigged and all lights focused and set. Then an additional unit is added – the worst case being an out of balance profile. The influence of the weight of the large lenses mounted at some distance from the C of G produces a moment about the mounting hook clamp which tends to rotate the bar causing all of the other lights that have been previously set to tilt downwards, much to the annoyance of the electrician that has to reset them all. Having established the desirability of having luminaires in balance, sometimes a compromise is required because the C of G might come in line with the gate, shutters or some other obstruction.

6.10 Ventilation

The importance of adequate ventilation in a luminaire cannot be overstated. An overheated lamp will give a short life, the internal electrical system and lampholder will deteriorate and the housing will become dangerously hot. The rules to achieve good ventilation are simple but are so often ignored. A common mistake is to believe that lots of holes in the housing will introduce a lot of airflow through it. In fact, the opposite may be true. A splendid example is a kiln, where a chimney is erected with hot air rising through it, creating a partial vacuum behind it, sucking the air into the kiln at the place where it is required to fuel the fire. The same is true for luminaires and an air path is worked out bearing in mind the working angles of the unit to determine the inlet and outlet path. One system is to have an inlet – scoop or mouth – positioned so that internal baffles can direct the air across the base of the lamp and then between the lamp and reflector and

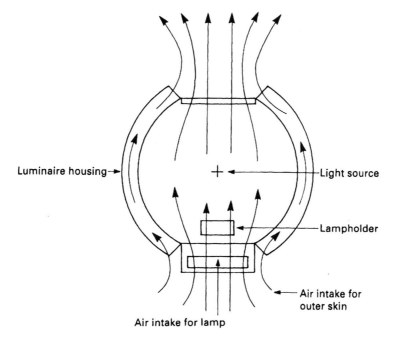

Figure 6.26 Luminaire ventilation air path

ultimately through an escape chimney. The chimney has to be designed so that water or foreign objects cannot directly enter, electrical safety has to be checked by using 'British Standard Finger' tests.

This system works well to maintain the correct lamp temperature, however other means are required to cool the housing. If a wall cavity is provided by placing internal baffles in the housing, a separate ventilating system can be adopted to keep the outer skin cool. By providing separate inlet vent holes between the two skins, the air can be accelerated through the cavity by positioning the outlet slots adjacent to the chimney outlet, the hot air rising through the chimney creates an air rush around it, sucking the air up through the two skins. A third ventilating system will be required around the lens and colour filter (see Figure 6.26).

6.11   The carbon arc

Most high efficiency carbons produce about 46 lumens/W, which is roughly double the efficacy of a tungsten halogen lamp and half the efficacy of a discharge lamp. All of the light is emitted from the centre of the positive carbon, the positive is constructed by an outer shell made from compressed carbon with a core injected under high pressure made of various rare earths and carbon. This enables the manufacturer to create the correct mix for maximum efficiency and the required colour temperature. This construction also provides a hollow in the centre of the core which is containing the crater – that is the centre of the light output. It is necessary with most

Amps	Arc volts dc	Size (mm)		Burning rate mm/hr	
		Positive	Negative	Positive	Negative
225	72	16	13.5	430	70
150	65	16	11	230	64
120	53	13.6	10	240	64
60	52	9	7	330	80
40	50	8	7	100	76

Figure 6.27 Carbon burning characteristics

carbon arc luminaires to have an operator present to keep a constant distance between the two carbons and this is known as trimming the carbons.

The correct burning position can be seen from Figure 6.27 where the tail flame is held in the vertical at the correct angle. If the positive or negative carbons are allowed to overfeed and become out of alignment, the tail flame will become unstable and create a flicker and ultimately the carbons will set up a squealing noise. One simple method of setting up a carbon arc when cold is to take a spent end of a positive carbon and use it as a gauge by placing it between the tip of the negative and the front edge of the positive carbon. In this way a reasonable running condition will result when the carbon is struck – that is the negative is raised up until it touches the positive and then allowed to drop immediately an arc is struck. As soon as the arc has been established the gap can be adjusted by eye through the coloured glass of the viewing port. The running speeds are normally adjusted by a motor drive which feeds the positive and negative carbons towards each other at a predetermined rate which can be varied by a potentiometer. The negative carbon does not rotate, however the positive carbon is rotated continuously to prevent the outer shell of the carbon burning away at the top and allowing the crater to spill out. Carbons always operate from a direct current which can be derived from generators or from a transformer rectifier unit working from a.c. mains.

If carbons are used in a confined space, adequate ventilation must be provided to extract the fumes and the large quantities of ozone which are produced. Arcs normally work with a controlling ballast in series with the supply to them, the ballast will provide high voltage to initiate the arc and then become self regulating as the arc starts to draw current through the ballast increasing its resistance and reducing the voltage. Arcs have mainly been replaced by the higher efficiency discharge sources which do not require adjustment during operation and can therefore be remote controlled. However, the arc still lives on and is still used in some rental departments throughout the world, due to the dramatic quality of light and by those practitioners who tend to use them for nostalgic reasons.

7
Lighting suspension systems

7.1 Suspension and why it is needed

In TV and film studios, the majority of lighting is placed at a reasonable height above the acting area. The reasons for this are quite simply that we do not wish the acting area to be full of equipment, additionally the floor area is also cluttered with cameras and sound booms.

When gas lighting over the stage was introduced it consisted of a 1.5 inch bore steel gas pipe with rat tail burners fitted along its length every few inches across the whole width of the stage. The pipe was suspended from steel ropes and fed by flexible hoses from the sides of the stage. It is interesting to note that $1^{29}/_{32}$ inch (48 mm) is the outside diameter of a 1.5 inch steel gas pipe and this was adopted as the standard for the industry. Ultimately theatres used the redundant gas pipes to hang their brand new electric lanterns.

The film industry tend to use single lights suspended by hemp ropes from block and tackles mounted on steel beams in the roof. On occasions, a platform with hand rails (called a 'boat') is suspended from two or more block and tackles above the studio so that the additional lights attached to its side rails could be attended by the electricians. Some film studios use long barrels to suspend lights. It is worth noting that the film industry tends to work from the studio floor 'up', as opposed to TV which works from the ceiling grid 'down'.

In 1936 when the BBC started TV transmission, all the lighting equipment came from theatre and film manufacturers, mainly using the rigging techniques of the film industry, such as hemp ropes and block and tackles.

By 1956 the BBC had introduced a motorised hoisting system for lighting, comprising a unit with a motorised gearbox and wire ropes to suspend a 2.4 m long, 48 mm diameter barrel.

With the introduction of commercial TV in 1955 a new type of suspension system had been designed, which consisted of an overhead walkover grid at high level with slots, running the length of the studio into which telescopic suspension units were placed and winched down to the required height from the grid.

Starting from this date, an argument ensued and persists of the merits and disadvantages of motorised barrels versus single point suspension. The motorised barrel protagonist will insist that the saturated lighting rig with two or three lights on each barrel provides enough choice of lighting positions and can be rigged from the studio floor at the same time as other trades are working on the set in comparative safety; whereas a single point suspension installation requires men to be above the grid for rigging. The LD, working in a single point suspension studio, will argue that he can be more precise and can place the luminaire of his choice at the point in space where he wants it, with independent height control of every luminaire.

7.2 Grid systems

The dictionary defines a 'grid' as a grating, a gridiron, a framework. It is also described as the 'framework above a theatre stage from which scenery and lights may be suspended'. The original theatre grids were usually wooden platforms suspended from the roof structure, providing a working level for men to walk over. The floor, which was slatted, provided a means by which ropes or scenery could be suspended. Additionally, the lighting bars were suspended from this platform.

In TV, the term 'grid' usually describes the roof structure that supports the lighting systems installed and these can be from very simple fixed barrel rigs to complex monopole grids. The TV industry tended to follow the example of the theatre, due to the need to suspend lights and scenery. The film industry has traditionally always built scenery from the studio floor upwards and any rigging of luminaires is usually done by block and tackles, suspended from RSJs at high level.

In a TV studio where motorised units are installed, the basic need to walk to the units installed at high level can be met by walkways adjacent to the units. However, some organisations have made the entire area at high level completely uncluttered by using self-climbing units, thus allowing unrestricted access to almost any point above the acting area. Monopole grids do require access by staff to move the units. One of the problems associated with walkover grids is that of safety. Obviously, no object must fall from the grid with personnel working on the studio floor and to this end, either pocketless overalls are worn by staff or any items that can be used at high level are usually attached to devices to prevent them falling through the grid slots. Arguments ensue all the time as to the viability of walkover grids, bearing in mind safety legislation, and most studios generally provide maintenance access only. The alternative to this safety problem is to clear the acting area of all other staff. Unfortunately this is time consuming and raises the operational costs.

The most basic design of grid from which we can hang a light consists of 48-mm diameter metal barrels suspended above the acting area. The height will generally be fixed although the use of spring pantographs or drop arms can be advantageous. When the lighting requires adjustment, steps or ladders have to be used to provide access to rig and derig the luminaires. If the position of the luminaires is correct then pole operated controls enable adjustments to be made quickly without much disturbance to the rehearsals. Power sockets are usually distributed in a uniform manner just above the fixed barrels.

To give more flexibility, at a low installation cost, a *roller barrel* system is often used; this allows barrels, about 2 m, long to run along a set of parallel tracks mounted at high level in the studio. It is usually the practice with this type of installation, to mount the trunking with the power sockets attached, between the trackways. As this requires the minimum of space, the trackways can be installed very close to each other, subsequently allowing the luminaires to be positioned with a high degree of accuracy. It is essential that the moving barrel units are provided with trolleys designed so that they run smoothly along the trackways when pushed or pulled at any point on the barrel unit. There is nothing more annoying to the operator than pushing a roller barrel along the trackway only to see it jam and then having to waste time and effort in moving the unit once again. It is often advantageous to fit a brake to the barrels so that they maintain their set positions in the studio.

The barrels must be installed so that they cannot be removed from the trackways without the use of tools; otherwise a hazardous situation can occur. This system, which allows very good positioning in the horizontal plane, still suffers the drawback that unless additional equipment is provided, the height of the luminaires is fixed. Also, when the barrels move over a reasonable distance, some plugging and unplugging of the feeder cables would have to take place due to the fixed socket arrangement. It is normal practice with the roller barrel system to suspend each luminaire from the barrels by a roller trolley, therefore movement in two planes is achieved. To make the system even more flexible, the luminaire can be suspended by a variable pantograph from the barrel trolley, giving a high degree of flexibility in three planes.

A system of suspension that has achieved a reasonable degree of success, is the use of pantographs, mounted on roller trolleys and moving along long single trackways. This gives extremely good height flexibility and when the trackways are positioned as near to each other as possible, also offers a very good coverage over the acting area; the spacing between the trackways is dictated by the maximum size of luminaires used in the installation. The system can use spring pantographs where the height can be easily adjusted by pushing the unit up and down (Figure 7.1). Spring pantographs are balanced for the load of the luminaire and the major

Figure 7.1 Pantograph

drawback is that special safety precautions have to be taken when changing luminaires on spring pantographs. It is preferable to use wind-up pantographs which are not load dependent and thus safer. Horizontal movement is accomplished by dragging or pushing the pantograph top trolley unit along the trackway. The power feeds to the individual pantograph units are often provided by a catenary cable system, rather like those used for overhead cranes. A modern advance, favoured by some large broadcasting organisations, is to use motorised pantographs where the height is adjusted by motor driven wire ropes and the horizontal movement accomplished by a motor drive onto the trackways. Catenary feeder cables for both the control system and the power system are essential. The system can be easily adapted for remote control and has the great advantage of overcoming the safety problems connected with spring pantographs and is very quick and easy to use.

The above systems have mainly allowed only one luminaire to move at a time. When we wish to move more lights at the same time, the systems become mechanically more complex. The most basic of these systems is to use a long barrel with the adjustment of height made by a counterweight system. In the theatre, these consist of very long barrels up to 10 m long, slung from several wire ropes. The lights are all at the same height and the weight on the barrel can be considerable when the power cables are attached. The counterweight system allows for the weight of the barrel, plus all the luminaires and cables mounted on it, to be balanced by a selection of special iron weights and provides an easy method of raising and lowering barrels with heavy loads. Counterweight barrels are mainly used in the theatre; although they have been used in some TV studios, they cannot provide the flexibility of other systems for this application.

An advance on the counterweight systems is the provision of motorised barrels. The motor unit can be separate from the barrel unit, or in the case of self climbers, integral to the barrel unit. The barrel itself is over 2 m long and enables several luminaires to be placed side by side along the bar. Power is provided by fixed sockets, mounted on trunking along the barrel so that the luminaires can be easily plugged into the lighting supply. The adjustment of height is totally flexible and the system inherently safe by its design. It is very easy to operate from a remote control.

Finally, we come to probably the most accurate lighting positioning system of all. The mono-pole grid, although expensive to install, allows monopoles to be positioned about 600 mm from each other in adjacent tracks and individually to be placed anywhere along the trackways. The height of the monopoles is either adjusted by personnel at grid level, using portable drive tools, or by remotely controlled integral drive motors. The main drawback of monopoles is that a reduction in the number of units used in a studio for economic reasons means more physical movement of the units themselves and this requires riggers working over the acting area, which with modern safety legislation, dictates that special arrangements have to be made. It is difficult to move the units in the grid area if they are permanently cabled so the electrical system has to be designed to cater for multi-positional use, allowing the units to be connected as necessary.

When discussing more sophisticated lighting suspension systems, there are certain items that are common to either monopoles, motorised barrels or motorised pantographs. If we cover the ground rules for the component parts, the understanding of the complete pieces of equipment becomes easier.

It is difficult to state which items have the most importance due to the reliance upon one another for the satisfactory operation of particular items of equipment. However, to stick our necks out, we plump for the electric motors first as without these we have to resort to muscle power.

Most modern barrel winch units today employ three-phase electric motors of about 1–1.5 kW rating (Figure 7.2). They also have a combined gearbox. The gearbox will have reduction gears so that the barrel unit moves up and down at a reasonable speed which is usually 8–10 m per minute. The gearbox is selected so that when maximum weight is applied to the barrel and the electrical system is 'off', the unit will not move, thus providing a self sustaining system of gearing. To prevent the barrel unit over-running when being raised or lowered, an integral electrical

Figure 7.2 Motorised barrel

braking system is installed on the high speed side of the gearbox. This brake is normally applied and only released when the motor is activated. Monopole motor units may use three phase, single phase or d.c. drive motors. Because a monopole has a maximum lifting capacity of about 60 kg only compared with a barrel of about 150 kg, the motors are generally smaller. It is easy to reverse a three-phase motor but single-phase motors have to have special drive circuits to allow forward and reverse operation. If d.c. motors are used, although they allow very easy control, they may present problems by becoming generators and supplying harmful voltage back into any control circuits. With any of the systems using motor drive units, it is essential that some form of manual drive is available in the event of electrical failure of the system.

There are two basic types of winding drum. The first being the scroll drum where the wire rope is wound on side by side in much the same way as a cotton reel. Due to the length of wire rope, together with the need to keep a low torque on the motor, the drums are usually reasonably small in diameter (200 mm approx.) and as only one turn of rope is used around 250 mm wide. It is important that the drum width is held as small as possible so that the horizontal angle where the wire rope meets the drum is kept within certain limits. Usually a groove is formed in the winding drum so the rope follows the correct path. A big advantage of the scroll drum system is that the speed of the barrel unit remains constant when being raised and lowered.

The other type of winding drum is the pile wind and this works rather like a large yo-yo. The rope is piled singly, several layers thick upon itself between two substantial metal plates. This means that as the effective diameter of the drum is changing as the rope piles the barrel unit's speed of travel varies from its highest point to its lowest. A problem for the designers of pile drum systems is that the torque is not constant and the system has to cater for the worst case, which is when the barrel is at its highest point where the pile drum provides maximum speed with reduced lifting ability. This means that larger motors have to be used on pile wind winches than will be used on a scroll drum winch of similar lifting capacity. The system also suffers from the tendency for the ropes to be easily damaged if the mechanical design is not of the highest quality particularly if the retaining plates on the pile drum are weak. With both scroll and pile wind drums the wire ropes have to be very positively anchored to the drum and two clamps are used for each rope. To ensure a margin of safety, a minimum of two turns of rope must be left on either type of drum when the barrel is at its lowest operating point.

It is preferable on self climbing winches to use scroll drums because, by keeping to a low torque, it will also enable the motor to be smaller – with obvious benefits. With a self climber, having the motor unit positioned approximately in the middle of the bar, with scroll drums either side, means that the unit will be wide and this might prove to be a problem. In practice, this does not appear to be the case. As an alternative it is possible to use scroll drums positioned so that they lay in the same direction as the barrel, but if this is used, precautions have to be taken to make certain that the unit, when winding up and down stays in the same vertical plane. Also, there is the danger that the motor unit sticks out to one side and causes an out of balance condition. It is very normal with self climbing winches to use four wire ropes to enable a better balance to be achieved and to meet current safety standards.

Diverter pulleys (used to guide the wire rope to the correct plane) which are generally made from steel for strength and durability consist of a grooved wheel running on bearings. When the wire rope leaves the winding drum it has to be guided via the diverter pulleys to the correct position. The diverter pulleys are grooved and it is important that the wire rope fits snugly in that groove. The diameter of the pulley is also important due to the wire rope having a minimum quoted bending radius so that damage to the rope is avoided. Current regulations call for a diameter not less than 20 times the ropes' thickness. The pulleys must run on properly lubricated bearings due to the high mechanical loads involved, and to keep noise to a minimum. As a general guide each diverter pulley in the system will reduce the lifting capacity by between 2% and 5% dependent on the type of bearings used.

Barrel winches normally have two ropes, each capable of supporting at least *six* times the total applied load. Self climbing winches generally have four wire ropes for suspension, however the rules for the breaking strain of the ropes remains at *six* times total load for each rope.

Monopoles and motorised pantographs which could be operated by a single wire rope, have to be provided with twin lifting ropes for safety. Each single rope must support the total load of the monopole or pantograph in event of failure of either of the two ropes. The minimum breaking strength of each rope must be able to cope with at least *six* times the safe working load (SWL) plus the weight of the suspension tubes and electrical cables. In the event of a single rope failure, free fall via the rope length compensator system should be no greater than 12.7 mm. It is extremely important that in practice wire ropes do not become frayed and damaged. If a wire rope gets nicked or crushed it is vital that the rope is changed.

Various functions on the motor unit have to be made automatic to avoid either damaging the equipment, or more importantly, injuring staff. The functions are as follows.

Limit switches generally consist of a striker which is driven along a finely threaded shaft towards a microswitch which activates a relay and switches 'off' the power to the motor. Rotational movement of the strikers is prevented by a retaining bar which is placed in slots on the strikers themselves. To adjust the strikers, the bar is simply raised and the striker is screwed along the thread to the pre-set position desired and then the retaining bar is replaced. The threaded shaft which activates the strikers is driven from the main gearbox usually by a belt, chain or set of gears.

A 'top' switch which will automatically disconnect the motor supply when the lifting assembly is raised to its highest set point. To avoid straining the motor gearbox, the diverters, wire ropes, etc. if the unit tries to drive itself to a dead stop, in the event of the *top limit* switch failing, current European standards require a second top limit switch situated just after the normal top limit. This system is generally used where an automatic overload cut-out is not provided. If an automatic overload system is provided, another solution under the European standards is to have a mechanical buffer which the barrel unit will hit before it reaches its highest point just after top limit thus causing the automatic overload system to trip causing the unit to stop. Either of these solutions has to prevent an overload to the unit of more than 1.4 times thus ensuring no permanent mechanical damage.

A 'bottom' switch which will automatically disconnect the motor supply when the lifting assembly is lowered to its lowest set point, which is usually 1 m above floor level. In the event of failure of the *bottom limit* switch, and if the ropes keep unwinding, the slack rope switch will operate.

If any of the wire ropes which suspend the units are allowed to slacken, usually by meeting an obstruction on the descent, a dangerous situation arises. If the unit does not automatically stop it may:

(a)   tangle its own ropes causing permanent damage to them, and
(b)   suddenly fall free under its unbalanced weight.

Obviously (b) is the more hazardous and to prevent any danger sensors are usually fitted to each individual wire rope which operate rapidly as soon as any slackness occurs. *Slack rope* sensors usually consist of a striking mechanism attached to a spring under compression and a short distance away from a microswitch. When the ropes slacken, the spring expands and forces the microswitch to operate.

Although not specified under European regulations, a sensing system should be provided so that if a load greater than the SWL is applied to the barrel unit, the motor supply will automatically shut off. The European tolerance for overload is 40% but some organisations ask for closer limits of about 20–25%. *Overload* rope sensors usually consist of spring biased pivoted diverter pulleys. Normally the spring keeps the diverter pulley assembly from striking the microswitch. On overload the spring compresses and the microswitch operates. Obviously the springs have to be selected to cater for the designated load of the particular unit.

In the case of standard winches or self climbers, the overload condition is dependent on the position of the load applied to the barrel. Some units are designed to assess the overload as if it were positioned in the centre of the barrel. Thus 100 kg will present a load of 50 kg on each rope, in the case of a two-rope system. If each rope were designed to sense a 100 kg overload, the system would not work; if however, the ropes were designed for 50 kg each, the system would work correctly. The main problem would arise when a load of 100 kg is off centre, thus presenting an overload condition to one rope most of the time. Most modern winch systems should attempt to use a design where the load is added, totalling the correct SWL irrespective of the load's position on the bar.

Both overload and slack rope systems are usually designed to automatically reset once the problem has been cured.

All of these sensors are fed to a purpose built electrical control box which contains the contactors for the raise and lower motor functions together with the control circuits for top and bottom limits, overload and slack wire rope sensors. Local control for raise and lower is usually provided for ease of maintenance. The system accepts remote control signals from elsewhere in the operational area.

Each unit has to be provided with labels to clearly indicate operational functions used by the staff. In addition, warning labels have to be provided to ensure staff safety. A reasonably comprehensive list is given below:

1   Unit number.
2   Lighting supply cable identification.
3   Lighting power socket identification.

4   Each control must be labelled i.e. Raise, Lower, Local control, Remote control, Supply on/off.
5   Warning labels must be provided to indicate the mechanical loading and the electrical loading.
6   Any safety hazards connected with the operation of the equipment.

The length of the barrel is dictated by the needs of the installation. The unit which would be capable of lifting loads up to 150 kg, is fitted with brackets so that the wire ropes from the winding drums may be attached. In line with the rest of the equipment connected with a winch the attachment brackets must have a sufficient safety factor and this is normally six times the applied SWL. The barrel, which may be steel or aluminium, will bend when loaded with lighting equipment and it is important that the barrel does not deflect more than recommended amounts. Therefore the barrel supports must also be capable of some deflection without permanent damage. The wire ropes must be attached to the brackets by correctly locked off shackles so that they will not loosen in operational use. The ends of the wire ropes where the shackles pass through must be permanently formed into eyelets by correctly splicing the ropes.

A trunking is usually fitted above the barrel itself for the termination of the power feeder cables and these cables usually go directly to sockets mounted on the front face of the trunking. The trunking is usually mounted approximately 300 mm above the barrel. Many configurations of sockets are used according to the electrical standards of the user country. In the UK most companies have now settled for 240 V, 32 A, BS 4343 sockets. This allows the connection of 5 kW lights and falls in well with the practice of using 5 kW dimmers. The BS 4343 16 A socket is also used for lower powered luminaires and sub circuits.

The power cables for the lighting socket outlets are fed from high level down to the trunking on the barrel unit. Over the years, many systems have been used but the two most popular are the 'curly cable' and 'flip-flop'. The first system uses cables formed into a coil which is wrapped around the wire ropes. The cables which are suspended from the high level structure adjacent to the winch units, tend to act like elongated springs. Either one or more of the wire ropes can be used and the curly cables are generally multi-core. Due to the weight of the cables, there is a tendency for the coils to compress immediately above the barrel unit. The flip-flop system, on the other hand, allows the cable to fold in a uniform and controlled manner. Each section of the fold is about 1 m long, the cables can be unsupported where each fold is determined by a mechanical clip or a device to form a radius. Although more costly, a system of lightweight support trays can be used as a definite route so that the cables fold almost perfectly. Plastic trays, although on the surface seemingly ideal for the job, will probably distort in the heat from luminaires hung from the barrel especially at the lower end of the flip-flops, just above the luminaires. Precautions have to be taken so that the trays will pivot at grid level to avoid damage if a barrel assembly is moved sideways, the cable system should never be allowed to become straight in its maximum travel thereby avoiding the sections of cable tray from attempting to fold in the opposite direction to normal.

7.3   Pantographs

Pantographs allow luminaires to have their operating height adjusted over a specific range. Manual pantographs come as two distinct types, either spring balanced or manually wound with wire ropes. The ones most used in practice are those which are spring balanced. The reason for this being that once the springs are adjusted to balance the weight of the luminaire on the pantograph, very little effort is required to raise and lower the luminaire and this system is extremely quick in studio use. The main problem with spring pantographs is that adjusting the springs is extremely hazardous if not carried out by trained staff. Wind-up pantographs, on the other hand, have little or no safety problems, but the disadvantage of this type is that they are slow in operational use due to the gearing via a pole operated system. Manual pantographs come with either two, four or six springs. The amount of springs has some bearing on the adjustment range for the luminaires. Obviously with more springs, a finer range of adjustment can be achieved. Spring balanced pantographs generally have a range from approximately 1.8 m to 4.5 m. The stabilising framework for pantographs can either be twin cross armed devices or a single cross armed device. Spring pantographs are always twin cross armed devices. The pantographs are usually fitted with cable clips, either side along the cross armed devices, to allow for cable routing from the trolley, where the unit is usually mounted on the barrel, down to a socket outlet at the base of the pantograph which can either be free or permanently fixed adjacent to the luminaire spigot holder. As the weight of pantographs are an additional load for the grid, they are generally made from aluminium. Due to the range of springs that can be fitted to pantographs, units come in various weight ranges, therefore during the planning of the studio installation, it is important to know the weight of the luminaires to be used.

The original motorised pantographs had one motor for lifting to ease the problems associated with spring and manually wound pantographs. However, without a traversing motor, it meant that the operators had to drag quite heavy units along the trackways.

Modern motorised pantographs are usually fitted with two motor units, one for lifting and one for traversing on its associated trackways. All the electrical cables are terminated in a box at the top of the unit. A socket outlet is provided adjacent to the luminaire attachment point. The unit is generally designed to occupy as little height as possible when fully raised to the grid. The pantograph must be capable of operating with any load between zero and its SWL plus the weight of all permanently attached components such as the stabilising framework, the electrical sockets, cables and cable supports. The luminaires are usually attached to the bottom of the pantograph by means of a female socket to accept a 28.58 mm (1$\frac{1}{8}$ inch) spigot or a 'C' clamp over a mini barrel. Normally they are designed for a SWL of approximately 40 kg. The speed of operation is extremely important with the 'raise and lower' being approximately 8–10 m/minute.

The pantograph's traverse speed must be slower than 15 m/minute. At speeds faster than this the unit is inclined to jerk, and the luminaire may oscillate in travel. Bearing in mind that the pantograph unit should be as compact as possible, the usual operating height range is around 7 m due to the length of wire rope needed and the subsequent effect on the size of the winding drums. The two motors are normally powered from an a.c. single phase supply. The unit for raising and lowering the luminaire will be approximately 600 W and the unit for traversing will be about 100 W. Brakes are required to stop the unit over running and these should operate on the high speed side of the motor gearbox units. The brake is automatically applied whenever the motor supply is switched off or interrupted and electromagnetically released when the motor supply is on. The gearbox as usual, should be self sustaining. For the purposes of maintenance the electric motors, gearboxes, brakes if fitted, wire rope winding drums, travel and load limit switches, must be accessible and easily replaced in the event of faults occurring. Provision must be made so that the units can be wound by hand in the event of failure of the electrical equipment or in order to facilitate maintenance. In a similar manner to monopoles, two wire ropes have to be fitted to meet current safety standards, and the twin drums will be either pile wind or scroll. The suspension system using the wire ropes on a pantograph is the same as that used on a monopole and to compensate for the differential in rope lengths a toggle bar is used for the rope attachment at the base of the unit. The pantograph should be fitted with slack rope and overload sensing systems, it must also incorporate vertical travel limits to stop the pantograph at pre-set positions at the top and bottom of travel. The traversing system consists of an electric motor, a gearbox and generally a friction drive system formed as an integral unit. The pantograph would normally be propelled along the trackway by a friction wheel or similar drive. The drivewheel, which is normally permanently engaged but must have a method of easily uncoupling it and manually traversing the pantograph in an emergency.

These types of pantographs rely upon remote electrical control. A termination box has to be provided and fitted close to the motor unit assembly. This box will accept the remote control supply system, together with a main luminaire supply for the particular unit. All of these signals will be supplied through a catenary cable feeder system. The remote control system has to provide 'raise', 'lower', 'traverse left' and 'traverse right' signals. To keep the complexity of the electrical system on the pantograph system to a minimum, it is preferable to remote the control relays and use mains drives direct to the motors. The unit should also be provided with local electrical control where the traverse and vertical control of the unit is accomplished by standard pole operation cups pinned to the shafts of biased rotary switches. Pantograph movement is obtained by turning the switches either left or right. It is obviously impossible in practice to have a left and right traverse, as it is dependent on the position of the operator in the studio, so the directions are called 'red' and 'white' and appropriate marker boards are fitted to the studio walls. The indicators for red and white direction and raise and lower must be clearly visible from the studio floor.

7.4 Counterweight bars

The counterweight bar is the primary means of support for everything above stage in the theatre (see Figure 7.3). The bars are adapted to lift scenery and lighting. The only special adaptation for the lighting bar is the provision of a distribution system of sockets running along its length with a terminal box at one end of the barrel supplied from a hanging multi-core cable system known as 'tripe'. The support cables or ropes travel via diverter pulleys to the side of the stage where they are connected to a counterweight box. The box is loaded with cast iron weights until it balances the intended load. At this point very little effort is required to raise and lower the bar. When the bar has been adjusted to the required position, a clamping device is applied to the ropes to hold them firmly in place. The rope brake is designed to hold with only a small out of balance load. This prevents a dangerous condition when either the barrel is overloaded or luminaires are

1	Head Pulley
2	Head Steels
3	Top Stop Channels
4	Weight Cradle
5	Space Bar
6	Caulking Bracket
7	Guide Channel
8	Bottom Rope Return Pulley
9	Bottom Stop Channels
10	Fly Gallery
11	Rope Lock Rail
12	Rope Lock
13	Hauling Rope
14	Loading Gallery
15	Suspension Cables
16	Grid Pulley
17	Grid Drop Channels
18	48 mm Counterweight Bar
19	Flyrail Cleat
20	Scenery Pack Rail
21	Guard Panels

A 76mm (Wall to Head Steels)
B 509mm (Between Head Steels)
C 1980mm (single purchase)
    2602mm (double purchase)
D 686mm
E 1118mm
F 990mm
G 610mm
H 1980mm
J 2750mm
K 1000mm
L 152mm

Figure 7.3 Counterweight system

removed by mistake i.e. the rope starts to slip with about 25 kg out of balance load. The counterweight bar appears to satisfy all of the rigging needs of the theatre, although it should be pointed out that the total weight load on the grid is double that of the lighting i.e. the weight of the lighting plus the weight of the counterweight system. It does however, present a problem inasmuch as the counterweight box is normally 2 m high which represents a loss of height by the time it reaches floor level.

When contemplating such a rigging system for lighting in a TV studio the height of the counterweight box and the ultimate height of the lighting bar must be considered. However, the main disadvantage of this suspension system in TV studios is that even if the bars are made half the width of the studio with counterweights on both sides, the bars are still usually too long to provide accurate lighting positions for other than one or two luminaires, in view of the fact that all of the rest of the lights on the bar are in a compromise height position. The exceptions to this statement are a row of top cyclorama lights at the side of the studio presenting a continuous length of barrel and banks of floodlights.

7.5 Motorised barrel winches

The main drive unit which can be mounted at high level in the studio, on a side gallery or at floor level, consists of a substantial framework to which is attached the electrical motor drive unit, gearbox, wire rope winding drums and the wire rope diverter pulleys. When the units are mounted in the grid the imposed weight load is that of the units plus the lighting. However, in the case of motor units attached to the side walls, most of the load on the grid is from the lighting only. The barrel unit, together with its associated lighting power sockets, mounted on an integral trunking system, is suspended from high level by wire ropes, which may be taken to the drive unit by additional diverter pulley systems. The associated electrical control box can be positioned adjacent to the unit or away from the unit in purpose made cabinets. However, a remote control unit would require more individual mains cables to connect it to the winch in the studio area.

The design of winches should provide for the lightest weight of support framework commensurate with minimum mechanical distortion. Any framework distortion may give problems with the mechanical sensing systems for 'slack rope' and 'overload'. It also may give problems with the pile or scroll drums. The physical size and weight of the unit is extremely important as this will have considerable impact on the support structure. A problem that always exists with conventional barrel winches is that of access to the motor units, usually solved by either walkways adjacent to the units or 'walkover' grids.

In essence a self climbing barrel winch is an upside down standard winch with the motor gear box mounted above the barrel on the same assembly. The main problem with self climbing winches is that in addition to lifting the normal SWL, they have to lift their own weight, bearing in mind that the weight of the unit is usually similar to that of the SWL, it would not be inconceivable that a self climber would have to be rated to lift something like 250 kg from the studio floor. This means, in general, that the power of the motors will be more on self climbing units, particularly so if pile wind drums are used, hence the motor gearbox becomes heavier which poses a design problem. The self contained unit consists of a motor and gearbox, wire rope winding drums, diverter pulleys and the sensing system for top and bottom limits, slack rope and overload. The unit is secured and suspended by the steel wire lifting ropes from the underside of a suitable ceiling or grid structure. All lighting and control circuits are fed from the ceiling or grid structure via flip-flop or curly cables. The barrel, which is usually from 2.0 m to 2.5 m long, and capable of lifting loads up to 120 kg, is suspended from the main housing which contains the motor gearbox unit, etc. With self climbers it is generally normal to integrate the lighting power sockets into the main housing instead of supplying a separate trunking system.

A major advantage of self climbers is that they do not require complex grid systems and are much less time consuming to install. Generally any maintenance can be carried out at studio floor level.

7.6 Monopoles

A monopole or 'a single suspension unit' is a means by which a luminaire can be raised or lowered by a wire rope winding system with stability being maintained by metal tubes which are telescopic and slide within each other. Due to the self-sustaining gearboxes employed, it would be a very tiresome business to manually wind a luminaire from studio floor level to grid level. Therefore, the units are generally operated by powered drive systems.

A manual monopole will be normally operated by a portable tool which could be driven by compressed air or electricity. Alternatively, the unit may be operated by a purpose designed integral electric motor gearbox unit and is designated a 'motorised monopole'. Generally, both types of monopole are mechanically much the same. The SWL of monopoles is approximately 45 kg with some specially designed units capable of loads up to 60 kg. Due to handling problems at high level, it is important that the weight of each unit does not exceed 80 kg and preferably should be a lot less. Each monopole generally consists of 7 or 8 interlocking steel tubes and are usually manufactured for a working height range of 10 m and all the tubes used have to be made to close dimensional tolerances and straightness. The telescopic sections should be provided with interlocking retaining tabs, which prevent the monopole twisting too much in operational use. Each tube locks into the one above to restrict rotational movement of the individual tubes to within ±2.5°. It should be noted that the telescopic sections are only to give stability and are not load carrying. The tube sets are always made longer than the wire ropes at their maximum extension and it is extremely important that the tubes do not stick at any point. If the tubes do stick at high level, and then suddenly become free, the energy transferred to the rope suspension system will probably be sufficient to cause considerable damage. Due to safety considerations, each monopole must be fitted with twin wire ropes and these can be contained within twin scroll or wire rope pile drums. The twin cables must be independently terminated on the winding drum assemblies and to a compensator attachment (to allow for differential in the length of the ropes) which should be fitted to the base of the telescopic tube assembly. All the wire rope terminations must have provision for a visual inspection at regular intervals to meet current safety standards. The gearbox on both motorised monopoles and manual monopoles must be self sustaining. Where integral electric drive motors are used, they are usually a special single phase type but d.c. motors are also used. Due to the lower SWL of monopoles together with their lower self weight, less powerful motors can be used.

In the case of monopoles with integral drive motors, electromechanically operated overload and slack wire rope devices should be incorporated into the units, together with top and bottom travel limit switches. In the case of manual monopoles, which employ drive tools, it is obviously important to have some form of torque limitation on the drive system, otherwise undue stress will be applied to the wire ropes and pile drums. The motor control units, which are generally mounted at the top of the monopole, normally require an a.c. supply. The control units should also provide a local or remote control facility which can be selected. Remote control circuits are usually by low voltage d.c. The local control can either be an 'up' or 'down' button or a centre biased 'raise' and 'lower' switch. In an emergency, or in the event of system power failure, the gearbox should have a spindle drive facility for the unit to be operated by hand or by suitable portable drive tools.

The monopoles have to be provided with a trolley which is purpose made to suit the grid slot system in use and will have to meet such safety standards as required by the installation and to the operators' satisfaction. Normally these trolleys are fitted with eight wheels to mount on the grid slots. The trolley should be braked, and can be fitted additionally with lifting mechanism for ease of rotation for direction changes when using transfer slots.

A spigot holder has to be provided at the lower end of monopole tube sets, generally to take a standard 28.58 mm (1⅛ inch) spigot as normally fitted to luminaires. For many years, the electrical supply cable to the luminaires suspended from monopoles was generally dropped from high level with a female socket attached so that the luminaire could be plugged in at low level. In recent years, some manufacturers have provided luminaire supply cables which are made in preformed coils and wrapped around the telescopic sections with a socket fixed adjacent to the spigot holder and in this way a much neater system has evolved. The supply socket would obviously need to meet the requirements of the particular studio.

7.7   System controls

It's no good installing motorised units in a theatre or studio without having some form of control. The simplest form of control is two wires that go to a unit, and say, 'go up' and 'go down'. However, doing this one at a time, is very time consuming. It is far better to have a certain number of units that could move up at the same time as another set could come down. In the case of the winch systems, the 'up/down' commands are the only ones needed. Unfortunately, if we are using motorised pantographs, or for that matter, motorised monopoles with a traversing system that requires control, then the system becomes more complex.

Let us now consider how we can control a fairly simple unit going up and down. It is obviously more economical if from the control console to each unit we use the minimum of copper wire, and to achieve this we use low power relays driving mains contactors. In the case of three phase drive motors, we use subsidiary relays to drive the 'up' and 'down' contactors. Today's systems usually employ 24 V relays. The mains power for the motors can be derived from a ring main going from unit to unit; if the power requirements of each motor are fairly small, then a reasonable size ring main will allow several units to be used at once, and most studios aim to control 20 units at any one time. This avoids a surge on the electrical supply caused by the motors all starting at the same time and prevents a large dynamic mechanical load being applied to the grid. For either standard barrel winches or self climbing winches where the installation is fixed, the electrical control system is relatively straightforward. If, however, there is a need to control monopoles from the studio floor, to reduce the amount of operational work at grid level, the monopoles would have to be provided with either extremely long electrical cables coming from the motors or a multiplicity of control points would have to be provided at grid level.

The most common consoles used today are equipped with a 'green' and 'amber' group control system; where each winch is capable of being routed to either the 'green' or 'amber' control. Therefore some units can be switched to green control, giving up/down commands, and other units can be switched to the amber, also giving up/down commands. The amber and green controls are completely independent of each other; therefore some winches can be going up while others are coming down. Where winch units are coupled together for operational reasons, some clear indication of this state must be made on the appropriate console. In the past this was often bits of sticky tape, or pieces of perspex coupling the switches together; in modern consoles this can be accomplished by electronically interlocking the system. The limitations placed on the number of winches to be used at any one time is generally occasioned by the dynamic mechanical load applied to the grid structures when the motors start. Some recent advances in the control of suspension units in studios include using microprocessor control with alphanumeric keyboards and VDUs to display the information. With some intelligence built into the system it is therefore possible to have sophisticated selection whereby units that are coupled together are easily recognised by the system and the studio should generally become more safe.

The large control consoles, which are mainly banks of switches, are usually positioned on a convenient wall in the operational area, but there are occasions when it is impossible to see what is happening when operating from the console, therefore remote control units are often used to allow the operator to walk to the area being lit and so have good sight lines to the equipment being moved. Originally these remote controls were by wire back to a point adjacent to the main console. Recent developments include radio and infrared transmitted control systems.

Remote control of monopole systems has never been developed to any degree, whereas motorised pantograph systems have become quite complex. The motorised pantograph requires control of 'up' and 'down' and its traversing motion. Units in use at the BBC in their regional studios also control on/off information of the luminaires as well; control being accomplished by a small portable handheld radio controller that can be carried about in the studio and used by the LD or senior electrician. The system is used for a rigging aid and not for total control of the luminaires. It does have the advantage that one man can move and adjust lights with relative speed. Control of motorised pantograph units is generally done from a base system, which sends mains signals to the motorised pantograph units, thus avoiding too many relays and subsidiary circuits within the units mounted at high level.

7.8   Rigging monopoles and pantographs

Pantographs, both manually and electrically controlled are normally mounted onto roller barrel trolleys or heavy duty 'C' section track. The method of mounting when using this track is to slide the pantograph unit into the track from one end making sure that the end stops are replaced in both ends of the track. When mounting pantographs onto a barrel roller trolley, the trolley is placed over the barrel so that the support wheels may traverse along the barrel. Safety bolts or plates are then fitted to the trolley to prevent it lifting off the barrel. Having mounted and secured the pantograph, the mains cable should be inspected to determine that none of the loops attached to the side of the pantograph can be trapped between the cross links which will act like a pair of scissors when the pantograph is opened and closed.

Load adjustment of spring pantographs is made by moving the position of the end of the spring up and down the outside rungs by use of hook plates attached to the end of each spring. This is a dangerous adjustment, and must be performed to the manufacturers' instructions to ensure that the spring is not released when it is moved from one rung to another.

When balancing the load it is a good practice to equalise the position of diagonally opposite springs to keep the pantograph from twisting. Extending the springs towards the base of the pantograph adjacent to the luminaire mounting point allows a greater load to be balanced. To load a luminaire onto a spring pantograph it is necessary to either climb up to the top position adjacent to the grid with the light which makes it difficult to adjust the springs for the applied load. A much preferred practice is to tie a piece of rope to the base of the pantograph and pull it down to floor level, where a sandbag or other convenient weight can be attached whilst the luminaire is being fitted to the base. The springs may now be adjusted until a perfect balance is achieved and the rope can be released. Extreme caution must be taken when unloading a spring pantograph to make sure that the reverse procedure is adopted to that of the mounting procedure, preferably with the rope, so that the pantograph is allowed to slowly close as the rope is played out. We have seen the results of a pantograph being released at floor level, allowing it to fly up to the top without a load and the result is quite dramatic and very dangerous. Springs become detached and links are broken, showering debris on those below with a real danger of the whole pantograph frame structure falling on the person responsible for letting go of it.

Motorised pantographs are much easier to mount in view of the fact that they are lowered by a motor and can be loaded at floor level, however the same procedure is required as in the case of the spring pantograph with regards to mounting and the path of the cables. If electrical traverse is provided, extra care is needed to ensure sufficient length of trailing cable and its safe routing.

Monopoles, because of their weight are difficult to handle, require at least two men and in the case of the motorised monopole, with its mains cable, three men to rig them. If it is practical, it is a better proposition to use a small hoist or tackle to get them up to grid level and then the most simple monopole may be lowered into the appropriate slot from above, having made sure that the grid end stops are in position. With more sophisticated grids, a transfer trolley is provided so that the monopole can be loaded into the trolley from the top gallery, pushed along to the appropriate slot, and then positioned in the grid.

When the monopole has been placed in the grid slot, it is necessary to guide the mains cable through the cable guide ring that holds it in the centre of the slot. This is to prevent the cable being trapped by the wheels of the trolley. Monopoles are positioned in the vertical and lateral position by motor drives in the case of the fully motorised unit, but in the case of the manually operated monopole these functions can only be performed from above the grid. Under no circumstances should the monopole be pulled along the slot from below by pulling the tubes. This will damage or break the tubes or at least, distort them, causing them to stick and bind when being lowered.

A good practice when installing monopoles is to determine the type of plug or connector being used at the luminaire end of the supply cable. Many types of 5 kW plug will not go through the standard grid slot of 2.5 inches (62.5 mm) and therefore must be fed through the end of the grid slot. This small observation before installation could save hours of shunting and moving monopoles around the grid when it comes to connecting up.

7.9 Loading barrel winches

Barrel winches come in a variety of types, they may be suspended by a counterweight system; they could be a standard winch unit where the motor is mounted at grid level or they may be a self climber where the motor unit is integral to the barrel. Two features that are common to any type of barrel suspension is that they have well-defined SWL; and being fairly long devices, occupy a large space in the grid system.

Generally with counterweight systems, it is almost impossible to overload them as the counterweight bucket usually only contains sufficient weights to balance the SWL on the bar. The overload warning system heard is probably the grunts and groans from the 'sparks' using the system.

Because of the larger lights used in TV, the spacing between barrels is fairly wide and this, together with the end to end spacing of the barrels, poses problems for the positioning of the luminaires. The position of the lighting has to be reasonably accurate and is dictated by the layout of the sets within the production area and the requirements of the LD to cover the action correctly. Many studios use a standard rig of luminaires which may be fastened directly to the barrel unit, or attached via a short spring pantograph so flexibility in height is provided. Where luminaires and pantographs are supplied as combinations, there is usually very little spare weight capacity on the bars, thus when additional equipment is required to be rigged to the bar, it may take the bar over its SWL limit. This poses real problems for the LD because he now has to make up his mind, whether to lose a luminaire or use another type of light. It may be possible to de-rig a pantograph leaving its luminaire in place, although with long barrel units it is preferable to keep the pantographs to allow flexibility between the luminaires attached to the bar. Another problem is that even if the bar was capable of taking the extra luminaire weight, it might be that the unit is too large to fit in the available space. At this point, the LD could use a short drop arm on the luminaire required so that it hangs just below the space occupied by the luminaires already present on the bar; although this may restrict the up/down movement of the luminaires on the pantographs.

What happens in TV studios when the barrel units do not provide the LD with his desired position for the luminaire? The only thing to do is to provide a temporary barrel that bridges two of the normal barrels. The two major problems with using cross barrels is that they tether two units together, inhibiting flexibility and the ends of the cross barrel attached to the standard barrel units impose extra weight. This load will be in proportion to the length of the crossbar between the attachment points and the point loads on the cross bar. For example, 50 kg in the centre of a cross barrel between two standard barrel units, will present a load of 25 kg to each barrel unit. At the other end of the scale, if the point load of 50 kg was positioned at one of the attachment points most of the 50 kg would be present at that point. It can be seen, therefore, that as the load moves along the bar, it moves proportionately between the two attachment points on the barrels.

The above case illustrates that it's not just simply a matter of putting a cross bar between two units. When using cross bars what happens when only one bar is raised and the other bar does not move? The bar that is moving in an upward direction will eventually take the total weight of the cross bar and attempt to pull it with itself. Just after this point in travel the cross bar will attempt to start raising the other winch barrel. Unless very good overload sensors are provided, it might be that the whole cross barrel structure is raised and eventually becomes dangerous because the luminaires are not hanging normally by the barrel clamping arrangement provided but have rotational stress applied. It may be that these exceed the mechanical tolerances as designed.

Conversely, the lowering of one of the main bars eventually means that one end of the cross bar becomes lower and lower and then will start to drag the other supporting bar into the moving unit. Once again, additional torque may be introduced into mechanical sections of the units. This case highlights the need for good overload protection but it is quite possible in practice that none of the loads on either the two original bars, or the cross bar exceeded the system specifications, only when the units were moved. In practice, it is therefore extremely important that any cross bar is clearly marked so that the electricians operating the winch control console will not raise or lower one bar without the other. This situation cited above involved two bars, with one crossbar attached, but in long experience in studios, we have seen several cross bars across several barrel units all at the same time; together with crossbars on crossbars, and one shudders to think of the complications this causes in practice.

The same rules apply to studios that employ self climbing units but unfortunately, an additional hazard exists. When using cross barrels in self climbing studios, not only would the cross barrel attempt to lift the SWL, it ultimately starts to lift the entire load of the barrel unit, and although it might not progress to a great height, it might get sufficiently high to suddenly swing free and act like a giant pendulum, which would be extremely dangerous to say the least.

In recent times, broadcasting organisations using motorised barrel systems, have examined more sophisticated control of their winch systems to prevent problems such as these occurring. Two methods can be employed; one of which is to *remove from any form of control* the two bar units with a cross barrel attached once they have been positioned; alternatively ensure that any movement of one of the normal bars will *guarantee the other bar moves in unison*, thus maintaining the status quo for the cross barrel.

Luminaires rigged directly on a bar require a safety bond that passes over the barrel as the second means of suspension in accordance with normal safety procedures. If however, a pantograph is used to support a luminaire a different technique must be employed. *If the pantograph is attached to the support system by a wheeled trolley which cannot be removed without a tool* then a safety bond will not be required at the top of the pantograph. However, the luminaire still requires bonding to the base of the pantograph. *Bonds are required at the top of portable pantograph units and drop arms*, and this must pass over the main barrel. At the base of any pantograph, where the luminaire is attached, either by a spud directly into a spigot holder or by a 'C' clamp onto a spade fixing at the base of the pantograph, the luminaire safety bond must pass over the permanently attached bottom section of the pantograph unit.

When using bars that are say, 2.4 m long, it is important that the roller trolleys used for the luminaires' horizontal adjustment do not entangle the cables, from the lighting power sockets adjacent to the bar, supplying the luminaires. Various methods have been employed over the years to prevent this happening, one of the most successful is to have a small subsidiary bar adjacent to the main bar with small runners attached so that the power cable is conveyed along out of harm's way rather like the power feeds used with gantry cranes. Another important point to watch when rigging bars is to ensure that the cable does not droop from the socket across the heat outlet at the top of the luminaire and thus get either too hot or melt completely. This may seem rather obvious, but unfortunately in practice happens too often and the cables do become very brittle and thus pose a safety hazard.

Many modern winch systems are fitted with a local barrel switch which enables the electrician, when rigging, to move the barrel up and down by using his operating pole in the cup of the operating switch. This allows very fine adjustments; which are only limited by the length of the pole used, and improves the productivity during the rigging period. The normal procedure for rigging bars in studios is to bring sections of the barrel system down to the studio floor level so the electricians can remove luminaires where necessary, introduce new luminaires, change filters and fit any other equipment as desired by the LD. This operation is usually done in groups of about 20 bars, this being the maximum amount that the winch system caters for at any one time and, by coincidence, is usually two rows across a production studio of about 800 m². While the rigging is taking place, it will usually involve a team of two electricians on the bars, one electrician fetching and carrying and another based near the winch console to move the bars up and down when requested. It is obviously extremely important that the communication between these men is good to ensure the correct weights are applied to bars, cross barrels are carefully noted and when the bars are moved they do not foul items of scenery and technical equipment. Additionally, on those occasions when temporary circuits such as a 10-kW feeder, is draped across several bars for convenience, that this is also noted to prevent accidents; as this fairly large cable acts like a *soft cross barrel*.

Other than additional luminaires or positions for luminaires which require cross barrels, there is also a need to provide facilities for slung video monitors and column loudspeakers in a standard lighting rig. In installations where permanent audience areas are allocated, although the seating may not always be in situ, it is customary to feed specified bars with sound and vision facilities. Sometimes special bars are provided to be used only for vision and sound audience facilities. However, if we have to rig a large video monitor onto a barrel, we will invariably have to move some of the existing equipment due to the weight of the monitor. If the equipment to be removed is a short spring pantograph, supporting a luminaire, it is essential that the spring pantograph is collapsed before removing the luminaire. Alternatively, it may be possible to remove the pantograph and luminaire as one combined unit in absolute safety. *Having removed any lighting equipment it is essential that it is transported safely to a secure area for storage thus ensuring no damage occurs.*

7.10   Rigging luminaires

The first consideration when rigging luminaires must be safety. Any light mounted above people is a potential hazard. Each suspension device will have a maximum SWL. This must be observed. Further, each luminaire is required to have its own safety bond made off around the primary means of support and the luminaire to arrest it in the event of it falling. The accessories such as barndoors and colour frames, also require their own safety retention device to prevent them becoming dislodged during movement. Having established that these requirements have been met, the electricians can mount the luminaire onto its support. In addition to the safety bond, a safety pin is also provided and this should be inserted into the top of the spigot when it has been passed through the spigot holder. The electrician connecting the luminaire to the supply is responsible for visually examining the cable and connector to establish that they are electrically safe before plugging the luminaire into its socket. The choice of luminaire is normally dictated by the lighting plot which will show the electrician the type of unit, its wattage and the colour of any filter to be used. A space is usually left on the lighting plot for the electrician to complete the circuit number used in the event that one has not already been allocated. It is normal practice to open the luminaire and determine that the correct size lamp has been fitted and then switch the luminaire on, focus and direct it to the approximate position as indicated on the lighting plot. These disciplines can save an enormous amount of time during rehearsals when in all probability, to get to a luminaire over sets and obstacles, it will be necessary to use tall steps or a portable tower. There will be occasions when it will be impossible to reach the luminaire after rigging is complete and rehearsals have commenced.

8
Dimming and control

Introduction

Before the introduction of electrical control of dimming, various methods of reducing the light level developed and many are still in use today. The two main disadvantages of electrical dimming is that by lowering the voltage to a tungsten lamp the colour of the light source changes, moving towards the red end of the spectrum, and secondly any colour filter that is placed in the luminaire will give a different result. The most exaggerated change will result with a heavy blue filter. When the source is running at full power it is producing light across the spectrum with some blue to penetrate the filter and provide blue light. When the source is dimmed down, the colour shifts towards the red end of the spectrum and produces very little blue, therefore the filter which restricts the red and green will pass little, if any colour. This is an important fact that all LDs learn early on in their career that the dimmer setting is just as important as the selection of the colour filter when designing the lighting plot.

Before we discuss the electrical methods of varying the voltage to the lamp, let us consider some mechanical solutions that have been used over the years that do not change the colour of the light from the luminaire.

A scrim can be a piece of wire mesh placed in the colour runners of a luminaire and normally available in order of the amount of light that it will allow through the holes in the mesh; 25%, 50%, 75% etc. If the required effect is to reduce the lighting level and to produce a softer shadow, the scrim could be a piece of cloth or gauze or a frost plastic filter, held in a frame and mounted at some distance in front of the light.

Plastic neutral density filters are available that work in the same way as the scrim, but of course, suffer deterioration with light and heat causing a change in the light output.

A thin box shape containing lateral slats, rather like a Venetian blind, can be mounted in the colour runners of the luminaire and the slats moved from the horizontal; where very little light will be obscured, to the vertical when the effect will be a total blackout. This movement can be a manual push/pull control or a more sophisticated control is obtained by gearing the blades to a motor gearbox device to provide remote control.

In profiles and follow spots the optical design provides an opportunity to place an iris in the optical path, normally between the objective lenses so that it will be well out of focus. In this position the iris will not affect the spot size and will produce an even dimming effect. The control can be a manual lever on the luminaire, or a motor gearbox will provide remote control.

Most of us associate a barndoor with a Fresnel spot. However, a little known fact is that a standard barndoor can be placed in the colour runners of a profile or follow spot, where it is out of focus, and used as a dimmer simply by bending in all four flaps to interrupt the light beam and adjust the intensity. This is a very useful ploy to balance the light output from follow spots that are mounted at different distances from the acting area. The barndoor will not affect the beam size and can be manually or remote control operated.

It is not that many years ago that most control from lighting consoles to dimmers was by a minimum of two wires for any individual dimmer, although by using a common return wire it is possible that 100 dimmers would have only required 101 wires. From the beginning of the 1980s digital control, using a pair of conductors was introduced, which had two distinct advantages:

1   the amount of wiring was reduced because it was possible to feed all the dimmer racks with a coded signal down one wire, and the dimmers would decode the signal that only applied to them, and
2   secondly, soft patching became extremely easy and dimmers could be grouped very readily, usually in real time, without having the need to resort to the pin patch panels provided in the 1960s and 1970s.

Recent times have seen digital control signals transmitted by radio and infrared across an area where direct cabling would have been difficult.

Other developments include small groups of dimmers being integrated into lighting hoists and suspension systems. However, if a group of dimmers have a common a.c. supply and a fault develops, the device protecting the main supply wiring to the dimmers could fail, thus losing not just one but several dimmers. The electrical installation must ensure that there is sufficient discrimination between the individual dimmer fuses or mcbs. There is little difference in weight between one heavy cable feeding three dimmers, or three smaller individual cables. It is important that dimmers mounted on the suspension system are audibly noise free. One very practical problem is that, when maintenance is required, how difficult is it to actually maintain the dimmers. Any dimmer should be capable of being removed, taken to a workshop and a replacement easily fitted.

There have been some interesting developments with dimmers. In the past, a signal went from the lighting console to the dimmer rack and only by observing the luminaires, together with hard wired indicator warning systems did the operator know the state of the studio or stage. Although in recent years, multiplex digital control signals to the dimmer room were employed, they still had to be decoded and converted to local d.c. control signals within the dimmer racks. Today, dimmers have been introduced where the digital signals are taken directly to the dimmer modules. This now allows much greater control of the individual dimmers. It is now possible to stabilise the output voltage of the dimmers to a high degree of accuracy, e.g. 196 V which represents setting '7' on a square law system. However it should be noted that we still can't make up volts, when the input voltage of the system falls below the set levels we can only go to the input voltage level, i.e. if the dimmer has been set for an output voltage of 240 and the input voltage falls to 230, we will still only get 230 V. From the console we can programme the dimmer laws with great ease, in addition to built in 'square', 'S' and 'linear' laws, it is also possible for the user to programme his own curves. Rather than having to remember that a certain keylight is channel 123, it's possible to use a 5-character alphanumeric name. The dimmers are clever enough to report back to the operator various problems. These are *no load present; no output volts present; there is an excess of d.c. in the system; there is no control available and the units have exceeded their normal temperatures.* Whether or not we need this intelligence is for the operators of the systems themselves to decide. The inescapable fact however, is that it is extremely easy for the manufacturers to design very elaborate controls for the entire system.

8.1   Theory of dimmers

A dimming device is one that reduces the flow of energy from a source to a destination and the source we are concerned with is electricity. The original control was by resistance but unfortunately caused power to be wasted. Ultimately auto transformer dimmers and saturable reactor dimmers were used to control lighting. One big advantage of a saturable reactor dimmer was that small d.c. control signals could be supplied from a remote point. Both the resistance dimming systems and auto transformer systems generally depended upon complex mechanical drive arrangements being provided to achieve any form of control.

The greatest advance in lighting control came about during the mid-1960s with the introduction of the *thyristor*. Because the thyristor is a uni-directional device, two have to be used for the control of a.c. supplies for lighting systems so that we control the positive and negative half cycles of the a.c. supply. A close cousin of the thyristor is the 'triac'. Whereas the thyristor is uni-directional, the triac is a bi-directional device, and by applying a signal to the gate, we can obtain full wave control of a.c. power. There are several advantages by using solid state devices such as the thyristor and triac, the power loss is exceedingly small, they are very easily controlled and the most important of all, that they are independent of the load across them. The major drawback to solid state switching devices is the fact that the period of time from its 'off' state to its 'on' state is extremely small, in fact of the order of microseconds, and it is this switching cycle that gives problems in practice. All the other types of dimmers that have been mentioned such as resistance, auto-transformer and saturable reactor, work on the principle of diminishing or increasing the sine wave with virtually no distortion. The thyristor dimmer output, as can be seen from Figure 8.1, chops the wave form into discrete quantities.

The input control signal for a thyristor dimmer is varied at the control console. The signal level reaching the dimmer is compared internally on the dimmer control circuit and according to that comparison, the dimmers are switched on at some time during the positive and negative half cycles. Thyristors automatically switch off when they pass through the zero point of the mains cycle; therefore a signal has to be applied to the thyristors controlling the positive and negative portions of the input mains every half cycle, to enable them to conduct continuously. If for instance, we are working on a linear system, and '5' on the fader literally means 50% power

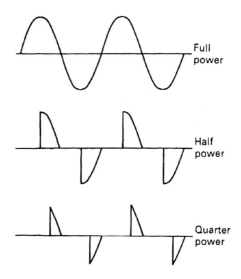

Figure 8.1 Thyristor waveform diagrams

output from the dimmer, the thyristors would conduct at the 90° point, which is halfway between the start of the half cycle and the completion of the half cycle. Solid state devices such as the thyristor depend on a flow of current to keep them activated, which is somewhat similar to the action of the holding current in the coil of a magnetic relay. Thyristors require a well defined minimum current to maintain a conducting state. When the current drops below this minimum level, which is known as the 'holding current', the thyristor will stop conduction and become effectively an open circuit. It is therefore essential that a minimum current has to flow in the thyristor circuits so that they are stable. In the earlier days of thyristors, it was felt practical that one short pulse applied at the nominated switch on point in the half cycle would be sufficient to keep them conducting for the remainder of the half cycle and in most practical situations this was true. It was found in practice however that dimmers used for tungsten lighting became unstable with small resistive and inductive loads. Several methods were employed to overcome this problem, one of which was to keep a continual stream of pulses into the thyristor gate during the nominated conduction periods of the negative and positive half cycles, so that there was no tendency to switch off. Another method was by applying a switching signal which consisted of a constant d.c. signal to the thyristor gate during the nominated conduction period, so that during the half cycle there was always a voltage present to ensure that the thyristor fired for the selected period of time.

When lamps switch on, the current flowing through a cold filament may be up to 15 times greater than the normal current. Thus a 5-kW studio Fresnel spotlight with a normal steady state current of around 21 A on a 240 V supply, would have a cold inrush current of anything up to 300 A. This obviously must have some effect on a thyristor being used as the dimmer. The main problem being that to cater for the short term high current, the thyristor has to be rated at a greater current level than would normally be expected.

A problem associated with thyristors is that, as the output power of thyristors increases, the gate requires a higher current flow and to ensure high sensitivity of input for large current devices, a subsidiary thyristor may be used to fire the gate circuit. The reason for this is that the small primary thyristor will require a very low current at its gate to conduct and its output, which will be several times greater than the input current, will quite adequately fire a higher powered thyristor. Most of the discussion taking place here relates to the practice of using two 'back to back' thyristors, rather than any use of triacs, which only tend to be used in lower quality dimmers. In recent times, it has become possible to obtain solid state devices which incorporate the two thyristors and some of the associated firing circuitry, all in one encapsulated package.

The past few years has seen the introduction of dimmers based on IGBT technology (Insulated Gate Bipolar Transistor) (See Figure 8.2). These high powered transistors have become widely used throughout the electrical industry for controlling supply switching, control of motors,

Figure 8.2 IGBT dimmer

battery charging, etc. The most recent development is to replace triacs and thyristors in circuits used for dimming lights. The advantage of a transistor over the thyristor, is that the current can be gradually varied through the device and not just a rapid switch on, as is the case with thyristors. Insulated Gate Bipolar Transistor dimmers allow the power to come on naturally at the beginning of the half cycle, but slowly turn off the current in a controlled manner on the falling waveform. The software controlling the dimmer is designed so that the switch off curve is tailored to reduce the rapid fall time of a thyristor dimmer. The benefits are that EM interference is reduced to a lower level and any lamp sing is virtually eliminated. One aim for many years has been to have a true sine wave dimmer where there would be no rapidly rising waveforms to create the problems associated with other types of modern dimming. The International Electronic Service (IES) of The Netherlands have developed a sine wave dimmer for powers of 3 kW, 5 kW and 10 kW. They are not pure sine wave, but are reconstructed smooth sine waves, using 40 kHz switching control systems. By using a high frequency, there are many steps in each sine wave, therefore it becomes practically smooth in practice. One of the best developments of modern IGBT dimmers is that short circuit protection can be performed by the electronic circuitry. The units will switch off on short circuits. The input is usually controlled by an mcb with the unit providing electronic overload and short circuit protection.

8.2 Problems in practice

Since the inception of modern electronic dimmers using thyristors, etc. all manufacturers have been trying to solve the problem of the chopped waveform and the associated electromagnetic interference. Several ideas have emerged from manufacturers to reduce that interference to manageable levels, and recently have seen the introduction of devices other than the thyristor as the power controllers. Unfortunately at the lower priced end of the dimmer market, the interference is only just contained to the general level set by the standards authority of the countries concerned, and is usually not good enough for professional installations where microphone cables and video cables are used. At the upper end of the market, manufacturers, at a cost, will make dimmers with very low interference levels from the point of view of audio and video circuits. The strict implementation of the EMC Directive by all manufacturers should ensure that dimmer interference is much lower in the future.

In practice, most thyristor dimmers are operated at about 80% of their full output and this is enough to guarantee that we will always have a rapidly rising current waveform which is the switch-on point of the negative and positive half cycles. We hope our readers will appreciate, without going into complicated mathematics that any waveform approaching a square wave, is made up of a multiplicity of other waveforms, varying from waveforms at fairly low frequencies to those at extremely high frequencies and it is the generation of these high frequency waveforms that gives us the most problems.

If we examine the effects of the lower frequency waveforms, we find that these can cause sympathetic vibrations to be set up in lamp filaments every half cycle and if these approach the resonance of the filament itself, we can have quite loud acoustic noises coming from the luminaires, which manifests itself in a high pitched buzzing – colloquially known as 'lamp sing'.

It would seem on initial inspection that to get around the problem of the wave shape output of thyristor dimmers is almost impossible. However, this is not the case in practice and a very simple trick can be employed. By introducing into the circuit a choke, which consists of a coil of wire wound on a fairly heavy iron core, the rise time of the leading edge of the waveform (the switch-on point) is slowed down and if we effect a change from the normal 2 or 3 microseconds switch on time to around 500 microseconds, then we will have overcome most of the interference problems. More recent developments use controlled switching sequences for the power devices;

thus instead of rapidly changing levels in a few microseconds a ramped switching is used to give a much longer transitional period thus producing less interference.

A method of measuring the amount of noise generated is required and the generally accepted standard for assessing interference from dimmers was that introduced by the BBC during the late 1960s which still holds true today. Various groups of people had experimented with measuring the amount of interference generated and the experiments included specific lengths of wire being laid adjacent to the dimmer power cables. Special coils were also used mounted adjacent to power carrying conductors, so to assess the electromagnetic radiation. One of the problems with these methods is that they are much too flexible and have too many variables, i.e. length of cables used, the position of the cables in relation to each other and how do we equate the current flowing with the interference received. Before making any measurements or standards it was necessary to establish the levels of noise that would cause problems in practice. In general, within controlled studio conditions, very few problems occur with the vision circuits – only on the audio.

The basis for the measurements to avoid audio problems was as follows. On the assumption that when a microphone is working at −70 dB, its normal operating point, quite considerable amplification has to take place before the audio signal is processed. It was found at that time that sound desks had a signal to noise ratio of about 50 dB, so a figure in excess of this had to be aimed at to avoid deterioration in the quality of sound.

It is very easy to keep the dimmer power cables away from the audio and vision circuits in the permanent installation, but it is extremely difficult where many flexible cables are used. At the time these experiments were taking place, Star Quad microphone cable with very superior interference rejection properties, came into use. This enabled quite reasonable levels of interference to be tolerated, and thus the dimmer manufacturers weren't presented with quite the problem they originally envisaged.

It should be noted that Star Quad cables have varied over the years, and the introduction of a thinner type of cable with lower rejection limits caused some concern during the early 1980s but does not seem to have proved to be a problem in practice.

To measure the interference accurately, it was decided that the best way would be to wire some form of measuring device into the circuit so that as many variables as possible were removed.

A solid state dimmer, which chops the waveform, when conducting at any level under maximum will generate on its output a string of interference pulses. These pulses are at a maximum amplitude when the dimmer is at 90° conduction. It was essential that the test circuit when placed into the power feeds disturbed these pulses as little as possible, so avoiding erroneous readings.

Ultimately the circuit as shown in Figure 8.3 was adopted as the most effective method of measuring the interference in dimmer circuits. Two main points have to be observed when making these measurements, and these are:

1   As any noise generated by a waveform is proportional to its energy content, a method of measuring the rms value has to be used.
2   As the test is to assess electrical interference which becomes audible, a method of weighting the reading to the ears' response has to be incorporated.

The measurement of rms is relatively straightforward as several test meters made by reputable manufacturers are available. Point (2) is covered by the circuit which electrically gives a similar response to the ear. Having decided upon a measuring technique, it was relatively easy to set the levels of permissible interference in the studio.

The measuring circuits have to be adequately encased within metal boxes so that external electric fields are minimised and no stray voltages are present on the meter readings. One other

Figure 8.3 Circuit diagram of dimmer test system

extremely important point is that the source impedance of the electrical supply to the test dimmer and load should be as low as possible because the interference readings may be artificially lowered on high impedance sources.

Having set up the test rig the sequence to be followed is:

1   Normal supply volts are applied to the dimmer.
2   The control level and hence the 'switch on' point of the thyristors is varied to give a maximum reading on the meter, and this generally occurs at a firing angle of 90° with maximum rated load.

To meet acceptable levels, the rms meter readings must not exceed 15 mV rms for 2.5 kW, 3 kW or 5 kW dimmers, and must not exceed 30 mV rms for 6 kW and 10 kW dimmers.

The figures given are for the interference limits in 240 V dimmer circuits. Both 120 V and 240 V systems generate interference, the problem with 120 V supplies is that the current for any given wattage is double that of a 240 V system. As the interference is proportional to the amount of current this will mean taking extra precautions on 120 V installations.

If the power cables going from the dimmer room to any of the luminaires run very close to other cables, then electrical induction takes place, and the 'rubbish' voltage from the dimmers is transferred on to all other forms of wiring. This might not be so bad if the wiring is the normal mains system around the premises, but it is obviously extremely bad if it is the vision or audio circuits that are affected. Of course, one of the unfortunate side effects of using a large choke in the output is that the choke itself can cause acoustic interference, and dimmer rooms can become quite noisy places, so much so that it causes problems in the rest of the installation.

8.3   Dimmer types

Dimmers come in various shapes and sizes, the most popular being 2.5 kW, 3 kW, 5 kW, 6 kW and 10 kW. Dimmers are available in two distinct types; those which are 'wired in' and those which have 'plug in' dimmer modules. Wired in dimmers are usually permanently installed inside some form of container, be it a small portable crate or a reasonably large metal enclosure rather like a filing cabinet. Plug in dimmers are often used where failure of particular dimmer modules causes problems with regard to the progress of rehearsals, transmissions and any live performance.

A plug in dimmer consists of a chassis, which these days may be metal or plastic, on which is mounted the control circuit, made as a removable pcb, the output power devices, which could be either individual thyristors or an integrated circuit power block. Filtering chokes are generally mounted on this chassis, although in some systems, the choke is mounted separately within the dimmer cabinet. When using plug in dimmers, it is important that some distinction is made electrically and/or mechanically in the inter-changeability of units within a dimmer rack. This is to avoid making the mistake of putting a low powered dimmer on a high powered source. One major problem that occurs with plug in dimmers is that of safety. It is obviously important when removing a dimmer module, which may be approximately the size of a shoe box, from a dimmer rack, that operator access to any live terminals is prevented, thus preventing any electrical shock hazards.

Wired in dimmer systems are usually supplied with master printed circuit boards, with the control circuits on it for each of the individual dimmers. The power thyristors or integrated circuit power blocks are usually separate from the mother board. Although a dimmer rack may contain quite a large number of dimmers, it is important that the printed circuit boards control only small numbers of dimmers from the point of view of failure. One master control circuit board failing could be quite disastrous if it is controlling 30 or more dimmers. Control circuits that are common to about six dimmers are preferable. High density wired in dimmers are mounted in cabinets where access is only possible by the use of a key or tool to open the door so that safety is maintained. Small six-way dimmer packs, which are very common in practice, usually have to be dismantled by removing screws and covers to gain access for maintenance.

Dimmer technical parameters

To avoid fluctuations in the light output of the luminaires when controlled by dimmers, it is important that the dimmers are relatively independent of the input voltage variations. Most good quality dimmers made today are usually supplied with 'feed back loops' so that the dimmer output is maintained within certain limits (usually 10:1). However, it should be borne in mind that a dimmer only works from the nominated output mains voltage downwards. Unless supplied with special transformers and control circuitry, it is not practical to have a dimmer which boosts the output, i.e. if the dimmer is rated at 240 V output and the mains input is only 210 V it is impossible to make the output any higher than 210 V.

In practice dimmer loads vary considerably and any type of dimmer may be required to work with loads of small power (i.e. our old friend the 60 W practical lamp). It is obviously essential that the dimmer should remain stable on such occasions and not go into any form of variation of output caused by say, internal oscillation. Dimmers are also somewhat abused by the operators and more than likely they will have isolating transformers plugged into them or many other inductive loads. On these occasions, it is essential that the dimmer does not lose its stability or for that matter, draw excessive current which might destroy the output thyristors.

If the output of the dimmer does not have a balanced output, the imbalance will be seen as a small direct current component. It is essential that this direct current is kept to an extremely low level so that it does not cause problems to any of the connected loads or for that matter on the mains supply to the dimmer room. The electricity supply authorities are not too happy with d.c. on their a.c. distribution system.

All dimmers have to meet normal electromagnetic spectrum interference regulations in the country concerned. Additionally, the dimmers must reduce the high frequencies present in the output waveform which would cause problems with the sound and vision circuits in any installation.

It is obviously important when controlling dimmers that the application of a control signal will produce a known response, in practice dimmers are required to respond instantly to any change of the control signal; the only limitation being the lag within the lamp filaments themselves.

A problem that exists with the larger light sources such as the 5 kW and 10 kW, is that of 'thermal shock', due to the large inrush currents. Modern digital techniques can vary the 'turn on' time to allow a build up of power over several cycles of the mains when the channel is switched to 'full' thus 'fading' the lamp up, although it appears to be 'instant'.

In the past dimmers were controlled by analogue, d.c. control signals, i.e. the application of a small control voltage from 0 to 10 V d.c. will produce the changes within the dimmer itself. Several disadvantages exist with analogue control signals; first and foremost is that each dimmer has to have one input control wire, thus if a control system of 240 ways is driving 240 dimmers, 240 control wires would have to be used, together with one or more common wires. Today, the application of digital control signals to dimming systems has become the normal practice. Digital control inputs are generally decoded on special cards situated within the dimmer pack and the control signal is conveyed either by co-ax cables or twisted pairs. Thus all the dimmer control signals are fed down one cable, the usual limitation being the digital system and this is 512 channels when using DMX 512, thus two cables are needed if this number of channels are exceeded.

A dimmer will obviously respond in some way to the control signal – that response will be dictated by the needs of the operators. It may be that a rapid fade-up is required over the lower portion of the control channel with a slower progression over the upper portion of the control channel; or the operator required very little light change from the luminaire over the lower portion of the fader characteristic with a large variation when the channel is raised towards its maximum. Dimmers have been made with built in 'laws' to cater for various tastes in the entertainment industry for many years. However, in recent times, with the advent of more sophisticated control from modern lighting consoles, it is possible to use 'linear' dimmers where the law shaping is done by variations on the input control signals. With digital control, it is possible to set the 'law' of the dimmers precisely to the operators' requirements by adjusting the 'dimmer programme'.

The square of the fader setting gives the percentage light output, as shown in Table 8.1, e.g. Fader at '6' equals light output of 36%.

In practice if we fade on an American system at 120 V or a British system at 240 V, we see little or no difference to the operation of the lighting system. However, if we choose to do comparisons of the parameters concerned, it is important to remember that each volt of variation will produce a change of 10 K degrees within a 120 V dimming system, whereas at 240 V, each volt change produces a difference of 5 K degrees. This is because of the relationship of Kelvin degrees to the current, and for the same wattage load a 120 V system will have twice the current of a 240 V system.

Table 8.1 Square law dimmer control

	Light		Output volts				
Fader	Output %	CT (K)	%	240	120	Current %	Power %
10	100	3200	100	240	120	100	100
9	81	3120	93	224	112	96	89
8	64	3040	88	211	106	93	82
7	49	2960	81	194	97	88	72
6	36	2860	74	178	89	85	63
5	25	2750	66	158	79	78	52
4	16	2600	59	142	71	73	43
3	9	2400	51	122	61	67	34
2	4	2200	39	94	47	59	23
1	1	–	23	55	27	46	11
0	0	–	0	0	0	0	0

8.4   Protecting dimmers

As far as the output of the individual dimmers themselves goes these can be protected by either mcbs or fuses.

Many mcbs that are used for circuits with much lower current capacity have fault current ratings of somewhere between 6000 A and 9000 A particularly in the type that we would select for dimmers. It is more than likely that the potential fault current of the circuits involved will exceed these values. It would seem at this point that an mcb could not be used to protect our outgoing circuits, however, in practice this is not the case, because we are allowed to use a device which is not quite adequate if we back it up with a fuse which adequately protects the complete circuit. Thus, if the prospective fault current was 8000 A and the breaking capacity of the mcb we had selected was 6000 A, we would have to back up the mcb with a fuse with a breaking capacity in excess of 8000 A so that the circuit was fully protected.

Before we go any further it would perhaps be better to introduce the term I^2t, which refers to the time/current characteristic and is a quantity consisting of the time period combined with the square of the instantaneous current passing through a fuse between the instant when the circuit fault commences and the instant of the fuse rupturing. I^2t is often described as the 'let through energy'. Both thyristor manufacturers and fuse manufacturers publish I^2t curves for their devices, and the manufacturers of dimmers simply have to compare these curves to select the correct type of fuse to protect the devices used. It is therefore essential to observe the manufacturers' choice of fuses for their equipment. Thyristors and triacs will also be damaged if an over voltage is applied in the reverse direction to the normal current flow and in most cases will only tolerate twice the peak value of the steady state voltage. Fuses to protect thyristors and other solid state devices in dimmers should meet the requirements of IEC 269-4 and BS 88 part 4. Fuses for 2.5 kW 240 V circuits usually are 10 A rating and those for 5 kW 240 V circuits are rated at 20 A. Any fuses used should be generally available and not specially made.

The problem with fuses is that, believe it or not, they take a finite time to operate. If a solid state device is rated at say, 40 A, it quite happily carries a current of 40 A indefinitely, and over short periods of time, it will carry currents in excess of 40 A quite safely, however a high current for long periods of time will be fatal for the device. The reason for failure of thyristors is that the semiconductor junctions within the device overheat and ultimately break down, thus if we overload the device well in excess of its normal current rating, for any period of time, we will destroy the thyristor. Therefore our first consideration when selecting a fuse is that it should adequately protect the thyristor circuitry. Additionally, the fuse must be capable of handling the cold current surge of the lamps without failing. Fuses operate extremely rapidly when a very high current is applied; or it might be a low current for a longer period of time. The time can be over the range from a few milliseconds to several thousands of seconds. It is therefore not possible to give the operating time for any specific fuse when the operating time is dependent on the value of the currents involved.

One problem that can occur with dimmer installations is that a 5 kW dimmer may be used to feed a practical light on a set and this practical light may only be a 60 W lamp fed via some lighting flex. In this case, the 20 A fuse would be well over the approved rating for the flex feeding the individual lamp; therefore some form of sub-fusing must take place. This sub-fusing must be inserted at a point in the electric circuit so that it adequately protects the wiring concerned.

8.5   Dimmer rooms and switchgear

If we are designing from scratch, we can obviously make allowance for some area within an installation which would house the dimmers, their racks and the associated switchgear to control those racks. In practice however, any broom cupboard seems to be the solution to the dimmer room. What do we require from a well designed dimmer room?

First and foremost it is space. Secondly, the room has to be either self ventilating or provided with proper means of ventilation. If we have a large area that can be used for the dimmers, it is possible to install dimmer racks containing a small number of dimmers per rack. As most areas allocated for dimmers are small, modern practice is to use high density racks, and these may be up to 192 dimmers per rack. The physical numbers in the rack does not necessarily create a problem, but the weight of the racks on the floor area does. The other possible source of concern is that by using one rack with many dimmers in it, controlled from only one piece of switchgear, any form of breakdown in the main supply would be quite disastrous on any transmissions, rehearsals or live performances. As a general rule, it is better to spread the eggs over more than one basket. Although this requires more pieces of switchgear, because each dimmer rack must be provided with a means of isolation, independent of all the other racks, it is obviously much more expedient from an operational point of view and also from a maintenance point of view. Another snag that occurs with high density dimmer racks, is that all the output power cables going to the stage or studio area have to be terminated somewhere within the dimmer rack itself and the greater the density, usually the greater the problem of termination. If we allow for a waste heat generation of approximately 100 W per 5 kW of dimmer power, it can be appreciated that in a high density rack quite high heat loads are generated. Thus the dimmer racks usually have to be force cooled by fans mounted within the racks, and in fact in one installation seen by the authors in America, the degree of cooling required in a room with several high density racks was so great that it was difficult to close the dimmer room door against the gale!

Dimmer racks will be designed for either single-phase input or three-phase input and this could be either by cables or some form of busbars. The dimmer rack itself should preferably be no higher than 1.8 m so that access to the rack is feasible without the use of steps or with the operators having to over reach, which in itself is dangerous. It is obviously easy to have the control and power connections made when there is access from the front of the rack together with access from the rear. If rear access is required, allowance must be made for additional space within a dimmer room as the rear access would no doubt have an opening door and a clearance of at least 600 mm must be provided. Many modern dimmer racks have front access only but the problem of front access is that all the input and output terminals must be accessible and this often involves the manufacturers in some conflicts of interests with regard to space within the rack. Where small dimmer racks such as six-way packs are used, the problems are not so acute, although each of these racks would have to be provided with a small isolator adjacent to the racks for safety reasons. Dimmer racks have to be clearly marked because there will be several circuits within a rack, all with fuses or mcbs which must be clearly marked. The dimmer racks must also have indicators which show that power is supplied to the rack and each individual dimmer must have some form of indicator to show that it is live. It is important that any form of earth leakage should be detected, although this is not usually provided on small dimmer racks. It is preferable that some kind of overheat detection is supplied within larger racks and this can be for two purposes. To detect firstly the generation of fire, and secondly the generation of additional heat which may be caused by fan failure within the racks. Although not a large danger within the premises, it may be that the failure of the fans causes the individual dimmers to fail by becoming excessively hot subsequently causing the semiconductor devices to fail.

It goes without saying that all dimmer racks have to meet high electrical and mechanical safety standards. Any form of electrical apparatus built within a rack or chassis system has to meet the requirements of the country of manufacture and also the country in which it would be used.

On the surface it would seem a very good idea to employ a residual current device (RCD) *formerly known as an earth leakage circuit breaker*, with a very low sensitivity (30 mA/40 msec) on the output of each dimmer which would ensure that any operator coming into contact with either of the live wires, i.e. the phase or the neutral, would be safe. Evidence exists that would indicate that any RCD must be carefully chosen so that it operates almost independently of the dimmer output voltage levels. A point to be watched is that RCD manufacturers don't necessarily endorse the use of their products when used with dimmed, chopped waveforms.

It's no good having a nice looking dimmer rack where, when faults occur access for maintenance is a nightmare. It is particularly galling to any operator to find that to change the simplest of components requires minutes and sometimes hours removing screws, nuts, washers, panels etc. often cutting one's hand in the process, accompanied by the usual quietly mouthed expletives. For ease of maintenance it is obviously essential to have good technical information which gives circuit diagrams, constructional details of the cabinets and a complete set of instructions of how to go about maintaining the equipment itself, and this must be totally unambiguous. Much modern equipment however, is quite sophisticated and any maintenance, other than first line, would probably have to be carried out by the manufacturer, but this usually entails extra expense when calling upon a service engineer from the manufacturer concerned.

8.6   Distributed dimmers

When dimmers were controlled by analogue signals, a centralised dimmer room was installed. The amount of cabling involved to have dimmers placed all over a studio grid, for example, would have been quite inhibiting to the normal operation. With the advent of DMX control, it is now possible, by using one very simple cable, to control many dimmers throughout the installation. Combined with the reduction in weight of dimmers, it is possible to either place dimmers on the lighting bars themselves, or integrate them into the luminaires. As most studio premises these days are equipped with vast quantities of dimmers, it now makes sense that the dimmers could be integrated into the lighting bars. Thus, if there were three outlets which in the past were fed from the dimmer room, the three dimmers could now be integrated into the assembly above the lighting bar itself.

As an example let us see how we can feed three 5 kW channels which are 50 m from the dimmer room. If we use conventional dimmers, we would require a circuit capable of taking 20.833 A at 240 V or 21.74 A at 230 V. The maximum volt drop we are allowed is 9.6 V. If we are using PVC cables in trunking, we could use 6 mm^2 cable with a current rating of 41 A. The voltage drop for 6 mm^2 cable is 7.3 mV per A per m; so for 240 V we have a volt drop of 7.6 V, which is well within the specified voltage drop limits. For an applied voltage of 230 V we would get a voltage drop of 7.94 V, which again is within the capability of the cable. However, in a normal dimmer installation, we are feeding several circuits down the trunking, therefore we have to apply a grouping factor. If we assume there are 20 active circuits down the trunking, our correction factor for grouping is 0.38, which means we are looking at a cable capable of taking 53 A. This means we will have to increase our cable size to 10 mm^2. The advantage is that we get less volt drop going to the luminaires from the dimmer room. If we now take the case of a triple 5 kW pack of dimmers in the studio, being fed by one cable, we require a cable taking a load current of 63 A. This fits in well with having a 63 A mcb protecting the circuit. For a single-phase feed to this dimmer pack, the cables selected would be 16 mm^2 capable of 76 A. The volt drop is only 2.8 mV per A per m, so the overall volt drop would be 8.28 A which is within our 9.6 V maximum voltage drop. If however, we group these feeder cables in trunking, we would then have to supply a suitable grouping factor. If we assume we are feeding three dimmer packs giving total dimmer outlets of nine, we would have to apply a grouping factor of 0.5 which means that the cables would have to be rated for 90 A, which means that we are required to install 25 mm^2 cable for each feeder to the dimmer packs. All the previous calculations are based on using single-phase a.c., but if we were using three-phase cabling within trunking, the current rating would be reduced slightly for all cables. The 25 mm^2 cable would still suffice for the triple dimmer pack. In the case of the single circuits, we would have to increase our cable size from 10 mm^2 to 16 mm^2. All of these calculations are based on all circuits being fully loaded. However we are allowed to reduce the cable size if, in fact, not all the cables in a group are used simultaneously, and generally in film and TV studios, this may be the case. All modern dimmers are capable of being selected as a numbered channel on a DMX decoding system, and in the case of distributed dimming, it is relatively easy to change the channel number controlling a dimmer in the studio.

8.7   Control systems

In the days of resistance dimmers, control of lighting was slow and cumbersome. The cues were accomplished by the electricians making several dimmers move in unison for effect and even to move one dimmer was a considerable task. The main problem being that the LD was not in control of the lighting system at all.

Eventually Strand Lighting introduced electrical controllers, driven from a rotating mechanical shaft system, that allowed the amount of current fed to the luminaires to be varied. The most famous of these were auto transformer dimmers which were driven by an up/down clutching system driven by a variable speed shaft drive arrangement. The system was relatively slow in operation and produced good fades but not as swift as those accomplished today. These earlier systems generally were 'two pre-set' which allowed two states for each dimmer, according to which of the pre-set channel controllers were in use. The consoles were provided with master controls for over-riding the pre-set states, so that fades could be accomplished with groups of lamps.

One of the drawbacks with systems such as these, was the fact there were no memory systems which memorised the on/off state of the channels – thus groups of channels could not be switched on and off at will. Strand Lighting came up with an ideal solution for the time by using the technology from the organ builders and pictures of old control boards looked like the consoles of cinema organs. The system of memory was extremely simple inasmuch as a small flexible contact pin was allowed to engage in a movable bar with contacts arranged as small notches along the bar, thus offering low voltage control of the particular channel and upon selection of the appropriate notch bar, would bring into play the group of channels. As can be well imagined to have many memories meant that the system required a multiplicity of contact pins and several notch bars, thus this type of console was usually limited to about 40 memories on the red pre-set and 40 memories on the blue pre-set. It was not uncommon in the early days of memory systems that the operators had to re-plot major portions of the action to take advantage of the memory grouping facilities. One problem associated with memory control in those days was if you didn't release your foot at the correct moment off the 'pre-setter' pedal on the console, you were in great danger of having a random selection of pins in the notch bars which caused rather a lot of soul searching by the operator concerned.

One of the biggest steps forward was the introduction of solid state dimmers, which allowed voltage control of the dimmer directly from a console rather than control via the electrome-chanical system. These lighting consoles were hard wired systems where the voltage or current output of a fader was taken down one individual wire to control a dimmer, using a common return. As has already been noted, the saturable reactor system allowed direct control but unfortunately the memory systems were extremely primitive when using this system.

Up to the late 1960s the majority of lighting control systems were based on a fader directly controlling a dimmer. In 1967, Tony Isaacs of Thorn Lighting devised a new type of control system, using logic circuits. These circuits were extremely crude compared with today's silicon chip devices and were constructed from germanium transistors, resistors and capacitors. The memory system was based on a ferrite bead matrix where a series of these beads carried the '0' and '1' magnetic information to give channel level and on/off instructions.

This console was capable of memorising several levels from one channel. For the first time a control system worked by sequentially scanning each piece of channel control information, from a dedicated controller capable of controlling any channel number input from a numeric keyboard. Whereas systems before this relied upon the setting of a fader; the fader on the Thorn console could be used to set one channel level, which was stored and another channel selected and another level set. This also allowed a multiplicity of levels for any single channel. The faders were servo coupled and always followed the selected channel level. The amount of group memories was limited purely by the fact that the ferrite bead matrix memories were expensive and difficult to construct. The original system comprised rather a neat control panel but tucked away in a little room adjacent were four bays of equipment. With the introduction of integrated circuits, the system reduced to two bays of equipment, but was very large when one looks at a system today where the actual electronics is no greater than that contained in a PC.

The Thorn system had dedicated control panels and not long after its introduction Strand introduced the MMS (modular memory system) console, where individual components of a console could be blended to give different alternatives for the various customers.

Changes between one lighting state and another can be incredibly complicated with variations of the speed of fade down or fade up of the lights all intermixed to provide a variety of effects, and all these can be programmed to be accomplished very quickly or very slowly. Due to the advances in microprocessor design and the use of PCs, it is possible to make relatively cheap lighting systems with an incredible range of facilities. Modern memory systems now have to control the intensity and colour of the light, and additionally the position of the luminaire and all its beam pattern and shaping functions.

Many consoles today are based on Pentium processors and these enable a lighting console to be fitted with the necessary hardware to cover for all eventualities and the software programme of operation, can be changed so that the desk operates in different ways. An important feature of consoles is that any operation should give a predictable result, therefore not confusing the operator. The ergonomics of design of the controls and their placement on a lighting console is extremely important; the physical size should be kept as small as possible so that one operator can get to all controls with relative ease. Due to the various operating philosophies adopted in different parts of the world, it is now possible for consoles to be programmed to take into account the customer preferences as to the way they wish the console to respond to their commands. Even consoles have entered the magic world of 'the net'. By using network systems it is now possible to access the control signals from various points on the network. In the past, distributed signals around a production area probably involved several multiway cables, co-ax cables and various other types of cables to accommodate the data necessary to provide remote control and remote viewing of console outputs. By using a modern network system it is possible to use one high grade cable system with the necessary termination points fitted and all signals run through this system. Previously, a LD and possibly the assistant, would have to draw on a large-scale plan the lights that are required, the various gels that may be used and the positional data for all the luminaires. Having done all this preparation, it was then necessary to transfer all this information to the lighting console when in the production area. Today, by using off-line editor programmes, which are capable of running on a fairly average PC, it is possible to prepare the production lighting and adjust all the necessary effects and balances, where this is possible, and to record them onto a disk which can then be used in the lighting console. Having recorded the necessary memories and any effects to be used, it is possible for them to be replayed in real-time on the PC and its associated VDU. It should be noted that the use of an editor does not necessarily give the positional information of the lights; this more than likely will still be prepared on a good old fashioned piece of paper.

Some companies now produce Windows based programmes which provide a virtual lighting console on a PC. To keep the screen information to manageable levels, it is possible to select on the VDU several different pages of pre-sets together with their master controls, e.g. channels 1–20, channels 21–40 etc. A drawback when using a 'mouse' is that you may be unable to independently move individual fader levels up and down at the same time. One advantage of this system is a small number of channels per page with the ability to change pages rapidly to gain access to other channels; although to simultaneously gain access to channels spread over several pages may be difficult and time consuming.

Although many modern lighting consoles are rather daunting in appearance, they still have to provide the following basic functions.

1   To be able to set the channels and hence the dimmers anywhere from zero to full light output.
2   The ability to switch a channel on or off at any level of its fader setting.
3   To group channels together.
4   To mix either individual channels or groups of channels together.
5   The ability to over-ride channels by 'Master' or 'Group' faders and by master switching.
6   The ability to collect the channel information which would be its fader setting and/or its on/off condition; either as individual channels or in groups or combinations of groups and consequently store in some form of memory system.
7   To be able to rehearse complicated fade sequences involving groups of channels or memories in a timed sequence and subsequently record this information.
8   To be able to recall settings, change them and re-record the result.
9   To replay the information stored in memory either manually or automatically in a sequence to suit the action.

Lighting consoles come as three distinct varieties, the first being the manual system, where each channel is individually fed from a fader; the second system is that of an 'enhanced' manual system where several faders are employed together with a very simple memory control so that the channel settings can be memorised and replayed and some or all of the faders can be re-used for other purposes. The third type of system is the fully automated control system where channel selection is invariably by a keypad; there are only one or two channel faders employed and these may exist in the form of a wheel rather than the traditional lever. The control console will have a memory system where anything is possible, and effects systems are built in (see Figure 8.4a,b).

Generally, in a manual system each channel is directly fed from a fader, thus a simple 60-way system uses 60 faders. If the system is two pre-set, this means that two faders are provided per channel with the ability using two pre-set master faders, to fade between either one of their preselected states; the highest of the selected states taking precedence when the two masters are fully on.

For example, channel X is set at '7' on the red pre-set and '5' on the green pre-set. With the red master 'up' and the green channel 'down', channel X is set to '7'; when the red master is 'down' and the green master is 'up', the channel is set at '5'. When the red master is at 'full', raising the green master to full will not change the state of the channel, as the red channel is the highest, the output will always be '7'. This gives simple twin-state (or pre-set) mixing. The state of each channel can be easily set on the lighting console and an over-riding master facility is available. For simple productions and the control of lighting of many types, this console is more than sufficient and generally is very fast in operation, as channels are very easily accessed. Most manual systems these days have a control where the cross fade is usually dipless, i.e. there is

(a)

(b)

Figure 8.4 Lighting consoles (courtesy of Electronic Theatre Controls (Europe)) a small amount of electronic control which provides for a smooth fade progression between the two pre-sets.

Small installations will use consoles with 12, 24, 36 or 48 channels and these are usually fairly simple two pre-set manual consoles, with one channel fader dedicated to each dimmer. One of the drawbacks of manual systems is that you cannot have more than two states of each channel with two pre-set systems, because otherwise you have to reset the fader lever.

The next step up from a basic, manual console are those where a limited memory system is also available. The method of recording a lighting scene is usually to use a specified pre-set of channel faders to set the various levels and when the scene has been lit, the submaster is then memorised, and this then records the current lighting state, allowing the next scene to be set up using the same set of faders, because of the enormous memory capability, it is now possible to set up several hundred cues which may be very subtle changes to the lighting states, but it enables the lighting designers and their assistants not to have to keep notes, as was the case in years gone by. The only thing needed now is an accurate cue sheet to ensure that the right lighting is selected at the right time during the production.

We finally come to the all singing, all dancing, memory control systems that exist today. Generally the system will have at least one or two channel controllers, each one of these having the ability to control any channel. It will also be quite possible that memories and groups may be introduced into the main system via the channel controller. Consoles of this type work on the principle that we select a channel on the controller, the level is set and stored away and we now move onto the next channel to be controlled. Thus systematically, one by one, we assign levels to the lights concerned, either on stage or in the studio. As the channels are switched on and the levels are set, we slowly build up the lighting within the scene. At the end of this period, it is possible, by using the memory system, to store all the channels at their various levels for future use. One advantage of this system is that if the same lights are used for a further piece of action within the scene, the LD can set completely independent levels from those already memorised without ever considering the information stored away. The control system does it all for him. To replay the scenes that have been memorised, they are usually recalled from the memory system by the selection of the appropriate buttons and subsequently played back via the master controllers which enable either cuts or fades to progress. Memories may also be added or subtracted and multiple effects can be combined before being introduced into the lighting output. Additionally, consoles provide facilities for controlling automated luminaires.

Talking to most operators, we generally find that they prefer a fader per channel which gives instant access, particularly on live events. One big problem with us humans is that we like all the little frilly extras that exist on any pieces of equipment. One of the difficulties that exists with very sophisticated consoles is how fast can the operator respond when a problem occurs. Is it really necessary, or so it seems, for the operator to require a science degree to be able to understand and operate many modern lighting consoles?

There is a tendency by manufacturers, because of the competition within the industry, to provide every 'bell and whistle' possible within their control system, the main reason being that they do not want their product to look deficient in any way. Quite often ending up with a console trying to be everything to everyone. There is a confliction of interests between the TV industry and their requirements; the theatre industry and their requirements and the 'pop' industry and its requirements. It is very difficult to have a hybrid lighting console to bridge the gap, and invariably we end up with the horse so designed that it turns out to be a camel!

Advantages however, do exist with modern consoles, inasmuch that effects can be immediately accomplished, without much of a problem. Most modern consoles have integral soft patching systems, which allows the control of many dimmers usually via a smaller number of control channels. They also have the ability to shape the input control characteristic of the dimmers themselves, thus different shaped characteristics can be provided for lamps that respond rapidly when switched on, such as 1 kW profile spot luminaires, compared with the 5 kW and 10 kW which have a much slower response time. It is now possible, within complicated fades, to tailor the curve of each individual light to gain a most harmonious result.

A typical modern console allows control of 512 channels, 60 channel faders, 450 memories, 15 active playbacks.

The channels can be allocated as Highest Takes Precedence (HTP) or Latest Takes Precedence (LTP). The console provides for:

- any channel to control multiple dimmers,
- individual response curves for each dimmer channel, and
- patching of dimmer and colour changers by typing a DMX number.

It is possible to arrange the functions of automated luminaires so that they appear on certain faders in a defined sequence. The console shows:

- channel output in % and 0–255 steps,
- DMX 512 output levels,
- channel usage with luminaire name (e.g. Superscan),
- patching information,
- preview of memories,
- preview of sequences and chases,
- chase speed and cross-fade settings,
- sequence information, and
- fade progression and other items of information to help the operator.

If we buy a console from a manufacturer together with that manufacturers' dimmers, no doubt they will nicely work together. However, this is not always the case when we would desire to buy dimmers from one source and a lighting console from another. It is absolutely essential that the console talks intelligently to the dimming system. In the days when systems used analogue d.c. control signals, this was more than likely possible, although over the years manufacturers all had their subtle variations, around a 10 V d.c. theme. With the advent of digital control systems, it is important that the digital signal is recognised by the dimmer units.

Although the lighting console is 'remote' from the dimmers in most installations, the term 'remote control' usually refers to additional methods of control other than the main console. Two types of remote control of dimmers are required. The first being a fairly simple type of remote control which generally consists of switching dimmers off and on only, which is used for rigging purposes by the electricians within the installation concerned. This might be a large panel mounted on the wall in a studio and often called 'an electricians panel' or it might be a small hand held controller. It is now possible to provide a 'mini console' adjacent to the studio winch control panel for use by the studio operatives.

The second, which is the LD's control, is required to be virtually an extension of a complete working console, thus enabling the LD to sit either in the stalls, or conveniently stand within the studio and plot his lights at first hand. Designers' controls generally will give access to all the channels and memory system.

If the power input to the installation fails the dimmers will not work and of course we have lost the ability to control them. If however the main lighting console fails what would we expect to be able to do? Possibly the best form of back-up system is where we virtually duplicate all the console facilities, and in fact, in some systems, this is actually done, although obviously at some premium. The biggest loss of facilities is when the memory system itself fails, because of the reliance upon the memory system to store all the channel information. In general, back-up systems are not really used with manual control and enhanced manual control systems, but are only used with the more sophisticated consoles. Obviously where a lever per channel is the operating method, the actual memory system is the fader itself. The most advanced back-up systems in use today allow for a monitoring of the main system and recording constantly all the channel levels to update the system in event of failure. If the back-up system allows for the selection of the memories together with some grouping and the ability to fade up and down from its master faders, then it is unlikely that the audience will notice any major differences.

DMX 512 is a world-wide standard signal which allows lighting consoles to send information to dimmers. The intensity level is sent as a digital code, using an 8-bit number providing 256 levels from zero to full intensity. In addition to controlling dimmers, it is also possible to control colour changers with DMX data sent to each unit. DMX signals are also used to control automated light sources and smoke machines. One DMX cable can transmit 512 individual data signals, each having a unique address number. Therefore, 512 addresses can control 512 dimmers. A motorised luminaire used for effect will probably have several attributes being controlled; if we use a channel of DMX for each attribute, we will obviously soon run out of control signals within DMX 512 control cable. Complex lighting rigs will use several DMX 512 cables to feed all the luminaires.

Typical attributes of an automated luminaire are as follows:

- Intensity
- Focus
- Iris
- Colour
- Cyan dichroic
- Magenta dichroic
- Yellow dichroic
- Gobo
- Rotating gobo
- Pan
- Tilt
- Speed
- Reset

8.8   Electromagnetic compatibility (EMC) Directive

If every piece of electrical apparatus in the world only used a sinusoidal waveform there would be no need for the EMC Directive. We are only too aware of the clicks generated by the refrigerator switching on and off affecting our radios; the buzzing noises from fluorescent chokes and if one takes a medium wave radio close to a PC, rather nasty noises emanate from the loudspeaker. Although these manifestations of electromagnetic disturbance are annoying, they are not necessarily in themselves, dangerous, however, in a world that is now full of radio communications and telecommunications networks, it is important that any forms of interference do not interfere with the safe working of systems. For many years several standards have been applied in the United Kingdom for the reduction of radio disturbance from household electrical appliances, portable electric tools, fluorescent lamps and luminaires and broadcast receivers and associated equipment.

The EMC Directive seeks to ensure that any electrical/electronic equipment throughout Europe adopts certain standards to define the permissible electromagnetic disturbance levels that the equipment is liable to generate. The Directive is extremely important to the lighting industry mainly because of the dimmers we use, the consoles and the discharge lighting all of which are quite complex electronic pieces of equipment and all capable of generating some form of electromagnetic interference. Additionally, mechanical equipment used is also controlled by electronic systems and it would be dangerous if these control systems suffered interference in such a way as to affect its performance.

9
Studio technical design

Introduction

The installation of lighting systems has a major impact on safety. It introduces large mechanical loads to structures. Heavyweight devices are hung over areas which may be populated by the public, artists or technicians. The lighting system introduces electricity to many areas and, particularly when this is on flexible leads feeding equipment, can be a source of danger. Most of the heat generated in the building will probably come from the lights being used. The electrical and mechanical systems installed can maim or even kill if we fool with them. Therefore, there is a necessity to install lighting systems as safely as is humanly possible.

Generally, systems have luminaires in one place and the dimmers that control them in another. Over the years suggestions have been made for the controlling dimmer of a light source to be within the luminaire itself. In the case of the standard arrangement, all that is required from the dimmer to the luminaire, are two wires carrying the live and neutral or the positive and negative. In the case of motorised luminaires, signals in addition to the mains feeds have to be provided. If a luminaire is used with a dimmer mounted within its casing, the mains can be taken either from a radial supply system or from a ring main, but one has to remember that with a large number of luminaires, the ring main conductors become very large indeed, and the weight of the cables will be a problem. Conversely, dimmers traditionally are not the lightest of objects and we suspect that each luminaire would have a reasonable weight addition to its normal configuration. This would then mean the luminaires themselves are getting heavier, consequently they may impose additional loads on structures that are inadequate. By using dimmers within luminaires, a careful approach would have to be made to the protection of the wiring feeding these luminaires, either by the correct fusing or choice of mcbs.

May we make a plea to all architects and end users to contact a reliable lighting consultant before deciding on the shape and size of any new facility. We have both experienced the problem of being called in at a late stage of construction and being presented with a *fait accompli*, having no regard for the technical requirements.

9.1 Project team

Before discussing the technical aspects of installing lighting systems we have to have a team of people who will be intimately involved with the planning and construction of such systems. Normally on large installations, a 'project team' would be formed consisting of senior key personnel. These

146

would comprise the *architect* who will be responsible for the overall planning of the building installation and its associated services. His major concern will be the construction of a pleasing building or conversion of an existing building, together with the correct installation of any technical plant. He will be aided in his work by a *quantity surveyor*, who will cost the work and thus enable the architect to make decisions with regard to the budget. One of the main concerns of the architect will be the size of the structure required to support lighting systems together with the weights involved. To solve the structural problems that will arise, a *structural engineer* will work very closely with the architect, and it is his calculations that will decide the structure of the building. The lighting produces tremendous heat loads in a structure and obviously from the point of view of audience or artists' comfort, these loads have to be successfully dealt with. The person concerned with this aspect of the installation will be an *air conditioning engineer*. One of his main problems will be that to move the vast quantities of hot air requires large amounts of plant and these have to be housed somewhere in or on the building; the other problem being that the air conditioning itself can generate noise. This brings us to another valuable member of the team – the *acoustic engineer* whose concern will be to ensure good acoustics for either the audience in the theatre or for the reception of sound in film and TV studios. Major concerns to him will be the shape of the building and the noise generated by equipment, such as air conditioning etc. and how this can be adequately dealt with.

Finally, we have two people who will work extremely close together; one of which is the *lighting consultant*, designing the lighting system and the *electrical engineer* concerned with the installation. One of his prime functions will be to interpret the needs of the lighting consultant for the wiring, the lighting power sockets and the power supplies needed for the lighting in the building. In addition, he will be concerned with the electrical supply for the air conditioning system and the general lighting in the premises, together with normal power sockets around the building. He will also be concerned with fire detection and emergency lighting systems.

Items to be considered by the project team are as follows:

1 Overall plan
   (a) What exactly is the requirement?
   (b) Is it a new building or modifications to an existing premises?
   (c) Is it a refurbishment?
   (d) Is this the final scheme, or is any allowance to be made for future expansion or development?
2 Building construction
   (a) Floor
   (b) Walls
   (c) Ceiling or roof structure
   (d) Access to working area
   (e) Ancillary and control areas
3 Studio size
   (a) Length/depth
   (b) Width
   (c) Grid height
   (d) Overall height
4 Ventilation/air conditioning
   (a) Position in studio
   (b) Capability
   (c) Plant and ducting routes
5 Power system
   (a) Method of supply i.e. single or three phase, 'Star' or 'Delta'?
   (b) Voltage and current capacity of incoming supply

6   Lighting requirement
    (a)   Light levels required
    (b)   Type of suspension
7   Studio requirements
    (a)   Scenic suspension facilities
    (b)   Main lighting
    (c)   Effects lighting (cycloramas, projection systems and automated luminaires)
    (d)   Special facilities e.g. remote control of lighting power
8   Control and Dimming requirements
    (a)   Type of lighting control console
    (b)   Location of lighting console
    (c)   Number of dimmers
    (d)   Location of dimmers
    (e)   Provision of power and switchgear for dimmers
    (f)   Provision of remote control consoles for scenery and lighting systems
    (g)   Switching of lighting in remote areas; or, remote control of the system from two or more
          points
9   Provisions for safety
    (a)   Smoke detectors/sprinklers
    (b)   Local authority requirements
    (c)   Users' requirements

9.2   Safety requirements

The requirements of safety have a major influence on the installation, and they will ultimately sway the decisions made by the project team.

One of the problems in any premises is fire. It is relatively easy to train the permanent staff manning a building and, for that matter, the artists concerned with the production the safest way to exit from the area of work. It becomes much more difficult with the public, because of the inability to train them in the direction of where to go safely, when a fire breaks out. Thus, there is a need for clearly marked 'exits', correctly defined passageways for staff, artists and audience to evacuate a building. Although sprinkler systems are commonly used in the theatre due to the fact they can extinguish fires very effectively, they are somewhat of a hazard in the film and TV industry as generally much more lighting will be involved together with a lot of technical equipment. There is obviously a need, if a fire breaks out, not to damage too much of the existing technical plant. To this end, smoke detectors and 'rate of temperature rise' detectors have been used in more recent years to warn the local staff of problems and these can also be coupled through via the telephone network to the local fire department.

With any planned development of any premises, either existing or proposed, it is most important to involve the local fire authority at an early stage so that they are consulted on what should take place within the building. There is a requirement that all the adjacent areas to a studio have to be safe as well, such as dressing rooms, control rooms, dimmer rooms, etc. A good example of applied safety is that of a dimmer room which may have a door opening into the active area itself, will require another access door, generally at the opposite end of the room so that operators can evacuate away from areas of potential hazard. In film and TV studios, there is a need to have defined fire lanes within the studio active area, so that people can exit safely from an area of great potential danger. Most modern studios are built with a marked fire lane, which has to remain clear of any obstructions, around the perimeter. They also have to be equipped with a certain number of exits according to size. In TV and film studios, acoustic barriers are often formed by having twin doors through a small lobby from the corridors adjacent to studios to the studio area itself. It is obviously important that these allow a safe exit.

An area of great concern for safety is the mechanical structure formed above the acting area. This will usually weigh several tonnes and will have pieces of moving machinery sitting on the structure itself. Thus, other than the static load of the weight of the equipment, we have the dynamic loads when the motors and lifting gear are operated, lifting scenery and luminaires from the acting area. Devices rigged to the mechanical structure such as the luminaires, pantographs, technical fittings of any description and scenery equipment all pose areas of potential danger. Almost on a par with the mechanical problems are the electrical problems. Although it is not very likely that an electrical socket will suddenly work free and fall to the studio floor in normal operation, it is possible that any malfunction of the electrical system may cause a fire. It is also important from the operators' point of view that the electrical system is installed to the highest safety standards.

9.3   Greenfield sites and the refurbishment of existing premises

The architect having been given a brief which may be that of a 'green field' site, which means building new premises from scratch, or the refurbishment of existing premises. In the first case, that of new premises, the architect obviously starts with a blank piece of paper and can incorporate many new ideas and suggestions. If, however, it is the refurbishment of existing premises, he is constrained by what he can do within the building, the limits being caused by the physical structure of the building and the loads that would be acceptable to that structure, how much space is there for the development or how can extra space be created within the development. Unfortunately, for the poor architect, every interested technical person has an input which usually conflicts with the rest of the team. For example, it might be that the lighting consultant, to meet the needs of his client, requires to make the area as large as possible, together with extremely high lighting and thus electrical loads, which will cause problems for the air conditioning and electrical engineers. With all these changes to the structure and shape, the poor acoustics specialist starts to tear his hair out with all the extra work that this is going to entail. The structural engineer, at this point, probably has his eyes firmly fixed on the ceiling thinking of all the calculations he has to make so that the architect will be convinced that the building won't fall down.

Having said this, of course, most project teams work extremely harmoniously and usually generate a good team spirit. It is more than obvious at this stage that a great deal of compromise will have to be reached on the installation itself. Thus, where do we start?

In an existing installation, the size of the studio will be fixed, and very seldom will it be changed. It might be that new mechanical devices are incorporated in the new installation or the electrical installation is changed, but generally the size and height of the area is fixed. This is probably a good thing from the architects' point of view because it places quite logical constraints on what can happen within the area chosen for development. It may be that the existing lighting grid structure remains unchanged, the only alterations being changing the luminaires supplied to the premises. If this is the case, the constraints already laid down by the lifting capacity of the equipment installed will dictate the type of luminaires purchased. If however, some of the facilities are to be changed so that greater lifting capacity can be used, this will have a knock on effect on the structural engineers' calculations, due to the devices imposing greater loads on the structure. It is quite conceivable that although the weight of the equipment doesn't increase, the power required for the equipment is higher, thus the electrical engineer will have to update his power system and the ventilation engineer will probably have a potential problem with the existing air conditioning plant. The room used to house the dimmers, if such a room exists, which was probably quite adequate, possibly now becomes inadequate by an increase in the number of dimmers required. All of this presupposes that the lighting consultant can actually do what he wants. Unfortunately, in any modern system, we also have to handle scenery. Therefore this places constraints on the disposition of lighting bars in a system, it also dictates the spacing between lighting bars or trackways. The size of the luminaires involved will also dictate spacing in the grid.

A modern controversy that reigns quite a lot these days, is where do we put control rooms? In the theatre, control rooms with a window having a clear view of the stage are obviously desired for those staff operating sound systems and the lighting control console. In television there is not an overwhelming need to see in the studio as the pictures from the cameras will tell the operating staff what is happening. There is however, a need for rapid access for the LD and people concerned with the production from the control rooms to the studio and to this end, many studios built today have control rooms at floor level. A walkover grid is highly desirable for the ease of suspending items of equipment from the grid itself. One of the major problems of walkover grids is the building is required to be higher, or in a fixed building, the proposed grid is forced to be lower. In an existing building, the walls may not be capable of taking additional loads and any new equipment installed would require either building alterations to the walls themselves so that the loads become spread or that structures are used that use the floor area as support. If we are building from scratch on a green field site, most of the problems can be taken care of, hopefully with the ingenuity of the architect and the structural engineer. The main requirement in a green field site would be that of the acting area and its associated facilities. There is always a need for large theatre stages, but common-sense has to prevail and generally the architect, having been briefed by the client as to what the requirements are, has to do his best within the budget to meet the planned objectives.

If we were building from scratch in the film industry, generally we would be building studios with very large acting areas i.e. around $1500\,m^2$ to $3000\,m^2$. In the film industry, the feeling generally is that a small production can fit into a large studio area but not the other way around. This might appear to be the case for the TV industry as well, but because the studios have defined purposes, such as small news areas, small presentation areas, medium-sized studios or large multi-purpose production studios, there are finite limits to areas required. Most of these are established by custom and practice within the industry itself. Another aspect of film studios is that they are not, generally, permanently equipped with lighting equipment but are usually provided with a fairly basic lighting grid and power supply system.

Television studios are generally integrated into production centres, which may vary from fairly small to very large such as the BBC TV Centre in London. By integrating a series of box like structures into a building, the design of the building is greatly influenced. In TV there is a need for many adjacent areas to a studio such as make-up and wardrobe areas, dimmer room, production, lighting, vision and sound control rooms. The disposition of all these areas has a bearing on access ways and vantage points to the studio. In the theatre there is not the need for so many technical rooms as the production is controlled from the stage area. Most of the support areas have to be close to the stage so that artists are provided with good access to dressing rooms and quick change areas. A requirement of theatre productions is to have complex mechanical stage lifting arrangements, possibly integrated with orchestral facilities. All of these will have to be considered by the architect so as to integrate the whole system to a meaningful production area and the following sections give the various parameters that have to be observed so that the various requirements of the building are met.

9.4 Building construction – how it can be influenced

In film and TV studios, the decisions are somewhat dictated by the needs of the set designer. Generally, in the case of the film industry, 'big is beautiful'. Large scale studios often have wide vista shots taking place, which dictate the height of any cycloramas used. A studio 32 m long will require cycs at least 9.5 m high and probably higher. If we allow a clearance above the cyc sight line so that luminaires do not intrude, we additionally need at least 1.5 m clearance from the top of the cycs to the grid. If, for instance, boats are used in the studio, then even more clearance is required above the cyc line and this would imply an extra 2.5 m, thus allowing operators to work at this level without hitting their heads on the grid structure. Film studios are not traditionally equipped with walkover grids, but they do require access at high level, even if it's only walkways to allow access for rigging and de-rigging of the block and tackle units to suspend lines for scenery and luminaires. There is obviously also a need to reach the electrical distribution system at this level where luminaires are being used or power feeds have been dropped from the grid down to lights which may be suspended on block and tackle or some other lifting device.

Attempts have been made in the past to provide some form of mechanised system similar to those used in the TV industry. The most famous of these was the installation of a monopole system in two studios at Pinewood in England. For most of the time however, the film industry is content to go on in the same way that it's practised lighting for many years. Thus the prime requirements of the film studio are suspensions trackways at fairly frequent intervals down a studio so that lifting equipment or 'boats' may be attached where and when desired. Due to the sheer physical size and subsequent weight of the luminaires used in the film industry over many years, the grid structures have had to be reasonably robust to take the weights of the equipment. However, it should be borne in mind that saturated lighting with its well distributed weight load, is not used in the film industry. One of their main requirements is high point loadings caused by several large high intensity luminaires, or a 'boat' with luminaires attached, in one small area of the grid structure.

With the construction of a new film studio, it might be that we would have to integrate its use for either film or video shooting. Much of the economy of the film industry these days is based upon the shooting of pop videos and commercials for TV. Film studios are fairly simple in their nature being rather large 'box-like' structures immune to outside noise if designed as sound stages, and constructed in such a way that almost any production can be fitted in them with the provision of high cycloramas. The actual lighting arrangements are extremely basic. The film industry occasionally use dimmer units for some control on productions. The one big advance that has helped in the film studio is the introduction of discharge lighting taking away the need for the large carbon arcs. These units, with their highly efficient output require much less power from the electrical system. Talking about power in systems reminds us that some film stages may still have d.c. voltage feeders, although in most cases these are being converted to a.c. systems. Generally there is no need to provide permanent dimmer rooms adjacent to film studios, although if new studios did evolve for dual purpose film/vision systems, then a provision should be made so that fairly large dimmer installations could be added at a later date in the studios' life. The general requirement in film studios is for large power distribution cabinets, placed at regular intervals around the studio from which can be taken all the temporary feeds to the lighting units themselves. Whereas in TV studios highly sophisticated air conditioning systems are used, the film industry is still fairly basic in its requirements. Due to the nature of filming, which may be a rehearsal period and then a 'take' with long extended intervals between, it is easy to allow the premises to cool over periods of time. Although it must be said, that in modern TV studios the use of rehearse/record techniques using a few sets at a time diminishes the requirement for the large air conditioning systems at present employed.

Due to the need to contain costs within the TV industry, it is strongly suspected that other than refurbishing existing studios, very few new studios will now be constructed, in either Europe or America. What may be required is the conversion of some premises for studio use.

Let us now turn our attention to the design of lighting systems for TV studios and how those designs will influence the building construction. Large TV studios generally use a complex grid which in itself poses installation problems but prior to that is the need to ascertain the height of the grid and clearance above for services and personnel. There have been cases over the years where the management and accountants were convinced by the arguments put forward by architects saying that for each 300 mm of additional height in a studio enormous additional costs were incurred. Thus certain studios were limited in height, only to find the programme makers were forever complaining about the limitations imposed in these studios. As a starting point it is extremely important to get the height of the studio correct and the following system gives the method of calculation. It is relatively easy to decide upon the acting area that is required and consequently the floor dimensions. However, an important parameter that can only be ascertained by examination of the camera viewing angles is that of the cyc height and its subsequent effect on wide shots in a studio.

In small studios, more than likely, the cyclorama track and hence the cloth hanging from it will be relatively close to some of the walls, the only space required behind is for the odd low level lighting outlet box with space to plug in sources without impeding on the cyc cloth itself. In larger studios it is normal to have a walkway behind the cycs where space is not so critical from the point of view of the cable outlet boxes. When designing lighting for a cyclorama, the question is often asked, is top or bottom cyc lighting the best? The answer is – neither – it depends what type of result is required. One of the main essentials is to have good coving arrangements at the base of the cyc to get a blend between the horizontal and vertical so that there appears to be one continuous surface from the camera's viewpoint. Top cyc lighting, which is plotted at 3.1 m away from the cyc at 2.5 m intervals, will give very good results from a height of 10 m down to floor level. However, bearing in mind that the light is striking the cyc cloth at a very acute angle, and striking the floor almost straight on, gives differentials between the base of the cyc and the floor which are very difficult to overcome. The great advantage of top cyc lighting is no floor space is required, and indeed, in small news and current affairs studios, almost essential to prevent problems with space in the studio.

Bottom cyc lighting, which is generally used 1 m away from the base of the cyc, with each individual source of light at 1.2 m intervals, can give a very even horizontal wash on the cyc but gives a very bright horizon effect at the base of the cyc and fades off rather rapidly in the vertical. If the units are taken out into the studio by the same amount as top units, i.e. about 3 m then we could generally expect a much more even result but as is obvious, this is not practical and it may be that the bright horizon effect is quite desirable. However, it is essential with groundrow units that they are hidden in some way unless the units themselves are not too unattractive to appear in shot. Two methods of hiding groundrow units are used; one of which is to have a short cove around the studio on the inside surface between the cyc units and the acting area, or to place the groundrow units in a well which runs parallel to the base of the cyc, which can be very effective in long shot, but unfortunately when cameras are used off centre, can pose a problem inasmuch that the well itself may become noticeable.

With a camera viewing aspect ratio of 4:3, if a 36° lens angle is used this gives a vertical angle of 27° (Figure 9.1). When using a 16:9 aspect ratio system the relative cyclorama heights remain the same but the horizontal angle will have increased.

Note: By knowing the aspect ratio and horizontal angle of view, the vertical angle can always be derived.

Assume a lens height of 1.8 m above floor level. Cyclorama height = (L × tan 13.5°) + 1.8 m (where L is the length of the studio). Cyclorama heights (in metres) for studios with maximum length (in metres) are shown in Table 9.1.

Figure 9.1 Camera angles

Table 9.1

Studio length (m)	Cyclorama height (m)	Studio length (m)	Cyclorama height (m)
6	3.2	20	6.6
8	3.7	22	7.1
10	4.2	24	7.6
12	4.7	26	8.0
14	5.2	28	8.5
16	5.6	30	9.0
18	6.1	32	9.5

As an example to see how the studio height has been influenced by the choice of the cyclorama height the following example is given.

Studio dimensions	$= 30\,m \times 24\,m$
Cyclorama height for 30 m	$= 9\,m$
Height allowance above the top of the cyc for luminaires and pantographs from the suspension system	$= 2\,m$
Therefore the grid height	$= 11\,m$
Allowance above the grid for maintenance	$= 2.5\,m$
Allowance for air conditioning and services above the grid maintenance area	$= 2.5\,m$
Total studio height	$= 11 + 2.5 + 2.5 = 16\,m$

The example quoted is for a conventional studio with a barrel grid. The figures still hold for monopole grids, but if no access is required above the grid, or ventilation is provided such that access is not impeded, then the total height could be reduced. In the smaller studios little or no access is required at high level, the only space requirements generally are for the air conditioning equipment and electrical services.

9.5   Structural loads

Monopole installations

Monopole grids consist of continuous longitudinal trackways at very regular intervals usually engineered from steel, because they will wear so much better than lighter weight materials such as aluminium. At right angles to the main trackways, again at regular intervals, are the change-over tracks to enable monopoles to be wheeled from one track to another.

The method of construction of a monopole grid is to have a series of oblong platforms, made from steel with aluminium decking infill, individually suspended from the under side of the primary steels which will generally be used to support the roof of the studio. The long sides of the platforms form the main trackways and the short sides are the cross over tracks. The slots provided in the grid for the monopoles are conventionally 63.5 mm (2.5 inches) wide.

In the monopole system the mechanical loads on the structure can move around the grid; in comparison, a barrel grid, because of the design of the system, spreads the structural load fairly evenly. If we take as an example a monopole capable of lifting 60 kg, it will have a self weight of approximately the same amount, thus its total overall weight will be 120 kg. Therefore the point loading on the grid is 120 kg every time one of these units is used. The next problem arises when considering how many units per linear run could we use and for TV it is quite possible that a high density of monopoles have to be provided and allowance has to be made for the units to work almost next to each other, although it is doubtful that more than about 20 would be used in any one cluster. For the structural engineer concerned, the problem is that these large lumps of metal can move around the structure and can appear almost anywhere. Therefore a monopole grid has to be extremely strong and thus tends to be quite heavy. All this creates loading problems for the structural engineer and the architect to incorporate in their design. To give some idea of possible loadings in a studio it may be that 120 motorised monopoles are used in a studio of some 600 m^2. This represents a load, just for positioning the lights, of 14.4 tonnes. If there is a need to cluster the light sources; as an example, 16 lights formed into a square would occupy approximately 4 × 4 m and present a load of 1.92 tonnes to that area, which of course is a high point loading.

Another problem arises inasmuch that if we started all the units up at the same time, the dynamic load on that portion of the grid would be quite considerable and we certainly don't want it springing and oscillating every time we move equipment. Therefore, it has to be reasonably rigid, and this requirement also dictates the needs for fairly massive grid structures. In addition to the basic grid, there will be a need for loading platforms adjacent to the grid for rigging monopoles into the trackways. Possibly suspended just below grid level around the studio, are walkways, used for access to power feeds and specially rigged peripheral luminaires. Approximately 1 m from the edge of the studio a permanent cyc track will be provided. Trap doors have to be provided for lifting equipment into the grid area: either built into the grid itself or provided at the side of the studio. Due to the highly flexible nature of monopole grids they only require a certain basic amount of luminaires because these can be moved around to suit the production. Figures for luminaire requirements are given in the next section.

Barrel installations

Many American studios are equipped with counterweight barrel systems where the length of the bar may be around 4–5 m long. Studios are generally equipped with a reasonable density of this type of barrel. The nice thing about counterweight bars from the structural man's point of view is that the load on the grid is usually the basic SWL of the bar itself and most of the weight is contained within the counterweight system, usually mounted on the studio walls. Some barrel studios have been constructed with bar units in the studio area with the support wires taken via diverter pulleys to the edge of the studio where the motor units are mounted on the walls. In most modern barrel studios where the scenery handling facilities are integrated into the grid structure the motor winding units for the scenery lifting system are generally mounted on the side walls of the studio. Most of the problems for the structural engineer with grid designs, usually arise with the heavy motorised barrel units which may be of the standard type with motors mounted at grid level or self climbing units with integral motors. Even if the system uses self climbing units, the total weight presented to the grid structure at any point is approximately the same.

Most barrel studios are usually constructed with the bar units approximately 1.5 m apart with an end to end spacing of approximately 1 m. Thus having been given the studio area which doesn't include the fire lane, it is relatively easy to work out how many bar units will be employed. To take account of cyclorama tracks which have a radius at the corners of the studio, short bar units may be employed in the four corners of the studio.

In a monopole grid, because the slots provided at grid level are very similar to those in the theatre, it is relatively easy to drop spot lines for holding scenery up or suspending scenery pieces. In barrel studios, it is important that provision is made for the use of scenery and many modern studios have specially installed scenery winching systems, which run in between the main bars themselves. It is fairly obvious that the easiest installation for scene winches is in the same orientation as the bars. Going crosswise across the bar system could pose considerable problems. Motorised barrel winch units when they are of the standard type, are usually supported lengthways along twin structural members.

In a studio of some considerable span, these members have to be supported at frequent intervals to take account of the load. Thus several upright members between the grid and the primary steels have to be used so consequently it is not totally unobstructed. This point has to be borne in mind when designing walkover grids so that access is reasonable. A typical barrel winch unit will weigh approximately 150 kg, with a lifting capacity of almost the same amount, so the total load on the grid from any one winch unit may be around 300 kg. The encouraging thing from the point of view of the structural engineer and architect is the fact these loads are fixed in position in the grid. The weights given here assume the use of bar units approximately 2.5 to 3.0 m long. If we use shorter units the relative weights are somewhat similar from the point of view of the structural man, i.e. a shorter bar unit may have only half the lifting capacity of a long unit and its motor unit, mounted at the grid, may be only around 75% of a big unit but we will use twice as many bars in the studio. Thus the total load on the grid is approximately the same.

Most studios fitted with barrel systems operate with a high density of lighting. It may be at the BBC where multi-purpose luminaires are rigged permanently to the barrels, or like some of the studios in America where many 2 kW and 1 kW luminaires are rigged per barrel, just for the ease of the general operation.

It is more than likely, in many of the studios that use motorised devices, for some restriction to be placed on the amount of units used at any one time, to stop dynamic loading problems on the grid.

Smaller studios such as those using motorised or spring pantographs will have long track-ways where rather like the monopole studio the loads can be grouped in areas. The weight of equipment in these studios is significantly less than motorised barrel and monopole systems. However, due to the nature of operations in studios of this type, their load is fairly well spread throughout the structure and of course, can be contained by loading notices which prohibit too much clustering within the studio area.

Perhaps only about 40 luminaires may be used together with 40 suspension points and of course this does not present the problems that exist in a large studio. Small roller barrel grids can also present a moving load to the main structure, although by not using motorised units, the weight on the structure is considerably less. In the larger studios such as those used with monopoles and motorised barrels which may have their motor units mounted at grid level, or be the self climbing type, special metal structures have to be arranged usually by the structural engineer in consultation with the architect, so that the rather heavy lighting grid system can be installed safely. This may require the use of special large beams being incorporated into the structure at high level. It must also be remembered that other than a lighting grid, air conditioning

(a)

(b)

Figure 9.2 Typical studio layouts: (a) fixed barrel grid; (b) roller barrel

Figure 9.2 *Continued* (c) motorised barrels

requirements exist and there will be a lot of additional weight from the power wiring system etc. In smaller studios it may be that grid attachments can be made to, for example, a concrete roof going over the studio which can be made sufficiently strong by the astute use of reinforcing rod. The saving grace in a smaller studio is that the spans are not so great.

So far we have discussed the installation of grid systems and their subsequent structural loading, on the assumption that we are in a new building and can influence the design. What happens if we require to put a lighting system in existing premises? First of all it is important to come up with the lighting scheme itself, which can then be presented with all its facts and figures to the architect and structural engineer concerned. They will obviously be able either to accept the scheme as it stands for the new design, or it may be that they are able to modify the building in some way to accept the new design. Therefore it's back to the poor old lighting consultant to come up with an idea to be contained within the parameters set by the architect and structural engineer. It's quite possible that the idea could be acceptable but with some change to the structure itself, such as spreading the loadings between the walls and the roof, not just using the roof itself. It may be that the roof structure cannot accept any load other than the one existing, therefore all the new installation would have to be supported from the side walls or from a structure built up from the floor level. The first of these requires that the walls are strong enough, and the second that the floor is also strong enough. Any of these solutions may be acceptable and it might even be a combination of any of them or all three. It must be remembered when discussing the structural arrangements with the architect and structural engineer, that these figures have to include for all the lights, all the rigging system, all the power system and any ancillaries that may be added at any time.

In addition to the structural loads presented by the lighting system in the studio, the structural engineer will also be concerned with the size of plant installed in areas adjacent to the studio. Generally, the weight of the switchgear will be spread out in a fairly uniform fashion. The input power cables to the switchgear and the cables from the switchgear to the dimmer racks will also be fairly well distributed throughout the area. Most of the problem will be concerned with the weight of the dimmer racks where in a large installation the structural engineer may be confronted with a room with up to 20 or 30 dimmer racks. Dimensions of dimmer racks vary quite considerably, and as an example, a lightweight rack of 200 kg from one manufacturer has base dimensions of 905 × 510 mm whereas another, which is a high density rack weighing 900 kg with base dimensions of 850 × 600 mm. The latter rack obviously gives floor loading problems, being a large weight over a small area. It would seem at first sight that the best solution to any of the loading problems in dimmer rooms is to keep the weights of the racks low and use more racks so that the loadings are well spread. However the size of the room dictates how many racks may be used and the economics of the situation is that more racks generally put up the cost. In a new building, the structural engineer would obviously cater for the high floor loading at the planning stage; in existing buildings however, special precautions will have to be taken, or it may be that additional building work is required.

In practice, over many years of experience, it is very seldom that we have found buildings to be so bad that they would preclude some form of solution being adopted albeit possibly far removed from the original concept.

9.6 Television studio requirements

The influence on the structure caused by the lighting grid has nothing to do with the amount of luminaires to be provided. Grids are there to hang lights, almost anywhere, using whatever quantities of luminaires that may be available. The basic requirement in any TV studio is for a certain amount of light to satisfy the technical requirements of the cameras. This quantity of light will be determined by the average reflectivity of scenery together with the exposure time of the camera coupled with the aperture of the lens in use. Based upon incandescent sources with an efficacy of around 26 lumens/W we can measure the amount of power required for the acting area to be adequately lit and this is given in Watts per square metre. At the present time, a figure of around 300 W of lighting/m^2 for the basic lighting is considered adequate for the majority of general purpose requirements in TV. Many TV studios today will use prompters mounted on the cameras; these reduce the reflected light to a camera by about half a stop and the incident light level has to be raised by 33% to compensate.

For example:

- Normal light level required: 600 lux.
- Prompter loss of 1/2 stop effectively reduces light level to 450 lux (75% transmission).

- Light level to achieve 600 lux = 600/0.75 = 800 lux, which represents an increase of 33%.
- Now the prompter loss of 1/2 stop reduces light level from 800 lux to 600 lux, the level initially required.

This is usually accomplished by utilising higher powered light sources or raising the dimmer output levels. It may be that the dimmer settings are quite high e.g. '8', '9', and it is impossible to achieve the correct incident light level. This may necessitate, for example, having to choose 2 kW instead of 1 kW luminaires. In larger luminaires, this can be overcome by using higher powered twin filament lamps or moving from 2 kW to 3 kW lamps.

Although the figure of 300 W/m^2 is satisfactory for most basic purposes, it should be borne in mind that additional requirements, such as cyc and effects lighting, will impose an additional burden. A colour mixing system used on cycloramas will probably require loads of anything up to 2000 W/m of linear run, thus a 40 m cyclorama cloth might require anything up to 80 kW being provided for adequate effects purposes. Although the cyc lighting power figure seems over generous it must be noted that when using highly saturated filter colours with transmissions as low as 5% the light output needs to be high to create the maximum effect and it is therefore suggested that a slightly higher estimating figure of around 450 W/m^2 is used on any studio above about 250 m^2. An important fact in the choice of luminaires is the size of the studio. Studios up to about 150 m^2 will generally work quite happily with a 1 kW fresnel as the highest power luminaire required. However, above this size of studio, the majority of luminaires will probably settle at 2 kW, 3 kW or 1.25/2.5/5 kW. These powers of course, are related to working distances involved between the lights and the various subjects.

Whatever estimating figure we use for the power requirements for a studio, be it 300 W/m^2, or 450 W/m^2, it is obviously relatively easy to work out the power requirement by taking the active area in square metres and multiplying it by the appropriate wattage figure. In the case of monopole studios, and the smaller pantograph type studios it is more than likely that the power requirements of the supply system will more or less match the available total wattage of the luminaires used. However, in the case of saturated lighting grids, the total power of the luminaires installed will probably exceed the power available by a factor of anything up to three times. As an example of this, a BBC studio of 800 m^2 will be supplied with approximately 450 kW of power. The 100 bars installed will each have two 3.75 kW luminaires rigged on them, thus the load presented by the luminaires to the system is 750 kW. In practice this is not a problem as only selected numbers of lights are used and therefore it is a basic requirement that the LD must have current meters and/or an alarm system indicating the maximum electrical load. The figures that follow have been worked out from typical studio usage over many years and represent reasonable requirements of any studio. It is obviously easy to start equipping a studio by covering the basic lighting requirements and in the fullness of time purchase more equipment to suit the installation. As an approximate guide, the 'luminaire power' required is divided into 2/3 hard sources and 1/3 soft sources.

9.7 The smaller studio

The smaller studio (those from 20 m^2 to 80 m^2) usually provides for 'fixed head' presentations.

They are quite often conversions of existing premises with little or no air conditioning. The floors are usually strong, but the walls or ceiling may require some modification to allow a simple grid to be installed and this is generally because of the imposed weight of the grid and luminaires. If the main grid can be suspended from the ceiling all that is needed at the sides of the studio are cyc rail supports. Or it may be that the cyc system is integrated into the main grid structure. On occasions, however, the ceiling will be not strong enough to support the weight of the grid and it will be necessary to either fix to the walls or have a floor standing structure to support the grid. Quite often height is a problem and deep primary support beams, for the grid, across the studio will make matters worse. The use of a light weight truss can be advantageous if a floor standing structure has to be installed.

---

50 m²
Minimum power required: 16 kW
12 × 1 kW Fresnel spots
 6 × 650 W Fresnel spots
 8 × 625 W tungsten softlights
or
8 × 220 W Fluorescent softlights
4 × 575 W Profile spots
4 × Floor stands
Cyc:
12 × 625 W single compartment
top units (1.2 m from cyc)

150 m²
Minimum power required: 50 kW
24 × 1 kW Fresnel spots
10 × 650 W Fresnel spots
10 × 1.25 kW tungsten softlights
or
10 × 330 W Fluorescent softlights
 6 × 575 W/1 kW Profile spots
 8 × Floor stands
Cyc:
30 × 625 W single top units
(1.2 m from cyc)
and/or
30 × 625 W 4-compartment
groundrow units

400 m²
Minimum power required: 180 kW
 3 × 10 kW Fresnel spots
 6 × 5 kW Fresnel spots
20 × 2 kW Fresnel spots
40 × 1 kW Fresnel spots
or
48 × 1.25/2.5 kW Fresnel spots
and
12 × 650 W Fresnel spots
24 × 1.25 kW tungsten softlights
or
24 × 330 W Fluorescent softlights
 8 × 575 W/1 kW Profile spots
20 × 500 W Par-cans
12 Floor stands
Cyc:
16 × 1.25 kW 4-compartment
top units (3 m from cyc)
and/or
40 × 625 W 4-compartment
groundrow units

100 m²
Minimum power required: 30 kW
18 × 1 kW Fresnel spots
 8 × 650 W Fresnel spots
10 × 1.25 kW tungsten softlights
or
10 × 220 W Fluorescent softlights
 6 × 575 W Profile spots
 6 × Floor stands
Cyc:
16 × 625 W single compartment top
units (1.2 m from cyc)

250 m²
Minimum power required: 75 kW
10 × 2 kW Fresnel spots
30 × 1 kW Fresnel spots
16 × 1.25 kW tungsten softlights
or
16 × 330 W Fluorescent softlights
 6 × 575 W/1 kW Profile spots
10 × Floor stands
Cyc:
20 × 1.25 kW twin top units
(3 m from cyc)
and/or
40 × 625 W 4-compartment
groundrow units

750 m²
Minimum power required: 320 kW
 6 × 10 kW Fresnel spots
10 × 5 kW Fresnel spots
35 × 2 kW Fresnel spots
70 × 1 kW Fresnel spots
or
85 × 1.25/2.5 kW Fresnel spots
and
20 × 650 W Fresnel spots
40 × 1.25 kW tungsten softlights
or
40 × 330 W Fluorescent softlights
12 × 575 W/1 kW Profile spots
40 × 500 W Par-cans
16 Floor stands
Cyc:
30 × 1.25 kW 4-compartment
top units (3 m from cyc)
and/or
70 × 625 W 4-compartment
groundrow units

The most basic grid is a fixed matrix of steel barrels, although if weight is a problem aluminium can be used at a cost premium. The matrix should provide a spacing no greater than 1 m and preferably 600 mm. However, the less the spacing the more the weight load and cost! A good alternative is to use roller barrels which allows for better positioning of luminaires and can cut down the amount of metal in the grid structure. Usually a twin cyc rail is quite sufficient and the cyc cloths will usually be lit from above to conserve the limited floor space. There will be a need for Chromakey backings which can be provided by a cloth or by a fluorescent back lit panel. Access behind the cyc cloth will be fairly restricted, but there will be a need for some power sockets at studio floor level for floor-stand mounted luminaires and effects lights. The choice of lighting can be made from tungsten for the best control of optical performance and lighting level which is controlled by a dimmer. Unfortunately this can cause problems with heat therefore a hybrid solution can be adopted by using a mixture of tungsten hard lighting with fluorescent softlights. The dimmers will be controlled by a very basic lighting console. The amount of facilities will depend upon the complexity of programmes, which in a small studio are very limited. The main requirement of the lighting console will be very rapid access to any channel as it is more than likely that rehearsals will be very brief affairs.

9.8 Air conditioning requirements

If we install 100 kW of tungsten lighting in any area, we have to expect that, ultimately, all of this will appear as waste heat and most of this will rise vertically. From the point of view of air conditioning, two effects take place. The first is that the luminaires will radiate infrared energy in the direction of the artists. This radiation is in direct proportion to the efficiency of the luminaires themselves, thus a luminaire with a claimed efficiency of 26% will have approximately 26% radiant energy in the light beam; the remainder will be contained within the luminaire and subsequently re-radiated from the luminaire body or as exhaust from the ventilation system on the luminaire itself. Generally older premises are never provided with adequate air conditioning systems and it always seems 'that you have to sweat to earn your money'! However, in new premises or where premises are capable of being successfully converted, it is possible to have adequate air conditioning installed. Thus, there are two important areas from the point of view of the air conditioning man: first of all, the conditions that create a comfortable atmosphere at the acting level and secondly, the conditions for people working either in the flies or at grid level itself, and it is at grid level where the maximum heat will eventually settle, assuming nothing is done to prevent it.

Heat loads are rather like the domestic electrical load and are somewhat subject to diversity of use. It is very seldom that *all* the installed lighting in any system will be used at the same time, and over a period of some years it has been established in TV, that an average load of 66% of the maximum installed kilowatts will be used over a period of time. So, for a studio using 400 kW of lighting power, we need to worry about 264 kW worth, thus easing the burden on the air conditioning man. In film studios, although large amounts of power are used on film sets, they are usually used for reasonably short periods of time with breaks between, which allows the temperature, although perhaps having reached high levels, to be dissipated fairly quickly by the use of large fans in the roof or walls. Television has changed greatly in recent years and the technique of rehearse/shoot, generally means that only perhaps one or two sets of the possible 10/13 sets in a large studio are in use at any one time, thus the load on the air conditioning system is considerably less and it may be in the future that the estimating figure of 66% needs to be looked at once again and possibly reduced.

It's all very well having air conditioning that works effectively and keeps the ambient temperature to reasonable limits, to the relief of everybody concerned; however air conditioning can only be achieved by moving a large volume of air down small ducting or an equal volume of air down a large ducting system. The latter will create, in general, much less noise, and in fact for TV use, we have to be extremely careful with the generation of noise from the air conditioning system. An interesting coincidence occurs inasmuch that by moving large volumes of air we don't create some of the air movement that causes problems in practice, such as a cyc cloth being moved by the sheer volume of air flowing around a studio. Other than the needs of the studio, air conditioning will be required in the dimmer room, as there is a reasonable amount of waste heat generated.

This is particularly important if the dimmer room doubles as a maintenance room for the electricians to use. In a large studio it may be that the air conditioning engineer concerned will be able to have a zonal control system so that when only one quarter of the studio is used only that quarter is air conditioned to any reasonable degree. The requirement for a large volume of air to be moved down large ducting, obviously implies a large space being occupied by the air conditioning system at grid level. Thus, it is extremely important when planning a studio, to integrate the air conditioning system and the lighting grid system together, so that a clash of interest does not occur and certainly access to the lighting equipment is not prevented. Others affected by the requirements of air conditioning are sound, vision and electrical technicians who also require the use of certain portions of the grid for some of their systems. Some air conditioning systems, when moving the volumes of air suggested in this section, require large rooms in which to put plant, and these rooms can almost approach the size of some of the studios they service. Further problems associated with air conditioning are that chilled water is required and if compressor units are used, it is important they do not create any undue noise in the studio. It also happens that introduction of air conditioning breaches the walls around the area which consequently cause problems to the acoustic specialist; this latter problem will be discussed in Section 9.10.

9.9   Power requirements

We are sometimes asked about the problems of interference with the use of discharge lighting in a studio as opposed to tungsten lighting with dimmers. Solid state flicker free discharge ballasts, although capable of generating high levels of interference are usually engineered in such a way that interference is minimised. At the present time the EMC regulations would ensure that all solid state ballasts conform to a low degree of interference capability in the same way that dimmers have to be treated.

Irrespective of whether we use 1 kW, 2 kW, 3 kW, 5 kW or 10 kW luminaires, or whatever type of dimmers drive them, power has to flow from one area to another, and this involves large numbers of cables which have to be routed from one area to another with absolute safety. The system that supplies the power has to be carefully worked out and this is conditioned by whether or not it is a new installation or the refurbishment of an old installation. Various parameters concern us when we move power from one location to another and most important of these would be cable size. What affects the cable size? All cables have a small resistance and the larger the cable the less they impede the flow of current. Therefore if we use cables which are high in resistance to the flow of current we will waste some power in the cables themselves and this can cause problems from two points of view; one of which is that the cables heat, which is dangerous or secondly, we lose valuable power in the cables and do not deliver it to the lamps, thus we get a volts drop and the lamps do not work at their maximum efficiency. How do we get around this problem?

The best method is to use generous sized cables and keep the distance from the dimmers to the luminaires as short as possible, bearing in mind possible acoustic noise problems. In film and

TV the luminaires tend to be used with reasonably short flexible leads attached so that most of the volts drop is in the fixed wiring. The heating of the fixed and flexible cables by not being large enough in current carrying capacity is, however, very serious. With new installations the present legislation in the UK prevents cables being used which are quite simply not up to the job. However, in old installations, it is more than likely, if refurbished, they will have to have a completely new electrical system.

It is preferable that all dimmers are grouped together in a purpose built room where the noise can be contained and ventilation controlled fairly easily. Circuits should be run as phase/neutral pairs usually with a common earth provided either by large cables to groups of sockets or by the trunking used to distribute the power system. Unswitched sockets should be used and at the present time in the United Kingdom plugs and sockets to BS 4343 are used in 16 A, 32 A and 63 A ratings, and these should be installed as a matter of course in a new installation and wherever possible used as replacements in existing installations. Parallel sockets are provided for convenience on the radial circuits used with the responsibility for the electrical loading of the system being placed on the operators.

Most dimmers in use today are the thyristor type, and we have already discussed the interference that these units can generate. In addition to the thyristor dimming circuits, independent or 'non-dimmable' circuits are also required. These are used for electrical loads such as the motors on effects lighting units, fan units and discharge lights including follow spots. It is relatively easy to provide such circuits from contactor switched power although most dimmer manufacturers offer 'non-dim' circuits through their dimmer racks, by either bypassing the action of the thyristors or having thyristor dimmers that, in full conduction, stay relatively stable when this type of load is applied. Other than the permanently supplied lighting power for the units contained within the premises, there is a need for additional power supplies when temporary lighting and sound equipment is provided by touring companies. From the point of view of cost, it is important that the dimmer room is as near as possible to the socket outlets used for the lighting system, thus cutting down the amount of cables required between the dimmers and the lights themselves.

The requirements of the film studio for luminaires and dimmers are less demanding than those for a TV studio and the majority of cables used will be flexible feeders and not part of the fixed installation. The biggest difference will be the provision of much larger power supplies. Whereas, for years, the film industry generated their own d.c. voltage, they now rely on the incoming a.c. mains supply.

For TV, in general, we are looking at light levels between 300 and 800 lux, with 60% from keylights; 40% from the fill to give a reasonable contrast ratio. Although in recent years there has reduction in incident light levels this does not reduce the number of luminaires required, only the size and power. In studios which are equipped with dual source luminaires, there is no effect on the luminaires, the only requirement is that lower powered lamps are fitted.

With a more energy conscious society and owing to the need of lower power in installations and heat loads, it is worthwhile considering fluorescent lighting, although this gives reasonable light levels, it is not as good for modelling as Fresnel spots. New installations are, quite often, a mixture of tungsten keylights and fluorescent softlights.

It is possible to use discharge lighting such as the MSR, HMI, etc., to give high light levels and less heat in an installation. One problem with using discharge sources is that they are only capable of being dimmed from a maximum down to 50% light output, and this somewhat limits the control available to the lighting designer, although they may be designated 'hot restrike' lamps, they only come on at full power if they have been off for a short period of time. When struck from cold, they still require a warm-up period to achieve maximum light output, which may be a minute or more. It is possible, of course, to fit some type of mechanical dimming to discharge sources and the drawback to this is the noise that may be generated. It is not possible to do lighting changes as such due to the fact that we can never go below 50% light output on the dimming curve. Therefore, discharge lighting is only suitable for studios where the lighting set-up is fixed, i.e. no lighting changes take place. To integrate discharge and tungsten lighting requires one or other being filtered to the correct colour temperature. Another problem that exists in this type of installation, is that all the devices require ballasts and a choice has to be made between standard and flicker free, and it is only the flicker free that allow the 50% dimming to take place; therefore the costs are much higher than would be with standard ballast units. Furthermore, when using flicker free ballasts, some care has to be taken in the installation so that the levels of electromagnetic interference are kept to a minimum. Generally the housekeeping concerned should be the same as when using dimmer systems, i.e. that the wiring feeding the fluorescents, etc. should be kept reasonably well separated from all the sound and vision circuits.

9.10   Acoustic requirements

It's no good having a wonderful building where we are unable to hear the artists perform or for that matter resolve the sound spectrum fairly accurately within a broadcast studio.

What has lighting got that influences the acoustics to any degree? In the film and TV studio there is a requirement to ensure that noise does not come from any of the electrical plant into the studio area. In film studios, generally, this shouldn't cause too much of a problem as dimmers are not the norm in this situation. They will probably have more problems with the use of discharge light sources on the sets themselves and the ballast units used with them. In TV however, there is a problem with the use of many dimmers which are usually positioned very close to the studio, and one of the problems we have is that we make holes in the walls by taking the trunking from one area through to the studio and hence allow some form of vibration to go through the structures. Even if we inhibit vibration by using rubber mounts, or even discontinuous pieces of trunking, it may be that the noise comes from around the hole made in the studio wall and this does cause a real problem in studios. It's very convenient to have a door from the studio through to the dimmer room, but in most cases these have to be carefully selected acoustic doors, and usually double ones, to prevent noise coming from the dimmer room to the studio. Studios are usually formed as rather large box like structures with a metal grid, some 3m below the actual roof. Television studios are generally designed to have a fairly 'dead' sound and any reverberation required is added artificially, thus the acoustic specialist has to provide some form of acoustic boxes on the ceilings above the grid where space is at a premium. There is little or nothing he can do below the grid owing to the nature of productions and the usage of the system. The acoustic specialist will also want to cover the walls in acoustic cladding of some description, but unfortunately is bedevilled by lots of trunking and large control consoles at fairly regular intervals around the walls of the studios. This would either be for the lighting system or the sound and vision system. However good the acoustic specialist is, matters are not always controlled by his skills. The biggest problem in studios can be the noise generated by the lights. If the choice of luminaires leads to creaking bodywork on heating up and cooling down of a luminaire, this is absolutely disastrous. *Lamp sing* can penetrate the quietest of conversations. So whether we like it or not, the lighting systems have a major impact on the acoustics and sound quality of any building used for entertainment.

10
Lighting for locations and sport

Introduction

The colour of the light sources selected for any location lighting have to blend with any existing lighting but most importantly must be capable of giving good colour rendition. A prime requirement of lighting for sports is that the sources are as efficient as possible due to the reasonably high light levels required.

When we started our careers in the lighting industry, it was quite common, particularly on sports events floodlit for TV, to see several huge carbon arcs positioned on top of scaffolding towers, nowadays we would get a similar result by using 2.5 kW or 4 kW discharge PAR sources.

In a TV studio the lighting system is usually permanently in position for the operators to manipulate according to the lighting plot issued by the LD. On film stages, lights tend to be introduced almost in the same way that location lighting is used in the film industry, i.e. the type of lights used are not normally present in the studio but only placed there according to the demands of the director of photography. However, when lighting on location for film, TV, special events and concerts, the luminaires, generators, and luminaire rigging systems all have to be specially supplied. At some events, there will also be a requirement to set up a TV studio, together with designated interview areas on televised events e.g. talking to ice skaters at the side of a rink.

10.1 Location lighting

With specially installed temporary sports lighting there are guidelines for either the participants benefit or for the filming and televising of sporting events, which will have a limiting effect on the choice of luminaires and the type of rig to be used. The suspension system will be very straightforward and is there just to get the lights in the right position. The main points being that, generally, the rig should not be too obvious and that the lighting will be fairly even. The other type of lighting required which has to be more artistic and generally more uneven by design, can be for:

1 special videos and films shot on location, and
2 televised events, which may be a major outside broadcast such as the Last Night of the Proms.

The lighting can be anything from a small fluorescent source up to 20 kW tungsten sources and 18-kW discharge sources. Television and film will use tungsten and discharge lighting for location and events, with discharge predominating due to its greater efficiency; thus providing a cooler environment for the competitors or artistes. This type of lighting will be balanced by the use of dimmable ballasts, scrims and gels, and can remain on for periods of time without dynamic lighting changes.

There are several questions that need to be answered when arranging the facilities for any location and these are:

1   Location of site?
2   Has the site been used before, and if so, are there records showing rigging arrangements, electrical supply, access routes, communication facilities and points of contact?
3   How much time is there to rig and de-rig the event?
4   Access to and from site?
5   There will probably be a need for a truss system to be erected to support the luminaires, sound systems etc. additionally there could be a requirement for scaffolding platforms for follow spots, etc.
6   Where is the technical equipment to be situated, i.e. lighting, sound and cameras?
7   Is there a requirement for a control position – if so, where is it in relation to the other equipment?
8   Does the location have a sufficiently large power supply or does it require power generation equipment?
9   If generators are required, where can they be positioned, bearing in mind they are very heavy and fairly noisy devices?
10 How do we get power from the generators to a fairly central position where it can be distributed throughout the venue or location without large volt drops on the long cable runs?

Many small outside locations used for film and TV probably only require the use of a few luminaires and the majority of these will be used on stands. Where more complex arrangements are required for this type of location, it is possible to hire trucks complete with generator and a working platform capable of going up to great heights, to enable lights to be positioned very high above a scene. These can vary from a single Fresnel discharge source on a jib arm through to more powerful sources such as the tower trucks made by Musco Lighting of America capable of raising an array of fifteen 6 kW discharge sources to around 35 m. Because each 6 kW luminaire is an open-faced fitting, its light output is more than twice that of a 12 kW Fresnel discharge luminaire. The trucks, which are fitted with soundproofed generators, weigh around 33 tonnes; the boom extension is fitted behind the driver's cab and towards the front of the generator. This obviously gives a very stable base for the heights required, with an extremely low centre of gravity. The lights can be controlled from a small handheld remote control unit or by an operator with levers at the base of the boom arm; and each light can be panned through 359°, tilted through 220°, flooded and spotted. Additionally, the boom arm is capable of rotating 180° on its base.

10.2   Electrical distribution

When designing a power distribution system various requirements will have to be taken into account. These are:

1   What are the production requirements?
2   What are the site conditions?

3   The design of a safe and suitable electrical system, which will have to take account of the fact that some systems may have large out of balance neutral currents.
4   Ensure that any installation meets the requirements of the local authorities such as the Fire Brigade, etc.
5   In areas where lightning is a high risk, it is essential that precautions are taken to prevent any unnecessary hazards.

The various connectors used must be approved to either a British Standard or an International standard to suit its actual use. The main requirement with connectors would be that they should only be used in association with a correct pin connections and relevant colour codes, etc. The main power distribution cables generally use large single pole connectors due to the high currents involved and it is essential to identify each of these connectors clearly to show whether it is a phase, neutral or earth conductor. It is fairly obvious that any misplugging can cause a huge fault, or a very dangerous situation. Several modern distribution systems do have sensing circuits to prevent any misplugging. Several distribution units in use today have all the necessary intake switchgear and sub-distribution fuses or mcbs contained within one unit, which makes the whole process so much safer by reducing the amount of inter-connections on site.

Generally, multicore connectors and cables are used for circuits up to 125 A, above this point single core connections are generally used. An important factor with the cable rating is that they may be taken to areas where the temperatures are extremely high and due to the installations, will probably be bunched or grouped in close proximity which can cause problems, and this is a factor which must be taken into account by the designer concerned. All items used on the temporary installation should have been tested for electrical safety prior to being delivered to site; they should be marked that the test was satisfactory. When routing the cables, it is essential when in the areas where the public are, that the cables are routed carefully, possibly up and over gangways so that there is no danger of anyone tripping over cables. A problem with temporary cables is that they may have to go through various doorways, etc. and it is essential that they would not break any fire regulations by breaching openings in the building which should be closed during a performance or normal working conditions. The power will be either from the public supply or from a generator and the distribution system will feed dimmers and other subsidiary equipment, which may be located in many places within the temporary installation. It is essential that all feeds to all these items of equipment are adequately fused or have the correct mcbs fitted to ensure protection for the cables and equipment. One of the problems with temporary installations is the variety of weather that may be encountered. For instance, outside events in very humid or wet conditions would no doubt require special precautions to be taken to prevent any safety hazards and the use of RCDs is encouraged. Most modern distribution units are fitted with RCDs and to prevent nuisance tripping they are also fitted with a bypass system accessed by the use of a key.

It is essential that when the temporary installation is complete it is fully checked to ensure, as far as possible, that all connections and equipment are installed correctly prior to the application of power to the system.

Multi-way connector systems together with multicore cables are used to supply from dimmer racks to points on a truss where 'fan out' cables are used for six dimmer circuits, each comprising a live, neutral and an earth connection.

With permanent installations, purpose built switch rooms and areas which are used for electrical supplies, can be built in such a way that they are not capable of being entered by members of the public. On outside broadcasts, locations or special events where temporary lighting is used, it is essential that the public are kept away from any source of electrical danger which might come from the distribution units or cable system. Most supply systems encountered are 'star' connected three-phase systems, but it is possible on some locations, to encounter

'Delta' connected systems and the best method to overcome any difficulties with the connected equipment is to employ 'Star' output transformers which are fed from the 'Delta' supply.

If the power requirement for additional lighting in any venue or premises is not too great, it is possible that there will be sufficient capacity on the house supplies to allow the extra luminaires to be used. However, in the majority of cases there is no slack capacity and the generator will have to be employed. Whatever the system of obtaining a power supply the fact is that it needs to be adequately fused, the cables need to be of sufficient size and they need to be run in such a manner that they do not cause danger to members of the public and/or artists. In the past, usually three-core cables were fed to each luminaire, usually from some switchgear or dimmers. The pop industry found this was too time consuming when they were on the road with the large rigs employed and resorted to multi-core cable systems feeding banks of luminaires. However, there is a finite limit to the size of cables used, due to the weight and flexibility. If they are heavy, it is important that the actual runs of cable, when coiled, would be within the handling capability say, a rigger or sparks on trussing etc. An important point to bear in mind is where are dimmers, if used, being placed in relation to the luminaires themselves. Obviously long cable runs should be avoided if possible and additionally, the power loads shouldn't be too far away from the generator due to the need to have large cables coming through any premises. Distribution can be broken down into three areas:

1 The main intake, where large cables are taken from a generator into subsidiary switchgear, probably of around 400 A per phase and then distributed from these units protected by mcbs.
2 To smaller units placed strategically in the premises and probably protected at around 125 A.
3 Finally these circuits would feed the dimmer racks with individual outputs anywhere between 2 kW and 10 kW.

Special arrangements have to be made to feed the ballast units associated with discharge sources. As well as the power feeds, there will also be a need for the control cables used with automated lighting systems, dimming shutters and hoist motors all placed in the temporary grid system. With tungsten lighting on dimmers, a power factor very close to unity will be achieved most of the time, however if using discharge lighting without power factor correction, it is possible to find that there are large neutral currents flowing and this can cause problems with the distribution system. Normally, with a three-phase supply if the load is balanced uniformly across the three phases, there would be no need for a neutral return, but with out of phase currents there is a need for a neutral. It's no good providing a small neutral in relation to the large phase conductors, it is essential that the neutral conductor is the same size as the phase conductors, and it may be with high harmonic content the neutral has to be twice the size of the phase conductors.

10.3 Generators

Generators come in various sizes, from the small Honda sets giving a few kilowatts to the large 1000 kVA generators. All modern generators are driven by diesel and are provided with large fuel tanks so that the generator can run for many hours without being replenished. One of the problems with diesels is that if it runs out of fuel, it would be necessary to bleed the fuel lines to allow the diesel to run again. On occasions, when it is necessary to run generators for long periods of time without switching off, it may be necessary to make special arrangements to introduce fuel from an external fuel tank system. The generators are normally three-phase and require that the phases are fairly well balanced to ensure that the diesel runs smoothly; the diesels used for the entertainment industry require to be silent running. It is essential that the frequency of supply is kept stable, and this is usually done by fitting electronic governor systems.

Normally, the rear of the generator contains a distribution panel which is fitted with voltmeters, ammeters and the various switches required to run the diesel itself. The normal procedure is to wire to the generator from the local distribution units, check all the electrical system is OK and safe and then run the generator, when the generator is running the main switches are applied and electricity is supplied to the system.

Although a generator may be rated at say, 1000 kVA, if this is not feeding units which have a good power factor, it can be that the output is considerably reduced and in the past with using discharge sources with standard ballasts, a 1000 kVA generator may be only worth 700 kVA with all the luminaires connected.

10.4 Trussing and support systems

Truss used for suspension systems comes in different sizes and lengths with a variety of joining pieces to enable intricate arrangements to be built. The physical size would be determined by the weight loads such as cables and luminaires imposed on the truss. The larger the load, the larger the cross section of the truss. The length of section will be decided by the maximum deflection under a load that can be applied safely without the truss being deformed. The size and length of truss may be decided by the ability to suspend only from a few points rather than regular intervals, i.e. a fairly long truss only suspended at its ends will obviously have a limit of deflection due to the lack of a central suspension point.

The first requirement of truss is that it should be lightweight but capable of taking quite high point loads on the structure with a pretty reasonable overall SWL. The sections have to be small enough to be manhandled and transported; they also have to be capable of being assembled quickly and safely. Truss comes in various sizes and various lengths. Having established the pattern of truss required, it is now essential to lift it to the height required in the venue by using inverted chain hoist motors, with capacities anywhere between 1/8 and 3 tonnes, the most favoured of these being 1 tonne. Obviously with just one straight section of truss, it may be possible to hoist it into place with two motors, but the first requirement of hoisting is the fact that the motors must run synchronously together so that it is easy for the operator on the control unit at floor level to ascertain the correct height and enable the unit to be positioned accurately. If three motors are used on a straight section of truss, it is essential that all three take the load simultaneously and no one motor ends up taking the majority of the load. As the rigs become more complex it may be that several motors have to be used simultaneously to lift a pre-arranged pattern of truss to a set position above the performing area.

Any chain hoist motor unit will probably be capable of up to 40 m of lift, be protected for overload and have upper and lower limit switches fitted to ensure safety when working with these units. They may be used on either single or three-phase supply; the majority being three phase.

The vast majority of the lights used on truss are Parcans, and these are usually in pre-wired groups on short bars, easily attached to the truss itself, and capable of being plugged to the multicore electrical feeder system very rapidly. However, there is a need to identify all the feeder cables so that the console operators concerned will know which dimmers control which lights. In addition to the Parcan, there is generally a multiplicity of automated luminaires to provide dynamic lighting effects on the set and there also may be a requirement for laser projection. Sound reinforcement loudspeakers may also be required to be rigged on the truss.

In addition to the chain motors which takes the truss to high level, once in position, it is essential that extra bonding is provided so that the system is absolutely safe. In addition to bonding the truss by a secondary means of support it is essential that all luminaires attached to the truss are also safety bonded to avoid any accidents, either to the performers, audience or technicians involved.

10.5   Lighting for sports

Most modern large indoor arenas will have floodlights fitted which provide lighting levels quite adequate for modern TV and usually are designed to do just this. Because the lighting levels for TV coverage are quite high, some venues will have a three-stage floodlighting system which provides for normal level of play, expert level of play and for TV coverage. Most floodlights have discharge lamps fitted because of their greater efficiency and in the past did not always have high colour rendition properties, however, most systems installed today will follow the guidelines set by the Sports Council in the United Kingdom and the CIE (Commission Internationale d'Eclairage) in Europe.

Floodlighting requirements for sports

(*Extract from Sports Council Guidance Notes for Floodlighting*)

Horizontal values at ground level

Sport	Class III		Class II		Class I	
	Lux	Ra	Lux	Ra	Lux	Ra
Association football	75	20	200	60	500	60
Athletics	100	20	200	60	500	60
Basketball	75	20	200	60	500	60
Cycle racing	100	20	300	60	500	60
Hockey	300	20	350	60	500	60
Lawn tennis (*court only*)	300	20	300	60	500	60
(*Total playing area*)	250	20	250	60	400	60
Rugby (League/Union)	75	20	200	60	500	60

Lux-Illuminance level. Ra-Colour rendering

Class III   Low level competition such as local or small club events. This generally does not involve spectators, but may include general training and recreational participation.

Class II   Medium level competition such as regional, county or local club events. This will often entail medium size spectator capacities and viewing distances, and may involve high level training.

Class I   Top level competition such as national and international events. This will often include large spectator capacities with long potential viewing distances, and top level training.

Floodlights consist of groups of luminaires aimed at the playing area with over-lapping beams to achieve a smooth result. In the past most of the floodlights were set by a team working to a drawn plan issued by the lighting designer after some laborious calculations, with luminaires having aiming sights. Today, it is more than likely that all the lighting calculations will have been done on a computer which then produces data which allows the luminaire settings to be pre-configured at the manufacturing plant. Once on site all that is necessary is to erect the masts at their designated positions, fit the luminaires and align them to the pre-set marks.

Lighting at sports events is quite often the application of reasonable illumination in a studied way onto an area. The skill generally is positioning trussing and lights so that they do not interfere with the *competitors' eyeline* and they also give a reasonable result on the playing area without affecting the *spectators' eyeline*.

Beyond the needs of the spectators, there is a need for the lighting levels to satisfy film and TV cameras and this is particularly true today when much sport is televised. In Europe the CIE have laid down guidelines for sports stadia lighting. These days, with many cameras used on sporting events, particularly small portable cameras that go anywhere in the playing area, any individual camera must have sufficient light level for its requirements wherever it may be. The Sports Council recommend that the Colour Rendering Index (Ra) for sports at the highest level should be at least 60. However, it is generally accepted that the Colour Rendering Index for film and TV coverage at the highest level of competition should be at least 65 and this is the recommended figure given by the CIE.

The CIE also state that vertical illuminance should be used to assess the lighting for good quality film and TV pictures. Vertical illuminance is used because all objects of interest are generally vertical to the playing area. The positions at which the vertical illumination measurements should be made depends on:

1   If the cameras are positioned along one side of the playing area then the incident illumination on the plane only facing the cameras has to meet the required light level (Figure 10.1).
2   Where the cameras are positioned anywhere around the playing area, it is essential for the illumination in all four vertical planes to meet the required levels (Figure 10.2).

Figure 10.1 Single plane incident light readings

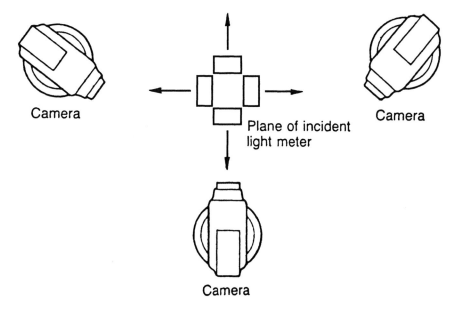

Figure 10.2 360° incident light readings

In isolation, each camera trained on a particular area may be able to correctly expose for a picture but the overall effect of the lighting has to be reasonably consistent to allow for those cameras which follow the action, for example all around a running track, and a figure of around 0.4 minimum to maximum vertical illumination is usually acceptable. As the illuminated horizontal area can form a large part of the field of view of a camera it is essential that a good balance is maintained between the vertical and horizontal lighting levels and a figure of between 0.5 and 2.0 is considered satisfactory. This figure is obtained from the ratio of the average horizontal illumination to the average vertical illumination. Acceptable illumination varies from 300 lux to around 1400 lux for events at the highest level such as the Olympic Games.

The figures given above reflect the illumination levels required for sport, they do not give any guidance as to glare and in practice most of the sports governing bodies have their own recommendations as to the way they prefer their individual sport to be lit. A good example would be fencing, where due to the nature of the sport, any small interference with the participants' eyeline from the lighting can cause problems. It is therefore preferable that the lighting is arranged parallel to either side of the fencing mat and sufficiently high to be out of the participants' eyeline.

11
Motorised lights

Introduction

Motorised lights were introduced on a large scale for the disco scene closely followed by the pop groups on tour, for road shows and live concerts. The idea of moving the light beams by either a mirror or moving the luminaire was a progression from purely placing colour and patterns in them. Eventually, TV and film borrowed the techniques to create, in their own media, a simulation of a live pop show.

The technical designers of lighting soon discovered that the pop/theatre and TV requirements were poles apart. The pop and theatre industry required extremely fast movement for effect with as many colour changes as possible, using multi-layer dichroic filters, all combined in a light-weight portable unit that could be rigged on overhead trusses. Theatre and TV systems do not always require the same degree of speed and number of colour changes, but do require accurate positioning. This is highlighted in the case of a motorised spot luminaire, with hard edged focus. With a projected distance of say, 10 m, the beam must stop within a repeatable accuracy of at least 10 cm.

In the case of Fresnel or PC luminaires, focusing from flood to spot does not require a great accuracy of setting, similarly hard edge to soft edge focus on a profile spot. In TV a motorised Fresnel with a set of barndoors requires movement of the four barndoor flaps together with clockwise/anticlockwise rotation. A colour changing system is an essential requirement, with a suggested minimum of 20 colours, which may be provided by a colour scroller or built in filtration. In a profile projector, two lenses have to be moved to change the spot size, a set of shutters with some degree of rotation are required to shape the beam with optical adjustments to produce the beam distribution required.

The acoustic noise associated with movement and accuracy of alignment can be overcome by either reducing the speed of movement, or by using very high grade drive systems. Motorised luminaires in TV are not always intended to stimulate emotional effects; the aim is to produce fast turn round times in a studio.

Ask any LD for a desirable list of requirements for a motorised luminaire and they will certainly cite all of the above controls, plus many personal foibles. They would also like to control the luminaires by standing in the middle of the acting area, pointing a magic wand at the appropriate luminaire and creating any number of effects. Added to these requirements is a memory system that would record every movement, the time of that movement and the position of the end result.

11.1   Luminaires

Modern fittings are capable of rapid lighting changes and although one light may be capable of several modes, by moving the beam around the acting area we get several incident light angles. As Francis Reid has said 'one of the most important aspects of lighting is the angle at which the light beam hits the artists'. From the point of view of changing the beam shape, light output and colour, there are many useful features in the modern generation of motorised luminaires. The multiplicity of colours available for one luminaire may obviate the use of two or three for effect (see Figure 11.1).

Figure 11.1 Motorised luminaire (courtesy of High End Systems)

There is a need to shape the light beam in many ways and to introduce a multiplicity of colour effects. In the luminaires provided by some manufacturers the movement of the light beam is created by the use of mirrors. Mirrors are used because they are extremely lightweight devices in comparison to the luminaire itself and to move luminaires at high velocity to achieve rapidly moving effects, requires sophisticated drive systems. For TV, the movements required are usually slower due to using larger luminaires.

With a motorised 'pan and tilt' mechanism, it is possible to remotely focus the luminaire. On the surface this seems relatively straightforward to achieve but there are several snags that have to be watched for and these are:

(a)   What is the speed of motion required?
(b)   How is the speed controlled?
(c)   Is it variable and does it have a finite maximum to avoid any structural damage to any component parts of the luminaire?

If the speed is too low it will be annoying to the operator controlling the result, and if too fast probably not very well controlled. How far do we take the directional movement? It would obviously be quite ludicrous to have a device that allowed the 'tilt' mode to keep travelling in the same direction and thus rotate within its yoke. This would cause rather a lot of damage to any power feeding cables or control cables for that matter. By the same token the 'pan' has to be restricted in some way with a feedback system that tells the control that it has reached a finite distance of travel. It is suggested that for 'pan' the motion must be restricted to just over 360° to cover for all situations. Is the device equipped with a system that allows control of 'pan and tilt' simultaneously and does the device have sufficient intelligence to work out its final destination from two co-ordinates being provided. Perhaps most important of all is how accurately does the device position itself and how noisy is it in operation?

As an example, let us take the case of an effects luminaire with a beam width of 30° with a throw of 10 m: the beam diameter would be 5.36 m. On the assumption of an error of 50 mm at the edge of the beam would not produce too disturbing a result, we discover that this would be caused by the beam being misaligned by 0.29°. In the world of digital electronics where the binary system is used, we find that 2 raised to the power of 10 gives 1024. As this would be a convenient number to use within our digital electronic control system, if we divide 360° (the maximum rotation within one full circle) by 1024 we discover it produces 0.35° and in fact most of the systems in use today work to an accuracy of roughly this amount; usually, in most manufacturers' literature, called 'one third of a degree'. This error, applied to our original beam at 10 m throw produces an error of 61 mm, which is just over 1% of the width of the beam. Obviously as the beam width becomes narrower, the proportion of error in relation to the projected beam is greater. With wide beam luminaires, the result would not be so noticeable. The accuracy of the electronics involved is still, however, greatly influenced by the mechanical coupling of the systems themselves and if much slack exists in either the 'pan' or 'tilt' mechanism accuracies such as those discussed will not be attained. The practical limitations of 'pan and tilt' would appear to be a fraction over 360° in 'pan' and 270° for the 'tilt' operation. One point to be observed when going through the 'tilt' angles is that it would be quite possible to exceed the lamp manufacturers stated operating angles when using tungsten halogen lamps, although possibly quite satisfactory for discharge sources. Because a fixed speed of movement would be a disadvantage it is preferable that it is a smoothly controlled variable, governed by the control electronics. One manufacturer publishes figures of a minimum velocity of 0.5°/second, and a maximum velocity of 120°/second, which translated into more mean-ingful terms means rotations varying from 3 seconds in duration to 12 minutes. Measures should be taken so that in the event of hitting an obstruction the unit will not drive against a motor. This avoids the possibility of either damaging scenery, the luminaire body or burning out the motors.

Having adjusted the 'pan and tilt' so that the luminaire is pointing in the right direction, or the direction of reflection from the mirrors, what type of beam do we require? There are two ways of varying the beam angle of a luminaire; one of which is to adjust the lamp in relation to the optics to give varying outputs. This would be the case with Fresnel lens type luminaires. If we were focusing projector type luminaires such as the profile spot, it would be desirable to have adjustment of the optics or if fitted, zoom optics, thus being able to give a continuously variable beam angle over the operating range of the optics. Another desirable feature on a luminaire is that we should be able to have a soft or hard edge to the light beam. With all types of luminaire in use, patterns or 'gobos' will be required and these should obviously be inbuilt to the device so that they are instantly available upon selection.

Many of today's effects luminaires are often fitted with discharge lamps; if this is the case and they have to be integrated with other units, it should be borne in mind that their colour output will probably be around 5600 K and to match with other sources within sets, they may have to be colour corrected to 3200 K. By utilising special short arc discharge lamps a very high light output is gained and, in fact, almost doubled for some luminaires.

Even allowing for the colour of the source, we would wish to change the basic colour of the light output for effects. There are two ways by which this can be accomplished, one of which is to put electromechanically driven colour changing units on the front of the luminaires or have integral colour changing usually accomplished by a 'dichroic' system. Electro-mechanical colour changers are invariably noisy whereas the use of integral dichroics may be less obtrusive from the point of view of acoustics. A dichroic colour changer has to be able to feature a wide range of colours; one manufacturer gives a range of 120 different colours.

If we are using tungsten luminaires obviously these can be dimmed by electronic dimmers in the normal way. However, if we are using discharge sources, even if they were of the 'instant restrike' type, they always have to go through a period of colour and intensity change upon any degree of warming up after being activated. Generally discharge sources require separate mains supply and do not work satisfactorily from dimming circuits, therefore the most satisfactory method is to use a mechanical dimming shutter to control the light output. This possibly would take the form of an iris which works in a similar manner to that of a still camera. Although the iris would give good control of the light beam, we would have to allow for complete blackout for effect and the time from maximum 'open' to maximum 'close' has to be carefully controlled. Two variations of operation occur, one of which is the appearance of the luminaire having been switched off, which implies a very rapid shutdown of the iris, or it might be programmable over a long period of time to give the effect of a very slow fade, as used in the theatre world. Being a mechanical device, it once again is a source of acoustic noise (see Figure 11.2). Motorised lights project patterns, colours and mixtures of the two. Most motorised light luminaires are usually fitted with a rotating gobo wheel and a fixed gobo wheel. A fixed gobo in position is fixed relative to the optical axis, whereas a rotating gobo, when its position is selected, the individual gobo can then be rotated and obviously it is possible to do combinations of either to give various types of effects (see Figure 11.3).

The units are used with a lighting console, using DMX 512 control protocol. DMX 512 is an 8-bit system that allows for 256 discrete levels. When used for dimmers, this is more than adequate but when it is needed to control motorised lights, the resolution is not high enough, therefore more than one DMX is used to extend the system from an 8-bit to a 16-bit. In a 16-bit system, there are 65536 levels available, which gives more than adequate control for the fine movements on some of the lights. If the number of channels required exceeds more than 512, then it is possible to use another DMX link.

Figure 11.2 Mechanics of motorised luminaire (courtesy of High End Systems)

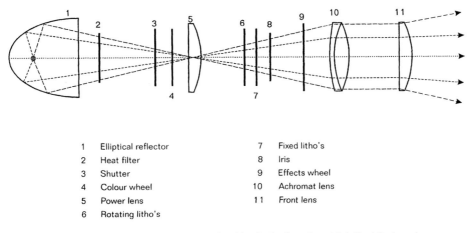

1	Elliptical reflector	7	Fixed litho's
2	Heat filter	8	Iris
3	Shutter	9	Effects wheel
4	Colour wheel	10	Achromat lens
5	Power lens	11	Front lens
6	Rotating litho's		

Figure 11.3 Optical system – motorised luminaire (courtesy High End Systems)

To give an example of a modern motorised effects light, we will look at the Studio Spot 575 made by High End Systems.

Studio Spot motors	
Pan	One 3-phase stepper motor
Tilt	One 3-phase stepper motor
Shutters	Two 2-phase stepper motors
Colour	Two 2-phase stepper motors
Gobo select	Two 2-phase stepper motors
Gobo rotate	Two 2-phase stepper motors
Frost	One 2-phase stepper motor
Focus	One 2-phase stepper motor
Iris	One 2-phase stepper motor

The unit possesses a full colour mixing facility using two colour wheels (see Figure 11.4). All the colour settings are programmable and can be recalled from the controller's memory. The unit is convection cooled, thus there is no fan noise. It is fitted with 10 rotating gobos/effects via two six-position wheels. Remote focus is provided together with a shutter that can give instant blackout. All the functions are controlled by a 16-bit DMX 512 and the functions include colour mixing, random gobo, gobo effects spins, variable frost, smooth mechanical dimming and a fade to black. The unit is fitted with a 575 W MSR discharge lamp.

Table 11.1 shows the colour combinations from the two wheels. The unit can be supplied with a 13°, 18° or 30° lens. The yoke fitted to the luminaire is capable of a 370° pan and 255° tilt, with an accuracy of 11.6 seconds (0.0032°).

Figure 11.4 Colour filter wheel (courtesy of High End Systems)

Table 11.1 High End Systems colour wheel combinations

Wheel 1	Wheel 2	Combination colour
Yellow	Cyan	Dark green
Yellow	Light cyan	Dark yellow green
Yellow	Indigo	Does not mix
Yellow	Pink	Orange
Yellow	Magenta	Red
CTO	Cyan	Moonlight blue
CTO	Light cyan	Blue green
CTO	Indigo	Dark indigo
CTO	Pink	Cherry rose
CTO	Magenta	Red rose
Aqua	Cyan	Primary green
Aqua	Light cyan	Indigo
Aqua	Indigo	Does not mix
Aqua	Pink	Does not mix
Aqua	Magenta	Does not mix
Pink	Cyan	Medium blue
Pink	Light cyan	Congo blue
Pink	Indigo	Indigo
Pink	Pink	Pink
Pink	Magenta	Broadway pink
Magenta	Cyan	Indigo
Magenta	Light cyan	Rose indigo
Magenta	Indigo	Indigo
Magenta	Pink	Broadway pink
Magenta	Magenta	Magenta

11.2   Digital projection

Most motorised lights rely upon changing gobos in the optical path and introducing coloured filters to get effects, but obviously those effects are limited by how many gobos and colour filters can be inserted into the optical train. If we look at some of the more complex drawing packages on the normal PC, such as the ones provided by Corel, we can form an incredible array of images and an almost infinite selection of colours. If we can now introduce that type of technology into motorised light sources, this would be an enormous step forward. In recent years, LCD digital projectors have taken over from the standard 35-mm projector used for video presentations, the advantage being that the output, usually from a laptop, can be fed to a video projector and hence onto a fairly large screen for presentations to a large group of people. During the 1990s Texas Instruments produced their Digital Light Processing system (DLPs), which has now taken over from LCDs, due to its superior structure. Digital Light Processing system works on the principle of a chip that is covered in minute mirrors, each mirror being one pixel, so for an 800×600 resolution we have 480 000 mirrors on a chip approximately 1 cm across. By tilting the mirrors, light can either go to the screen or not, and by introducing red, blue and green filters, for the primary colours, it is possible to produce an extremely wide range of colours. At the present time, projection systems which are adequate for projecting film in cinemas are now in use but unfortunately the light output would not be quite sufficient for effects in a TV studio. The LSD Icon is one of the first units that uses a DLP but at the present time, suffers from a low light output which will no doubt be overcome in the not too distant future. The advantage of this technology is that by using a simple DLP projection system which is controlled from a computer, any image in any colour can be rapidly programmed and presented. Even more importantly, to be able to do it in real time. Digital Light Processing systems have an advantage over LCD due to the fact the pixels are more closely packed than those of an LCD. Other than a much better resolution of images, the digital light mirror produces a brighter image. The digital light mirror chips have had extended life cycle tests, simulating 20 years of use. After these tests, no evidence was shown of any broken hinges on the mirrors in the devices. At the present time, the LSD Icon is the only integrated unit on the motorised light market, but no doubt all manufacturers are vigorously researching into this new development.

An interesting alternative development from High End Systems called VertiGo uses a standard video projector mounted in a motorised yoke. VertiGo is designed to utilise the versatility of video based image projection with all the finesse of control of a motorised light. All parameters of VertiGo are controllable from any standard DMX 512 lighting desk in real time. The system offers total control of the lights position, its colour and shape of the projected beam. It is possible to provide shutters of any shape, irises of any shape and patterns derived from any standard picture or image file. VertiGo uses as its light source any standard video projector with smooth 360° movement through a twin periscope mirror head and software to manipulate any image through DMX 512 protocol.

The VertiGo System consists of:

1   VertiGo periscope mirror head fitted to video projector,
2   rack containing control electronics for mirror head and DMX interface,
3   video effects computer and all image storage, and
4   connection to projector via standard SVGA or S video.

VertiGo operates with any standard video projector fitted with an SVGA input. High End Systems recommends using a 3-chip based projector for optimum operation.

The system provides:

- full colour playback,
- all control via standard DMX 512,
- all effects are available in real time,
- still image or video from any source including live video,
- compatible with all standard image formats (MPEG, JPEG, QuickTime, BMP, TIFF etc.),
- instant selection of image from choice of thousands (Full David Hersey Associates and High End Systems gobo libraries included),
- rotation of image in all three planes,
- scaling of image in all three planes,
- full keystone correction,
- image pre-distortion onto any surface,
- image transparency,
- image trails,
- full anti-aliasing of image,
- overlaying of images,
- blending of images,
- colour mixing,
- graded colour (fountain fills),
- full pan and tilt movement, and
- control of projector zoom and focus where applicable.

When using video projectors we have to have some method of determining the light output and this is measured in *ANSI lumens*. This is ascertained by projecting an image 1 m^2 onto a screen, which is then divided into nine equal areas. Light is measured at the centre of each area and is then averaged. This is the brightness quoted for all digital and LCD projectors.

11.3   TV lighting

If we are using motorised lighting for TV, the larger luminaires used will always have barndoor systems fitted. Although some barndoors come with either four flaps, each with adjustable width of flap, or for that matter, eight independent flaps, we will examine the effect of mechanisation on a four-door system. Because barndoors are made with two small and two large flaps, the orientation of the doors allows oblong shapes at various rotational angles to be projected onto the sets. We must be able to regulate this rotation and it can be seen immediately that we will have to have some method by which the rotation is carefully governed so that we do not exceed a reasonable operating range and run into problems with control cable feeds, etc. Thus the rotation of the barndoor flaps is similar to that of the 'pan' system which allows for just over 360° of rotation. Each of the individual barndoor flaps has to be capable to being adjusted from fully open to fully closed and one of the problems with this would be that if two flaps are allowed to operate simultaneously, and they have to intermesh, there must be some safeguard so that they intermesh safely and do not cause mechanical jamming. This obviously requires a great deal of feedback from the angle of flap movement to the control system to compare the angle of each flap to ensure correct intermeshing. How far do we take the control of the barndoor system? Should we be able to rotate and adjust all four flaps at the same time? If so this probably poses bigger problems for the control system.

One of the biggest problems with having small motors attached to the flaps of barndoors, is that the barndoor system regulates the light beam, which unfortunately is one of the hottest parts of the luminaire, thus all the devices used on the doors have to be either carefully insulated or be in such a position that they are not affected too much by the light beam and hence heat. Having said that, the same would be true of any motors that are close to the body of a high powered light source in use, due to the radiant heat from the luminaire body.

In a manner similar to that of the 'pan and tilt' the repeatability of barndoor positioning must be obviously high. If for instance, a set of barndoors were used to project an oblong shape on a doorway within a film or TV set, the accuracy of that type of positioning needs to be extremely high.

Any luminaires used in TV and film would invariably have to be supplied to go with rigging systems and the whole has to be integrated very carefully. In TV one luminaire without lateral movement will not be able to take the place of three other luminaires. One of the problems in TV and film is that we've always got an obtrusive object called a boom microphone that hovers around creating rather nasty shadows if the lighting is not correctly positioned; therefore the position of the luminaire is extremely critical. In TV the control of the lights is relatively easy because the LD will have camera preview monitors to see the effect of any adjustments made, however in the film industry, this might not be the case although some systems do use combined video/film techniques. The biggest snag in the TV and film industry is the fact that the units would probably be too noisy for the quiet conditions demanded by the realisation team in any studio.

11.4   System control

We have talked at great length about the luminaires but somehow all their functions have to be controlled from a console of some description. It's more than likely that the console we use will bear a great similarity to a lighting control system and in many cases, the two are integrated as one unit. With more functions requiring control, the system has to be more complex which brings us to the point of how do the control signals go from the console to the functional parts on the luminaires? Well, we turn to our friend the 'digit' which rapidly goes down pieces of wire from the control area to the luminaires themselves. If the control system used means that a luminaire has to wait until another luminaire has finished all its functional movements, then this is much slower than a system which allows two or more luminaires to be adjusted simultaneously. The limiting point in the speed of operation is that, as more functions are required, each luminaire needs more control signals. These take a finite time to be accepted and made operable. If a large number of adjustments are having to be made at the same time, the system itself may become slow and cumbersome. Thus, the effects are observable and not acceptable as far as the LD is concerned.

Having decided that we require to get signals from point A to point B to control the luminaires, how are these distributed in the premises? It's impractical to take an individual feed to each luminaire therefore a superior way is to provide a digital control 'bus' such as DMX 512 with provision made for take off points for the luminaires involved. This then means that each luminaire plugged into the 'bus' has to have a code number which is recognised by the control system itself. If any luminaire is changed within the lighting rig due to possible failure or a requirement change, a definite code has to be sent, on substitution, so that the system recognises the type of luminaire in use and its position in the system.

One of the reasons for using motorised systems is the requirement to reduce operating costs, and as can be imagined the cost of motorised lighting systems is fairly high. The cost of any system will be dictated by the complexity of the luminaires concerned: if simple functions such as 'pan and tilt' only are desired to be automated then this is obviously much cheaper than a TV studio full of multi-purpose luminaires where many functions would have to be controlled.

An interesting method of control from Whybron of America is the Auto-Pilot system. The system is designed to send signals through a system of luminaires so that the luminaires will track the performer as they move around on the stage. The Auto-Pilot system consists of a DMX compatible system controller, four belt packs and eight ceiling receivers. The system controller is connected between the lighting console and the automated lights. The controller receives DMX 512 data from the lighting console and passes along all the lighting parameters except the pan and tilt information to the luminaires. A performer wears a belt pack powered by a 9-V battery which sends signals to the receivers overhead. The system controller then uses this data to generate and insert the necessary pan and tilt information into the DMX data stream. As the artists move around, so is the pan and tilt information updated and thus the lights respond, following the performers' every move. The system can accommodate up to four performers, using the same eight receiver array; the system is capable of controlling up to 24 lights simultaneously and it can be adjusted to suit performers of different heights.

11.5   Studio installations

Applying controlled mechanisation to the luminaires is not new and attempts were made in Europe during the 1970s to achieve some crude form of control. The units themselves were fairly cumbersome, utilising standard drive systems, such as small a.c. or d.c. motors.

What type of studio is suitable for a motorised lighting system? If we start at the lower end of the scale with small interview situations, there is probably no need to automate any small studio that has only two or three handed interview situations as the lighting could be left for the majority of the time and even when changes are desired, these would be small and relatively insignificant. Studios of this type often run with little or no electrical staff involved and in fact the lighting may be adjusted by any of the vision operators concerned. Moving up a notch, we get to a small studio of approximately 150 m² which would be the type used for local programmes. In this type of studio the programmes are usually based around an anchor man/woman sitting at one position with two or three set-ups to cover for much of the news intake of the day and local current affairs programmes. They have, on occasions in the past, been used for small dramas and for small audience participation shows – all of which lead to variations in the lighting rig itself. Owing to the repertory nature and repeatability of the lighting over quite long periods, possibly over a programme period of 13/26/52 weeks, there is a definite need for a repeatable rigging system and an automated lighting control system in a studio such as this is highly desirable. The idea is that the LD could, in fact, have the studio rigged with about eight basic but different set-ups to cover most the situations he is likely to encounter on a day to day basis. Having received the information as to the programme content on a day to day basis, it would then be very easy for the LD to dial up 'Set 1', 'Set 2', etc. until he has the combination of sets so desired for the programme content of the day. If the luminaires are generally fixed in their application, such as a 'key' light, these will invariably be Fresnel spotlights, together with a requirement for softlights as fillers. However, to allow the LD a greater degree of flexibility, the use of multi-purpose luminaires is to be encouraged so that any luminaire can perform any function, within reason. Subsequently, there will probably be a reduction in the overall rig. This type of installation lends itself to the use of the motorised pantograph working within a reasonable range of lateral flexibility and height, together with a multi-purpose luminaire. This system, as already noted, allows space for luminaires to move alongside each other so accuracy of rigging is reasonable. It might be that the control system is clever enough to know if one luminaire is not within striking distance of another luminaire, it can move to a new position thus allowing accurate rigging. It may be an operational requirement that all luminaires are parked at one end of any trackway and the system should be intelligent enough to allow this operation to take place without any problems.

What happens when we go to a main line studio, say of about 500 m², where we would expect to cover any production such as drama, dance, music, light entertainment, audience participation, comedy shows, etc. If we take drama, it is quite possible that we will not necessarily be confined to single storey sets, but we may have multiple storey sets which causes problems because of their height. There could be scaffold arrangements built in studios of this type, which might be for high cameras, for example. It might be that we need special follow spot positions rigged which again involves scaffolding towers and special positions within the studio. There will be a need to light the cyc cloths to a higher degree of evenness than would be required in a smaller studio and this would therefore require special cyc lights to be rigged at high level. There will also be a need in the largest studio for scenery to be suspended from the grid itself, this necessitates the use of spot winching systems, lines and supplementary barrels or drapes to be positioned; all of which conspire against the movement of luminaires along the grid system, thus traversing becomes extremely difficult. The problem can be eased in a monopole studio by restricting the lateral movement of the units themselves. If we're considering a barrel rigged studio the problem is not so acute because the basic barrel system allows spaces for the scenery suspension system. It is only where supplementary barrels have to be placed, possibly at right angles to normal, that there could be problems.

The major drawback to automation in studios of this size is the fact that the programmes are not repertory by nature and are usually 'one offs'. A series of six situation comedy programmes will be different in their content on a weekly basis. It's no good pretending that although we have a 'stock set' every week, such as a police station in a series of programmes, that lighting within that set will stay the same, because it will vary according to the action within that area. Therefore 'normal' lighting does not exist. This highlights the main problem when trying to apply automated systems to large studios. The lighting is extremely varied, there are difficulties in moving the lights themselves and this also requires that on every individual programme the LD would have to re-programme all the lights in the studio, or most of the lights, on that production, even on the repetitive week to week series that may be shot in the studios. If the system could be made as sophisticated as possible the LD would have the pleasure of sitting at home with his computer, working out the lighting plot and then sending it down the modem to the studio centre to have it rigged automatically. The problem comes – when does it get rigged? We are certain the Scenery department will be most indignant while they are rigging to find that lights keep moving around. Do the Scenery department have to say to the lighting man's computer 'We've finished, you can carry on now'?

Large studio productions rely for speed and efficiency upon scene and electrical crews largely integrating their work output so that time is reduced in the rig and pre-light session. If we have to have a situation where the lighting has to be allowed to reset itself to new positions, is this done before the sets are placed in position? Because this is not the normal way of doing things. At the present time, sets are rigged and the lights are dropped in to suit the action on the sets. What happens if the scenic designer has made a change or for that matter the sets have been placed off their marks in the studio. This actually happened to one of the authors where the whole studio had to be relit from scratch, due to a design mix up prior to the first day of rehearsals. Would the lighting man's computer know this? And when his luminaires position themselves, would they be able to ascertain this? Not without extremely good intelligence which would require enormous computer capacity with a very sophisticated feedback system from the luminaires.

It would seem therefore that there is a case for automation in the smaller to medium sized studio but its application to large production studios is probably a remote dream and will probably never be realised. Even if we could have equipment of the intelligence required to solve many of the problems, could we actually afford all this equipment. Would our capital costs be recovered by the savings on the operating costs? Possibly with some of the clever young accountants of today this might be the case; but we believe in actual practice this is unlikely. With regard to the larger studio, what is desired is a better degree of control of the luminaires to help the LD. Remote control of the functions on a key light would allow the LD to adjust the effect while sitting in the correct viewing position. This applies equally to all forms of entertainment lighting.

One of the aims of lighting systems automation is that the LD would be able to sit at his desk, hopefully at home, and via his computer, draw a lighting plot which will then be rigged automatically at the touch of a button. It would also be possible to store and replay lighting plots on a 'repertory' basis so that set rigs could be rapidly brought into use.

A TV studio using 100 motorised luminaires would have its installation costs quadrupled. The difference in costs from using normal luminaires, would have to be paid back over a reasonable period of time to keep the accountants happy. The labour saved may produce a reduction in operating costs, but we may be confronted with a higher maintenance cost. Based on the experience of lighting control systems, which these days are extremely robust, it is more than likely that the system will give little problem over a 10-year period. If the new luminaires are more complex than the luminaires they have replaced, they will obviously have to be taken out for longer periods of time for maintenance.

The standard luminaires used in the TV and film industry, although they have generally high power outputs, give very little trouble if relatively basic maintenance is performed annually. In the case of automated luminaires, this maintenance will have to be much more stringent. In discussing maintenance, we have to bear in mind that this is generally only required because of breakdowns. What actually happens if a fully automated luminaire breaks down? If it was replacing three luminaires, the loss would be most noticeable.

Finally, and most important of all, what happens when the systems malfunction and every cue is uncontrollable?

11.6   Grid system functions

Control of lighting breaks down into three distinct areas:

1   control of the intensity of luminaires and their on/off function in some combination,
2   the elevation and positioning of the luminaires themselves by motorised lifting systems, and
3   control of the directional properties of luminaires and further functions for effect such as iris, shutters and barndoors together with the control of the colour output.

First of all, what is the basic function we require if we apply mechanisation to a grid system? It would be nice to be able to control the hanging of any luminaire in three planes i.e. its attitude across and along the acting area, coupled with the height of the luminaire over the acting area. The control of height is very straightforward. When using motorised pantographs and motorised monopoles, control of direction in either the x or y co-ordinates of the studio is extremely easy as the unit will invariably only have to motor backwards and forwards along a fixed trackway consisting of either barrel or RSJ, or a 'C' section channel system. Movement in the other plane would be more difficult to accomplish although not impossible. When rigging a monopole, and its associated luminaire, the only problem that exists for the operators is to have a nominated position for the luminaire to be hung in the studio and also sufficient space to hang it in the position required. Motorised barrel systems require a slightly differing technique inasmuch as there is no individual control of any single luminaire except when using short barrels, other than by use of supplementary spring pantographs on the barrel unit.

The height of a motorised barrel unit is generally dictated by the LDs requirements. The luminaire on its associated trolley is then moved along the bar to a point as near as possible to the nominated position in the studio rig. As has already been stated, this is somewhat of a compromise in practice. Where a horizontal bar some 2.5 m long is raised and lowered in a studio, its position in relation to the scenery is extremely important and in fact, it might be impossible to put the bar at the desired position due to the height of intervening scenery.

Motorised pantographs pose similar positioning problems to the motorised monopole with one big distinction. Where necessary, monopoles can be removed from their associated trackways and either lifted out to another trackway or by using crossover point systems between trackways, be diverted to adjacent trackways. The motorised pantograph system is generally permanently installed to the trackways and is not normally rigged or derigged in practice.

If we motorise the elevation of monopoles, barrel winches or pantographs, the safety cut-out systems employed on them should guarantee not too many mishaps in operational use. The slack wire cut-out operates very rapidly on these devices when meeting an obstruction on their downward travel: however, when individual units are not fully loaded, the overload system may not trip even when starting to pick up inadvertently, a relatively large piece of scenery. This highlights one of the major problems with total mechanisation of winching systems in that dangers are always inherent with scenery flats and other obstructions in the acting area, which really do require human supervision to ensure no malfunction of the system.

It is obviously relatively easy to add a motor to allow a unit to traverse along its trackway, but what happens to the luminaire at the base of the lifting device? Does it know that a scenery flat is in the way or that a luminaire in the trackway is in the position which we've nominated for the new luminaire. At what speed will our nominated luminaire approach the fixed luminaires within the rig? If we are using barrel systems and to avoid problems, it might be that only one motorised traversing unit has to be fitted to each barrel. However, to cover the studio area adequately, we would have to provide a large number of short barrels all over the studio. If we extend this principle of restricting the movement of the traversing system, would it not be sensible to restrict the movement of the monopoles in their trackways and the motorised pantographs in theirs, so that they are only allowed to travel in 'safe space'. It is strongly suspected that this would be operationally extremely undesirable.

Let's look a little closer at the individual systems themselves and the problems they may pose and primarily look at the barrel system.

Barrels which may be 2.4 m long or a shorter one at 1.2 m long are installed to give as much coverage as possible within the studio. The length of the bars dictates the actual operational flexibility of the system. The more short bars are obviously preferable to fewer long bars. The BBC, for instance, use systems where two luminaires are permanently rigged to 2.4 m bars and one luminaire is permanently rigged to a 1.2 m bar, but there is always the provision to add extra lights to any of the bars in use for special requirements within a production. How would we get over the problem of the peak demand of studios where we do not necessarily always require the largest number of luminaires to be permanently rigged.

This brings us to the point as to how do we set about rigging a studio with motorised luminaires which are attached to barrel units. Although the barrel unit only has the problem of finding its nominated height as dictated by the LD, the luminaires, if motorised, would have to pan and tilt to meet the requirements of the LD. Two problems exist with motor driven pan and tilt with luminaires on barrel systems used in this way. One, is to avoid a luminaire on panning around crashing into its neighbour; and secondly, if the starting torque is high, it is more than likely this would impart motion to the barrel unit itself which would probably react by swinging like a pendulum for some time during the rigging period. The problem comes when adjustments are made to the lights in the rehearsal period, where motion is totally undesirable and would be extremely annoying from the point of view of the LD and even more so from the programme director's viewpoint.

Barrel units always have a tendency for some motion generally caused by their position near the floor which involves relatively long wire rope drops from the grid level. This statement holds true for standard winches with motors at grid level or for self climbing winches with integral motors. Other problems exist with installing mechanised luminaires on barrel rigs. Firstly there is the cost of installing fully automated luminaires on the bars themselves and secondly, what functions are required and how are these units actually controlled? The existing barrel systems usually have a reasonably generous SWL but it is marginal when additional temporary equipment is rigged. The additional loads presented by the motorised units may prohibit some types of temporary equipment being used.

The BBC have installed studios, varying from 140 m^2 to 220 m^2, with motorised pantograph systems. The reasons for their introduction are twofold: one of which is that they are much safer than the traditional spring pantographs used in small studios and secondly, if they are motorised for elevation and track position, they can be controlled from a remote point by one man, relatively easily. The basic premise of the original system installed was that if each motorised pantograph unit was fitted with a multi-purpose luminaire, a man with a pole in one hand and a remote control unit in the other, could rig and adjust the lighting in the studio with consummate ease. This system, although mechanised, has no inherent positional memory provided and thus cannot be claimed to be an automated lighting system. Additionally, the luminaires chosen for use have no motorised functions and are standard multi-purpose units.

The pantograph trackways are spaced at intervals so that the luminaires can pass each other when moving along their associated trackways, generally, with the barndoors open. It is possible to obtain greater flexibility to have the trackways spaced at smaller intervals but the barndoors may have to be closed when units pass each other. It is also possible to lower the luminaire to the floor so that its supporting pantograph, which is smaller in cross section, can pass between adjacent luminaires. Grids, in this type of studio are approximately 6 m above floor level, thus extra long pantograph units are not necessarily required. The pantograph only needs to reach 1 m above floor level so that luminaires can be rigged and derigged with ease. The signals coming from the control system, could be in many forms, but in the BBC were chosen to be a.c. mains signals, so that the amount of control gear built within any pantograph unit was kept to a minimum, thus reducing the possibility of operational failure. The electrical signals required for any unit is the 'up/down' function and for the 'traverse' function. In the event of control system failure, it was felt necessary to provide a pole operated control switch on the pantograph unit that could, by injecting mains signals, replace the incoming control signals and allow for local control of up/down and traverse motion. To avoid damage to adjacent units, buffers were fitted to the trolley units at the top of the pantograph rather in the style of an elongated version of buffers as fitted to railway locomotives. It is important that the traversing speed is not too high, so that the units themselves do not swing when in a lowered condition. To this end, all the pantographs have to be fitted with pivoting mechanisms at high level to avoid damage.

If either of the motor units fail, this is a severe operational problem in practice and to that end, the unit should be relatively easy to move off the trackway if the need arises. They would be rather unwieldy for the operational personnel to manhandle without safety problems being encountered, so this operation will probably require the use of a small local winch unit to raise and lower the old and new pantograph units into position. In practice, however, this type of unit has proved to be extremely reliable.

As the units are fitted with one luminaire, only one 5 kW supply cable and socket for lighting power is needed at the base of each pantograph unit. The controlling a.c. mains feeds together with the lighting power, are fed to the motor unit at high level by a catenary cable system rather like those used with overhead electrical cranes.

At the moment it sounds as though we're discussing one unit in the track, which of course in practice is not the case, and more than likely six motorised pantograph units will be used in each trackway. If we assume three units would be fed by catenary cables from each side of the studio, then some degree of flexibility has to be inbuilt to the cabling system. It has to be noted that to reduce the amount of trackways for the cable systems, bunches of cable are suspended from either one or two trackways. These trackways are adjacent to their respective pantographs and carry one set of triple cables from one side of the studio and another triple set from the other. The flexibility requires that all the units have to be able to be positioned anywhere along the trackway, the only limitation being the space taken up by adjacent units. To achieve this means that the cables themselves have to be sufficiently long to allow any unit to reach its maximum towards the other side of the studio, allowing for parked luminaires, and that the cable between each unit also has to be long enough (say 8 m) to allow precise positioning of the luminaire.

The operator in charge of the rigging is provided with a small hand held controller. This controller, although it could be connected by flexible cable back to a wall termination point, is much better for use if it is not constrained by a length of cable. The hand held unit which could be infrared, rather like the controller for TV/video systems, but generally is radio controlled, the reason for this being that some problems have occurred in practice when using infrared systems and their reception, usually occasioned by flats and cloths and other devices being in the way in the studio area. The intensity of lighting itself however, has proved little or no problem for IR systems in the studios and experiments did take place where receptor units were exposed to the light of a fully spotted 5 kW luminaire and still were able to distinguish the infrared signals being received.

The small hand held controller is used to select the luminaire required in the studio and its associated pantograph and controls the luminaires 'on/off' function. It also enables the control of the 'up/down' and 'traversing' motion of the pantograph unit while the channel is selected. It is possible that, having selected the channel to be 'on' or 'off', to leave it in either state so that all the lights on any one area can be controlled easily. Initially, it was felt desirable to control the mechanical functions of only one unit at a time, thus avoiding any dangerous situations, such as a unit being moved inadvertently out of the operators' eyeline. It would be possible, however, to control more units if it is assumed that the operator has a clear view of all units selected.

If radio control is used in an area, it is essential that the control unit is not operated outside of that area as the signals will be received by the base station and this would mean that the units in the studio would be controlled by somebody having no idea of what was happening. In practice this is overcome by ensuring that only trained operators use the system and they have strict instructions that *under no circumstances is the controller to be used outside the studio*. To prevent malpractice, the operators have to input an access code to the system.

Upon completion of the rigging period, the studio control system is switched off and the normal lighting control console takes over control of the luminaires themselves. The actual rig is now in position and unless small adjustments are required is left unattended.

The biggest advantage of the motorised pantograph unit is the fact that springs are not required, thus the unit itself is not load dependent. Any luminaire from the smallest to the largest allowed on the unit may be rigged and derigged in absolute safety.

We now come to studios which are utilising motorised monopole units for mechanisation. One of the problems with monopoles, as has been noted elsewhere in this book, is the problem that to move them around requires personnel working at grid level, possibly above artists and other personnel during rehearsals. In recent times, with the advent of stricter safety legislation, this practice has had to be tightened up considerably and quite often people are moved away from the area in which monopoles are being rigged and derigged, for safety reasons. It would be difficult to move the monopoles in their x and y axes without very complicated mechanical arrangements being made and it is preferable that they only traverse along sections of trackway. It would be desirable to limit that movement to certain sections of trackway, due to the need to avoid one unit hitting another or the possibility of fouling other pieces of studio equipment. If we limit the traversing of units to a specific distance, what distance should be involved? Probably, as a guide, it could be similar to that of the barrels on barrel winches, and therefore approximately 1.5 m. Monopole studios are usually constructed with trackways that are very close to each other to enable luminaires to be positioned almost anywhere. If we have a system where traversing is allowed even over short distances, we have to make allowances for luminaires to pass each other for overlap purposes and this would dictate the spacing of the trackways and invariably make them wider spaced. By doing this, we have negated one of the great advantages of monopole rigs, the fact that luminaires can be positioned anywhere. If we follow this argument to its logical conclusion, it would seem more acceptable to rig monopoles incapable of traverse in a standard monopole grid and only use 'up and down' motors on the units themselves. Having done this, we have taken away another advantage of monopole systems, the fact that rigging still has to take place to a considerable degree, requiring a reasonable number of electrical staff.

If we make the systems more efficient, it is the reduction of staff that is important from the point of view of cost saving. Rigging is the situation where the most staff are required, but any studio, once rigged, requires very few electricians to do the fine 'trim' that is desired by the LDs. If we automate a monopole rigged studio, what type of luminaires should be used? A motorised version of a multi-purpose luminaire seems to be the most logical choice. The ICARUS system is the first one introduced into general studio use that offers control of the luminaires and also suspension equipment. The controls are as follows: it is motorised trolley with point suspension (telescope pantograph or scenery hoist together with one fully automated luminaire); horizontal movement on the trackway; vertical movement of

Figure 11.5 Icarus system (courtesy of DeSisti (UK) Ltd)

the suspension; luminaire pan, tilt and focus; barndoor rotation and barndoor positioning (see Figure 11.5).

The capacity of the ICARUS system, using self climbing or conventional winches, is for the control of up to 336 hoists each one equipped with three motorised luminaires giving a total of 1008 luminaires. There is no system limitation to the grouping arrangements, but it has to be borne in mind what would be the dynamic loads on the supporting grid system by the simultaneous movement of a large number of units.

The control console uses the standard PC using Windows programmes with appropriate graphics of the various modes selected and these are as follows: positioning luminaires – singly or in groups; the system also allows for live and preset settings. The various pre-set functions of the luminaires and winches or support systems can be memorised by simply giving it a file name and recording in the PC. The system also allows for hand held remote control units for setting up in the studio.

The trolley is driven by one motor drive wheel with a torque limiter which provides a degree of protection if the unit hits an object and comes to a stop. Feedback to the control system warns the operator and the software stops the motor after a few seconds. Information is input into the control system on installation which imposes a minimum distance between two or more moving trolleys, which is maintained even when they are moving. This is obviously necessary to prevent luminaires clashing.

The accuracy of trolley movement which is controlled by optical incremental encoders gives an accuracy of +/− 8 mm on 10 m of travel. The motors are equipped with soft start and soft stop functions to avoid any jerky movements. Telescopes are also equipped with optical incremental encoders for height information with an accuracy of +/− 8 mm on a 10-m extension.

The following table gives the conductors within the electrical track system. This works by sliding contacts on copper conductors similar to those used with overhead cranes, and the following figures are for 18 m of track. Each conductor rail is rated for 80 A.

	Motor side of trolley			Opposite face	
Rail	Function	Circuit	Rail	Function	Circuit
1	Dimmer phase	Channel 3 (blue phase)	11	Dimmer phase	Channel 4 (red phase)
2	Dimmer phase	Channel 2 (yellow phase)	12	Dimmer phase	Channel 5 (yellow phase)
3	Dimmer phase	Channel 1 (red phase)	13	Dimmer phase	Channel 6 (blue phase)
4	Dimmer neutral	Channels 7 and 8	14	Dimmer phase	Channel 7 (red phase)
5	Dimmer neutral	Channels 4, 5 and 6	15	Dimmer phase	Channel 8 (yellow phase)
6	Protective conductor	Earth	16	Dimmer neutral	Channels 1, 2 and 3
7	Protocol bus	RS422	17	Motor phase	Blue phase
8	Protocol bus	RS422	18	Motor phase	Yellow phase
9	Protocol bus	RS422	19	Motor phase	Red phase
10	Protocol bus	RS422	20	Motor neutral	Neutral (three motors)

12
Electrical distribution

Introduction

In the past and indeed up to quite recently, film studios often generated their own power. This was in the form of a d.c. voltage, usually at 120 V and mainly used because of the need to supply carbon arc sources used in the film industry. The basis of the 120 V was the importation from America of the lighting technology used in film studios. As the public supply authorities did not in general, supply d.c. voltage, it was necessary for the film studio to install large diesel driven generators. Associated with the 120 V systems used was the need to have much larger copper feeder cables than would be normal in the UK, due to the current being used. With the advent of much more sophisticated d.c. power supplies, particularly of a size such as the film industry would demand, it was easier to supply systems with a.c. voltage and transform and rectify it to the 120 V needed.

Nearly all TV and film premises these days use a.c. power supplies provided by the local electricity authority. In the smaller installation one three-phase transformer will usually be fed from an 11 kV high-voltage main. In the larger installations, it is quite possible that a high voltage ring main will be used with several sub-stations to transform from 11 kV to 415 V within the building and positioned adjacent to the areas of maximum demand. A big problem for supply authorities these days is the fact that the supply system itself contains a high proportion of harmonics and this has been created by the use of discharge lighting systems such as fluorescents and, in many cases, solid state semi-conductor equipment such as computer power supplies. Unfortunately in large premises using lighting systems, we do have a high proportion of fluorescent lighting in the offices, we may have a high proportion of discharge lighting on the sets and we certainly have many dimmer racks full of solid state equipment generating harmonics. In theory, in a balanced three-phase system all the current will flow in the phase conductors and not in the neutral. Unfortunately in the situations quoted, it is possible to have as much current in the neutral as contained in the phases themselves.

So far we have discussed the supply of power for use from the public supply system, but of course it is possible to have a back-up generator used within the premises to prevent any problems if the public power supply fails. If back-up power systems are used only for technical equipment then the loads may not be too great and small diesel generators are a good proposition. When applied to the lighting systems where considerable amounts of power are required, it is not always economically viable to install standby power equipment. Most TV companies install a small generator, sufficiently large to keep a small amount of crucial equipment operating and capable of being used for transmission; with sufficient power spare to enable say, captions and one announcer to be lit.

In very large installations, it is more than likely that two incoming supplies from the local 11 kV distribution system are provided to the premises and obviously there has to be an arrangement made to have changeover facilities in the event of failure. It is extremely advantageous in a large building to use a ring main for the high voltage supplies so that in the event of damage or faults on any equipment, an alternative supply route can be utilised. In premises such as a large TV studio complex, there is a need to keep the studios working as much as possible, therefore when maintenance is required, it is important that the local transformer can be bypassed and the area supplied from another area so that essential maintenance is carried out. Routine maintenance will obviously have to be carried out on all the switchgear on a regular basis.

Within any installation, the siting of the main transformers and switchgear either connected with high voltage or low voltage systems has to be carefully considered and the installation carefully planned. In the smaller installation, only one low voltage sub-station will probably be provided, additionally one switch room will be installed close to the incoming supply and within this room will be a factory built assembly from specialist manufacturers which will incorporate the circuit breakers, fuses, mcbs and metering systems. A very important point in the selection of the electrical power systems is the fact that the electrical designer concerned should ensure that most equipment is fairly standard, therefore any problems can be quickly overcome and the spares holding is reasonable in size. Usually the lighting power is controlled by a special switch on the lighting console, probably remotely engaging a large contactor in the switch room. Although it would be nice to think that this contactor would be operated as a 'no load' device, thus ensuring that the contacts within the switchgear are not burnt by opening under large electrical loads and thus causing arcing, there is no guarantee that this will not happen. In practice therefore the switchgear has to interrupt large currents.

In general, it's not a good idea to install systems that would automatically shut off the supply in the event of an overload. Systems are generally designed to have warnings displayed for overloads so that the operating staff can take avoiding action. The installed capacity of luminaires can quite often exceed that of the power allowed for any installation, therefore generally the discipline of the operators is required to ensure there is no overload of the system.

For ease of operation and to ensure the minimum disruption in the event of any faults, generally with lighting installations, it is wise to have several small pieces of switchgear feeding dimmer racks, thus ensuring no one item of equipment on failing would take the whole system out of action. One good thing about most modern dimming equipment, is that it is generally well protected by fuses or mcbs and therefore faults are contained within individual parts of the system and not reflected back.

In film and TV studios, lighting creates the greatest single demand for electricity. With demands ranging from hundreds of kilowatts to possibly even thousands of kilowatts, lighting generally has to be considered almost separately from the rest of the installation. The loads it can impose on a three-phase system can have quite severe effects on the rest of that system.

Most installations in the UK use BS 4343 plugs and sockets in either 16 A, 32 A or 63 A rating. One great advantage of using this range for plugs and sockets is that they are very readily available from many sources and are relatively cheap. In practice, they have proved to be extremely rugged and very adaptable. One problem to be considered when using BS 4343 connectors in a grid system, is that they will not pass through the grid slots which could change the way in which the electrical distribution is routed.

There are no hard and fast rules with regard to the provision of lighting power outlets in any installation. The numbers involved will require liaison for the individual installation between the lighting consultant and the user of the premises. The factors however to be taken into account include maximum usage of any premises so that on installation all needs are catered for because it's so much easier and cheaper to do it in the first place than modify systems at a later date.

Film studios are a slightly different case when compared with TV, because their power intakes do not generally feed dimming systems. So the main requirement is to have banks of switchgear with individual contactors or isolators supplying large distribution frames somewhere within the studio. These are usually at floor level although there could be some power distribution at high level if a grid is installed or a gallery is provided around the studio itself. Film power distribution tends to be rather flexible in nature using long leads to distribute power to various parts of the sets involved. These days, the requirements of British Standards for power distribution, be it on outside broadcasts or filming, involve the use of specified distribution units so that an installation is somewhat safer than the old style of production. These distribution units contain circuit breakers, fuses and at times RCDs to prevent any harmful electric shock. Other types of power connectors are also allowed for under British Standards for the distribution of power on film and TV, but generally it is preferable to use the BS 4343 range because of ease of replacement.

A frequent problem that often emerges with installations is the possibility of induced electromagnetic interference, either on the vision or sound systems in TV studios, and the possibility of hum on audio in other installations. The most important factor to avoid hum loops is to use a star point connection for the earth conductors within the installation, i.e. all earth conductors within an area should be taken to a common terminal. From our experience, it is very easy to blame the dimmer system for problems, whereas the electrical installation within the building is often the root cause. As an example, in a studio in Milan, northern Italy, there were severe three-phase hum bars on the vision system and a high degree of hum on the audio. Upon investigation, it was found that due to the dryness of the soil in the area, causing poor conductivity in the earth spikes, the electrical contractor had laid a continuous conductor around the building, which was approximately 300 m long, with several earth rods spaced at 20 m intervals. The various parts of the installation, such as the electrical, vision and sound, were all connected in a rather haphazard way to the loop around the building. Between the earth conductor and neutral there was about 37 V of hum on a system used for 220 V mains. The supplier of the dimmers, a world famous English based lighting company, were accused of problems with their thyristor dimmers. One of the authors travelled to Milan with a representative of the lighting company and, having assessed the situation, persuaded the customer to disconnect the ring either side of one of the earth points and to take one earth from the central apparatus area down to this point. Immediately, the three-phase interference on the vision disappeared and the audio became satisfactory. Although the solution was relatively easy, the cost of getting the installation up to a good technical standard was reasonably high, which proves that some consultation, when building or planning installations, is extremely valuable and avoids unwanted costs at a later date.

12.1 Sub-station and switchgear

When using powers of hundreds of kilowatts, it obviously makes sense to have large transformers very close to the areas concerned. This enables high voltage feeds, say 11 kV, to be fed to local sub-stations and then be transformed down to a 415 V three-phase system. One snag with having the transformer very close to the dimmer room is that the impedance of the cables between the dimmer cabinets and the transformer is extremely low and allows very high fault currents to occur. This means that the dimming equipment supplied will have to meet exacting tests.

In the smaller installation, it will obviously not be practical to allow the lighting system to be fed from its own transformer and it will have to share power requirements with the remainder of the building. In larger installations however, it is preferable that the lighting system has its own transformer and when systems are of the order of 500 kW this makes life so much easier. It may also be possible in the very large installation that two studios can share a transformer and even bigger transformers can be installed. It can be advantageous to have a dimmer room with two sets of switchgear, fed by a common transformer, covering two studios.

Lighting loads in a studio; when the console is being used in anger, on some types of shows, might vary from the solo spotlight on a performer perhaps at 2 kW, to a complete lighting change on the other hand of 300–400 kW of power and this imposes enormous surges on the power system. Thus, the inherent stability of the lighting power system has to be good and this requirement is met by high quality transformers on one hand and modern self stabilising dimming systems on the other.

If we take the distribution in a large dimmer room the main incoming power from the adjacent transformer will be fed through armoured cables to the switchgear and then via a busbar system through the switchgear. The switchgear provides for an isolator per dimmer rack. This is for (a) safe isolation for maintenance and (b) to isolate parts of the equipment in the event of a major fault. It is important to have individual isolators for the equipment and not a common isolator to more than one piece of equipment which could cause a problem during the normal operation of the premises; and of course it is not very useful when you have to shut down the entire system just to maintain one dimmer. All of the lighting power will usually be under the control of a contactor on the input to the switchboard, so that lighting power can be remotely switched from the lighting control room. This contactor will have be quite large: it will also have to be rated for live working conditions. There is no guarantee that 'no load' conditions will exist at the time the contactor operates.

It is usual to feed from the isolators on the switchgear to the dimmer racks with armoured multi-core cable and as this has a definite bending radius, it is often advantageous to use parallel multi-core cables of a slightly smaller physical size so that they may be manipulated easily within the dimmer room. Generally dimmer racks are fed via the top of the units which makes access fairly easy although on some occasions we are likely to find the air conditioning installation technicians trying to impose their trunking in the most awkward places. Other than armoured cables, the use of trunking to enclose PVC power feeder cables can be advantageous, due to the fact that PVC cables are much easier to manipulate then their armoured counterparts. It has already been mentioned in Chapter 8 that it is extremely important to provide sufficient space for the termination of the mains input cables. The racks' incoming cables may range from 16 mm^2 cables on smaller installations up to 400 mm^2 cables or the equivalent on very large dimmer racks.

12.2   Power and balance for three phases

In the past, due to the British regulations pertaining at the time, which treated single and three-phase working voltages differently, it was very difficult to feed the lighting system effectively from three-phase supplies, owing to the need for defined limits of separation between socket outlets on different phases. In practice, this often meant that all floor sockets were on the same phase as the technical equipment. In trunking arrangements with socket outlets fitted and especially on barrels, it was difficult to prevent clusters of equipment appearing on the same phase causing large imbalances over the three phases. The main reason was that studios had to have the individual barrel outlets on the same phase; thus one third of the barrels would be connected to the 'red' phase, one third to 'yellow' and the remainder 'blue'. Generally, the barrels were interspersed as sets of three for phase distribution. Thus barrel 1 would be red; barrel 2 blue, barrel 3 yellow and so on. Sometimes to get around loading problems in an installation, yellow and red phases would be used for lighting and blue for the remainder of the installation. Due to a change of IEE specification, which defines *any voltage up to that of 1000 V a.c. between conductors, or 600 V a.c. between conductors and earth, as low voltage*, we are now covered for both 230 V and 400 V in one voltage range and the requirement for separation has lapsed. We can now quite happily design the lighting distribution to be spread over three phases for the ease of balancing the power system. Although it's possible to design the studio to work on three phases, and for that matter to arrange some form of uniform distribution throughout the grid system and lighting sockets generally, we have no guarantee that the luminaires will be plugged in a balanced way or that the use of the lights controlled by the lighting console will not, by coincidence, only use those on one phase only, by some chance of fate.

When the lighting director is producing his lighting plot for the electricians to use in the studio to plug the luminaires into the electrical supply system, he will have to bear in mind the phase of the various lighting power socket outlets in the area concerned so hopefully he can ensure a reasonable balance over three phases. If systems are using any form of 'patch' it may be that the LD indicates the lighting positions that he requires and allows the electricians to plug these into appropriate sockets. With a soft patch system in use it may be that the LD upon being given the dimmer numbers, can programme his console to suit the channel numbers in use. The main point that the LD will have to watch is the maximum capacity of each phase.

How is the lighting apportioned over the three phases so that one phase is not highly loaded in comparison to the others? It may be that the maximum current allowed on a phase dictates the amount of luminaires that the LD may use at any one time. Thus it is not always a simple matter for the LD to ask for various combinations of lighting equipment without having some regard for the supply concerned. For example, if the maximum current allowed is 200 A per phase, it will not be possible to allocate more than ten 5 kW luminaires to that phase. If there were some guarantee that diversity was applied, i.e. all the dimmers were never to be higher than say 8 then more luminaires could be allocated per phase due to the lower individual current consumption.

These days where many installations do not have permanent LDs but most are brought in on contract, it's more than likely that any LD doesn't have an intimate knowledge of the premises concerned. It is extremely important therefore, that any technical literature that may be given to any guest LD in any premises, is extremely accurate and reflects faithfully the lighting electrical system together with details of the lighting console installation and any quirks within the installation with regard to the general power supplies. In practice, it's no good calling for six 10 kW luminaires to be used when the system does not even have any 10 kW dimmers or, for that matter, sockets supplied.

12.3 Distribution systems

Probably the best place to start in our distribution system is to look at an individual circuit and see the initial effects of lighting power in a practical way and then how it affects the rest of the system. The current carrying capacity of a 4 mm^2 PVC cable is 30 A and a 240 V 5 kW circuit will draw 20.83 A, therefore superficially it would appear that this cable would be sufficient for our purposes; but unfortunately that's not the end of the story. It is important in any installation that the volts dropped by the current flowing down the cables does not exceed certain limits. The concern with voltage drop is that items of equipment might cease to operate correctly and therefore constitute some form of danger. In UK regulations, the maximum stipulated voltage drop is 4% of the nominal voltage, which is 9.6 V with a 240 V supply.

Obviously with the majority of lighting equipment, we are not so much concerned with the volt drop to the luminaire as the tungsten lamps will operate on any voltage from zero to their maximum. Our problem, in practice, if we lose too many volts down the cable is that the lamps will commence to burn at a lower colour temperature than that desired even at maximum applied volts, and although not critical in a theatre, this might prove to be a problem with aligning cameras. Voltage drop on a domestic installation will not be very high as the length of cables involved are relatively short. However, let's take a practical example in an installation using a 240 V 5 kW dimmer, feeding a socket in the acting area and the cable from the dimmer to the socket is 80 m long.

PVC single-core cable (in trunking)		Voltage drop for 80 m (V)
4 mm^2	11 mV/A/m run	18.3
6 mm^2	7.3 mV/A/m	12.2
10 mm^2	4.4 mV/A/m	7.3

It will be readily appreciated that the first two voltage drops exceed the limit as laid down by the present regulations, and only the 10 mm^2 cable would be acceptable.

A further problem now arises. Most luminaires are fed via flexible cables and if we assume this to be a 4 mm^2 three-cored flexible cable, then even a short lead, 5 m long, will give us 1.3 V of voltage drop on a 5 kW luminaire. This has to be added to the 10 mm^2 figure.

An even bigger problem occurs when the 80 m of 10 mm^2 cable is terminated at grid level, instead of going directly to a socket in the acting area. This is usually to allow the inter-connection of a 4 mm^2 flexible cable from the termination point, via a flip-flop cable system, down to a socket on a suspension bar. If this cable was 15 m long, we would get a further voltage drop of 4 V. If we run all the figures together, which might be quite possible in a TV studio installation, we therefore have, using 10 mm^2 cable, a loss of 7.3 V. We have a further loss of 4 V on the feeder from the grid system to the bar outlet socket and the luminaire lead will also have a loss amounting to 1.3 V, so our total loss is 12.6 V, which is above the desired IEE technical parameters. However, in the studio, this might not give a problem with the intensity of light, but we do have to bear in mind that if this was a 240 V system, we would have a colour temperature change of 5 K/V. When calculated this gives $12.6 \times 5 K = 63 K$. It is not unknown in practice, unfortunately, that lamps are delivered from manufacturers with low operating colour temperatures and these may be around 3100 K for a nominal 3200 K lamp. So instead of our system now producing a start point of 3200 K, it may be we are closer to 3000 K, and of course we intended lining the TV cameras up around this point. If we reduce the dimmer to 7 which would be our normal starting point for technical line up, we would have a colour temperature output from the lamp of about 2850 K, which is really at the lower acceptable limit of the video camera and thus does not allow for any further dimming of the light sources if we are to maintain the cameras colour integrity.

Thus it is extremely important that cables between the areas and on the equipment themselves are as generous as possible to avoid voltage drop. It is, of course, possible to have the input transformers feeding the switchgear and dimmer racks adjusted so that they deliver high volts on input, say 250 V, to offset some of the voltage drop in a system, but this is a practice which should not be encouraged. By starting with high volts, which would be presented to the dimming system, and by suddenly getting a voltage surge, it might be that we rapidly exceed safe limits on the dimmers and this would be quite disastrous.

In most installations these days, electrical services will be generally conveyed by trunking or cable trays. Due to the amount of cables used in installations which may be pairs of single conductors or multi-core cables, it requires that the trunking and tray systems installed will have to be prefabricated from steel, due to its strength and rigidity. Cables fed by either system at high level in the premises will unfortunately be in the area of the highest temperatures. It may be that the use of cable trays is more advantageous with the cables being exposed to the air, particularly if not bunched, and probably not having the same electrical requirements of those that are totally enclosed. However, due to the need to keep the EM interference as low as possible, it is preferable to keep all cables from dimming systems in trunking rather than on trays and this is particularly important when the dimmers are feeding low level sockets within the premises where they may be in close proximity to sound circuits. As a guide, if separations of approximately 300 mm or greater are used between the lighting power cables, and any other installed cables, there generally will not be a problem. Another major advantage of metal trunking systems is that it can provide an extremely good earth continuity throughout the installation and in addition affords a high degree of mechanical protection to the cables. In the theatre, the trunking systems will be provided generally to the periphery of the stage area so that power feeds can be taken across to the lighting bars on flexible cables. In film studios, as already noted, most of the distribution will be at floor level. In TV studios however, nearly all the distribution is at high level and this means that the system has to be carefully integrated with the layout of any monopole bar, motorised pantograph or even a fairly simple lighting system such as fixed barrels. If we require clearance above a grid for access, it is important that trunking is not put in the most awkward places, thus creating possible hazards to the operational staff working in the area. Most systems will use trunking at high level, dropping it down to outlet points on a fairly regular basis and usually this will be a central box feeding four winch units at the same time. In the case of monopoles, quite complex socket arrangements are provided.

One problem with using dimmer systems is that the harmonic content of the waveforms is extremely high when they are in 90° conduction, and if we are not careful, we will have high circulating currents in the neutral and earth conductors.

Two basic rules are extremely important.

1 *All circuits wired from the dimmer room to the acting area should be wired as live/neutral pairs of conductors in the same conductor size.* The use of several small independent phase conductors with a large common neutral is to be deprecated, because this in itself can cause a problem. For example, in one large broadcasting studio that was converted from saturable reactors to thyristor dimmers using common neutral systems, the circulating harmonics caused severe eddy currents in the trunking in the studio and created conditions where it was extremely difficult to hold a conversation against the noise, other than the fact the trunking was getting rather hot. It's worth noting that it cost quite a lot of money to correct this design error.

2 *Equally important, and at times capable of causing more problems, is the correct earthing of the system.*

It is essential that the earthing system does not form a ring conductor within the system but all earths should be radial conductors, and if possible, taken to a nominated star point. To avoid problems on most installations these days, it is usual practice to adopt a 'clean earth' policy where the technical equipment is on a separate earth system to the dimming system – if this is at all possible. Any circulating earth currents can cause a greater problem with the sound and vision equipment than the electromagnetic interference radiated by the cables from the dimmers.

In addition to the power cables for the individual circuits from dimmer racks, there is a need for the control system inputs from the control room to all dimmer racks and these will be conveyed in either separate trunking or by small flexible cables fed within the racks themselves. On the whole the control cable is relatively immune from interference problems. The main precaution to take with analogue signal cables is to ensure that the cables are well screened internally. With digital inputs becoming more normal these days, control system interference is virtually non existent, as any random signals can be prevented from causing problems by checking all the data for error signals.

Other than the power wiring in the studio, there will be a need for additional trunking which provides for the control cables to and from the various control consoles within the studio and these would be as follows:

1 Local electricians' panel.
2 Lighting hoist control panel.
3 Scenery winch control panel.

These may be placed anywhere at studio floor level for the ease of the local operators, but in general they will tend to be grouped, particularly those for the electricians' panel and the lighting hoist panel.

12.4   Distribution problems

The following example actually occurred in a small TV studio, where the windows over-looked a waterfront which was used as backing to the camera shots.

The air conditioning was not functioning as effectively as it should have been, the movement of air in the studio was not enough and the ceiling area was accumulating a pocket of very hot air. This was mainly caused by the use of several 5 kW tungsten sources, fitted with IL Blue correction filters to counterbalance the daylight, rather than using IL Orange on the windows to correct to 3200 K or using discharge sources of a quarter the power for the same light level. There were also some 2 kW circuits in use for effects lighting.

The studio had originally been wired with flexible cables from the dimmer room, mounted on cable trays. However, it was felt that the cables could be tidier and the tray was replaced by PVC cables in trunking. It was then discovered that the trunking and cables were running at around 80°C.

In normal circumstances, the cables installed from the dimmer room to the studio may possibly have sufficed, if all the circuits were not selected simultaneously, thus avoiding a grouping problem. However due to the need to light the studio to a high level, all the luminaires had to be used and thus no diversity took place.

Taking into account the ambient temperature, together with the grouping factor of the cables in the trunking, it was essential to increase the cable size for the 5 kW circuits, which also had the advantage of reducing the voltage drop to the studio where even 5 V lost represents around 5% light loss in the studio.

There were two solutions to the cable heating problem – assuming no other changes.

1 Leave the existing trunking and cable for 2 kW circuits only and remove the 5 kW feed cables. Install new 100 × 100 mm trunking for the 5 kW circuits with the cable size increased to a minimum of 10 mm^2.
2 Remove all the existing trunking and cable and rewire in rubber flexible (85°C) cable on perforated trays. No more than a double layer with a minimum of 6 mm^2 for the 5 kW circuits and 4 mm^2 for the 2 kW circuits.
   Note: The use of tray allows a smaller cable size for the 5 kW circuits.

The second course of action was adopted as the solution to the problem. As can be appreciated, this merely reverted the situation to 'Square One'.

12.5 Distribution sockets

With a limited number of dimmers, it is possible to have a power patch system so that the sockets to be powered in the 'active lit' area can be connected to dimmers as appropriate to the area concerned. This is often done in smaller installations where perhaps 24 dimmers are provided feeding 48 sockets. A good thing about patch systems is the fact that, usually, the power from the dimmer to the socket is on a 'one to one' basis with very little chance of circuit overloads occurring. If however, the dimmer units are provided with parallel sockets on the front panels for convenience, there is the danger of overloads if the operators are not careful.

Due to the flexible nature of monopole grids, it is necessary to provide a reasonable number of dimmers which cater for the maximum size of production in the studio but, because of the need to keep continually repositioning monopoles and to prevent long flexible leads, several parallel sockets at high level are required. Either we have a very clever switching system to prevent any of the individual circuits being overloaded or we rely upon the operators making the right decision when plugging up the various luminaire feeder cables.

In pantograph systems, when permanent catenary systems are employed feeding the individual luminaires on the base of the pantographs it is very seldom to find circuit overloads. This is because the system is strictly 'one to one'.

Motorised barrel systems will employ a variety of sockets mounted adjacent to the suspension barrel for the luminaires. In general, the circuits will be 5 kW and the minimum number usually supplied per 2.5 m bar, for example, will be three circuits. It is possible that one of these circuits or more, may be installed with parallel sockets across the dimmer circuit so that two small luminaires can be patched to one dimmer from the bar itself. In addition to the normal outlets for the Fresnels and softlights used, there will be a requirement for either additional standard sockets or for special sockets for cyclorama lighting units.

The distribution system will also feed floor outlets but the circuits are generally connected directly to the dimmer units. On occasions, it may be advantageous to switch between floor lighting power sockets and high level lighting power sockets, but if this is switched in the correct manner the power can only be in one place at any one time, therefore a circuit overload is avoided.

In a TV studio, other than the need for the power sockets for the normal lighting on any of the types of suspension used, there is a need for additional sockets to be used for effects lighting, cyc lighting and discharge lighting which may require connection to a three-phase system, and this is usually provided by special sockets in selected locations to suit the installation.

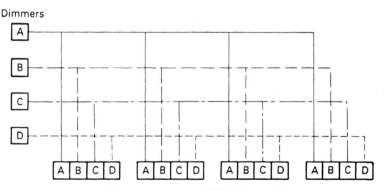

Four-compartment CYC lighting units

Figure 12.1 Cyclorama lighting distribution

One area where special sockets are required is for the lighting of cyclorama cloths (Figure 12.1). Groundrow cyclorama units invariably are supplied with 625 W lamps per compartment. If we use 4-compartment groundrow units for 4-colour mixing, we can feed a string of eight of the same colour compartments from one dimmer, i.e. $8 \times 625\,W = 5\,kW$ (Figure 12.2(a)).

Special cables are supplied by manufacturers to allow the linking of several groundrow units. These may be integral to the unit itself or supplied as separate pre-formed cables in eight, four and single connector configurations. The cyc end of these cables are usually fitted with 9-pin connectors to mate with the cyc units; the other end is split into four standard studio plugs for circuits A, B, C and D (Figure 12.2(b) and (c)).

Cyclorama lighting units when employed at the top of cycs invariably use 1250 W lamps and we could therefore light four of the same compartments from one dimmer, i.e. $4 \times 1250\,W = 5\,kW$ (Figure 12.3). Top cyc units can be supplied by manufacturers with input cables to suit the installation power sockets. They can vary from a single cable and plug attached to each compartment to a 9-pin male connector, used for the four circuits, going to special sockets provided in the grid system.

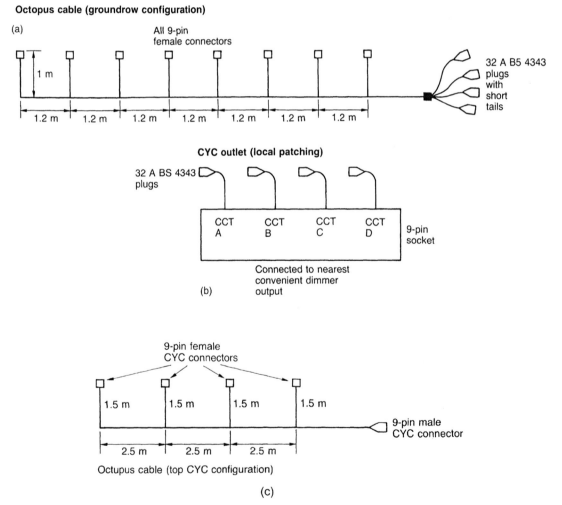

Figure 12.2 Cyclorama electrical distribution

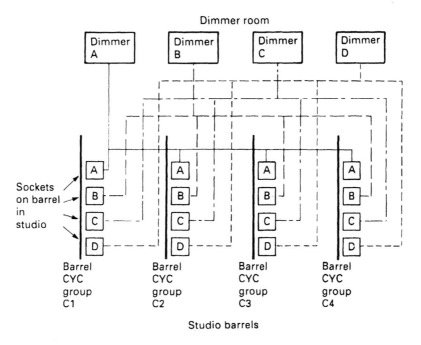

Figure 12.3 Permanently installed cyclorama distribution

As an example, let's take the case of overhead cyc lighting with four units used, each with four compartments fed from four 5 kW dimmers.

Dimmer A feeding the first colour, Dimmer B the second colour, Dimmer C the third colour and finally Dimmer D the fourth colour. In the case of groundrow units, obviously the four dimmers are still required but we now can feed eight sets of four compartment units rather than the four used at high level. For convenience, we can install sockets in groups of four representing A, B, C, D, for use by either cyclorama system. It may be that the barrel system at high level also has a permanent cyclorama lighting installation which would utilise groups of 9-pin 'A, B, C, D,' sockets where the sockets would be paralleled in groups of four, where each group, i.e. 4 × A, is fed from one dimmer output; 4 × B from another dimmer, etc. As an alternative, the 9-pin cyc sockets can be fed by four flexible cables, the ends of which are fitted with standard plugs, allowing them to be patched to any standard studio socket.

In addition to this type of socket used in the studio, there will be a need for distribution, in some studios, of 10 kW sockets when higher powered luminaires may be required. When the 10 kW socket is not being used, it is preferential to supply two 5 kW sockets in parallel, switched from and adjoining the 10 kW socket and all fed from the same 10 kW dimmer, thus upon selection, one 10 kW socket could be used or two parallel 5 kW sockets. These 5 kW sockets would have to be subfused on the adjacent panel next to the selection switch.

12.6   Fuses and circuit breakers

There are two functions required from the protective devices we use, one of which will protect for normal overload conditions, such as lamps failing or incorrectly plugged luminaires creating too much current on a circuit. In addition, the devices have to be adequately rated so that they safely stand fault currents caused by short circuits.

The wiring going from the switchgear to the dimmer racks has to be protected by either fuses or some form of circuit breaker. Before we go any further it would perhaps be wise to look at the magnitude of currents that flow from the main switchgear to the dimmer racks. In a fairly straightforward simple installation using packs of 6 × 2.5 kW dimmers each pack, which would probably be connected to 240 V single phase, would consume 62.5 A on full load. At the other end of the scale, using a high density dimmer rack containing 192 5 kW dimmers, spread over three phases, we would have 1333 A per phase on full load. With smaller systems it is probably just as easy to protect the input to the dimmer racks by fuses. However, with higher current systems, it is more than likely that the electrical installation engineer will install circuit breakers of sufficient rating to meet the demands of the dimmer racks. As far as the output of the individual dimmers themselves goes these can be protected by either mcbs or fuses.

At this point it would be worthwhile looking at fault currents. What do we mean by fault current?

If we are stupid enough to place a piece of wire across a 240 V supply and switch on, the wire disappears rather quickly. By using a simple bit of Ohm's law it will soon be realised that the current is governed by the resistance of the piece of wire and if the piece of wire does not have much resistance the current can become quite large. For example, if a piece of wire with a resistance of 0.01Ω is placed across a 240 V supply, the current flowing through the piece of wire would be 24 000 A. In practice we wouldn't just be concerned with a piece of wire across the 240 V supply, because in addition to the resistance of the wire will be the resistance of all the cables feeding to the initial point where the wire is inserted in the circuit. Thus, the nearer we are to the point of supply the greater will be the fault current. On the input to the main switchgear from the sub-station and its transformer we can get very high fault currents indeed. If, however, the fault occurs at the end of a 100 m of cable run the fault current will be relatively low. Although in practice it would be rare to have a short circuit at the output of a dimmer for example, the rules and regulations regarding protection state that we have to protect for a short circuit at this point. Thus the prospective fault current has to be verified for this point. Why should we be worried about a short circuit in the wiring system? We are concerned with avoiding short circuits in our lighting feeders because of the danger due to the magnetic and thermal effects it can produce in the conductors and on busbar systems. We must therefore place protective devices in the conductors which must operate sufficiently quickly and in absolute safety to prevent this kind of danger. If we are going to use a fuse, we can meet the fault current requirement by selecting fuses with a high rupturing capacity, for example BS 88 in the United Kingdom allows for a rupturing capacity of 80 kA. Another method of protecting circuits is by using an air circuit breaker (acb) or a moulded case circuit breaker (mccb). These will also have to be rated to meet the prospective fault current.

Thus the switchgear feeding the dimmer racks will be provided with, say, fuses to handle 400 A running current and if a normal overload occurs will rupture relatively quickly. In addition, they will have to fuse immediately with a fault current of around 20 000 A. Acbs and mccbs are often specified for high current applications of about 400 A and greater on switchgear. Fuses are generally used below this point.

Many mcbs that are used for circuits with much lower current capacity have fault current ratings of somewhere between 6000 A and 9000 A particularly in the type that we would select for dimmers. It is more than likely that the potential fault current of the circuits involved will exceed these values. It would seem at this point that an mcb could not be used to protect our outgoing circuits, however, in practice this is not the case, because we are allowed to use a device which is not quite adequate if we back it up with a fuse which adequately protects the complete circuit. Thus, if the prospective fault current was 8000 A and the breaking capacity of the mcb we had selected was 6000 A, we would have to back up the mcb with a fuse with a breaking capacity in excess of 8000 A so that the circuit was fully protected.

Most of the devices to protect the installation will have to be carefully selected. We have to bear in mind that there will be more than one device protecting the circuits so the protection devices have to be carefully integrated with each other so that discrimination is achieved. For example, it's no good having the mccb feeding the dimmer rack failing when only one outgoing dimmer circuit has a fault.

12.7 Meters

It's fairly obvious that the fault conditions can be calculated and appropriate measures be incorporated in the switchgear, dimmer racks and any ancillary equipment feeding a stage or studio area. Overload conditions are catered for by the selection of devices that disconnect the supply when a certain current level is reached.

From an operational point of view it is important that we monitor the parameters of the supply so that we do not create overloads on the main power intake. It may be that if you are on a special tariff, going 'over the top' costs real money. By putting voltmeters across the phases it will be possible to see the state of the voltage within the premises, although in general these are somewhat of a luxury because even if the volts are wrong you can do little or nothing about it. One of the problems with supplying voltmeters is: 'where do you actually take the reading?' If it's taken at the switchgear, it's quite possible that the voltage will be reasonable, if we took it at a studio socket it's more than likely it would be several volts lower and due to the varying lengths of run in a studio, it would be highly impractical to adopt a policy of looking at socket voltage outputs. Therefore the best voltage guide is probably the one provided by the switch-gear but, due to the various volt drops within the studio, this can be rather misleading in practice.

What can be done however, is to ensure that the capacity of the system is not exceeded by trying to draw too much current. If ammeters are supplied which monitor the current of the total system, and individually monitor supply to various parts of the system, then we can ensure an overload does not take place. On any lighting system it is preferable that an ammeter is placed in the incoming supply to the dimmer rack installation so that the total current can be monitored. This can then be displayed on remote metering systems in control rooms and in the dimmer room and at stage or studio floor level. The ammeters are also necessary for the operators to see the current in each phase so that the lighting load can be balanced across all three phases to avoid heavy neutral currents and the financial penalties imposed by supply companies for 'out of balance' loads. Modern metering systems use low volt signals to convey the information from special transducers built into the equipment. The metering systems should be placed for the operators' benefit as it is essential that the operators can read clearly what is indicated. It is very frustrating to have a meter with a red segment indicating the overload area, when you actually can't see the needle and where it's pointing. Generally, if meters are supplied they will require little lights to illuminate the panels. Of course, self illuminating meters could be used and in recent years some use of gas discharge bar graphs have been used where rising columns of bars indicate the voltage and current levels reached. On the whole, analogue meters are preferable, although there's much to be said for a digital display where the current level is clearly displayed in figures and not open to the operators' interpretation.

It's not a good idea to have a trip system which, on sensing an overload, would shut down that phase to avoid any further problems, because from an operational point of view this would be highly undesirable. Warning systems have been incorporated into metering systems in the past which, for instance, give some indication of either approaching the danger point or the actual overload condition per phase, but unfortunately the buzzers themselves can become a nuisance in practice and they have never been brought into general use.

It is essential to ensure there is no leakage of any currents down to earth, they should always come back up the correct paths. To ensure this, it is preferable that the earth leakage currents are monitored at the input to each dimmer rack and this can be achieved by having a current transformer mounted at the input of any rack where the input cables are taken through and then terminated. This ensures that the current flowing into the rack should equal the current flowing back up the return conductors and thus cancel out. Any imbalance would indicate a current flowing elsewhere and hence a fault condition. Earth leakage can be monitored in each rack and then, if a fault occurs a local indicator is activated. All the individual rack EL warning systems can be fed to a central unit which in turn sends a master warning signal to all interested parties. Isolating the problem is simply achieved by going to the dimmer room and seeing which individual rack has the fault.

12.8   Distribution on the 'set'

In addition to the suspended production lighting, there will be a need for luminaires mounted on floor stands around the sets, together with small luminaires on special clamps attached to the top of scenery flats for local lighting in the sets. There will also be a requirement to have 'practical' lights. These will be similar to those found in any normal house or business premises and consist of table lamps, fluorescent fittings, wall mounted units and pendant fittings hanging from a ceiling. The use of these fittings is to give a realistic effect to the scene. However, the general lighting effect will not be provided by the practical lamps but by the main lighting being used cleverly by the LD to supplement the effect of say, a 100 W bulb.

We have to be careful with this 100 W practical lamp, because it will no doubt be fed by relatively small electrical flex so that it looks right as far as the viewer is concerned, but unfortunately in practice the circuit may not have the correct back-up protection if anything goes wrong. It has already been noted in the section on dimming that it is very important to select the correct fuse for the circuit involved. If we take the standard studio or stage set-up, the 240 V dimmers will be fused at about 10 A or 20 A, or possibly even more on some occasions. The problem that occurs when the practical is plugged into a lighting power outlet is that the cable size has reduced considerably with the use of flex for the practical and we must insert a subsidiary fuse at this point where the cable sizes change. If the practical is supplied from a wall outlet and the flex has to progress several metres across the acting area this also constitutes a source of danger. Our best bet is to ensure that we get as near to the practical as possible with well rated cable and then introduce an additional fuse at this point so that only a short piece of flex is used. The best method is to use special extension leads, but whereas the normal lead will just have a socket at the end of it, the special leads for practicals will have fuses fitted adjacent to the final socket.

Obviously for convenience when two practicals have to be used together in a room, the extension cables should be supplied with parallel sockets, each one of these fitted with a small local fuse. Thus, the 20 A fuse used with a 240 V 5 kW dimmer, will protect the cable all the way down to the sub distribution outlet. This can then be sub-fused at 5 A to supply the final piece of flex and the subsequent 100 W lamp.

Other than practical lamps, it is quite possible that some of the lights used on the scenery flats are also low wattage sources. These luminaires may be supplied from within the premises or are hired pieces of equipment, but in most cases they will be supplied with small mains leads fitted. Once again, we have to ensure that they are only plugged into a circuit that is correctly protected by a subsidiary fuse rather than directly plugged into the main lighting circuits.

With set dressing lights, which are often supplied from overhead sockets, it may be more convenient to have an adaptor unit with a plug that goes into a bar outlet, is sub-fused at that point and provides a smaller connector on its output. As an example; a 32 A BS 4343 plug may be used to go into the 32 A socket on the bar but the outlet from the adaptor unit would be a 16 A BS 4343 socket supplied via a fuse fitted in the adaptor.

Having said that we need to protect the circuits by the choice of the correct fuses, we must also ensure any cables feeding either set or practical lights are routed in such a manner that they are protected from mechanical damage at all times. This will require special covers over cables at floor level together with a careful choice of route through the scenery labyrinth.

On occasions, there may be a need to use an isolating transformer to give a higher degree of protection to some of the circuits appearing at floor level. Generally these will be those circuits used for musical instruments and of course, these will not be dimmed circuits. However, it is important to ensure that at any time any load such as a transformer, or motor, when plugged into the system is going to work correctly with the dimmers installed in that system. Some hired-in equipment may not be the same voltage as the supply system in the premises and it would be somewhat disastrous to put a 120 V hired-in device across the output of a 240 V dimmer.

The main lessons to be learnt are that:

(a) Check every point of detail at any time with regard to the disposition of small pieces of lighting equipment within sets.
(b) Check particularly on their ability to handle current and that they are suitable for the system voltage.

Finally, it's no good having protected a 100 W lamp with a small fuse to have the cable draped across a corner of the set in such a way that the first person going that way trips over and breaks a leg!

13
Working lights and emergency systems

Introduction

In any area used for entertainment, there will be a requirement for four types of lighting:

1   Lighting for performance.
2   Lighting for working practices when the performance lights are not in use.
3   Lights provided for the benefit of audiences.
4   In the event of failure of the performance lighting, the working lights or the house lighting, an emergency lighting system has to be provided.

Houselights and working lights tend to describe lighting systems that may be achieving a somewhat similar result. In theatres, we would describe houselights as those used to illuminate the auditorium for the benefit of the audience. Working lights are used in the more technically orientated areas of the installation. In TV and film studios, houselights describe the fittings provided in a studio for general illumination and they are also the working lights.

When not using the performance lighting, we need to be able to see to work on rigging sets and to make changes to the production lighting within a building. In the so called 'good old days' this seemed to be answered, if one views any Hollywood movie, with a 60 W lamp stuck in a stand in the centre of a stage. Unfortunately, in this day and age, that's not good enough, because with the advent of measures to increase safety within working premises used for entertainment, light levels have to be sufficiently high so that hazards to staff and artists are avoided. There are no hard and fast rules for light levels for working lights and it is generally left for the users to decide what is best for their installation. Guidance for light levels in various areas is usually given by the Code of Practice issued by various authorities for the country concerned.

13.1   Types of sources

Before we discuss where to put working lights in any premises, perhaps it would be a good idea to review the light sources available, their advantages and disadvantages.

For many years, tungsten lamps have been used for house lighting and working lights and there really is not much of a problem when using this type of source. By choosing the correct lamp it is possible to get a reasonable light level commensurate with a reasonably long life. It is helpful if lamps don't have to be changed too frequently, because they are invariably in slightly inaccessible positions. The main snag with tungsten lamps is that their efficiency is low and they produce quite large amounts of waste heat. In film and TV studio installations a considerable amount of power can be used for the house and working lights and in fact, in some studios, this might be as high as 30 or 40 kW.

It would seem advantageous, therefore, to go to other sources of light and first of these would be the fluorescent lamp. Fluorescent lamps, which are more efficient, generate much less waste heat, which is advantageous from both the electrical and air conditioning viewpoints. One of the problems however, of fluorescent lamps, is that unless used close to the working area they provide broad sources of illumination and are not as convenient as focused down lights which may be required when the working area has a high grid. It would seem fairly obvious that we might be able to employ high bay lighting, such as in factories, using mercury discharge lights. The advantage of this type of lighting is that it is more efficient with much less wastage of power. But, mercury discharge lights have one major drawback – they take time to reach full light output; and if they fail whilst they are burning – and thus are hot – they take a long time to cool down. This means a long wait before the lamps can be restruck.

In the past, the BBC experimented with the use of discharge lighting for houselights in a studio at Television Centre in London. The installation made use of reasonable quality mercury discharge lamps in parabolic reflectors aimed down to the studio floor area.

To get around the problem of the warm up time of a discharge lamp, a tungsten lamp was positioned adjacent to each of the discharge sources. Upon initial 'switch-on' the tungsten light was activated as well as the discharge lamp; after about 10 minutes; the tungsten lamp was extinguished because, by this time, the discharge lamps had reached their stable working condition. In normal use, if the supply to the discharge sources was interrupted, either by the operators switching 'off' the working lights, or by failure of the incoming mains, the tungsten lamps were re-activated and the control circuits waited for the discharge lights to cool down for a set period of time before re-applying their ignition pulses. This required a reasonable amount of intelligence to be built into the control system for the studio, particularly as the working lights were split into four quadrants and each was treated independently.

Several facts emerged from this experimental installation, one of which was the lamps used did not maintain a good colour over their operational life and therefore some distortion was caused in the colour rendering of materials and drawings in use, being particularly troublesome to the lighting and scene crews involved. There was also a reasonably high degree of flicker present from the discharge sources. The periods of changeover from tungsten to discharge were annoying in practice and the operators much preferred the tungsten light, although it had a slightly lower light intensity. Finally, but not least, the installation of the system incurred high capital costs and although it was felt that these would be recovered in a reasonable period of time, this was not the case in practice.

A major operational problem nowadays is the need to have an emergency switch to isolate the production lighting in the event of any electrical hazard occurring in the working area. When the main production lighting is removed, the working lights need to be activated immediately, and discharge sources take too long to come up to full light output.

Having looked at the light output of sources used for working lights, what about the colour? We find tungsten lights will invariably give good colour rendition and cause very few problems in practice. If we choose to use fluorescent tubes for lighting the working area we have to be careful in the choice of tube so that the colour rendition is of a high order. Modern discharge sources can now be obtained with very good colour rendition and greater stability throughout their working life. In all cases it is important to avoid strobing and flicker.

For TV and film studios (working/houselights) a light level of between 200 and 400 lux is generally acceptable: but it should be borne in mind that when it is lower than this, the working conditions can become hazardous.

13.2   Integrating the system

Having decided upon the type of light source that we will use for a working light, where will we provide it? In the theatre, the main areas will be in the wings, above the grid, on the fly galleries and a general illumination on the stage itself. In all these areas a reasonably high illumination is required so that the operators can see clearly what they are doing, thus avoiding any accidents when handling scenery, luminaires and counterweight sets. Other than the working lights in any area, there is also a need to have some level of lighting backstage during the performance. This is to enable the stage operatives to react to cues and thus perform lighting and scene changes. It's fairly obvious that this shouldn't disrupt the performance lighting on the stage itself and thus interfere with the effect intended by the LD. This background lighting must be of a sufficiently high level so that it too avoids any safety problems.

All of this activity is occasioned by the 'live' performance. In TV and film this is not the case! Having set up the scene, movement is then restricted to keep background noise to a minimum while the scene is recorded on either film or via TV cameras. Thus, the need in TV and film studios is for working lights over the whole area to enable sets to be erected, dressed and lit and then ultimately used for production shooting, when the working lights will be switched off. In film and TV, if there is a need for some special working lights within a production area, due, for example, to quick change dressing room facilities being required, localised lighting is usually provided.

In the larger TV and film studios fluorescent lights are not generally used, tungsten sources being preferred and these are usually in the form of long life 1000 W linear lamps mounted in floodlight fittings pointing downwards or in the general direction of the acting area. This enables a reasonably high illumination level in the main area. In smaller studios, it is quite possible to use fluorescent fittings to provide an adequate light level on the studio floor. However, it may require several twin units to produce the light level required as it is more difficult to provide focused beams with fluorescent lamps as a source. One of the problems of mounting any form of working light in a grid system is the fact that there are so many objects hanging from the grid, obscuring the working light. In a large studio, we get the crazy situation when all the winches are raised towards the grid level, we have unobstructed lighting of the studio floor, but when we lower the winches to their operational height, which would be the main requirement when rigging and setting, the working lights are obscured.

When illuminating the acting area it's bad enough trying to position a small floodlight fitting about 300 mm square within a grid system, but when trying to install fluorescent fittings up to 2 m in length, it's almost impossible. Small lighting units can be installed between the ends of barrel winch units and not interfere with the main production lighting layout. Fluorescent fittings, however, can only be positioned between rows of production lighting units and this, of course, in practice means valuable space is occupied.

Other than the fittings below the grid level which illuminate the main area, there is also a requirement to illuminate above the grid for operators working at that level, although these lights will only be used occasionally and not permanently switched on.

In large studios there is a provision for some emergency lighting that is left alight all the time, usually fed from a central battery power supply. This has to be carefully integrated with the rest of the system, although the light level provided is low in comparison to the main house lighting and therefore generally does not affect the production lighting.

We've now got lights all over the place! How do we switch them on and off, because it's pretty obvious that switching them all off at the same time may be inconvenient and possibly dangerous. Most studios have the lights switched in four quadrants, thus it is possible to have a quarter of the working lights on, with three quarters off and this switching arrangement can be in any combination for convenience. One big problem with a high light level from the working lights in a studio is the fact they are also a major source of illumination and can project quite obtrusive, unwanted shadows. So although the lighting can be removed in certain segments, it is usually necessary to switch off most of the working lights during a production so that any undesired effects are avoided.

It is necessary to have an emergency 'off' button which operates the main lighting power. This is provided to remove the power from the active area in the event of fire or any electrical hazard. The application of this switch, which removes the main lighting, could plunge the area into darkness and so that this does not happen, an interlock system has to be provided so that when the production lighting is switched 'off', the working lights are immediately switched 'on', thus avoiding any danger. The emergency 'off' buttons operate on a latching system and therefore are not allowed to be reset until an authorised person investigates the problem and clears the situation for normal operation again.

Whatever type of lights we choose for our working lights, there will be a need to maintain them. This might be simply changing a lamp when it fails or cleaning the fittings on a regular basis to ensure maximum light output. This requirement means we have to carefully consider where we put the fittings and how they are accessed in normal use. Obviously in a small studio, using tungsten or fluorescent fittings, a pair of steps or a reasonably short ladder may be used by operators to gain access. In premises where high grids are installed, there will be a need to provide access to the working lights, generally from the grid system itself to avoid the use of high portable towers. On occasions there will be a need to lower the fittings to the floor and this requires lifting devices to be installed for every lighting unit.

Tungsten working lights and house light systems usually have thyristor dimmers to control them. Some modern studio installations have sophisticated control systems in an attempt to save power. The method of control is to generally have a period when the lights are fully on which is usually worked out from normal rigging practices and this amounts to say, 4 hours. At this point the lights will slowly fade down to half brightness, thus saving some energy. If the operators are still working and require the higher light level, the action of touching the 'on' button of the system, re-activates the circuits to maximum and a further 4 hour cycle commences.

On all types of working lights where there is a lamp involved we obviously have to take safety precautions. It is rather unnerving to have a lamp explode above members of staff or the public. Having only a mesh in front of any of these working luminaires is insufficient, and it is essential that no material escapes from one of these fittings when it is above people. In the case of tungsten or discharge fittings, it is possible to have safety glasses fitted which are toughened and in addition to the safety glass to also have a mesh to prevent pieces of the safety glass falling to the floor level. With fluorescent fittings, specially designed units can be obtained that are generally safe in most aspects. It goes without saying that all these fittings have to be fireproof!!

We have already mentioned that around the edge of a stage area there will have to be working lights left on to enable staff to perform some of the functions during a live performance. In TV particularly, there is a need for items of equipment to be illuminated around the edge of the studio for normal use, but which must not be too obtrusive when using the studio for recordings or transmissions.

Many TV studios are often fitted with cyclorama cloths that at times can encompass 2/3 of the periphery of a studio and this can pose a problem inasmuch that direct access towards an exit doorway is not possible, and an alternative route has to be available. There are strict rules concerning how much of a studio can be encompassed by pieces of cloth or sets and there must be definite access ways provided for safety. A problem that often occurs in TV studios is that the exit lights have to be left on and if a cyclorama cloth is hung across the face of the exit light the camera will see the outline of the 'exit' sign through the cloth, thus the exit sign has to be obscured in some way. The safest method, by far, in these circumstances is to hang some form of material in front of the sign but this must be hung as near to the cyc cloth as possible, so that the normal sight line to the 'exit' from the fire lane at the rear of the cyc, is maintained.

Additionally, around the edge of the studio there will be consoles for local control of the winches, pantographs, monopoles, together with controls for switching lights on and off. All of these need illumination for the operators to see what they are doing, and this is generally accomplished by having fluorescent downlighters mounted above the panels which can be obscured from the view of the camera. Unfortunately at times the outline of the panels can be seen through cyc cloths and therefore local switching arrangements have to be provided so that the fluorescent units can be switched off if the camera is looking in that direction. A fire lane will invariably be provided all the way round the edge of the studio and to ensure that illumination is sufficient for rapid access in the case of an emergency, fluorescent lights are provided at frequent intervals, attached to the studio walls. These also require baffles so that the cameras cannot see this illumination.

In a theatre, there will be permanent arrangements for an audience, this being part of the normal operation. However, in film and TV studios, audiences are not the 'norm'. When they are there, it is essential that the safety arrangements made are as good as those in theatres. Special arrangements have to be made to indicate clearly the exit routes; although in most modern studios the audience seating is generally integrated into the building, so there are definite access routes. If, however, the audience seating is placed in the area on an 'ad hoc' basis, then special arrangements have to be made. This is particularly important with regard to the lighting. In the event of an emergency it is essential that the audience is safely conveyed away from the technical area being used for the production, which is the high risk area. Thus special temporary lighting arrangements have to be made to light the exit routes, particularly around the audience rostra.

13.3   Lighting in control areas and dressing rooms

Although not usually of direct concern to technical consultants planning lighting systems, they should be aware of the requirements for control rooms and dressing rooms. In the control room used by the LD, there will be a need for downlighters onto the desk adjacent to the lighting console so that they can interpret the prepared lighting plot for the production in question. It may be that they have used colour coded symbols to indicate cyc lighting colours, for instance; therefore, in addition to a reasonable light level, there is also a requirement to have faithful colour rendition. In TV, the LD is intimately involved with the technical picture quality from the cameras and therefore has to use high grade monitors; in good viewing conditions, which implies almost dark surroundings. The only areas of light will be those on the control desk. Desk lighting these days is usually achieved by having fluorescent fittings to give a general background illumination along the working edge of the desk, with small tungsten spotlights to pick out areas of special interest. Both the fluorescent and tungsten lighting have to be provided with dimmers so that a balanced working light level is achieved.

Traditionally, dressing rooms are lit by banks of tungsten lamps around a make-up mirror. In recent times, however, fluorescent lighting has been used in an attempt to give a more even illumination which is kinder on the performers' eyes and also helps to save energy. The most important aspect is that the fluorescent tubes chosen must be a very good quality from the point of view of colour rendition.

This latter fact also applies to the fluorescent tubes used over control desks.

13.4   Emergency systems

Emergency lighting can take two forms:

1 *'Standby lighting'*   Where essential work is allowed to continue (this would obviously be more applicable to a hospital operating theatre). In general in the entertainment industry, standby lighting is not normally installed. It may be provided on occasions in those areas concerned with TV master transmission suites which have generators backing the public electrical supply systems, feeding the technical plant, so that a minimum 'on air' presence is maintained.
2 *Escape lighting*   This is required in areas occupied by staff, artists and audiences so that a rapid, but controlled, exit can be made from an entertainment area in the event of fire. It is the most important form of emergency lighting as its main requirement is to ultimately save life.

The essential requirement for emergency lighting is that it will operate reliably from an independent source other than the mains supply. The light level required for safety lighting is remarkably low and in fact for most areas a level of one lux is considered sufficient. However, the light level is really up to the installers and operators of the premises to review, and if necessary, increase upon this base level. Other important purposes of emergency lighting are:

1 It must clearly define the exits and all the emergency exits.
2 All escape routes must be clearly indicated and adequately lit so that people can see their way to exits.
3 It is essential that the lighting along escape routes is relatively even and does not have wide variations in light level.
4 It is absolutely essential that, having got out of the building, all the people evacuated don't blunder into pitch blackness, therefore outside illumination must be provided.

One of the most onerous requirements of emergency lighting is the fact that it has to reach the desired light level within 5 seconds of failure of the main lighting system. It is possible that the response time of the emergency system can be increased up to 15 seconds with the permission of the local authority, providing people in the building concerned are very familiar with their surroundings. However, in most cases it's preferable if the 5 seconds is maintained. Due to the 5 second limitation, it would obviously be impossible to use discharge sources for emergency lighting, and in fact the only types of lamps preferred for emergency lighting are from the tungsten and fluorescent families.

It is also extremely difficult to use a generator for the emergency lighting system due to the fact that they, also, need a finite time to run up and in most cases will probably exceed the 5 second limit. The main source of supply for emergency lighting is a battery system, this can be either a central system where the emergency power is distributed to the areas concerned, or self contained systems where each individual luminaire used comes complete with its own battery. In the past many large installations used large banks of batteries contained within a battery room in the premises to provide d.c. voltage to the emergency lighting systems. In essence, the battery system works rather like the battery on a car; in normal use, any drain on the battery systems by maintained exit signs or maintained house lights would be catered for by a charging plant in the same manner that the alternator on a car keeps a battery topped up. With failure of the mains, the batteries are always in a state to provide an emergency power source for a reasonable period of time. Battery powered emergency lighting is usually designed to be activated for a period of up to 3 hours, according to the size of the premises and with due regard to all the problems of escape from the building.

Battery backed luminaires used for emergency systems are usually reliant upon the normal mains input to provide a trickle charge so that the batteries are maintained in a working condition at all times. Luminaires for emergency systems come in three types:

1   The first of these is where a lamp is 'off' until any emergency arises, in which case the lamp will be powered from the internal battery pack. Normally the mains feeding the unit will trickle charge the battery pack.
2   The second type of unit is where the lamp is always in use and under normal circumstances powered from the mains, but in an emergency situation will use the internal battery supply. Once again, the incoming mains trickle charges the battery.
3   It is possible to combine the two types of operation in a third sort of luminaire for emergency systems, and this luminaire contains two lamps; one which is used normally, powered from the mains and a second lamp for use only in emergency conditions, powered from the internal battery pack. In the event of mains failure the second lamp will switch on. As before the unit relies upon a trickle charge from the normal mains to keep the batteries in good condition.

A problem that arises with emergency lighting luminaires is that if the lamp in the fitting is used all the time it is in a constant process of ageing, hence some notice must be taken of its life cycle so that lamps are changed to avoid failure in emergency conditions. Units that employ lamps which are only switched on in emergency conditions need to have these lamps checked at fairly frequent intervals to ensure no possible malfunction when used. It is also extremely important that all units installed in the premises are switched onto the emergency state at fairly frequent intervals to ensure that the batteries are working correctly.

In the entertainment industry the members of staff working in the premises will be aware of the escape routes, exits and emergency exits. Unfortunately, members of the public may come into these premises and will be totally unfamiliar with the layout of the building. This requires that the operators of any premises have to ensure that all exits, be they permanent or temporary, have to be clearly marked. As well as the need to have clear exit signs and lighting for the emergency routes, there is a need for additional lighting where hazards may exist along a route, such as stairways and any other type of obstruction. Obviously these must be clearly lit so that no additional problems are caused by people tripping over obstacles. It goes without saying that, if in doubt, put more emergency lighting in.

14
Safety

14.1 General measures for safety

Electrical

Research has shown that voltages below 50 V a.c. do not generally cause problems. From 50 V up to 1000 V a.c. (which is termed Low Voltage), the problems will be in direct relationship to Ohms Law which states 'the greater the voltage for a given resistance, the higher the current'. However, it must be realised this is an extremely simplistic view and the human body is quite complex but is generally considered mostly resistive. An electric shock results from the victim touching a part which is live or charged with electricity so that their body completes the electrical circuit to ground. At higher voltages, actual contact is not necessary because the current can jump appreciable distances. For a given current path through the human body, the danger to persons depends mainly on the magnitude and duration of the current flow. If recovery is not spontaneous or produced by prompt emergency treatment, the shock can prove to be fatal.

Muscular spasm may prevent the victim from letting go if they are touching a live part, the contracted chest muscles may prevent them from breathing and shouting for help and the pain and panic may cause sweating. With wet skin, the effects of the shock will be aggravated. The effect on the heart generally depends on the magnitude and duration of the shock and at what stage in the heart cycle the shock occurs. Generally, alternating currents will affect the heart to a greater extent than direct currents. At radio frequencies, burning is the main effect and fatal shock less likely.

In the United Kingdom about 50 people die each year, at work and in the home, from shocks from the normal 240 V domestic supply. In the majority of cases the victim received a shock between an exposed live part and earth. There are also a few accidents in the United Kingdom on lower voltage supplies in the range of 110/125 V and experience in countries where the supply system lies between 110 V and 120 V shows that electric shocks at these voltages can also be fatal.

Shock prevention

Electric shocks may be prevented by taking some of the following precautions, such as:

(a)   using low voltages,
(b)   insulating and/or enclosing live parts,

(c)   preventing conducting parts, not normally live, from becoming live:
    (i)   by earthing and automatic disconnection,
    (ii) by double insulation, and
    (iii) by separating the supply from mains and earth (isolating transformer).
(d)   selecting equipment suitable for the environment in which is to be used,
(e)   using equipment as directed in the manufacturers' instructions, and
(f) ensuring that the electrical equipment is tested and maintained.

Residual Current Devices

If someone receives an electric shock from a part which is live, the current flows to earth through the victim's body. RCDs can be obtained which are sensitive enough to detect this current and will trip the supply in a few milliseconds. However, it should be noted that the RCD does not prevent the person getting a shock nor does it limit the magnitude of the current, but it will limit the duration of the shock.

    Most RCDs are designed for 50 Hz sinusoidal a.c. mains currents. Conventional RCDs designed for 50 Hz supplies will probably not trip should an earth fault occur when used with dimmer circuits. Some manufacturers do make a much higher grade of RCD which can sense fault currents of around 30 mA at all dimmer settings above 50 V, however, it must be noted that the tripping time may vary as a result of the dimming.

Note: Never bypass any RCD if the equipment it is protecting causes it to trip – investigate why it has happened and take any necessary remedial measures.

Emergency systems

The IEE regulations requires that a means of interrupting the supply for the purpose of emergency switching shall be capable of cutting off the full load current of the relevant part of the installation. The regulations go on to state:

Where practical a device for emergency switching shall be manually operated directly interrupting the main circuit. A device such as a circuit breaker or a contactor operated by remote control shall open on de-energisation of the coil, or another technique of suitable reliability shall be employed.

The operating means (such as handle or push button) for a device for emergency switching shall be clearly identifiable and preferably coloured 'red'. It shall be installed in a readily accessible position where the hazard might occur and where appropriate, further devices shall be provided where additional emergency switching may be needed.

The operating means of a device for emergency switching shall be of the latching type or capable of being restrained in the 'OFF' or 'STOP' position. The release of the emergency switching device shall not re-energise the equipment concerned.

The re-energising of the equipment has to be carried out by approved personnel, such as engineers or electricians, to ensure that the hazard that caused the 'emergency' has been dealt with correctly.

Fire extinguishers

Extinguishers come in various types:

1 water extinguishers,
2 foam extinguishers,
3 dry powder extinguishers,
4 carbon dioxide extinguishers, and
5 vaporising liquid extinguishers.

Ensure that the correct type of extinguishers are placed where they are immediately available and clearly marked to ensure that the wrong one is not used. It is essential for staff to be familiar with the colour codes of the various extinguishers and to know what it contains and how it works.

Fire lanes and evacuation procedures

Safety law is framed to preserve life rather than property and therefore the law demands a fire certificate which carries details of how to escape in the event of a fire. It also demands that the staff should be familiar with the means of escape and the escape routes, which must be clearly marked. In studio premises there will always be fairly well defined safety procedures issued by the management but when on location it is very easy to fall in the trap of putting bits of temporary scenery in the way so as to obscure possible safety routes and these should be carefully thought out prior to doing any work.

Working platforms

Scaffold platforms are a very convenient method of getting to high positions with relative safety. Having said that, the safety only comes about by following carefully *all* the instructions with regard to scaffolding, portable towers, etc. We are not so much concerned with permanent working scaffold platforms, but mobile platforms, which are used to gain access to a lighting grid to work with the electrical system and the luminaires. The height of a mobile scaffold tower must not be more than three times the base width, if used out of doors, or three and a half times, if used indoors. When considering the base width this must also include any outriggers which are used. The cardinal rules is that mobile scaffold platforms *must not be moved whilst any person is on the platform* and movement must be accomplished only by pushing or pulling *at the base* of the platform. A sobering thought is the statistic that about 1100 people each year suffer from accidents due to falling from scaffold platforms.

14.2   Luminaires and EN 60598-2-17 (BS4533)

The following suggestions and remarks regarding safety considerations in the design and operation of luminaires should be taken as a guide to help you through EN 60598-2-17 which is now harmonised across Europe (EEC and EFTA) and Canada accepts it as an alternative to CSA standards, however, the USA will only accept UL 1573 which is considerably different to the European standards.

The main basis of the following is EN 60598-2-17 with an overlay of good practice accumulated by the authors over many years of experience. However, it is up to the individual to determine his own interpretation of the standards because the authors cannot accept responsibility for their accuracy. It is also assumed that the reader already has a sound knowledge of good electrical practice.

A luminaire should be designed in such a way that in the event of a lamp exploding, fragments of glass or quartz 3 mm in size should not escape directly in line, from a lamp, through a ventilator or other aperture. If the ventilation system is designed with a labyrinth or fitted with a mesh to prevent pieces of glass or quartz 3 mm in size coming out from a directly exploding lamp in such a way that the glass is caught within the labyrinth or by the mesh, this is accepted within the standard.

Open faced luminaires require either a safety glass with a minimum thickness of 3 mm or a safety mesh that will not permit pieces of glass or quartz 3 mm in size to pass through it. Luminaires that have a single lens require a safety mesh in front of the lens of such a size as to prevent pieces of glass 25 mm passing through it, however luminaires with more than one lens do not require a mesh, but it is our opinion that it is good practice to fit one. Luminaires that have a safety glass require a safety mesh in front of it, of such a size as to prevent pieces of glass 12 mm passing through it. The glass and mesh must be captive in the luminaire. In the event of a safety glass or lens cracking, its mounting must retain the broken pieces in position. The mechanical heat test for the safety glass is carried out by placing the luminaire in the horizontal position and burning it until it reaches a stable temperature, then water at a temperature of 15°C is sprinkled onto it by hand. The unit is allowed to cool and reheated and the test is repeated three times; the glass can crack, but it must be retained in its position in the housing. Tests for halogen lamp shields require that they withstand an exploding lamp and to ensure that any hot fragments that do escape do not ignite a gauze placed under the luminaire.

The mechanical connection between the yoke and the luminaire must be locked against loosening. This is to prevent the pivots working loose, during operational use, by tilting the housing. Forms of locking may consist of either fitting a locknut or drilling and pinning the pivot shaft.

The yoke must have earth continuity to the housing if there is a risk of a single electrical fault.

The mechanical safety of the yoke requires a 10:1 safety factor on each leg of the yoke so that if one side of the yoke is disconnected from the housing the remaining leg provides a 10:1 safety factor. The test procedure is to hang the luminaire from its spigot and apply a test load to the luminaire. Since the safety factor is to 10:1, a weight of *nine times* the total weight of the luminaire (including all accessories) is added to the housing, making a total of *10 times* the original weight. The yoke may deform under test, but it must not break. Discussions have taken place over a period of time to ascertain whether the safety factor could be reduced.

The size and type of spigot to be used can be determined from the following: Luminaires weighing up to 7.5 kg may use a 16 mm diameter spigot and it can be made of either steel or aluminium. Over 7.5 kg a 28.6 mm spigot is required and it must be manufactured from steel (aluminium is not permitted). A hybrid spigot has been developed which dimensionally suits the German DIN specification together with the British and USA standards.

A dedicated anchor point must be provided on the housing (unless it is intended for floor mounting or to be used as a hand held luminaire) whereby the safety bond can be passed over the primary means of suspension, through the yoke and terminated at the anchor point. In this way the housing will be arrested even if the yoke breaks. The test procedure is as follows. The unit will have all its accessories attached and lifted 300 mm and allowed to free fall until it is arrested by the safety bond. This procedure is repeated 30 times. During the test it is not

Figure 14.1 Spigots

permitted for any part of the luminaire or its accessories to become detached although they may become deformed.

A German DIN specification exists for the size of receptacles for colour frames and barndoors. This is to ensure a good mechanical fit of component parts together with ease of interchange-ability with other manufacturers' items of equipment. Although this is not a formal requirement it represents a very desirable feature.

If possible, luminaires should be designed to cater for the sizes quoted in these standards. The major manufacturers in Europe have already adopted these sizes.

Nominal size of colour frames – German DIN standard No. 15-560 part 38

The following dimensions (in millimetres) can be the diameter of a round colour frame or the size of a square frame: 120, 150, 160, 180, 210, 240, 270, 360, 390, 450, 480, 540.

The top latch which is normally provided for retaining the colour frame and barndoors must be self applying so that it does not rely on the operator to close it. In this way, the operator is obliged to hold the retaining clip out of the way whilst he withdraws the barndoor or colour frame. On letting go of the catch, it returns to its locked position.

PVC or other plastic cables should not be used on luminaires. This is because the cable will deform with the heat if it touches the side of the housing. The mains input cable must have a sleeve of insulation where it is clamped at the cable entry.

Any cable passing through a hole in sheet metal must be protected by a secondary sleeving to avoid mechanical damage to its insulation.

All electrical components such as switches, cables, terminal blocks, lampholders, etc. must be manufactured to the appropriate standards for the individual items concerned. Otherwise the luminaires could fail acceptance tests due to the use of unsatisfactory component parts.

The termination point of the incoming earth should be in view when the mains input terminals are exposed to enable an inspector to see that the earth is connected. The international earth symbol must be used adjacent to the incoming earth terminal. This must be punched into the metal or stuck onto it, so that it cannot be removed. The earth symbol must be a minimum of 5 mm high. Earthing washers are to be used to cut through the paint and ensure a good earth. The earthing screw is to be a minimum of 4 mm diameter with a machine cut thread, self tapping screws are *not* acceptable. The screw size will increase with electrical current requirements but cannot be reduced for mechanical strength reasons. The screw must be plated steel or manufactured from brass or copper.

All metal parts that can be touched on the outside of the luminaire, that could come into contact with a live part under a single fault condition, must be earthed. The lamp carriage must have a direct earth continuity wire, a scraping earth conducted along tracks is usually insufficient. Under no circumstances can push-on terminals be used for earth connections to luminaires that draw more than 3 A from the mains supply.

The terminal block should be designed so that it would allow one strand of wire to turn back from its connection by 8 mm and *not touch* adjacent terminals or metalwork in the luminaire. If the terminal block employed does not automatically perform this function, an insulating material must be placed under the block or used as a barrier between terminals so that isolation is achieved.

Warning labels required on the housing

The following recommended warnings are so numerous that it would require a larger housing just to display them on small luminaires. However, they are being quoted verbatim from the standards.

- *Before opening disconnect all poles from the electrical supply.* (The minimum height for the lettering is to be not less than 2 mm and 5 mm for graphical symbols.)
- *The top of the unit must be indicated to prevent it being mounted upside down.* (A broad arrow symbol may be used with the addition of the word 'TOP' or 'OBEN' in German. The minimum height of the arrow symbol is 5 mm.)
- *Replace any cracked protective shield.*
- *To be serviced by qualified personnel.*
- *State the distance from the lens to a flammable surface.* (When the temperature in the centre of the beam is $\leq 90°C$ with an ambient temperature of 25°C. Use the international symbol.)
- *The burning angle must be stated x° above horizontal, y° below horizontal.*
- *Observe the lamp manufacturers recommendations.*
- *Maximum voltage with an a.c. or d.c. symbol.*
- *The maximum current.*
- *The maximum wattage.* (State if there is more than one lamp used i.e. 4 × 1250 W.)
- *The frequency of the supply* (which may be in the instruction leaflet).
- *The maximum case temperature in degrees Celsius.* (This is defined as the hottest part of the housing that could be touched from the outside, also the maximum ambient temperature (Ta) if it is not 25°C.)
- *The weight, complete with lamp and all accessories.*
- *The manufacturers' name and type number.* (The label must have permanent print and must be attached to the luminaire with rivets or stuck so that it cannot be removed.)

Safety instruction sheet

This must be provided with every luminaire when it is sold. The sheet must describe all the hazards involved with lamps and luminaires (see Operating & Safety Instructions).
   The following should also be noted:

- *Ambient temperature*   All luminaires should be designed to work in a maximum ambient temperature of 45°C (good practice but not a standard).
- *Fuses*   The value of an integral fuse must be stated adjacent to the fuseholder, so that it is apparent to the operator when changing a fuse what value it should be.
- *Luminaire data sheet*   This must be enclosed with each luminaire and include the following:
   – The same information that appears on the warning labels.
   – The fixing instructions of how the unit should be mounted or suspended.
   – A description and location of the safety bond anchor point and how to correctly attach the safety bond.
- In addition, a description and reference numbers for the following items:
   – Safety glass
   – Wire guard
   – Lens
   – Safety bond
   – A list of all lamps that can be used in the luminaire with details of their voltage, wattage, life, colour temperature and any other parameters that are relevant.
   – A list of all accessories
   – Recommended stands
   – Spares.

Note: It is not a standard requirement to provide spares information, because the sheet will be particular to each unit. It is however, a good opportunity for the manufacturer to identify the spares at this time.

Additional requirements for discharge source

- *Luminaires*   These require the same standards as the tungsten halogen units, plus the following:
   – *UV Protection*   Where a luminaire is not fitted with a glass lens it is recommended that a safety glass is provided to absorb the UV radiation from the lamp. The glass should have a minimum thickness of 3 mm to provide adequate mechanical strength. However, with higher wattage luminaires, an increased thickness of glass will be required to give added strength.
   – *UV Radiation*   It is prudent for a manufacturer to have an independent test certificate from a test house such as the National Physical Laboratory to determine that luminaires do not exceed any dangerous UV radiation levels or to conduct the UV tests themselves and 'self certify' to the appropriate standards.
- *Warning on housing*   For UV protection, the safety glass must remain in position and be replaced if it is cracked, broken or has deep scratches.
- *Door opening*   The lens door may be screwed closed, in which case it would not require a safety switch. In the event that the door can be opened without a tool, then a double pole mains isolation switch can be used (good practice but not a standard) which must be

activated by the glass of the lens so that the unit will not work if the lens is removed or the door is open. The activator must be designed so that it cannot be operated by hand, i.e. enclosed in a tube with a push rod to prevent the operator holding the switch closed and operating the unit. Some manufacturers use a trip relay that does not re-activate until it is manually reset. The same safety requirements apply to open fronted discharge luminaires that are fitted with a safety glass.

● *The following warning is required*: *'Do not open for "x" seconds after switching off'*.

Note: This is due to the hot lamps having high internal pressures and seeks to avoid explosions caused by cold air blowing on the lamp. This instruction is only required on luminaires declared by the manufacturer 'a danger when hot', particularly xenon lamps.

Operating and safety instructions: Lamps and luminaires

Manufacturers are required to provide the following information for the safe operation of luminaires and their associated lamps in the entertainment industry.

It is in the interests of every person purchasing or operating luminaires to read the following *typical* instructions, because the manufacturer is making you aware of the possible safety problems. This will prevent you being in the unenviable position, after an accident, of the manufacturer saying 'I told you so!'

1 Luminaires should be marked with the maximum operating current. Observe the following colour code (Europe).
   Brown wire – live
   Blue wire – neutral
   Green/yellow wire – earth
2 When connecting the luminaire to the mains supply, ensure that it is effectively earthed, that the mains supply is at the rated voltage and that the correct polarity is observed.
3 Each circuit must be protected by rapid acting, high rupturing capacity fuse or miniature circuit breaker of suitable voltage and current rating.
4 Lamp replacement must only be carried out after the luminaire has been disconnected from the electricity supply. Allow sufficient time for the lamp to cool before removing it from the equipment. (Cooling could take as long as five minutes.)
5 Only use lamps of the recommended type and observe the maximum wattage limitation marked on the luminaire. Observe the lamp manufacturers' recommendations relating to lamp type.
6 Insertion of the lamp into the lampholder by holding the envelope may cause mechanical breakage of the lamp and/or seal. For safety, install by holding the lamp cap or protective sleeve and use eye protection where appropriate.
7 Do not handle the quartz envelope with bare hands. Oil or grease from the skin may contaminate the surface of the envelope and in operation reduce performance and cause premature failure. If the quartz is accidentally handled, clean it before operation with a cloth moistened with alcohol or methylated spirit.
8 In certain circumstances, items made from quartz or glass may shatter. Prevent water droplets splashing onto a hot lamp as they may cause the envelope to break.
9 A suitable safety mesh or glass must be fitted to protect persons and property in the event of a lamp shattering – this is most important when lamps are used in open fronted luminaires. If the safety glass or lens should become damaged with deep scratches or chipped edges, they must be replaced.

10 The lamp shall be changed if it has become damaged or thermally deformed.

11 At the end of life, lamps should be broken in a suitable robust container or wrapped to retain quartz fragments. The gas filling has a slight toxic content and large quantities of lamps should only be broken in a well ventilated area.

12 Direct exposure to discharge and high intensity tungsten halogen lamps can cause UV irritation to the skin and eyes. The use of glass or other UV filters is advised if the lamp is used in close proximity or for a prolonged period. When reflector fittings are used to concentrate the light in open fronted luminaires, the safe exposure period will be reduced. Appropriate screening of people and surroundings must be provided.

13 The luminaire must be mounted on a firm support or stand and positioned at a safe distance from any flammable material, e.g. curtains, background paper or scenery.

14 A high amount of radiant heat is produced and high surface temperatures are developed. Avoid operation in close proximity to human skin, as burns could result.

15 Avoid improper operation of the lamp e.g. over voltage, or at burning angles not designed for the lamp type.

16 Luminaires must not be operated in explosive or flammable atmospheres or other hazardous areas.

17 All luminaires that are suspended must be fitted with a secondary independent means of support i.e. a chain or bond. Removable accessories must be retained to prevent them falling if they become dislodged.

18 A dedicated anchor point should be provided on the housing so that the safety bond can be passed around a firm support through the yoke and terminated at the anchor point on the housing.

19 The top of the unit has been indicated to prevent it being mounted upside down.

20 Special care must be taken with portable luminaires and hand held lamps. When demounting the luminaires, allow them to completely cool before standing them on a flammable surface or placing them in a carrying case.

21 For replacement parts, refer to the manufacturers' parts list for the recommended type of safety glass, wire guard, safety suspension bond and any relevant accessories.

22 Service and repairs must only be carried out by a qualified person.

14.3 The Supply of Machinery (Safety) Regulations

For any person engaged in the lighting industry who is involved with luminaires and grid systems, these regulations have to be fully understood as they are not just recommendations but Statutory Instruments where failure to comply could lead to imprisonment and/or a heavy fine. *It is also important to fully understand the implications of the Regulations for the Safe Use of Lifting Equipment (LOLER) and the Safe Use of Work Equipment (PUWER) issued by the Health and Safety Commission.*

It is obviously impossible in this publication to cover the documents completely but the following is given as a brief guide. It is strongly recommended that the full regulations are obtained and studied in full.

Definition of 'responsible person'

(a) the manufacturer of the machinery
(b) the manufacturer's authorised representative in the Community
(c) the person who first supplies the relevant machinery in the Community

Definition of Machinery

(a) an assembly of linked parts or components, at least one of which moves, including, without prejudice to the generality of the foregoing, the appropriate actuators, control and power circuits, joined together for a specific application, in particular for the processing, treatment, moving or packaging of a material;

(b) an assembly of machines, that is to say, an assembly of items of machinery as referred to in (a) above which, in order to achieve the same end, are arranged and controlled so that they function as an integral whole notwithstanding that the items of machinery may themselves be relevant machinery and accordingly severally required to comply with these Regulations; or

(c) interchangeable equipment modifying the function of a machine which is supplied for the purpose of being assembled with an item of machinery as referred to in (a) above or with a series of different items of machinery or with a tractor by the operator himself save for any such equipment which is a spare part or tool.

There are exclusions regarding certain types of machinery and the Regulations should be consulted with regard to these.

General requirements

No person shall supply relevant machinery or safety component unless the requirements of regulation 12 below are complied with in relation thereto.

Where a person –

(a) being the manufacturer of relevant machinery or relevant safety component, himself put that relevant machinery or safety component into service in the course of a business; or

(b) having imported relevant machinery or safety component from a country or territory outside the Community, himself puts that relevant machinery or safety component into service in the course of a business.

Requirements for the supply of machinery

12 The requirements of this regulation are that:

(a) the relevant machinery satisfies the relevant essential health and safety requirements;

(b) the appropriate conformity assessment procedure in respect of the relevant machinery has been carried out;

(c) the responsible person, at his election, has issued either –
  (i)   an EC declaration of conformity, or;
  (ii) a declaration of incorporation;

(d) the CE mark has been properly affixed by the responsible person;

(e) the relevant machinery is in fact safe.

Machinery manufactured for European standards

The responsible person must:

(a) draw up and forward to an approved body a technical file;

(b) submit the technical file for verification that the standards have been correctly applied; and request that a certificate of adequacy is issued; or

(c)   submit the technical file together with an example of the relevant machinery for EC type examination.

The 'Technical File' must include the following:

(a)   An overall drawing of the machinery and control circuits
(b)   Fully detailed drawings together with calculations, test results and any other data that may be required to check the conformity of the machinery with the health and safety require-ments
(c)   A description of methods adopted to eliminate hazards presented by the machinery
(d)   A copy of the instructions for the machinery
(e)   For series manufacture, the internal measures that will be implemented to ensure that all the items of machinery are in conformity with the provisions of the Machinery Directive

CE marking

For the purposes of these Regulations, the CE marking shall not be regarded as properly affixed to relevant machinery unless:

(a)   that machinery –
      (i)   satisfies the relevant health and safety requirements; and
      (ii)   is safe; and
(b)   the responsible person who affixes the CE marking to the relevant machinery –
      (i)   has carried out the appropriate conformity assessment procedure and issued an EC declaration of conformity in respect thereof;
      (ii)   affixes the said marking in a distinct, visible, legible and indelible manner; and
      (iii) in the case of relevant machinery which is the subject of Community Directives other than the Machinery Directive, which also provide for the affixing of the CE marking, has complied with the requirements of those other Directives in respect of that machinery;
(c)   No markings which
      (i)   are likely to deceive any person as regards the meaning and form of the CE marking; or
      (ii)   reduce the visibility of legibility of the CE marking shall be fixed to relevant machinery.

Modifications

Where the responsible person complies with one of the conformity assessment procedures he must inform the approved body of any modifications, even of a minor nature which he or, where the responsible person is not the manufacturer, the manufacturer has made or plans to make to the relevant machinery to which the technical file relates.

14.4   The IEE Regulations in practice

In any installation that a lighting consultant is concerned with, the electrical engineer appointed will in the main ensure that the current regulations are adopted and enforced to ensure that the system is built to any required standards. There are however, some aspects of the regulations which have to be borne in mind by the lighting consultant as well. The first of these is the selection of the equipment that meets the requirements of the permanently installed lighting system such as the dimmer racks. It is obviously no good having a piece of equipment that has a reasonable metal shell around it but leaving it possible to poke your finger through a ventilation louvre enabling you to touch a live terminal or a busbar.

There are several aspects to the safety of equipment such as this. Some of these items may seem very obvious but it's very useful to ensure that equipment meets some of the basic parameters. Any item of equipment selected must meet the requirements of the voltages present in the installation, together with the normal current consumption and additionally has to perform satisfactorily and not create any danger by the abnormal current flow during fault conditions.

IP ratings

In the case of dimmer systems, it's obvious that we have to be aware of the voltage and frequency of the mains used. Dimmer racks are defined as 'factory built assemblies' and the rules for these must be complied with. There are various degrees of protection required in a dimmer rack and without going into all the details, the first of these that we are concerned with is a degree of protection to IP2X. This means that the rack is protected against the entry of solid objects greater than 12 mm across and is defined as a 'finger' or a similar object not exceeding 80 mm in length. This can be checked by using a 'standard test finger'. This degree of protection is required on all vertical surfaces of a dimmer rack. On the horizontal top surface however, an even greater protection is required and this is IP4X, where the top surface must be protected against the entry of solid objects greater than 1 mm. The definition refers to wire or strips of metal in thickness greater than 1 mm and solid objects exceeding 1 mm in diameter. This requirement is to protect against the dropping of small screwdrivers through slots on the top of a rack or

IP ratings

First number	Second number
Protection against solid objects	**Protection against liquids**
0 No protection	0 No protection
1 Protected against solid objects over 50 mm e.g. accidental touch by hands	1 Protected against vertically falling drops of water
2 Protected against solid objects over 12 mm e.g. fingers	2 Protected against direct sprays of water up to 15° from the vertical
3 Protected against solid objects over 2.5 mm (tools and wires)	3 Protected against sprays 60° from the vertical
4 Protected against solid objects over 1 mm (tools + small wires)	4 Protected against water sprayed from all directions – limited ingress permitted
5 Protected against dust – limited ingress (no harmful deposit) permitted	5 Protected against low pressure jets of water from all directions
6 Totally protected against dust	6 Protected against strong jets of water e.g. for use on ships' decks – limited ingress permitted
	7 Protected against the effects of immersion between 150 mm and 1 m
	8 Protected against long periods of immersion under pressure

For example, IP31 – protected against solid objects over 2.5 mm and protected against vertically falling drops of water.

strands of copper wire being used for the installation penetrating the slots, thus 'shorting out' equipment within the rack, possibly causing an electrical explosion.

The IEE regulations state that 'where an opening larger than that permitted for IP2X or IPXXB is necessary to allow the replacement of parts' two requirements will apply:

suitable precautions shall be taken to prevent persons from touching a live part unintentionally

and

it shall be established as far as practicable, that a person will be aware that a live part can be touched through the opening and should not be touched.

It is this particular requirement that makes the use of 'plug in' dimmers particularly onerous. When a 'plug in' dimmer is removed from a rack, quite a large space is left and terminals at the rear of the dimmer are exposed. Most dimmer racks these days have dimmers that are totally enclosed with terminals that are either very difficult to reach from the front surface of a dimmer rack or meet an IP2X requirement.

One of the most important regulations that concerns us with dimmer racks, is the one that states:

where it is necessary to remove a barrier or open an enclosure, or to remove a part of an enclosure, one or more of the following requirements shall be satisfied:

(i)   *the removal or opening shall be possible only by use of a key or tool.*
(ii)   *the removal or opening shall be possible only after disconnection of the supply to the live part against which the barrier or enclosure affords protection, restoration of the supply being possible only after replacement or reclosure of the barrier or enclosure.*
(iii) *an intermediate barrier shall be provided to prevent contact with a live part, such a barrier affording a degree of protection of at least IP2X or IPXXB and removable only by the use of a tool.*

Item (i) is generally met on dimmer racks by a front door being fitted which is usually locked with a key, and by the fact that any rear access requires screwdrivers or special tools to remove screws or nuts. Item (ii) is met by an automatic disconnection of a supply, probably realised by having a microswitch operating a contactor for example, but this is not usually used in our installation systems although a micro switch on the lens door of a discharge luminaire is somewhat similar in operation. An example of an intermediate barrier such as quoted in (iii), would be a perspex cover such as that provided to enclose the terminals on a transformer or across terminals at the input of the rack.

Each of the pieces of equipment that we wish to install will have to have a label or other suitable means of identification to indicate what the purpose of each item is. There will be wiring going to and from any apparatus installed and this must ensure that colour codes for identification of cables meet the requirements of the country where the system is to be used. It is essential that correct colour codes are maintained so there are no misunderstandings as to their purpose.

In a lighting system we have to make many electrical connections and there are strict rules with regard to these. The most obvious one is the fact that the terminals should be large enough to make a good connection with the type of cable in use. Thus the means of connection has to take into account the following:

(i)   *the material of the conductor and its insulation*
(ii)   *the number and shape of the wires forming the conductor*
(iii) *the cross sectional area of the conductor*
(iv)   *the number of conductors to be connected together*

(v)   the temperature attained by the terminals in normal service such that the effectiveness of the insulation of the conductors connected to them is not impaired
(vi)   where a soldered connection is used the design shall take account of creep, mechanical stress and temperature rise under fault current conditions
(vii) the provision of adequate locking arrangements in situations subject to vibration or thermal cycling.

Items (i), (ii), (iii) and (iv) cover the size of terminals including the provision of two or more parallel connections; Item (v) covers for high temperature switches where deterioration of the insulation will cause problems in practice; Item (vi) prevents the melting and breaking of soldered connections which could lead to wires floating about in cabinets; Item (vii) seeks to prevent terminals being loose either by the extremes of being cold and hot or by vibration which again could lead to wires floating about.

When using armoured cables for the input circuits to dimmer racks, there are strict rules regarding the type of cable used. One of the most important is that single core cables armoured with steel wire or tape should not be used, thus preventing any eddy currents being induced in the armour system. At the input to the dimmer rack, which is usually constructed from steel, an arrangement has to be made so that the individual conductors are not surrounded by a ferrous material thus preventing eddy (induced) currents. It's fairly obvious that any system using electrical conductors should provide a method of self cancellation to prevent harmful electromagnetic fields.

Conductors of a.c. circuits installed in ferromagnetic enclosures shall be arranged so that the conductors of all phases and the neutral conductor (if any) and the appropriate protective conductor of each circuit are contained in the same enclosure.

Every cable has to have adequate strength and be installed so that it can withstand any electromechanical forces caused by high fault currents or any other current that may occur in service. The same principle is applied to any busbar systems within dimmer racks.

As well as having regard for the regulations when we take the cables from the dimmer room to the production area and this has already been discussed but another point to be borne in mind is that any outlets either at the bottom of bars, along bars, attached to monopoles or pantographs, are all governed by regulations to ensure electrical safety is maintained.

An important element of the installation is the ambient temperatures that the racks and wiring can be subjected to, and there are rules regarding the limits and these have to be kept. The type of fusing, or protection afforded by mcbs, has to be carefully integrated with the size of cables and the loads that they are handling, although in practice the use of say a 20 A fuse on a 240 V 5 kW dimmer circuit will more than adequately protect the wiring installed which will invariably be generous in size to prevent voltage drop.

Another important element covered by regulations that we would be most concerned with is the mechanical strength of the equipment. We have to be aware of areas of high humidity, which although not usually a problem in the United Kingdom can be a problem with equipment in other countries. Much of the equipment used for entertainment will be subject to vibration, and this is another area which is governed by modern regulations.

If we could ensure a balanced distribution through our three-phase network, we wouldn't have to worry too much about the neutral conductor and it could be of a reasonable size in relation to the phase conductors. However, in many of our installations, we will have out of balance three-phase systems, therefore the neutral conductor must always have a cross sectional area appropriate to the expected value of the neutral current. In general this means the neutral conductor and the three-phase conductors are of similar size.

We are obviously concerned with the spread of fire within the systems we install, and another regulation states:

where a wiring system passes through elements of building construction, such as floors, walls, roofs, ceilings, partitions or cavity barriers, the openings remaining after passage of the wiring system shall be sealed according to the degree of fire resistance required of the element concerned (if any).

In addition

where a wiring system such as conduit, cable ducting, cable trunking, busbar or busbar trunking penetrates elements of building construction having specified fire resistance it shall be internally sealed so as to maintain the degree of fire resistance of the respective element as well as being externally sealed to maintain the required fire resistance.

The two regulations quoted cover for the instances when we go from one area to another and thus create holes in the structure. The first covers for unenclosed wiring systems where it may be just cables going from one area to another. The second regulation quoted covers for the fact that we might have trunking going through a wall and the trunking itself is sealed to the wall surround but unfortunately the internal part of the trunking allows fire to move from one area to another and this, of course, would be just as dangerous.

Additionally the regulation that covers all of the above states:

each sealing arrangement used in accordance with the regulations shall comply with the following requirements:
(i)   It should be compatible with the material of the wiring system with which it is in contact.
(ii)   It shall permit thermal movement of the wiring system without reduction of the sealing quality.
(iii) It shall be removable without damage to existing cable where space permits future extension to be made.
(iv) It shall resist relevant external influences to the same degree as the wiring system with which it is used.

and that

Each sealing arrangement shall be visually inspected at an appropriate time during erection to verify that it conforms to the manufacturers' erection instructions and the details shall be recorded.

Regulation (i) above seeks to prevent harmful chemical reactions between the wiring system itself and any materials used for fireproofing, (ii) is fairly obvious that it would be no good having fireproofing that with gradual movement allowed gaps to appear. Unfortunately fire doesn't need too much of a gap to go from one area to another, (iii) covers for the situation where it would be quite easy to spray, for instance, around cables with some foam which would be fire retardant but unfortunately, if you then needed to do anything with the cables, it would be physically impossible because they'd all be glued together, and (iv) prevents the use of materials which would be less robust than the cables themselves.

Thus we have to be careful with the methods used for fire prevention because by covering for this eventuality it may make life difficult when expansion of a system is required.

During an installation temporary sealing arrangements have to be provided as appropriate and when any work is done, any sealing that has been disturbed has to be re-instated as soon as possible.

In lighting systems we have the normal mains supply cable going to the luminaires, in addition we will have low voltage multi-core cables or smaller digital signal cables provided for the control systems. This type of situation is covered by the regulations which state that we are not allowed to mix cables with various voltages present unless the insulation of all of the cables used is insulated for the highest voltage present in any of the cables or, alternative methods are adopted.

(i)   Each conductor in a multi-core cable is insulated for the highest voltage present in the cable, or is enclosed within an earthed metallic screen of a current carrying capacity equivalent to that of the largest conductor enclosed within the screen,

or

(ii)   the cables are insulated for their respective system voltage and installed in a separate compartment of a cable ducting or cable trunking system, or have an earthed metallic covering.

It is obviously extremely dangerous to pick up a conductor where we expect to find safe low voltage and in fact find mains, and the above regulations seek to prevent this happening.

The two methods are either to have good insulation of the systems so voltages can't travel from one cable to another, or conductors that are surrounded by an earthed shield where any harmful voltage will be conveyed safely away.

In practice, we generally run the mains feeds around the building separately from the control feeds, the only time where they may come into close proximity is perhaps on monopoles, pantographs or motorised barrel units where technical cables for the sound and vision system are installed in addition to the lighting circuits.

In places of entertainment and for those concerned with the production of entertainment we have a multiplicity of plugs and sockets used. These may be the normal 13 A supplies for domestic use, special sockets concerned with lighting outlets and there will invariably be provision for three-phase supplies for portable machinery. We have to be extremely careful that we don't intermix any of these socket outlets or plugs so that people are not placed in danger or machines receive voltages for which they are not designed. The main requirement for plugs and socket outlets is as follows:

(i)   It shall not be possible for any pin of a plug to make contact with any live contact of its associated socket outlet while any other pin of the plug is completely exposed.
(ii)   It shall not be possible for any pin of a plug to make contact with any live contact of any socket outlet within the same installation other than the type of socket outlet for which the plug is designed.
(iii)   Every plug and socket outlet shall be of the non-reversible type with provision for the connection of a protective conductor.

Finally but certainly not least, is the provision of devices for emergency switching. The regulations require that a means of interrupting the supply for the purpose of emergency switching shall be capable of cutting off the full load current of the relevant part of the installation.

means for emergency switching shall consist of:

(i)   A single switching device directly cutting off the incoming supply, or
(ii)   A combination of several items of equipment operated by a single action and resulting in the removal of the hazard by cutting off the appropriate supply; emergency stopping may include the retention of supply electric braking facilities.

The regulations go on to state:

where practical a device for emergency switching shall be manually operated directly interrupting the main circuit. A device such as a circuit breaker or a contactor operated by remote control shall open on de-energisation of the coil, or another technique of suitable reliability shall be employed.

The operating means (such as handle or push button) for a device for emergency switching shall be clearly identifiable and preferably coloured 'red'. It shall be installed in a readily accessible position where the hazard might occur and where appropriate, further devices shall be provided where additional emergency switching may be needed.

The operating means of a device for emergency switching shall be of the latching type or capable of being restrained in the 'OFF' or 'STOP' position. The release of the emergency switching device shall not re-energise the equipment concerned.

Although it is possible, in a further qualified part of the regulations, to allow an automatic reset under specified conditions, we in the entertainment industry are mainly concerned with the fact that nearly all of the operatives involved with a production could de-energise the system by operating the emergency switching. The re-energising of the equipment has to be carried out by approved personnel, such as engineers or electricians concerned, to ensure that the hazard that caused the 'emergency' has been dealt with correctly.

14.5 Electricity at Work Regulations in practice

The Regulations are mandatory, and are enforceable by law. The intention of the Regulations is to require precaution to be taken against the risk of death or personal injury from electricity in the place of work. Whilst the Regulations cover all electrical supplies and equipment, we will restrict our coverage to portable items that can be plugged into the mains via a plug and socket. These are obviously the most vulnerable to damage and are by their description the most likely item to be handled.

The Regulations cover every portable item to be found on the premises from luminaires to kettles, from typewriters to electric drills, in fact every item fitted with a plug must be included. The wiring of the premises and permanently connected machinery and apparatus are also included, but are not being considered by us at this time. The following notes are our interpretation of some of the requirements and should not be taken as a statement of the Regulations.

The statement that all portable electrical equipment must be as far as possible electrically safe is the starting point and it really means *all and every item* found on the premises and does not take into account who owns it. It can be a personal radio or a rented item, it still comes under the umbrella of the Regulations. When the area safety officer calls to inspect your premises, he will ask to see the duty holder. This is any responsible person that has been nominated to keep a register of every item of electrical equipment; he will ask the duty holder for the register and expect to find certain information in it. Identify the item, the date that it was tested, the result of the test, which can only be pass or fail, action taken and the date of the next test. The period between tests can only be established by the duty holder and the operator and will depend on how often the appliance is used and the history of damage that can be sustained by the environment in which it is used. Examples could be: an electric drill being used every day, all day on a production line, in which case three-monthly tests could be deemed appropriate; equipment in frequent use and subject to transit damage could be every six months, and so on. Until a history is built up in the register no definite period can be established.

Most portable items in entertainment that are not out on rental or travelling shows, and are normally used in the same premises, could be considered to have light duty and might be considered for an annual test. Portable electrical equipment can be divided into three groups:

● *Class I*   Requiring an earth connection to any metal part that could become live in a fault condition.
● *Class II*   A totally insulated electrical device where no part can become live in the event of a fault condition. This type of equipment does not require an earth wire.
● *Class III*   Low voltage equipment that has special regulations.

A typical test for Class I equipment could be a visual inspection of the cable, the plug top, the cord grip at the plug and the cord grip at the appliance and an inspection inside the plug top to determine that it is correctly wired. Any damage to these items would fail the test and the equipment would not be allowed to continue to the electrical test. The reported accidents show that 80% of electrical accidents could have been avoided by a visual inspection. If the equipment passes the visual test it will be tested electrically for earth continuity from the plug top to the frame of the appliance and the earth resistance will be recorded and must be within the Regulations' requirements. The insulation is tested from the plug top through the earth and live conductors and must have the required resistance. Finally, a run test is conducted to determine that the equipment conforms to the Regulations in its working state. Other tests are available on some products, a high voltage test might be carried out, normally 1500 V for Class I equipment and 3000 V for Class II, but these are made at the discretion of the electrical engineer conducting the tests.

14.6   Safety checklists and inspections

Much of the equipment used in the entertainment industry is well built and a superficial examination usually would lead one to expect the equipment would work safely for long periods of time with little or nothing going wrong. However, life is not as easy as that and modern legislation requires that moving equipment such as monopoles, winches, pantographs and devices used to suspend equipment over stage areas, studio areas and particularly above audiences is regularly inspected to see no danger is present. Many items concerned with mechanical safety can be verified by visual inspection, but this is not necessarily the case with electrical equipment when the fault may lie in a piece of copper somewhere. All items of electrical equipment also have to undergo routine checks to ensure that they are not posing any hazard.

To ensure that the necessary inspections are carried out correctly, all items of equipment must be coded and numbered and a register of equipment and tests kept on the premises. When items of equipment are purchased, they must have a CE mark (including year of construction), name and address of manufacturer, designation of series or type, an identification number of the particular piece of equipment. All equipment must be accompanied by clear operating and maintenance instructions.

Routine testing (which covers many of the points of the EEC Machinery Directive) of lifting equipment has to provide checks against the following items:

1   Undue wear of any part.
2   The wire ropes used for lifting must be inspected to ensure they haven't been damaged in any way and that no strands are broken.
3   The points where wire ropes are made off to provide permanent anchor points to other parts of the structure are to be inspected to ensure they are not loose or damaged.

4 All parts of the motor assembly are firmly in place and not loose in any way.

5 All pulleys or scroll drums to be examined for undue signs of wear which would indicate possible problems with the winding of the wire ropes.

6 All diverter pulleys to be examined for signs of wear and the fact that they are free to rotate.

7 A visual inspection of the top and bottom limit system in addition to visual inspection of overload and slack wire system.

8 To apply load tests to ensure that the slack wire and overload system works correctly. In addition to traverse the unit from top to bottom to see that limit switches are operating correctly.

9 Ensure that all warning labels are present and all indicators are fully functional.

10 Ensure that the equipment is capable of being controlled from all nominated control positions, e.g. studio floor level or on the local controls at grid level.

11 All covers and guards are correctly positioned and fastened securely.

Electrical safety is covered, in the main, in the United Kingdom, by the Electricity at Work Regulations which would cover for items of equipment that are portable and in addition the latest edition of the IEE regulations pertaining to the installation of the electrical system in the building. As well as the regular checks for electrical safety under the Electricity at Work Regulations, it is also wise to check for the mechanical safety of any luminaire or other type of light source used in the entertainment industry. Most premises will, on a fairly regular basis, do some maintenance to ensure the equipment works correctly, and this obviously makes life much easier from the point of view of the electricians concerned with lighting equipment. At the time these checks for maintenance are made, it is very easy to go over some of the mechanical items to ensure that they are not damaged in any way. Testing the pan and tilt mechanism for movement and slackness might reveal problems in this area. A visual examination of a yoke for instance, would not necessarily indicate problems with the devices used to lock the yoke to the body of the luminaire. A fairly careful examination of the bodywork of any luminaire would reveal any loose parts that may be suspect and therefore in danger of falling off.

Therefore a suggested checklist for luminaires is as follows:

1 Is the yoke functioning correctly and are the pan and tilt controls, if fitted, working satisfactorily.

2 Do all locking knobs fitted correctly tighten the moving part so it can be held in the position as set.

3 Examine the spud fitted to see that it hasn't become loose from the yoke assembly.

4 Check internally for any loose parts, particularly with regard to reflectors and lamp holder assemblies.

5 Check internal wiring for any signs of wear.

6 Check all switches fitted to see that mechanically they function correctly. Although they may appear to be satisfactory from an electrical standpoint, it might be that they are not mechanically perfect. This generally avoids any arcing problems within switches, caused by springs or levers being slack.

7 Check to see that all accessories attached to the luminaire are not loose, i.e. barndoors, colour frames, etc.

8 Check all louvres which allow air flow through the luminaire for signs of damage and ensure they are working correctly to make certain that the luminaire does not get over hot. This can usually be ascertained by signs of burning on the bodywork.

9 Check to see that barndoors function correctly and are sufficiently tight to do the job needed.

10 If a base or feet are provided to stand a luminaire on, ensure they haven't become damaged in any way.

11 Luminaire leads and plugs should be tested *at least* once a year but it's quite useful to inspect them on a more frequent basis to see that no arcing is occurring on any of the pins, which would also indicate deterioration in any of the permanent sockets fitted in the system.
12 A useful point is to listen out whilst in operation for any nasty frying noises, which would indicate lamp contacts arcing and thus a lampholder would need replacing.

Although all the foregoing seems a bit of a chore and probably most people generally say, 'it's not my responsibility', if most of the tests listed above are carried out, it ensures a safe working environment in which it is easier to work because all the equipment is functioning correctly.

15
Maintaining and hiring lighting equipment

15.1 Standardisation for maintenance and spares

Maintenance can be in house or in the case of hired equipment, the hirer does the maintenance. What follows applies to anyone concerned with maintenance. One of the problems with a variety of equipment used, is the fact that to maintain it requires different procedures for each type of equipment. This generally poses a problem for the maintenance engineer and, secondly it can lead to items being overlooked by the staff being unfamiliar with all the equipment concerned. It therefore follows that is advantageous to keep the various types and makes of equipment to an acceptable minimum.

15.2 Maintenance rooms and test equipment

If we are given an opportunity to plan our own maintenance area, what should we look for?

The first requirement is an area large enough to store the spare lights and equipment plus enough room to stack the equipment requiring repair, leaving room to test luminaires and have enough racking for spares and consumables such as lamps and filters. Obviously we would require a good electrical supply terminated into a purpose built distribution board which will provide all the types of socket outlets required together with a three-phase outlet; a large bench, with an equally large vice, covered in a thick linoleum that is also a good insulator. A large lock up cupboard stocked with taps and dyes and nuts and bolts of all sizes, complete with all of the normal tools including an electric drill, soldering irons large and small and an adequate supply of various plugs, sockets and cables. Test equipment should also include a good quality multi-meter, an incident light meter and a tri-stimulus colour meter to perform light tests. To comply with the Electricity at Work Regulations, each piece of electrical equipment must be entered into a register and periodically tested. Purpose built electrical test instruments are available offering all the test facilities required and are a good investment for everyday use and to use for the periodic tests. To be given these conditions and a good lock on the door, is no more than the electrical staff deserve to enable them to keep a well ordered house in good working condition.

15.3   Luminaire maintenance

A common misunderstanding of maintenance is that the electrician walks round with a duster and flicks dust from lights and repairs the ones that do not work. Nothing could be further from the truth. Electrical maintenance is a legal requirement, laid down in the 'Electricity at Work Regulations'.

Over and above the electrical safety tests, there are three main problem areas to be considered when carrying out luminaire maintenance: heat, mechanical damage and the ingress of dirt. It is inevitable that luminaires are going to attract the dust and dirt that is in the air by virtue of the fact that the instrument is designed to have a cold air intake to cool the lamp and electrical equipment, which also sucks in the associated grime. As it does so, it deposits the dirt on the lens, reflector and any other surface which is subject to change of temperature. Therefore, periodic cleaning is required to maintain the efficiency of the luminaire. Most reflectors are made from brightly polished anodised aluminium. These are surface reflectors and should only be cleaned by wiping them with a damp cloth and liquid soap, a conventional wipe down with a wet rag afterwards to remove the soap will suffice and dry with a lint free rag. The same method can be used to clean the lenses, however, in the case of the tungsten halogen lamps which have a large deposit of grime on them, these should be wiped clean with alcohol and then polished with a clean lint free rag. Finger marks must be avoided on tungsten halogen lamps to prevent the fingerprints becoming etched into the envelope when they are hot, causing hot spots which can collect extra heat and form a blister on the envelope.

Regular examination of the internal cables, which are flexed when the unit is focused, are needed to determine if the insulation has been damaged. Switches and lampholders are a target for excessive heat. One indication of a lampholder overheating is to remove the lamp and inspect the pins. If they show signs of 'arcing' then the lampholder must be replaced, because if a new lamp is inserted into a lampholder that already has arcing on the contacts, it will transmit the same problem to the new lamp. The safety bond must be visually inspected for damaged or frayed strands. Any bond or chain must be replaced if it has arrested one fall of the luminaire. Barndoors and colour frames are retained by safety catches which must be in good working order. If cables are to be replaced they must be of the recommended temperature range, do not be tempted to use just any old cable. Lenses must be examined for chips or cracks, the most obvious place is around the edge of the lens which when continuously heated and cooled progresses the chip into a crack and the lens will ultimately fracture. Change any damaged lenses. Look for dents in the housing that could cause problems to the electrical internal switches and wiring. The yoke must be examined to determine that it is mechanically sound.

15.4   Suspension system maintenance

Trusses, counterweight bars, motorised barrels, telescopes and pantographs are basically the same device, a means of supporting luminaires from above with variable height. They may employ electrical drives, with various sensing switches together with cable support systems or alternatively, spring balanced. We can therefore generalise about support systems and state that a secondary means of support should be provided. This usually takes the form of a wire cable (safety bond), as a means of arresting the device if the primary means of support is broken. Therefore the first step in mechanical maintenance must be to inspect these areas which provide the ultimate safety.

Well designed winches allow inspection of the cable termination on the winding drum and at the bottom end of the cables. Look for loose or frayed ends, examine the whole length of the cable as it is wound in and out for any loose threads. If any such signs are seen, the cables must be changed. Each lifting apparatus has a SWL stated on it, a periodic inspection must include the application of a test load to determine that the unit is safe. Many insurance companies require such tests annually. Most designs employ a top and bottom limit, the unit should be run through the whole range to determine that both limits are working and also the overload and underload limits. These are normally provided to switch the device off in the event of it picking up an additional load such as a piece of scenery or a safeguard against the operator placing too many luminaires on the barrel. The underload switch is required if the luminaire is lowered onto the top of a set where cable would be spewed out until the luminaire toppled off the set and presents a real hazard. This test can easily be simulated by lowering the luminaire onto a rostrum where it should cut out immediately it touches the floor.

In the case of traversing monopoles and pantographs, they are normally fitted with end stop switches for traverse, which must be operated and the electrical cables should be examined for damage, particularly in the case of pantographs where cable are laced up the side of the links and can easily be caught between them. In general gearboxes should not require maintenance, unless they have been stripped down for repair. Care should be taken on the type of grease or oil used, some types of gearbox rely on a heavy lubricant to help them to become self sustaining to avoid the luminaire running away under a no volt condition. Any lubricants used must be at the recommendation of the manufacturer. A good guide to all lifting devices is that two turns should be left on the hoisting drum when the device is at the bottom limit. This will determine that the cables retain the load and not the end fixing. The cables used in lifting devices are special and normally of a flexible nature. Only use the manufacturers' replacements. Pantographs should be inspected for mechanical damage of the links and the hinge pin retaining clips, these have been known to pop off and not affect the operation until the pin slides out. The springs used on pantographs normally have a 10 000 cycle working life, this doesn't meant they will fall to pieces in 10 000 cycles but an early warning of fatigue can be found by inspecting the edge of the springs, which show small cracks developing along the edges towards the end of life. Any sign of fractures, the springs should be replaced. Extreme caution must be taken in removing the springs from pantographs, with a pantograph on a bench, the spring should be pulled down by the ring provided and allowed up slowly until it touches its winding drum. In this state, the spring will be stationary and can be released. The assembly can be removed from the pantograph. Under no circumstances attempt to remove the spring from the drum, it is under considerable tension and can only be removed from the drum by the manufacturer. Barrel roller trolleys have stops screwed to them which engage under the barrel to prevent the trolley jumping off. On inspection ensure that the stops are present and undamaged. Where monopoles are concerned, sticking tubes are often caused by external damage. If this is the case, it is recommended that a complete set of tubes is replaced, in view of the fact that these are mated during manufacture for not only size tolerance, but the bow that occurs in their length. Any attempt to replace one particular tube could result in many hours of work and problems of fit and alignment that you were not aware of.

15.5 Holding spares and expendables

The seemingly simple task of holding spare parts and replacement items is anything but simple. The problems are mainly trying to identify the parts required and the quantities to hold in stock and monitoring the usage of expendable items.

Major items of equipment, such as winch systems, dimmers and luminaires will be changed with replacement of worn out plant programmes and these may vary in length of time from a 7 to 20 year cycle. However, on a day to day basis, we have operating costs that are concerned with the maintenance of plant and the use of lamps, filters and certain types of accessories.

With a new installation it is a good policy to ask the manufacturer for a 'spares list' identifying all of the likely parts that will be required to keep the product in good repair. This request in itself, causes some manufacturers to research their own products to determine the likely spares requirement for the future; whereas other manufacturers produce pictorial spares sheets, with photographs of the parts for easy identification. This practice also helps the user to determine his particular model in the years to come after the product has undergone several modifications and upgrades, and also overcomes the language problem when trying to describe the parts that are required. If your make of equipment does not provide this luxury it is expedient to ask for a written parts list which will identify your model and the parts required at that point in time.

If you are fortunate enough to be at the planning meeting when the products that are to be ordered are chosen, then it will be expedient to include the spares at the same time and as a condition of the original purchase. That part is easy. The question is: how many spares should be held?

Manufacturers have often taken part in discussions with the user to determine a sensible spares holding. In the first place this can only be an educated estimate from past experience and a percentage applied to the purchase order. A typical spares list for a luminaire could be as follows, with a percentage applied for orders from 100 to 300 units.

Lenses	5%
Lampholders	6%
Switches	5%
Internal electrical harnesses	3%
Yokes	2%
Reflector	6%
Wire guard	2%
Barndoors	4%
Colour frames	10%
Housing	1%
Mains cable assembly	5%

This could be a good starting point but don't forget that paradoxically, the older the equipment gets, and therefore the more likely to require spares, the less likely they are to be available; because the manufacturer has moved on to other designs. However, most reputable manufacturers keep spares for seven years from the first model – so beware if you have purchased in the last year of manufacture.

Holding spares in an existing installation reduces the problem of how many to stock, because a good record of purchases over the years will give a good guide to the likely requirement. The main problem is availability, because many luminaires are kept working long after their useful life. If this is the case and the original equipment manufacturer cannot supply the spare parts, there are specialist companies that carry out repairs and make special parts for old products.

Expendable items are much easier to predict. With a good record of purchases a working quantity can be arrived at. Some of the most expensive items are the lamps. In many organisations the advent of computer databases has enabled the recording of faults and replacement items a relatively easy chore, which enables an analysis to be made of problems encountered. Fortunately, there are several main stockists that hold the large range of lamps used in TV, film and theatre, so the spares holding can be reduced to a nominal amount to cover day to day needs and calling on the stock of the main stockists for unscheduled requirements. From records, a guide of lamp usage in theatre and TV studios is approximately 1.3 lamps per year per luminaire. This is assuming that the lamps are supplied from dimmers. In the theatre the lamps will be providing different light levels, but the average dimmer output level could be similar to that adopted in TV, where it is common practice to line up the cameras with the dimmers set to level '7'. In both cases this has the effect of greatly extending the life of the lamp. However, in film lighting the lamps are normally run at full voltage, resulting in a much shorter life. Typically for a tungsten halogen lamp, rated at 3200 K, this is likely to be from 200 to 400 hours. One way of easing the pain of the lamp costs in the first 2 years of a new installation is to order two lamps for each luminaire at the same time that the equipment is purchased. In this way it is paid for out of the capital investment and does not come out of the expendable budget. By the second year, sufficient experience will be gained to determine a fairly accurate expendable requirement.

Whereas lamp manufacturers supply figures of typical life in use, filter manufacturers don't. This is obviously extremely difficult to do, because the life of filters is dependent upon the light source being used. However, from the customers' point of view, it's very useful to do some tests to ascertain which filter material has a good life. This can be done very simply by putting up similar colours on the same light source and seeing which one deteriorates the most.

Stocking colour filters can be a big problem; the variables being 100 different colours sold in sheets and rolls. Although there are several good stockists who can normally respond quickly to your needs, it is expedient to keep a working stock of filter to call on. To remove one of the variables, it is normally a good practice to stock colour filters in rolls, this makes racking simple, with a colour swatch and number attached to the end of the roll. Rolls are also more economical because different sizes can be cut with the minimum of waste. However, the second variable of 100 colours needs a lot more thought. If one applies the 20/80 principle which seems to work in most cases, then 80% of the filters used will be in 20% of the colours offered. This would appear to be a simple solution; just stock the 20 most popular colours. After much discussion and heated exchanges with the LDs, you might arrive at a compromise short list but be prepared for a long and arduous debate.

Filters used for colour correction are, of course, out of this category and are stocked separately as the need dictates.

Some accessories disappear as if they were expendable items and require special attention, otherwise a constant state of annoyance will persist. Barndoors usually suffer from damage preventing them from rotating and the flaps suffer from that infuriating malady known in the trade as 'a droopy flap'. This is when the hinges have become so weak that they cannot support the weight of the flap. Replacements will save a lot of aggravation between the LDs and the electrical staff. Safety bonds have a habit of disappearing, whether an alternative use has been found for them that we have not yet discovered or a private hoard is hidden somewhere in the building, we will most likely never find out, but one thing that is certain is that every luminaire must have one to meet the safety requirements, so good replacement stocks must be maintained. Colour frames suffer from the same problems but have the additional requirement in theatre to be 'gelled up' between shows, so a complete set of spares is required as well as replacements.

Control and dimming should not require a large spares stock; the modern systems are very reliable and offer electronic card replacements and dimmer modules which should suffice. However, do not forget that when a tungsten halogen lamp ends its life with an arc-over across the filament, that it draws a large current and normally blows the fuse, so it is necessary to keep a good stock of spare fuses. Finally be sure that you have made your case for expendable items by submitting your budget for next year in plenty of time. No one else in management is going to remind you to spend their money.

15.6   Monitoring equipment usage for replacement programmes

It is quite common for a lighting manufacturer to be asked for spares to repair a luminaire that is 30 years old, not for a sentimental enthusiast to restore the instrument as an antique, but by necessity to keep the luminaire working long past its useful life. It is normally not too difficult to get management to replace a control system after some years of service, because there is always a good case for having the latest development in 'thingummy bobs and wotsits' that the designers of lighting control systems are constantly adding to their products. The simple luminaire or lifting device stands very little chance of becoming more desirable because it is a new model so the attitude of some management is 'light still comes out of it' or 'it still lifts up and down, doesn't it?', mainly brought on by the sudden realisation of a big capital investment. Whilst we can blame the management for not wanting to invest more money, what have we done over the preceding years to develop a replacement programme. In most establishments, the accountant will depreciate the capital equipment by 25% per year, in this way the book value will reduce to 23.72% of the original value in 5 years.

This method of amortisation will never remove the item from the books, but will show the management that the equipment that will be scrapped when it is replaced has very little capital value so that it can be written off. It is therefore a good practice to keep records of your own in the maintenance department of purchases and the date and cost, and make this information part of your inventory. To support your argument for replacements, you should keep a record of breakdowns, cause and effect and so build up a case for replacements because of the nuisance to the production. Other factors are its size, weight and performance compared with a modern equivalent. In this way additional items can be introduced into your capital replacement budget each year in the hope that some money will be made available. If this is not forthcoming, keep the running total and add to it each year, then if you eventually get a percentage of your requested capital investment allowance, it will at least be a percentage of a much higher figure. The last question that management cannot ignore is 'does it conform to *current* safety standards?'

15.7   Hired equipment

At some time or the other, most lighting people will require the services of a rental company to supply the extra equipment for a particular occasion or to provide a total installation on a temporary basis. There are many good rental companies available, providing an excellent service to the industry. Rental companies tend to specialise in film, TV or theatre; normally dictated by the specialised equipment required in each of the lighting disciplines. A film company normally registers a film as a business name and trades as a Limited company for the duration of the film. This sometimes makes it advantageous for equipment and cameras to be hired from a rental company and are therefore costed directly to that film. If the equipment had been purchased, it would present a problem at the end of the film of what to do with the equipment. In theatre, most professional houses have a small complement of lighting and control but do not provide the quantity or choice of equipment for a large production. This dictates that the production company rents the additional lighting control and dimming required. The advantages are that the desired type and make of equipment can be chosen with the cost paid weekly from the takings or at the worst the equipment can be returned in the event of a disaster.

In TV the main requirement is for outside broadcast lighting, and on occasion to supplement the normal studio lighting with special units used for effects lighting.

While the rental system is most helpful and seems to fill a very real need it should not be entered into lightly, without reading the small print, usually found on the back of acceptance delivery notes and contracts issued at the time of ordering. Each rental company has its own conditions. The following are some of the more important ones found by the authors.

The customer hiring the equipment must check and test it before it is used and satisfy himself as to its fitness for the purpose. Further the customer must have adequate insurance cover to protect the rental company from claims against it for its products or personnel employed by the rental company for legal actions, proceedings, costs, charges, expenses and indemnity of third parties. The equipment must only be operated by people with the appropriate qualifications. If the customer uses labour provided by the rental company, the customer is responsible for them whilst on site, including any damages done, expenses or consequential indirect loss.

Finally, many an expensive argument can be avoided by determining if the cost of the hired lighting equipment also includes the lamps.

Appendix I
Glossary of terms

A Ampere.

Abbott A manufacturer of single-conductor connectors used on feeder cable.

Absorption filter A filter which transmits selected wavelengths. The absorbed energy is converted to heat which raises the temperature of the filter.

AC (1) Alternating current. (2) Camera assistant.

Ace A 1 kW Fresnel light.

Acting area That portion of a stage used by the actors during a performance.

Adapter A device used to convert from one type of connector to another.

Additive colour mixing The superimposition of light beams, usually consisting of the primary colours, whereby the resultant light is the *addition* of the various wavelengths concerned (see *Subtractive Colour Mixing*).

Alligator clip, Crocodile (croc) clip, Bulldog clip Metallic spring loaded clamp, similar to a clothes peg, with pointed teeth on the jaws of the clamp. Used for making temporary electrical connections. Also used to hold gels to barndoors.

Alternating current (a.c.) Electric current whose flow alternates in direction. The time of flow in one direction is a half period and the length of all half periods is the same. The normal waveform of a.c. is sinusoidal.

Ambient light General background light.

American National Standards Institute (ANSI) An independent association that establishes standards to promote consistency and interchangeability among manufacturers. This organisation was formerly known as the United States of America Standards Institute (USASI or ASI) and previously as the American Standards Association (ASA). Three-letter ANSI codes are used to identify light bulbs (e.g. EGT is a 1 kW bulb).

Ammeter A meter for measuring amperage.

Ampacity Current capacity of cable, connectors, etc. (USA).

Ampere A unit of current. One ampere will flow through a resistance of 1 Ω under a pressure of 1 V.

Ampere-hour A measure of a battery capacity equal to the number of amperes times the number of hours of charge that a battery can deliver.

Anode A positive electrode.

Apple box A reinforced plywood box used on the set for many purposes, including to raise an actor who is too short or to raise furniture. Apple boxes come in four sizes: full (20 × 12 × 8), half (20 × 12 × 4), quarter (20 × 12 × 2) and pancake (20 × 12 × 1) – measured in inches.

Arc   The discharge created between two electrodes usually with a fairly low voltage and high current. Has to be controlled by a ballast arrangement (see also *Carbon Arc*).

Arc light   Old term for a luminaire using a carbon arc discharge as the source of illumination. Also describes modern discharge sources such as MSR, HMI, CSI, etc.

Articulated arm   An adjustable device consisting of short pieces of tubular metal joined together by ball and socket joints. Used to hold gobos or flags, normally attached to a stand or rigged on other grip equipment or scenery.

Artificial light   Light coming from any source other than the sun, sky or moon.

ASA   (1) American Standards Association (now the ANSI). (2) The exposure index (EI) rating of a film emulsion, also referred to as ISO.

Aspect ratio   The ratio of the width to the height of any imaging system. The standard aspect ratios are 4:3 (standard TV), 16:9 (high-definition TV), 1.66:1 (European film standard), 1.85:1 (American wide screen standard) and 2.36:1 (Anamorphic 35 mm).

Atmosphere   The mood of a scene created by the lighting, set design, costumes and make-up. Additionally, influenced by sound effects, music, etc.

AWG (American Wire Gauge)   These sizes are based on the diameter of the wire expressed in mils (1/1000 in) or its cross sectional area (CSA), expressed as circular mils (Cmils) (see *Cmils*).

Baby   1 kW Fresnel luminaire.

Baby stand   A stand with a 5/8 inch stud.

Baby stud   A 5/8 inch mounting stud that mates with a 5/8 inch receptacle.

Backdrop (Backing)   A scenic painting or enlarged photograph transparency used to limit the view of the audience or a camera through openings such as doorways or windows.

Backing lighting   The illumination provided for scenery and backdrops.

Back light   A luminaire used to light the subject from the rear to help separation from backings and to increase the three-dimensional effect.

Bail   U-shaped part of a lighting fixture that attaches the fixture to the stand (see *Yoke*).

Bailing wire (USA)   A thin flexible wire used as safety wire for barndoors, snoots and other luminaire attachments.

Balance   (a) The relationship of light and shade in a scene to establish the mood and atmosphere e.g. high key or low key. (b) The maintenance of lighting levels between scenes to prevent exposure differences (see *High key, Low key*).

Ballast   The electrical device, required for all discharge lamps, that limits current through the lamp. Additional functions may be incorporated in the basic unit such as starting circuits and dimming control.

Banded cable   Several single-conductor cables banded together at intervals, formed into a bundle.

Bank   Used to describe groups of lights, such as several scoops or softlights. Also luminaires containing several PAR lamps.

Barndoor   Movable flaps attached to a Fresnel or PC luminaire to shape the light beam.

Barrel (Colloq. Bar)   A metal tube, generally 48-mm diameter, for suspending luminaires or scenery. Usually manufactured from steel or aluminium.

Base   (1) The basket on the underside of a fixture. (2) The base of a lamp is the porcelain part. (3) The lamp socket is also sometimes called the base.

Base light   The basic intensity of 'soft' lighting required to satisfy the minimum viewing or technical requirements.

Basher   A small luminaire of around 500 W used as a kicker.

Bates   A common name for three-pin connectors (20 A, 30 A, 60 A, 100 A).

Batten   (a) Horizontal pipe on which luminaires or scenery can be hung. (b) Compartmented multi-colour floodlight unit for theatrical lighting. (c) Refers to 3 × 1 inch timber.

Battery belt   A battery pack mounted on a belt that can be worn around the waist during location shooting.

Battery pack   Used on location where an electrical supply from the mains is not available. The most popular batteries for size to weight ratio are nickel–cadmium. Typical luminaires used with battery packs have open-faced reflectors, containing a tungsten halogen or discharge lamp.

Bazooka   An adjustable extension tube with a 1⅛ inch spigot for mounting luminaires on catwalks. It is similar to a small stand minus its legs.

Bead board   Styrofoam used to make soft bounce light.

Beam   The unidirectional flow of total light output from a source, usually a luminaire.

Beam angle   Those points on the light output curve which are 50% of maximum output. The included angle between these two points is the beam angle.

Beam light   Lens less luminaire with a parabolic reflector to give a parallel light beam.

Beaver board   A nail-on plate mounted to an apple box.

Best boy   The assistant chief lighting technician or second electrician. The best boy is the gaffer's chief assistant.

Big eye   A 10 kW incandescent fixture with an extra large lens (Mole Richardson).

Black wrap   Thick aluminium foil painted with matt black to control spill light from luminaires.

Blackbody   A body which completely absorbs any heat or light radiation falling upon it.

Blackbody radiation   Radiation that comes from an ideal blackbody. The distribution of energy is dependent only on the temperature of the blackbody and is governed by Planck's radiation law.

Blacklight   Radiation in the near ultraviolet (320–400 nm) used to make paints, dyes and materials fluoresce. As UV radiation is invisible to the eye, it is possible to use it for special effects where apparently, in darkness, materials glow as though they were normally illuminated. As with any other UV radiation, it is important that it does not cause any hazard to human beings.

Blackout   To switch all channels to 'off' on a lighting console. Also refers to switching off all illumination, except the exit lights.

Blackout switch   A master on/off switch used for controlling the overall production lighting for either stage or studios.

Blind   Refers to changes made on a lighting console which do not affect the 'live' console output (usually called *Blind Plotting*).

Blonde   A 2 kW open faced luminaire.

Board   A name for a control desk (derived from *switchboard*).

Boom   An extendible arm fixed to a stand to mount small lighting fixtures which may be moved to adjust the lighting on the subject.

Boomerang   A device attached to the front of the luminaire holding sets of filters. They are generally provided at the front of follow spots for colour changing.

Bounce lighting   Directing light onto a large diffuse surface to produce a soft reflected light.

Bracket   The small supports on the front of a luminaire which hold the barndoors, colour frame, scrims and other accessories.

Brail   To pull a lighting suspension or piece of scenery out of its normal hanging position by means of attached rope lines.

Branch circuit   As defined by the American NEC, circuits that are downstream of the last overcurrent protection.

Branchaloris   A branch of a tree or bush held in front of a light to create a moving or stationary foliage pattern.

Bridge   A narrow platform suspended over the acting area. Luminaires and projection devices mounted on the bridge are accessible during performance.

Brightness   See *Luminance*.

Brightness ratio   The ratio of maximum-to-minimum luminances occurring within a scene.

British Standards Institute (BSI)   Produced technical specifications and other documents which are made generally available. The main aim of the Institute is to maintain standards, quality and safety in goods and products.

Broad   A wide angle floodlight.

Brute   A 225 ampere d.c. high intensity carbon spotlight with a 24 inch diameter Fresnel lens.

Bubble   Slang term used in the TV and film industries to describe lamps of any type.

Build   A gradual increase in light level or in the number of light sources used.

Bulb   An old term describing the bulbous glass envelope of an electric lamp.

Bull switch   A main switch used on the main feeder or on sub-feeder lines.

Bump   To briefly flash lighting channels 'up' or 'down'.

Busbar   Copper bars (1/4 inch thick) to which lug connectors are attached.

Busbar lug (USA)   A small electrical 'G-clamp' made from brass used to attach large cables to busbars. Has good electrical conductivity and high current rating.

Butterfly set   A frame used to support a net or silk over the top of the action. The silk reduces and softens direct sunlight.

'C' Clamp   See *Hook clamp*.

CCD (Charge coupled device)   A charge coupled device is a solid state chip covered in several hundred thousand photosensitive cells. Each photosensitive cell represents one piece of picture information (*pixel*). All CCDs have the same colour sensitivity, therefore filters for the red, green and blue component have to be used.

CCT (Correlated colour temperature)   Many sources of light energy do not have the same characteristics as black body radiators, but sources which have a mainly white light output can be given a correlated colour temperature. This is defined as that temperature of the blackbody radiator which *most closely* matches that of the light source in question. It therefore gives a rough guide to the blueness or redness of the source.

C-stand   A multi-purpose stand used for setting flags and nets. Short for Century stand.

CID   Metal halide discharge lamp with a correlated colour temperature of 5600 K.

CIE   Commission International de l'Eclairage. The international body which regulates standards applied to lighting, with various committees comprising representatives from all over the world.

CIE Diagram   Shows the mixture of colours within the spectrum (see *Tri-stimulus*).

CSI   A discharge lamp which approximates to sunlight for colour balance (CCT 4000 K).

Cable crossover   A special rubber ramp used to protect cable from being damaged by being run over and to protect pedestrians from tripping over cable.

Cam-lok   A type of single pole connector used for feeder cables.

Camera light   A luminaire mounted on a camera for lighting along or near the optical axis, usually to provide catch lights for the subjects' eyes.

Can   Permanently installed switch gear containing busbars on a sound stage.

Candela   Unit of luminous intensity.

Candlepower   A term that was used for intensity but has been replaced by the candela.

Carbon arc   A d.c. arc source in which the arc is produced in air between a pair of carbon electrodes. These electrodes burn away and must be advanced during operation.

Cathode   A negative electrode.

Catwalk   A metal or wooden walkway usually used in the film industry to provide access and additional suspension points for luminaires.

Celo cuke   A wire mesh painted with a random pattern and placed in front of a light to throw a subtle pattern.

Chain vice grip   A mounting device that uses a bicycle chain and vice grip to create a tight clamp around pipes, poles, or tree limbs.

Channel   The circuit from the lighting control console to its associated dimmer.

Channel number   Reference number entered by a key pad; or used by dedicated faders.

Chase   A series of programmed sequential steps activating channels from a lighting console.

Chaser lights   A linear string of lamps wired and controlled so that the lights appear to be following in sequence.

Chiaroscuro   A strongly contrasting treatment of light and shade in drawing and painting. Translated from the Italian, the word means 'half-revealed'.

Chicken coop   An overhead suspended light box that provides general downward ambient or fill light. Also called a *coop*.

Chimera   A specially designed, lightweight, collapsible soft box manufactured by Chimera Photographic Lighting.

Chroma   In TV, the information which gives the colour of the image as distinct from its luminance (brightness).

Chroma key   A TV special effect which uses a monochromatic coloured background to allow electronic switching to another picture. Deep blue is commonly used for the background when the foreground involves people.

Chromaticity   The colour of light, as defined by its chromaticity co-ordinates, generally using the CIE diagram.

Cinevator stand   A heavy-duty stand used for the largest types of lights. The mechanism that raises and lowers the light is driven by an electric motor.

Circuit   The electrical path from a dimmer to the luminaire.

Circuit breaker   An electrical switch positioned in the circuit that will automatically operate to break the flow of current under abnormal conditions.

Cmils (USA)   A Cmil is the cross-sectional area of copper wire 1/1000 of an inch in diameter.

$$\text{Area} = \frac{\pi D^2}{4} = \frac{\pi (1^{-3})^2}{4} = \frac{3.142^{-6}}{4} = 0.00000079 \text{ sq. in. or } 0.784 \text{ sq. mil.}$$

One square inch will consist of 1 000 000 square mil or 1 273 240 cmil.

Cold mirror   A dichroic coated glass surface which reflects visible light but allows infrared energy to pass through the reflector so that the reflected light contains less heat.

Colour   A sensation of light induced in the eye by electromagnetic waves of a certain frequency – the colour being determined by that frequency.

Colour balance   Usually describes the effectiveness of film when exposed under various coloured light e.g. daylight film is balanced for 5600 K light, whereas tungsten film is balanced for 3200 K. Can also describe a slight bias introduced by filters to create a warmer or cooler picture.

Colour chart   A chart of standard colours filmed at the head of a roll of film as a colour reference for the lab.

Colour compensation (CC)   A reading obtained from a colour meter indicating the amount of green or magenta gel needed to neutralise off-colour hues, usually present in fluorescent lights.

Colour correction

1   The use of special filter materials to correct for: (a) daylight to tungsten, (b) tungsten to daylight, and (c) spectral aberrations in light sources.

2   Colour correction is also used for film processing to ensure that the various scenes blend together for continuity of picture quality.

Colour filter   A translucent material used to change the colour and quantity of light passing through it. The original filters were made from gelatine – hence all filters tend to be known as 'gels'. Modern filters are manufactured from high grade plastics and glass. With tungsten luminaires of 2 kW and above it is usually necessary to have stand off colour frames to prevent the filter from bleaching and burning.

Colour frame   A frame used to support colour media at the front of the luminaire.

Colour media   Any coloured transparent material that can be placed in front of a luminaire. These are often referred to as 'gels' (for gelatine). Glass and other plastic materials are also used.

Colour meter   A tri-stimulus colour meter contains three photo cells which are filtered to detect the primary values of blue, green and red light. The incident light level can be derived from the output of the green photo cell as this relates to the photopic curve. To obtain the colour temperature of a source, meters of this type will compute a point on the spectrum locus from an analysis of the red, blue and green receptors.

Colour rendering index (Ra)   The evaluation of the effect of a light source on a set of coloured test pieces representing portions of the visible spectrum. The higher the Index towards its maximum of '**100**' the better the colour reproduction. Sources in general require an Index greater than **90** to prevent noticeable colour distortion.

Colour scroller   A device fitted as an add-on extra to a luminaire to provide a colour changing system. Usually consists of around 16 colours glued together and activated by a motor in linear motion and controlled by a digital input signal.

Colour temperature   A method of specifying the colour of a source which emits light in a continuous spectrum. Expressed in Kelvin units, the range used in media lighting is from 2600 K (white lights with a high red content) to 6000 K (white light with a high blue content). *Note*: Cannot be used with discharge sources, although sometimes used as a guide to approximation of colour (see *Correlated Colour Temperature*).

Colour wheel   A circular mechanism holding several different colours mounted in front of a luminaire which can be rotated by hand or by a motor drive.

Combo stand   A junior stand with a $1\frac{1}{8}$ inch receptacle used to hold reflector boards and larger lights.

Complementary colours   A pair of colours in the additive colour mixing system which combine to make white light.

Condenser   A lens or mirror used in an optical system to collect the light being radiated from a source, which is then directed onto the gate of the projection system.

Condor   A vehicle with a telescoping boom arm used as a platform to position lights 30–120 ft in the air.

Console   Name for a control desk (derived from *organ console*).

Contactor   An electrical switch used within an electrical system to control the on/off state of the supply. Usually operated by an electromagnetic coil.

Continuity (Electrical)   The unbroken flow of electricity through various conductors.

Continuity tester   A device that runs a small amount of voltage through a conductor and lights a small bulb or makes a sound if the conductor is continuous.

Contrast range   This is the ratio of the brightness between the lightest and darkest areas in a subject. In a video system, it is the range between the maximum signal which can be satisfactorily handled without distortion and the acceptable electronic noise level of the system.

Contrast ratio   The ratio of the intensity of the key light plus the fill light to the intensity of the fill light alone.

Cookie   See *Cucaloris*.

Cosine law   The equation which allows the calculation of illumination on a surface which is at an angle to the incident light.

Counterweight system   Mechanical system for flying scenery in which the weight of the pieces of scenery is balanced by adjustable weights in a cradle running up and down in guides in a frame normally at the side of the stage. The system is also used for lighting bars.

Cove (Coving)   Portable scenery placed on floor with a curved section to allow a visual smooth transition between the floor and cycloramas. Main purpose in TV is to hide groundrow cyc units. The film industry usually provide deeper coving constructed on set by the plasterers and immediately adjacent to the vertical surface.

Crank-up stand   A heavy duty stand provided with gears and a cranked lever to raise and lower heavy luminaires.

Cribbing (USA)   Blocks of wood used to level camera tracks, lighting stands and props.

Croney cone   A cone-shaped attachment fitted with diffusion that fits on the front of a light to soften and control the beam.

Cross barrel   Used between barrels to allow accurate positioning of luminaires.

Crossfade   A gradual change in the lighting where one lighting set-up *completely* replaces another. Obviously, only one crossfade can occur at a time (see *Move fade*).

Crosslighting   Illumination from two luminaires at approximately 180° to each other on opposite sides of the subject. They are generally hard sources.

Crowder hanger   A fixture mount that fastens to the top of a set wall and provides two spigot holders (studs).

CTB gel   A blue gel that corrects a tungsten source to daylight.

CTO gel   An orange gel that corrects a daylight source to tungsten.

Cube tap   A device that allows three Edison plugs to plug into one Edison socket.

Cucaloris   A wooden cut-out pattern placed in front of a light to create a pattern.

Cue   A signal, which may be written, verbal or by action, that causes motivation of artists or technical staff. Also refers to changes in the lighting set-up.

Cue light   (1) A flashing or rotating light positioned outside the studio/set to warn people when a film take is happening. In TV, during rehearsals, blue lights indicate activity and red lights indicate transmission or recording conditions. (2) To activate the performer at a specified moment.

Cue number   The reference number given to control system memories which contain the lighting set-up information.

Cup blocks   Wooden blocks ($5\frac{1}{2}$ in. square) with concave indentations. They are usually used under the wheels of lighting stands to prevent them rolling away.

Current   The rate of flow of electricity measured in amperes.

$$I = \frac{V}{R}$$

where I = current in amperes, V = applied voltage and R = resistance.

With a.c., resistance is replaced by impedance (Z) or reactance ($X_L X_C$).

Cutter   A long, thin flag used to make cuts in the light.

Cyclorama   A backing, mounted in the studio, to provide a continuous surface and an illusion of infinity.

Cyclorama (cyc) lights (cyc strip)   A set of open-face luminaires used to light a cyclorama. The lights are often wired from two, three, or four separate circuits to provide individual control of different colours.

Daylight   Light commonly considered to have a colour temperature of between 5500 K and 6000 K. Daylight-balanced film renders colours naturally when lit with 5600 K light.

Daylight filter   (a) A blue filter used to change the colour of a light source from tungsten at 3200 K to approximately 5600 K. (b) A blue filter used on a camera to allow daylight balanced film stock to be used with tungsten lighting.

DC   See *Direct current* (also d.c.).

Dedolight   A small, special light fixture with a wide range of beam angle adjustment.

Delta-connected system   A system that provides a three-phase supply where the coils are connected to form the Greek letter delta (Δ).

Depth of field   The depth of the scene that will be in focus on the screen. Depth of field varies with the camera's aperture, focal length, and distance from the subject and the film format.

Deuce   A 2 kW Fresnel.

Deuce board   A fused AC/DC distribution box having two high-amperage contactors that can be controlled from remote switches.

Devitrification   The process which causes a change from a 'glassy' state to a crystalline state.

Dichroic filter   A filter which reflects chosen wavelengths and transmits the remainder. Usually for colour correction. Are used in moving light sources for colour mixing.

Diffuser   Sheets of frosted plastic or spun glass fibre used to soften the shadows produced by the light beam.

Dimmer   An electronic device used to reduce current flow to a lamp and therefore allow its light intensity to be adjusted.

Dimmer curve   A graph which shows the light output or voltage output of a dimmer against the channel control setting.

Dimmer room   The area which has been allocated for the equipment racks which contain the dimmers and associated equipment.

Dinkie   A small Fresnel luminaire which nowadays has been largely superseded by Dedolights which give a much higher light output.

Dipless crossfade   When channels with the same level in different lighting set-ups do not vary in intensity during a crossfade.

Direct current (d.c.)   Current that does not alternate in polarity.

Director of photography (DP)   The person in charge of the lighting and camera departments. The DP has direct creative control of the image.

Discharge sources   Light produced by the passage of electricity, through a gas, across two electrodes enclosed in a quartz envelope e.g. Xenon, CSI, HMI, MSR lamps (see *Arc*).

Discontinuous spectrum   A light source with a discontinuous spectrum, such as a standard fluorescent bulb, that does not emit light evenly across the color spectrum, but instead has spikes at particular wavelengths and emits little or no light at others, resulting in poor colour rendering.

Distribution box   An electrical box with circuit protection used to change cable and connector sizing and provide assorted outlets.

DMX   Multiplex protocol for transmitting digital information from control consoles to dimmers and automated luminaires. DMX 512 is the most used and when the system requires more than 512 control circuits, further DMX 512s have to be used.

Dog collar   A short length of aircraft cable used to secure lights hung above the set. The collar is fitted with a loop at one end and a clip or karabiner at the other.

Dolly grip   The grip in charge of laying dolly track and executing dolly moves and crane moves.

Dot   A very small, circular flag, net, or silk used to alter only a small portion of the beam of light.

Double broad   This is a twin lamp floodlight generally used on studio floors as a local filler.

Double purchase   A suspension system used on counterweight bars which gears the movement of the counterweight bucket to half that of the bar itself (see *Single purchase*).

Doughnut effect   The aberration in the centre of a luminaires' projected beam associated with Plano-Convex lens systems, follow spots and open faced luminaires, caused by the positioning of the lamp within the optical system.

Douser (Dowser)   A small metal flag used in follow spots to cut off the light beam without having to switch off the electrical supply to the source.

Down-fade   The portion of a fade that involves only channels that are decreasing in level.

Downlighter   Usually refers to small ceiling mounted luminaires in control areas.

Downstage   The stage or studio area which is nearest the audience.

Dress a light   To neaten up the light or cable.

Drop arm (Trombone) A device used to hang a luminaire lower than the normal suspension system permits. Allows the luminaires to be positioned at differing heights on lighting bars. Drop arms can be of fixed length, e.g. 0.5 m, 1.0 m, 1.5 m or variable in length where one tube slides inside another and holes are provided at 150 mm intervals to fix steel pins, thus providing a variety of heights.

Duck bill A vice grip with a baby stud on the handle and two 6 sq inch plates welded to the jaws. Used to mount foamcore and bead board on a C-stand.

Dummy load It is sometimes necessary to provide an electrical load to be able to test equipment. For example, when testing dimmers the load could be a resistance rather than a luminaire. Dummy loads are also used to balance electrical circuits for power distribution (see also *Ghost load*).

Duvetyne Thick, black cloth used to block the light beam.

Ears The metal brackets on the front of a luminaire that hold the barndoors and scrims (see *Bracket*).

Earth (Earth continuity conductor) A conductor bonded to earth, other than the neutral, to provide a safety connection for metal components which are not in the electrical circuit. It is accepted to be the point of zero potential.

Effects (a) Lighting to provide atmosphere. (b) Sequence of lighting, usually pre-programmed to give a visual effect (chasers etc.).

Effects projector A focusing luminaire used to project slides or shapes. The effects can also be motor driven.

Efficacy This is the efficiency of a light source in converting the electrical input power to light and is expressed in 'lumens per watt'.

Efficiency This is a measure of the *useful* light output in lumens against the total lumens generated by the light source.

Eggcrate A device consisting of small cross baffle plates to restrict the spread of the light beam on a soft light.

Electromagnetic spectrum Electromagnetic waves consist of radio waves, infrared, the visible portion of the spectrum, ultraviolet (UV), x-rays and gamma rays.

Electronic ballast A solid-state ballast. The term electronic ballast is synonymous with flicker-free low frequency square-wave ballasts for discharge sources such as the HMI, or high frequency units for fluorescent discharge sources (see *Ballast, Square Wave*).

Ellipsoidal spotlight (profile projector) A luminaire which uses an ellipsoidal reflector and a reasonable quality optical system to project shapes and patterns with a hard edge.

Elvis Gold lamé stretched on a frame and used to bounce light.

Equipment grounding (USA) (*Europe – Equipment earth*) The grounding of conductive parts of equipment, such as the outer metal casing, via a green grounding wire (*Europe – Green/yellow stripes*).

Ethernet Data transmission system for computer networks; also used for inter-connection of lighting consoles, dimmers and VDUs in remote locations (see *DMX*).

Expendables Supplies, such as tape, that are used up during the course of a production.

Extension bar This is used to extend lighting barrels for accurate positioning of luminaires.

Extension cable Used where the luminaire cable is too short to reach the nearest source of power. Generally 3-core, although for high current applications may be several single core cables.

Eye light Used to create a twinkle in the eye of the subject.

F-number A set of numbers used to express the aperture of a lens which represents its light transmission. It is worked out by dividing the focal length of the lens by the diameter of the opening in the lens diaphragm. It is also colloquially known as the *stop*.

Fade   A gradual change in light levels from one set of intensities to another.

Fade time   The time between the start and end of a lighting change. Can vary between a few seconds and anything up to 60 minutes; occasionally the time may be over a longer period in theatrical productions.

Fader   A control device for indirectly setting the current output of a dimmer and thus varying the light intensity. Originally were levers, but are often 'wheels' in modern lighting control systems.

Fall-off   The diminishing intensity of light across the beam of a luminaire. Also, the reduction in light output over distance due to the inverse square law.

FAY   An incandescent PAR lamp with dichroic coating that creates daylight-coloured light.

Feeder cable   Large single-conductor cable or multi-core cable used to run power from the power source to distribution boxes on the set (see *Extension cable, Distribution system*).

Field angle   Those points on the light output curve which are 10% of maximum output. The included angle between these two points is the field angle.

Filament   The tungsten coil inside a lamp that glows when voltage is applied to it creating light.

Filler   Light used to control shade areas. Usually a soft light but can be controlled hard light.

Film speed   (a) A measure of the film's sensitivity to light expressed in numerical terms to give an 'exposure index' which is used in the ISO and ASA system on light meters. (b) The velocity of film passing through movie cameras or projectors and is measured in frames per second or in metres per minute.

Finger   A very small rectangular flag, net or silk, used to control small portions of the light beam.

Five K   A colloquial term for a 5 kW spotlight.

Fixture   General term for a luminaire, light, or lantern.

Flag   A sheet of metal or card mounted in front of a luminaire to give a relatively sharp cut off to the light beam. The cut off is dependent upon the distance from the luminaire and improves as the distance increases. Very effective with focused luminaires such as the Fresnel but when used with open faced luminaires often requires greater distances to achieve sharp cut off. Also black Duvetyne cloth stretched over a metal frame.

Flag box   A wooden box in which flags, nets, and silks are stored.

FLB filter   A filter used to remove the green hue of fluorescents.

Flex arm   A small jointed arm used to hold fingers and dots.

Flicker-free ballast   A solid state ballast that provides square-waves of around 100 Hz to eliminate variations in the light output of discharge sources, thus avoiding problems with synchronisation of film shutters and TV field frequencies.

Flood   By focusing a lamp close to a lens, the diameter of the light beam is enlarged and thus gives the widest field of illumination.

Floodlight   A luminaire which has only a reflector to control the beam and has wide angle distribution (see *Soft light* and *Cyclorama light*).

Fluorescence   The ability of some materials to convert ultra violet energy into visible light.

Fly   To suspend scenery or equipment above a stage or studio floor by means of a suspension system which can be manually operated or driven by motorised units.

Focal length   The distance of the focal point from the lens is called the focal length of the lens.

Focal point   The point where the incident parallel rays, which are bent by a lens, meet in focus.

Focus   In optics, the adjustment to give a clearly defined image. Originally used in the lighting industry to indicate the process of 'spotting' or 'flooding' the light beam of a luminaire, but is now used to indicate the general setting of a luminaire on the stage or in a 'pop' rig.

Follow spot   A narrow angle, focusing hard edged spotlight used to follow moving artists.

Foot candle   An old unit, now superseded by 'lux', used to describe illumination which was measured in 'lumens per square foot'.

Foot lambert   The old unit for luminance (brightness) which has been replaced by the 'nit'.

FPS Frames Per Second.

Frequency The number of cycles per second of a.c., measured in Hertz (Hz).

Fresnel lens A convex lens built with concentric steps to enable its thickness to be reduced.

Fresnel spotlight (colloq. Fresnel) Luminaires fitted with Fresnel lenses of varying sizes, the width of the beam can be changed by varying the spacing between the lens and the lamp/reflector assembly.

Fringing Chromatic aberration in simple lenses creating dispersed colour effects around the light beam, similar to the colours of a rainbow in appearance, blue being the most predominant of the colours.

Frost Translucent gel or plastic used to diffuse light sources.

Fuse A protective device for electrical circuits; originally a piece of special wire but nowadays nearly always a metal link contained in a ceramic cartridge.

Gaffer Term used in the film industry to describe the chief technician.

Gaffer clamp/grip A clamp with two jaws fitted with rubber pads and equipped with a mounting spigot to temporarily attach fittings to scenery flats, suitable horizontal and vertical surfaces and lighting equipment e.g. lighting barrel (see *Mafer clamp*).

Gaffer tape Heavy, fabric-based tape that rips cleanly in the direction of the weave. It is used for securing cables and luminaires on the set.

Gamma A measure of the contrast in image reproduction. In TV overall gamma relates to the receiver screen luminance and the brightness of the original scene.

Gate The optical centre of a profile projector where the shutters are positioned and an iris or 'gobo' can be inserted.

Gator grip See *Gaffer clamp/grip*.

Gel See *Colour media*.

Generators A diesel powered unit used to generate power on location (also used in some film studios). They are sound baffled and provide either busbars or other feeder connectors. Also called *genny*.

GFI Ground Fault Interrupter.

Ghost load A load that is not used to light the set and is placed on a circuit to balance the various legs of power or to bring the load on a resistance-type dimmer up to its minimum operating wattage. Also called *dummy load* and *phantom load*.

Globe (USA) A lamp or bulb.

Gnats (Gnats whisker) Slang term used in the United Kingdom to describe a very small amount (**American** – *Scosh*).

Gobo A mask placed in the gate of a profile spot to shape the beam. It is a simple form of outline projection.

Gobo arm The arm which can be attached to a gobo head on a stand on which to mount gobos. Typical lengths of arm are 500 mm and 1 m.

Gobo head The metal knuckle that attaches the gobo arm to a stand. The unit consists of two metal plates with grooves to hold various sizes of arms, e.g. 1/4 in, 3/8 in, 1/2 in and 5/8 in.

Grandmaster The device (*wheel* or *fader*) which has overall control of the output of a console.

Grey Scale Chart showing gradations from white to black.

Grid (1) (USA) A resistance unit used with a carbon arc light. (2) The structure of metal tubes suspended above the stage floor for hanging luminaires (see *Lighting grid*).

Grid clamp A clamp that attaches to standard lighting grid barrels (48 mm OD). Several varieties are available for either bottom fixing or side fixing to the bar together with various configurations for suspension.

Grid cloth   A white nylon diffusion fabric with a grid-like weave. A similar filter material is also available.

Griffolyn   Trade name for plastic material. Griffolyn sheets come in 6′ × 6′, 12′ × 12′ and 20′ × 20′ available in black/white, white/white and clear. They are used as a bounce for fill. Also called *griff*.

Grip   A crew member responsible for the non-electrical aspects of lighting and rigging, and for the camera dolly and other camera platforms.

Grip clip   A metal spring clamp resembling a large clothes peg and used to clamp various materials together, e.g. tensioning cloths across wooden battens.

Grip truck   (USA) The lighting truck that houses the luminaires and grip equipment during location shooting. Will hold a considerable array of equipment, some of which is there 'just in case'.

Ground Fault Interrupter (GFI) (USA)   A special type of circuit protection. There are a number of different types of GFIs. One type compares the outgoing current of a circuit to the returning current. If it detects a difference in the two (indicating a ground fault), it trips a switch to disconnect the circuit. They are also called Ground Fault Circuit Interrupters (GFCI) (see also *RCD*).

Grounded wire (USA)   The grounded, white, current-carrying wire (neutral) of an American a.c. circuit.
(*Note*:   Do not confuse this term with the *green grounding wire*).

Grounding wire (USA)   The green, equipment grounding wire of an a.c. circuit (see *Earth*).

Groundrow   A lighting unit with multiple compartments, usually arranged in linear fashion, for lighting from the base of cyclorama. The units are provided as single, twin, three or four way. The three and four way units are used for colour mixing fitted with red, blue and green filters, the fourth compartment can be fitted with 'clear' to dilute the colour output. A cove normally hides them from view (see *Cyc lighting, Cove*).

HMI (also CID and MSR)   Discharge lamps which have a daylight colour balance (5600 K).

Half scrim   A semi-circular scrim used to attenuate part of the light beam (see *Scrim*).

Halogen cycle   The cycle by which halogen in a lamp returns tungsten deposits back to the filament thereby preventing blackening of the inner lamp wall.

Hard glass halogen lamp   A tungsten halogen lamp with an envelope of borosilicate glass.

Hard light   A luminaire that produces well-defined shadows, normally a spotlight.

Harmonic distortion   When a wave shape departs from being purely sinusoidal with a sharp rise or fall in its characteristic, such as a square wave or the chopped wave form produced from thyristor dimmers, it will contain harmonics of the original frequency.

Head   A luminaire (**USA** – *light fixture*).

Head cable   The power and control multi-core cable which connects the ballast to a discharge source luminaire. The plugs and sockets used vary in size and pin configuration according to the various manufacturers and the power requirements.

Heat filter   A filter which removes infrared from the light beam to reduce heat from the source of illumination.

Hertz (Hz)   The unit of frequency which is measured in cycles per second. Other units are kilohertz (kHz) and megahertz (MHz).

Hi boy (USA)   An extra tall stand for mounting luminaires.

High key   Describes a scene containing mainly light tones well illuminated without large areas of strong shadow.

High leg (USA)   The 208-V leg of a delta-connected three-phase system (see *Delta connected system*).

High roller (USA)   An extra tall rolling stand, often used to fly an overhead frame.

Highest takes precedence (HTP)   On a lighting control system, where the highest setting will win, when two or more pre-set levels are simultaneously selected for that channel, e.g. if '7' then '5' is selected for a particular channel, '7' will win (see also *Latest Takes Precedence*).

Hoist   Old term used to describe either manual or motorised lifting equipment (see *Winch*).

Hook clamp   A clamp used for suspending luminaires from lighting bars (see *C-clamp*).

Hot spot   (1) Usually produced by luminaire optical systems not using Fresnel lenses. The beam centre of PCs and some effects units are prone to hot spots unless the lamp is carefully focused or the manufacturer takes steps to prevent problems in practice. (2) A shiny spot or glare reflection that is distracting to the eye.

House lights   A lighting system permanently installed to either illuminate an audience area or provide worklights in studios.

Housing   The metal casing that encloses the lamp, reflector and optical system of a luminaire.

Hue   The quality by which one colour is distinguished from another as a result of their wavelengths. It does not take into account the brightness or intensity of the colour.

Illumination   The luminous flux falling on unit area of a surface. The unit of illumination is the lux (1 lumen/m^2) and it is the measure of the quantity of *incident light*.

Impedance (z)   A measure, in ohms, of the opposition to current flow in an a.c. circuit. Includes resistance and reactance.

Incandescence   The emission of light by raising a material to a high temperature.

Incident light   See *Lux*.

Incident light meter   A light meter that reads the light falling onto the subject.

Independent   Channels in a control system which only respond to one master and are 'independent' of the rest of the console.

Inductance   Opposition to current changing in an a.c. circuit, which causes the current to lag behind the applied voltage. Inductance is created by turns of wire with or without an iron core.

Infrared (IR)   Wavelengths below the visible wavelength of light, felt as heat.

Inky   A 100 W Fresnel luminaire manufactured by Mole Richardson Co.

Instrument (USA)   Name used for a lighting fixture (luminaire).

Internal reflector   An integral reflector formed on the inner rear surface of the envelope of a lamp and is usually parabolic or elliptic in shape.

Inverse square law   The equation which is used to calculate the illumination at a given distance from a source of light.

Iris   A series of adjustable metal plates arranged to give a variable circular aperture. Used in lighting projectors to alter the size of the light beam.

J-box (USA)   A junction box fitted with Socapex connectors and used to connect an extension cable to the existing head cable of a discharge luminaire.

Jockey boxes (USA)   Metal storage containers on the underside of a truck. Jockey boxes usually store sandbags, cable, and so on.

Junior stand (USA)   A stand with a 1⅛ inch spigot holder.

Junior stud (USA)   A 1⅛ inch spigot used for larger items of lighting equipment.

Junior (USA)   A 2 kW Fresnel spotlight.

Kelvin   The SI unit of thermodynamic temperature. It uses the same size of degree as the Celsius scale. (Zero K $= -273\,°$C).

Key light   The principal modelling light, usually a spotlight.

Kicker   Generally a hard light source used to provide obvious highlights.

Kilowatt   Electrical power term for 1000 W.

KVA (Kilovolt Amperes)   Whereas wattage is a measure of power consumed in a circuit, KVA gives the total of voltage applied and current flowing. With unity power factor, 1 KVA = 1 kW.

LD   Abbreviation for Lighting Designer or Lighting Director.

Lamp   A glass or quartz envelope which contains filaments or electrodes. The term lamp is often used to describe a luminaire, which is to be avoided as it can cause confusion (colloq. terms include globe, bubble, source).

Lantern   See *Luminaire*.

Latest takes precedence (LTP)   On a lighting control system, where the last selected level for a particular channel will win, e.g. if '7' then '5' is selected for a particular channel, '5' will win (see also *Highest Takes Precedence*).

Leko   A slang term used in America to describe ellipsoidal spotlights.

Life   Usually refers to the manufacturers' rates life in hours of a lamp at its normal voltage and is based on the average life of a number of lamps which have been tested.

Light meter   A device for measuring reflected or incident light. Many modern meters also measure the colour of the source (see *Luminance meter* and *Colour meter*).

Lighting balance   See *Balance*.

Light centre length (LCL)   The distance from the centre of the filament to a standard point at the base of the lamp.

Lighting batten   A barrel assembly with integral power feeders for luminaires.

Lighting control console   A unit which contains the controls for adjusting the channel levels and thus the dimmer outputs, 'group channel' control, memory control, playback system and special effects.

Lighting Designer (Director)   The person who creates and implements the lighting design for a production.

Lighting grid   In film and TV a structure mounted at high level above the operational area, usually made from steel or aluminium or a combination of the two, for the purposes of suspending luminaires and ancillary lighting equipment.

Lighting plot   The instructions and drawings of the various lighting set-ups for a production, used by the LD and electricians. (Sometimes simply known as the *Plot*)

Lighting ratio   The ratio of the light level on the keylight side to the light level on the filled side.

Limbo   Describes a state of lighting where the background details are suppressed. In TV this is usually created by 'blackness' whereas the film industry tends to use a white background.

Linnebach projector   A lighting unit, basically a box without a lens, which contains a small point source of illumination to project soft diffused images of cut-outs or glass slides.

Louvres   Thin black metallic strips located on a luminaire to reduce spill light (see *Eggcrates*). When fitted in front of a luminaire may also be adjustable at various angles to provide dimming without colour change (see also *Shutters*).

Low boy (USA)   A very short stand (see *Turtle*).

Low key   Describes a scene containing mostly dark tones with large areas of shadow and is often used to create a dramatic mood.

Lug   A very heavy-duty connector for attaching feeder cables to busbars.

Lumen   The lumen is the unit of 'luminous flux' and is defined as the amount of light which falls on 1 m^2 of a surface at a *constant* distance of 1 m from a source of one candela.

Lumens per watt   The light output in lumens produced by a source for each watt of electrical power supplied to the source.

Luminaire   A general term for a complete lighting unit. It includes the housing, the reflector, lens and lamps. (Colloq: light, lantern, fixture, unit, instrument, fitting).

Luminance   The measure of brightness of a surface, it is measured in 'nits'. The old unit was the 'foot lambert'.

Luminance meter   Luminance meters are used for the measurement of a light source or surface brightness. A normal luminance meter will be calibrated in candela/m^2 and alternatively foot lamberts (see *Spot meter*).

Luminous intensity   A measure of the energy from a light source emitted in a particular direction. It is measured in candelas.

Lux   The unit of illuminance (illumination). It is the unit of measurement for the incident light arriving at a surface. The old measuring system used foot-candles. (One foot-candle equals 10.76 lux).

Mcb   Miniature circuit breaker.

Mccb   Moulded case circuit breaker.

MR-16   A small projector lamp with a self contained reflector.

MT-2   A colour-correction gel used on carbon arc lights with a Y-1 gel to correct the colour temperature of a white flame arc to 3200 K.

MacBeth   A blue glass filter used on some open faced luminaires which converts tungsten sources to daylight.

Mafer clamp   All purpose grip clamp which can utilise different mounting attachments.

Master/Group master   Usually refers to a lighting control system fader which overrides by electrical means a group of individual faders.

Matte   An opaque shape used in front of a camera lens.

Matte process   A shape derived on film from subjects in front of a dense, coloured background (usually blue). This image is subsequently used as a matte in the optical printing process to allow two images to be combined. With the advent of computers, the image manipulation is carried out electronically.

Matth pole (USA)   A pole that braces against two opposite walls to provide a structure from which to hang a lightweight luminaire. Poles originally manufactured by Matthews as grip equipment.

Maxibrute   A large rectangular luminaire fitted with either nine 1000 W PARs or twenty-four 1000 W PARs, capable of being switched in segments to provide variable light output. Often used with Full Blue filter to provide fill light when shooting in daylight on location.

Maximum overall length (MOL)   The overall physical length of a lamp including all electrical contacts.

Meat axe (USA)   An arm mounted to the pipe of a catwalk or to the basket of a boom platform that provides a method of placing a flag in front of a luminaire.

Meltric (USA)   A five-pin, heavy-duty connector used in some power distribution systems.

Memory   The term used to denote electronically recorded information which contains the lighting set-ups.

Memory effect   Usually found in Nickel–Cadmium (Ni–Cad) batteries. Caused by insufficient discharge, where the battery upon recharge will only accept a limited level. In practice, shows as poor battery life.

Mickey (USA)   A 1 kW open-face luminaire manufactured by Mole Richardson.

Midget (USA)   A 200 W wide-beam Fresnel luminaire manufactured by Mole Richardson.

MIDI (Musical Instrument Digital Interface)   A communication protocol used to link control consoles for both lighting and automated luminaire systems.

Mini   A 200 W Fresnel luminaire manufactured by Mole Richardson, or a miniature soft light manufactured by LTM.

Minibrute   A rectangular luminaire fitted with either six 650 W PARs or nine 650 W PARs, capable of being switched in segments to provide variable light output. Often used with Full Blue filter to provide fill light when shooting in daylight on location.

Minus green gel   A magenta gel used to take the green out of fluorescent light.

Mired (MIcro REciprocal Degrees)   A filter causes a constant shift in the reciprocal value of the colour temperature of the source, and to acheive a more manageable number the reciprocal value is multiplied by 1 million.

Mirror ball   A motor driven ball with its surface covered in small mirrors. When rotated, with spotlights shining to it, it produces moving points of light.

Modelling light   The terms is used to describe any luminaire, generally a hard source, that reveals the depth, shade and texture of subjects.

MoleFay (USA)   A lighting unit consisting of a number of 650 W FAY lamps manufactured by Mole Richardson.

Monopole   A telescopic suspension unit used to suspend one luminaire. Their length is adjusted by internal wire ropes on winding drums at the top of the unit.

Motorised luminaires   Motorised effects luminaires which provide a multiplicity of projected moving images and colours. Units tend to be of two types – the light beam is modulated by a moving mirror with the luminaire stationary, or, the luminaire moves to create motion.

Move fade   A fade from one lighting set-up to another where only those channels with a new intensity change; the other channels remaining static. Several 'Move' fades can occur at the same time (see *Crossfade*).

MSR   Single ended discharge lamps made by Philips (see *HMI*).

Multiplex   Control signals passed in serial digital format down a pair of screened wires. The most normal form is DMX 512 and is used to control dimmers and motorised luminaires.

Munsell values   The Munsell system enables three qualities to be quantified and these are:
1   **hue** – describes the basic colour such as red or blue;
2   **value (or brightness)** – refers to how light or dark the colour appears (it is a measure of the amount of reflected light); and
3   **chroma (or saturation)** – refers to the intensity of colour; as a colour moves away from white it becomes more and more saturated.

ND   See *Neutral-density*.

NEC (USA)   National Electrical Code – the American version of the UK Electrical Regulations.

Nanometre (nm)   A unit of metric measurement equal to one billionth of a metre, which is used to measure light wavelengths.

Net   A black honeycomb netting material sewn onto a rod frame that is used to reduce the intensity of part or all of a light's beam.

Neutral density filter   A filter which attenuates the light passing through it without affecting the colour of that light.

Ni–cad batteries (Nickel–Cadmium)   Ni–cad have the advantage of being easy to handle, robust and accept very fast charges using specialised equipment.

Nine-light   A luminaire comprising nine PAR lamps used on exterior lighting.

Nit   The unit of luminance, which is one candela per square metre of surface radiation. It is therefore the measure of the *brightness* of a surface (see *Foot lambert*).

Non-dim   Describes the circuit which replaces the normal dimmer function, where the circuit is switched 'on' or 'off' *only*, either by a switch or relay system.

Nook light   A small lightweight open-face luminaire using a double-ended lamp and a V-shaped reflector.

Objective lens   See *Projection lens*.

Offset   A piece of grip hardware used to hang a luminaire out to the side of a floor stand.

Off-stage   Areas that are out of the eyeline of an audience.

Ohm (Ω)   The unit of electrical resistance equal to the resistance through which 1 V will force 1 A.

On-stage   In view of the audience.

Opal   A popular, thin diffusion.

Opaque   Absorbance of electro-magnetic radiation at specific wavelengths, generally refers to the fact that light is not transmitted.

Open faced luminaire   Describes luminaires with no lens system, such as the 'Redhead' and 'Blonde' (see *Focusing reflector light*).

Overcurrent device   A circuit breaker or fuse.

Overhead set   A large frame with one of several types of material stretched across it, including a solid, single net, double net, silk, or griffolyn.

Pan   Term describing the horizontal movement, about a point, of luminaires or equipment.

Pancake   The thinnest of the apple box range used for mounting equipment at a very low level.

Pantograph   A mechanical cross-armed device for varying the height of luminaires or other fittings. It is generally spring balanced but can be operated by a motor or manually driven gear system.

PAR   A lamp with an integral parabolic reflector, similar to a car headlight. PAR lamps are available in a wide variety of physical sizes with differing front lenses and power outputs.

Parabolic reflector   A reflector shaped like a parabola, giving it a focal point from which the majority of the light rays will be reflected outward in a parallel beam.

Parallel circuit   Connection of two or more devices or loads so that the current flowing through each one follows a separate path (see *Series circuit*).

Parcan   A simple luminaire, basically a metal tube, with a PAR lamp mounted in it. The type of lamp determines the beam spread.

Patching   A term describing the connections made between channels on lighting consoles and dimming systems. (Usually accomplished by software – known as *Soft patching*).

Patch panel   A system rather like an old telephone operators' interconnection system (switchboard) to connect low voltage circuits or high voltage circuits. (Known as *Hard patching*).

PCB   Printed circuit board. Individual boards are supplied with all components mounted on them and will be produced for a specific purpose e.g. a pcb for dimmer control circuits.

Peppers (USA)   A line of relatively compact tungsten luminaires manufactured by LTM in sizes of 100 W, 200 W, 300 W, 420 W, 500 W, 660 W, 1000 W, and 2 kW.

Phantom load   See *Ghost load*.

Phase   (1) An energised single conductor. (2) The positioning of an a.c. cycle in time, relative to the other two phases. Most electrical services are either single phase or three phase (see *Alternating current, Wye connected system*).

Photoflood   A lamp that has a colour temperature of 3400 K. These lamps, which are similar in size to household lamps, have over driven filaments to achieve the high colour temperature. Hence they have very short operating lives (see *Filament*).

Photopic curve   This gives the standard sensitivity for the eye for wavelengths from 380 nm to 760 nm. The peak sensitivity is at 555 nm, whereas the sensitivity at 400 nm is about 1/1000th of the highest level.

Piano board (USA)   Originally, a portable dimmer switchboard or road board. This term has come to be used for many types of portable dimmer switchboards.

Pigeon plate   A small metal plate attached, generally to apple boxes, for supporting small luminaires.

Pin matrix   A method of coupling control channels into groups by the insertion of special pins into a 'x' and 'y' matrix, where the 'x' axis may represent channels and the 'y' represent groups.

Pipe clamp (USA)   See *Hook clamp*.

Pixel   A picture element which is the smallest element of a CCD array. The definition is governed by the number of 'pixels per area', the higher the amount the better the resolution.

Plano-convex lens   A lens which has one flat side and one convex side.

Plano-convex spotlight (PC Spot)   A luminaire that gives a reasonably even beam with a very sharp edge. The PC uses a Plano-Convex lens and circular reflector and is similar to the Fresnel in construction and performance.

Plate dimmer (USA)   A resistance-type dimmer commonly used with d.c. circuits.

Playback   That part of a lighting control system where the lighting memories and/or other lighting states are combined and controlled by output master faders or switches.

Plugging box (USA)   A distribution box. May also refer more generally to any outlet box.

Plus green gel   A filter used to add green to the light output of normal lamps to match their colour to that of fluorescent lamps.

Polariser   A polarising filter removes some of the planes of polarisation and allows the subject to be seen clearly.

Polarity   The orientation of the positive and negative wires of a d.c. circuit or the phase and neutral wires of a.c. circuits.

Polecat   Lighting support system consisting of sprung metal tubes capable of extension onto which luminaires can be mounted. Used between two surfaces, floor and ceiling or two walls. Also called *pogo stick* and *Matth pole*.

Pole operation (Colloq. Pole Op)   The control of electrical and mechanical functions on luminaires and suspension equipment by means of a long metal pole. The end of the pole is fitted with either a hook or loop.

Power assisted systems   Suspension equipment under the direct control of an operator, e.g. winch control motor systems.

Power factor   In a.c., the ratio of the actual or effective power in watts to the apparent power in volt-amperes, expressed as a percentage.

Power   The total amount of work, measured in watts. One watt is equal to 1 J/second; one horsepower is equivalent to 746 W (see *Ampere, Volt*).

Practical lamp   A luminaire or any fixture that is shown in a scene. e.g. table lamp, that can be effectively switched on and off by an actor.

Prefocus   Denotes special lamp caps so that the filament lines up precisely to the optics of a luminaire.

Prelight or prerig   To rig and set the lights in advance, as close to the intended lighting scheme as possible.

Pre-set   A group of faders on a manual desk which are connected to the dimmers and controlled by a 'master fader'.

Primary colours   The primary *additive* colours are red, green and blue. The primary *subtractive* colours are cyan, magenta and yellow (see *Additive colour mixing, Subtractive colour mixing*).

Prime fixture (USA)   A focusing, open faced luminaire such as a Redhead or Blonde.

Priscilla (USA)   A silver lamé stretched on a frame and used to bounce light.

Profile spot   See *Ellipsoidal spotlight*.

Projection lens   A lens specially designed to project slides or shapes onto a surface with considerable enlargement of the slide or original material (see *Objective lens*).

Pup   A colloquial term for a 1 kW spotlight.

Purkinje effect   The change from 'cone' vision during daylight to 'rod' vision at night.

Putty knife (USA)   Decorators' putty knife which has a 5/8 inch spigot fixed to its handle. The knife can be inserted into the slot of a door frame or windowsill and the spigot will support a small luminaire.

Quartz   Crystalline silica which is glass like and used to make envelopes for lamps. It is generally transparent to ultra violet radiation.

RCD (Residual Current Device)   Formerly known as an earth leakage circuit breaker.

RMS   Abbreviation of Root-Mean-Square. The rms value of the current is a measure of its effectiveness in producing the same heating effect in a resistance as a direct current.

Radiant flux   The amount of light energy that is given off by an object each second and is measured in 'joules per second' (the physical unit of measurement is known as a watt).

Rag (USA)   The cloth part of an overhead set.

Rain tent   A tent to cover luminaires and electrical equipment in case of precipitation.

Reactance (X)   A measure, in ohms, of the opposition to a.c. due to capacitance (X_C) or inductance (X_L).

Receptacle   An in line female electrical connector or a socket mounted on a distribution box.

Record   The action of recording (memorising) a lighting set-up on a control system.

Rectifier   An electrical unit that converts a.c. to d.c.

Redhead   A 800 W open faced luminaire.

Reflectance (reflection factor)   The ratio of the reflected light to the incident light falling on a surface, measured in lumens.

Reflector   The component in luminaires that focuses the light rays towards the lens. In a Fresnel it will be a spherical reflector whereas PAR lamps use parabolic reflectors. Effects projectors (Leko) generally use ellipsoidal reflectors.

Reflector boards   Silver-covered boards typically used to bounce light, usually sunlight. Also called *shiny boards*.

Remainder dim   A lighting console instruction which maintains the levels of selected channels, while forcing all other active channels to zero.

Rembrandt lighting   Lighting style emphasising the subject by strong modelling of light and shadow. This style is reminiscent of Rembrandt's paintings, hence its name.

Remote   A method of controlling the lighting from a position away from the main control system.

Resistance (Ω)   A measure, in ohms, of the opposition to current flow in a conductor or device. In d.c., volts/amperes = ohms. For a.c., see impedance.

Rheostat   A resistance dimmer to control the voltage applied to a lamp. Also used to control the speed of motors.

Rig   (1) Any assembly designed to support luminaires, cabling, dimmers and effects units etc. (2) To set up scenery equipment and lighting.

Riggers control   A remote portable hand held control unit for controlling either luminaires or winch systems.

Rigging (USA)   Collective term for suspension equipment.

Rigging bible (USA)   A set of circuit diagrams showing the power layout of a studio's sound stages.

Rigging gaffer (USA)   The gaffer in charge of designing and installing the cabling and electrical distribution for a large set.

Rim light   A backlight that makes a rim around the head and shoulders of the subject from the perspective of the camera, enhancing the separation from the background.

Rise time   In an electronic circuit the time taken for the current to rise from 10% of its amplitude to 90% of maximum. The rate of change of current influences the amount of generated voltage in an inductive circuit. The rate of change of current in a falling waveform also affects the generated voltage.

Riser   (1) An extension tube to add height to a lighting stand. (2) A wooden platform used to raise the set, luminaires or the camera.

Risers   The flat surfaces on the Fresnel lens rings that form the division between segments.

Ritter fan (USA)   A large effects fan used to blow snow and rain; also to give the appearance of wind or speed.

SCR   A **S**ilicon **C**ontrolled **R**ectifier. A solid state current switching device, used in dimmers for lighting systems. It comes from the *thyristor* family.

SPD   Spectral Power Distribution.

SWL   The safe working load of a piece of lifting equipment usually quoted in lbs or kg.

Safety (USA)   A safety bond, wire, chain or rope looped around the yoke of a luminaire to prevent it from falling should it come loose from its fixing point.

Safety bond (also Safety Chain)   A short length of wire rope or chain formed into a loop around a suspension point, to act as a secondary means of suspension in the event of failure of the primary system. With wire rope safety bonds, regulations require that the bond should not allow a fall of more than 300 mm.

Sandbag   A sand-filled bag used to stabilise stands and equipment by adding dead weight or counterweight.

Saturated rig   A lighting installation where luminaires are installed in sufficient numbers to cover the total acting area without rigging and de-rigging.

Saturation   A term used to describe the density of a colour between the pure colour concerned and white, i.e. a deep red or pink.

Scaffold platforms (Parallels – USA)   Scaffold platforms, as used by builders, are quite frequently used as mobile lighting towers. They are quick and easy to assemble as they come in preformed sections, and if used properly can be safe.

Scene machine (USA)   A lighting unit that projects an image on a screen, usually from the back. The image can be made to move by scrolling through the machine or to rotate by using adjustable-speed motors. Scene machines are often used to create moving clouds across the cyclorama in theatrical productions. Known as back projection unit in the United Kingdom.

Scissor clamp   A device that provides a means of hanging luminaires from a false ceiling such as those found in many modern commercial buildings.

Scissor lift   A self-propelled, battery powered hydraulic lift. With a lifting capacity of between 300 kg and 600 kg and capable of heights between 6 m and 12 m. Normally used by the building industry, they have been adapted for use as mobile lighting and camera platforms.

Scissors arc   A special carbon arc device used to create a lightning effect. The carbons are touched together by a flexible drive device which is actuated in a similar manner to grass shears. This has been superseded by lightning effects generally produced by xenon tubes driven from electronic generators.

Scoop   A simple elliptical shaped floodlight usually fitted with a large GLS lamp giving a soft light output. Due to the type of lamp used, is prone to 'lamp sing' when used with thyristor dimmers.

Scrim   A scrim usually consists of wire mesh placed in front of a luminaire. The size of holes and thickness of wire determine the amount of light that will pass through the mesh.

Secondary colours   Those colours produced by mixing either two additive primary colours or two subtractive primary colours.

Sealed beam   A lamp with an integral reflector and lens (see *PAR*).

Senior (USA)   A 5 kW incandescent Fresnel luminaire manufactured by Mole Richardson Co.

Series circuit   Connection of two or more devices or loads in tandem so that the current flowing through one also flows through all the others (see *Parallel circuit*).

Service (Electrical service)   This term refers to the types of circuits installed, for example, single-phase, three-phase.

Service entrance   The main switchboard into which the power lines running to a building terminate.

Set   Scenery constructed for lighting and the shooting of scenes for film and TV.

Shock   The nervous sensation imparted to a body by the passage of an electric current. The severity of shock is dependent upon the current flowing, the path through the body and the time for which the current flows (see *RCDs*).

Short circuit   Unwanted current flow caused by low impedance between conductors. Usually controlled by fuses or circuit breakers.

Show card   Thick card stock, usually white on one side and black on the other, used to bounce light.

Shutter   Pieces of thin black metal, of varying shapes, used within a luminaire to block light. They are used to shape the light beam projected from effects spotlights and follow spots.

Shutters   Venetian blind type metal slats mounted in front of a luminaire as a blackout device or dimmer (see *Louvres*).

Silk   Originally was voile, a type of very fine silk netting used as the veil around ladies' hats. It is used to soften and cut the intensity of light and is available in several sizes, from very small dots and fingers to very large 20 × 20 ft overheads. Today, other materials with similar properties are used.

Silver bullet (USA)   A 12 kW or 18 kW discharge luminaire manufactured by Cinemills Corp.

Single purchase   A suspension system for counterweight bars where no gearing is used. The distance of travel of the counterweight bucket will be the same as the barrel (see *Double purchase*).

Sister lugs (USA)   See *Lug*.

Sky-cloth   Scenery used to convey the impression of an open sky (see *Cyclorama*).

Skypan   A very shallow scoop used in the film industry, which is rather like a metal dustbin lid with a bare lamp in the middle. Used for general fill, using either 2 kW, 5 kW, or 10 kW lamps.

Snoot   A conical metal tube fitted to the front of the luminaire to enable a reduction in beam size.

Snot tape   Sticky adhesive substance used to attach gel to a frame.

Socapex   Multi-wire cable connector used (1) on discharge source head feeder cables and (2) on multi-core cable for dimmer circuits.

Soft box   A device used to create very soft, diffuse light.

Soft patch   Electronic system on a lighting control desk to allocate dimmers to control channels.

Softlight   A luminaire designed to produce virtually shadowless light and is generally used to control contrast. The larger the source size the softer the shadow so the design of a softlight is always a compromise between the largest source that can be achieved and the size that can be tolerated in practice.

Solid   A black 'rag' stretched on a frame and used to cut light.

Sound stage   An enclosed area with smooth level floors and a high roof with lighting grid. It is sound proofed by having thick walls and special door arrangements.

Spacelight   A large cylinder consisting of a diffuser with an array of lamps inside to give soft ambient illumination.

Sparks   A nickname for set lighting technician.

Specular   Describes a mirror like surface. Highly reflective.

Spider box (USA)   An in line connection box fitted with short busbars enabling feeder cables with lug terminations to be joined in series.

Spigot   The male member attached to a yoke used for the suspension of the luminaire and also for insertion into a floor stand. Smaller luminaires used 5/8-in spigots and larger ones use a 1⅛ in. Colloq. 'spud' (see *Stud*).

Spill light   Extraneous uncontrolled light from a luminaire. May come from the rings on a Fresnel lens or escape from the aperture between the barndoors and colour frames.

Spot   To focus a luminaire by moving the lamp and/or reflector away from the lens, giving a narrow beam (see *Flood*).

Spot meter   A type of reflected meter having a very narrow angle of acceptance (1° to 20°) used to determine the light value of a specific point of interest.

Spotlight   A luminaire with a focusing system which allows concentration of the light beam, thus giving greater operational control of the light level.

Square law   Light is governed by a formula called the *Inverse Square Law* which states that the light falls off as the distance is squared.

Square wave   Alternating current with a square wave shape rapidly switched between positive and negative half cycles. In lighting, they are generated by an electronic ballast which enables discharge sources to be flicker-free.

Squeezer (USA)   A dimmer.

Stage box (USA)   A distribution box with sockets that accept a male connectors. Stage boxes are normally referred to by the number of sockets they have: one-hole, two-hole, four-hole, or six-hole boxes.

Stage extension (USA)   A high current extension cable. It has a male connector at one end and a single or twin at the other.

Stage left/right   The performers left and right as they face the audience.

Staging area   The area on the sound stage or location selected as a temporary place to keep the lighting equipment and technical equipment trolleys.

Stand   A telescopic floor mounted tripod device which provides a means of adjusting the height of luminaires above floor level. Can be manual lift, or by a geared wind-up system.

Stick-up (USA)   An extremely small, lightweight luminaire that can be taped to the wall.

Stinger (USA)   An extension cable usually fitted with Edison plugs and sockets.

Stirrup   Stirrup shaped receptacle, generally fitted at the base of extension arms and pantographs, allowing the attachment of luminaires by C clamps.

Stop   An f-stop or a t-stop (see *F-number*).

Strain relief   A rope tied to a cable to take the weight and reduce strain on electrical connectors.

Streaks and Tips (Trade name) (USA)   Cans of hair spray that are often handy for darkening reflective surfaces.

Strike   (1) To dismantle a set or to take down and put away a piece of equipment. (2) When referring to an arc or a discharge source, to strike the light means *turn it on*.

Strobe light   A light that creates short, bright, regular flashes of light at an adjustable speed. Speeds around 17 Hz are highly dangerous and can induce epileptic fits.

Stud   Term for piece of cylindrical metal which is attached to the yoke (*bail*) and used for mounting luminaires onto stands, etc (see *Spigot*).

Studio area   The total floor area contained within the walls of a studio which may not always be used as the acting area, due to fire lanes, etc.

Sub-master   A controller (usually a linear slider) on a dimmer board that allows manual control of groups, effects, cues, or channels.

Subtractive colour mixing   The removal of light of various wavelengths, by filtering or reflection, e.g. a magenta filter *subtracts* the green from the light path, whereas the pigment of yellow paint reflects the red and green components of the incident light but absorbs (*subtracts*) the blue. To change the colour of a light source for effect or colour correction, some form of coloured filter will be placed in the light path.

Suicide pin (USA)   An adapter with two male ends.

Sun gun   The term used for any small battery powered luminaire, originally a small tungsten source, now used to describe any tungsten or discharge source.

Swing (USA)   A crew member who performs the tasks of both grip and electrician, as needed.

System grounding (USA) (Neutral)   The grounding (earthing) of the electrical system by the neutral wire to the star point of the main power transformer and also to earth.

T-bone (USA)   A metal T-shaped base with a junior receptacle, used to place larger luminaires at ground level. In the United Kingdom known as *Turtle*.

T-stop   The f-stop is based upon the diaphragm aperture and focal length and does not account for overall transmission, therefore t-stops indicate the effective f-stop in terms of how much light passes through the lens system (see *F-number*).

Taco cart (Equipment trolley) (USA)   A special cart that carries grip equipment, such as C-stands, apple boxes, wedges, mounting hardware, and grip expendables.

Talent   On-camera people and subjects.

Telescope   A grid mounted device made from retractable sets of tubes that is used to suspend luminaires at varying heights in the studio. Older types of telescopes were driven by portable power tools, modern systems are generally equipped with integral electric motors.

Three-fer (USA)   An adapter that provides three female connectors from one male connector.

Three-phase   A type of alternating current that has three legs. The alternating voltage cycle of each leg is a third of a cycle apart (120°) (see *Harmonic distortion*, *Wye connected system*).

Three point lighting   Traditional lighting set-up using a key light, fill and back lights.

Three-riser (USA)   A stand that has three extensions.

Throw   Generally describes the direction of light from a luminaire and also the effective distance between the luminaire and the area being lit. The light arriving at the subject will also be influenced by the angle of incidence ($\cos \theta$).

Tie-in   The connection of temporary distribution cables to a facility's electrical service panel.

Tilt   Term describing the vertical movement, about a point, of luminaires or equipment. Can also refer to camera mounting heads.

Titan (USA)   A 350-A carbon arc luminaire manufactured by Mole Richardson. Known as Super Brute in United Kingdom.

Tower   A temporary platform usually made from scaffolding, on which to mount luminaires (see *Scaffold platforms*).

Tracing paper   Thin, translucent paper used to white out windows.

Transformer   Consists of a set of insulated windings on a laminated steel core that is used to transfer energy of a.c. Current transformers are used to sample high currents for feedback circuits in equipment such as dimmers and electronic control ballasts.

Translucent   A material that, although allowing the passage of light, does not allow a clear image to pass through.

Transmission   Given in percentage, is the amount of light passing through a material, particularly colour filters, scrims and diffusers. Its practical application is to give guidance as to the incident light level and exposure in stops, as an aid to balancing the overall lighting and hence the picture.

Tree   A tall stand or tower that has horizontal pipes on which luminaires can be hung. Used a great deal in theatre and concert lighting.

Tri-stimulus   The CIE system is based upon using a standard observer who is seated in front of a white screen. On one half of the screen is projected some arbitrary light source, on the other half of the screen is projected a combination of the three primaries. The observer has to adjust the intensity of the three primaries until both sides of the screen match exactly in colour and brightness. The amounts of red, blue and green used to match the arbitrary light source can be used to calculate *the tri-stimulus value* of the colour and this can be plotted on the CIE diagram.

Tripe   The groups of flexible cables from a theatre lighting bar to the permanent power outlets around the periphery of the stage area.

Trombone (USA)   Term for an adjustable Drop Arm (see also *Drop Arm*).

Truss   A framework, generally made from alloy bars together with cross bracing, to provide lightweight rigging structures. Trusses are used predominantly in TV temporary lighting rigs and concert lighting to support luminaires and other equipment at high level. The size of the truss dictates the amount of weight to be supported without dangerous deflection.

Tungsten halogen   Describes a family of lamps with either hard glass or quartz envelopes, *tungsten* filaments and *halogen* (usually iodine or bromine) fillings.

Tungsten halogen lamp   A lamp designed to maintain an almost constant colour temperature and a high lumen output throughout its life. The halogen cycle is a regenerative process that prevents the blackening of the inside of the bulb.

Turtle stand   A very low stand to position luminaires at ground level.

Tweenie (USA)   A 650 W Fresnel luminaire manufactured by Mole Richardson Co.

Twist-lock   A connector for which the plug inserts into the socket and then twists, locking the plug to the socket.

Two K   A colloquial term for a 2 kW spotlight.

Twelve-by (USA)   12 ft square butterfly, made from silk or net.

Ultraviolet (UV)   Ultraviolet radiation covers the range 4–400 nm and it begins at the short wavelength limit of visibility (violet) and extends to x-rays. It is divided into near (400–300 nm), far (300–200 nm) and extreme (below 200 nm). The near ultraviolet energy is known generally as blacklight.

Underwriters laboratory (UL) (USA)   An American independent test laboratory that ensures minimum safety standards of equipment.

Undo   A memory system feature for cancelling the last instruction and returning the console to its previous set-up.

Unilux (USA)   A manufacturer of strobe lighting equipment that can be synchronised to a motion picture camera shutter.

Up-fade   The portion of a fade that involves only channels that are increasing in level.

Variac   An auto-transformer dimmer.

VEAM connector   Multi-pin discharge source head feeder connectors and single conductor feeder cable connectors.

Velum   See *Tracing paper*.

Visible spectrum   The narrow band of electromagnetic radiation which lies between ultraviolet and infrared with wavelengths from 0.0004 mm (400 nm) to 0.0007 mm (700 nm) is detectable by the human eye and is known as light.

Visqueen (USA)   Plastic material used to protect equipment from rain and snow.

Volt (V)   A unit of electrical force. One volt is required to force one ampere of electricity though a resistance of 1 Ω.

Voltage drop   That loss of volts which occurs through energy wastage when a current passes through a cable or electronic device.

Volt-ampere (VA)   Voltage times current. In d.c., volts × amps = watts. In a.c. circuits, inductance and capacitance will introduce reactance, causing a discrepancy between the watts and volt-amperes (see *Power factor*).

Voltmeter   A meter used to measure voltage difference between two points in a circuit.

Wall sled (USA)   A luminaire-mounting device that hangs from the top of the set wall and rests against the wall.

Wall spreader   Hardware that mounts to either end of a piece of timber, creating a span from one wall to another from which luminaires can be hung.

Wash   General ambient light on the acting area.

Watt (W)   A unit of electrical power, the product of voltage and current.

Wattage   The power consumption measured in watts or more commonly kilowatts. Is used to rate the power of equipment such as lamps, luminaires and dimmer capacity.

Wedge   A triangular wooden block used to level dolly track.

Welding cable   A flexible electrical cable once widely used for power distribution. Welding cable is now prohibited, except for its use as an earth wire.

Western dolly (USA)   A flat-bed camera platform with large inflated tyres, steerable at one end and useful for moving heavy luminaires and cable.

Wiggy (USA)   A continuity or resistance-testing device.

Winch   Term used to describe either manual or motorised lifting equipment.

Wind-up stand   See *Crank-up Stand*.

Wire rope   Ropes formed from fine wires woven in complex patterns to give great strength.

Working lights   See *House lights*.

Wrap   The process of taking down luminaires and coiling cable that begins after the last shot of the day has been completed successfully.

Wye-connected system   A common type of three-phase transformer arrangement, also known as a *Star* system. Voltage reads 415 V (208 V) between any two of the phases and 240 V (120 V) between a phase and the neutral.

Xenon lamps   A discharge lamp which provides a very small source. It can be accurately aligned in an optical system to give a high output efficiency. There is a safety problem with xenon lamps, because of the high internal pressures which can be from 6 to 8 atmospheres when cold and 15–20 atmospheres when hot. The manufacturers recommend that protective gloves and goggles are worn when handling the xenon lamp and special precautions are taken when transporting it.

Xenon luminaire   A discharge luminaire that has a colour temperature of 5600 K. Because the arc is very small, the light output is extremely efficient.

Yoke   The suspension frame of a luminaire; possibly containing the drive mechanism for pan and tilt. Colloq. fork, stirrup, trunnion.

Zoom   Used in profile spots and scenic projectors, consisting of the relative movement of two lenses in an optical system to change beam width and focus.

Appendix II
World mains voltages

Country	Supply voltage	Supply frequency
Afghanistan	220	50
Albania	220	50
Algeria	127/220	50
Angola	220	50
Anguilla	110	60
Antigua and Barbuda	230	60
Argentina	220	50
Australia	240	50
Austria	230	50
Azores	220	50
Bahamas	120	60
Bahrain	230	50
Balearic Islands	220	50
Bangladesh	220	50
Barbados	115	50
Belgium	230	50
Belize	110/220	60
Benin	220	50
Bermuda	120	60
Bolivia	115/220/230	50
Botswana	230	50
Brazil	110/220	60
Brunei	240	50
Bulgaria	220	50
Burundi	220	50
Cambodia	220	50
Cameroon	220	50
Canada	120	60
Canary Islands	127	50
Cayman Islands	120	60
Central African Rep.	220	50
Chad	220	50
Channel Islands	230/240	50
Chile	220	50
China	220	50
Colombia	110	60
Congo	220	50
Costa Rica	120	60
Croatia	220	50

Table – *continued*

Country	Supply voltage	Supply frequency
Cuba	110/220	60
Cyprus	240	50
Czech Republic	230	50
Denmark	230	50
Djibouti	220	50
Dominican Rep.	110	60
Ecuador	120/127	60
Egypt	220	50
El Salvador	115	60
Eritrea	220	50
Estonia	220	50
Ethiopia	220	50
Fiji	240	50
Finland	230	50
France	230	50
French Guiana	220	50
Gabon	220	50
Gambia	220	50
Germany	230	50
Ghana	230	50
Gibraltar	240	50
Greece	220	50
Greenland	220	50
Grenada	230	50
Guadeloupe	220	50
Guatemala	120	60
Guinea Rep.	220	50
Guyana	120/240	50
Haiti	110	60
Honduras	110	60
Hong Kong	220	50
Hungary	220	50
Iceland	220	50
India	230	50
Indonesia	220	50
Iran	220	50
Iraq	220	50
Ireland	230	50
Isle of Man	240	50
Israel	230	50
Italy	220	50
Ivory Coast	220	50
Jamaica	110	50
Japan	100	50/60
Jordan	220	50
Kazakhstan	220	50
Kenya	240	50
Korea	220	60
Kuwait	240	50
Laos	220	50
Latvia	220	50
Lebanon	110/220	50
Lesotho	220	50
Liberia	120	60
Libya	127/230	50
Lithuania	220	50

Table – *continued*

Country	Supply voltage	Supply frequency
Luxembourg	220	50
Macau	220	50
Macedonia	220	50
Madagascar	127/220	50
Madeira	220	50
Malawi	230	50
Malaysia	240	50
Maldives	230	50
Mali	220	50
Malta	240	50
Martinique	220	50
Mauretania	220	50
Mauritius	230	50
Mexico	127	60
Monaco	127/220	50
Mongolia	127/220	50
Morocco	127/220	50
Mozambique	220	50
Myanmar	230	50
Namibia	220	50
Nepal	220	50
Netherlands	230	50
New Zealand	230	50
Nicaragua	120	60
Niger	220	50
Nigeria	230	50
Norway	230	50
Oman	240	50
Pakistan	220	50
Panama	110	60
Papua New Guinea	240	50
Paraguay	220	50
Peru	220	60
Philippines	125	60
Poland	220	50
Portugal	220	50
Puerto Rico	120	60
Qatar	240	50
Romania	220	50
Russia and its Reps.	220	50
Rwanda	220	50
Samoa	120	60
Saudi Arabia	127	60
Senegal	220	50
Seychelles	240	50
Sierra Leone	230	50
Singapore	220	50
Slovak Republic	220	50
Slovenia	220	50
Somalia	110/220/230	50
South Africa	220/230/250	50
Spain	220	50
Sri Lanka	230	50
St Vincent	230	50
Sudan	240	50
Suriname	127	60

Table – *continued*

Country	Supply voltage	Supply frequency
Swaziland	230	50
Sweden	230	50
Switzerland	230	50
Syria	220	50
Taiwan	110	60
Tanzania	230	50
Thailand	220	50
Togo	220	50
Tonga	240	50
Trinidad and Tobago	115	60
Tunisia	127/220	50
Turkey	220	50
Uganda	240	50
United Arab Emirates	220	50
United Kingdom	230	50
Uruguay	220	50
USA	120	60
Venezuela	120	60
Vietnam	220	50
Virgin Islands	110	60
Western Samoa	230	50
Yemen Arab Rep.	220/230	50
Yugoslavia	220	50
Zambia	220	50
Zimbabwe	220	50

Lamp tables

Incandescent lamps

In general, incandescent lamps for film, TV and theatre in Europe can be divided into three groups, having the codes of CP, P and T. The designations are given by the Lighting Industries Federation (LIF) and are broadly described as follows:

CP   Originally stood for Colour Photography, because the first lamps were imported from the USA by the film industry. All CP lamps are 3200 K and are single ended, ranging in size from 300 to 20 000 W.
P   This class of lamps are also 3200 K but they are linear, double ended types, ranging in size from 250 to 2000 W.
T   Indicates lamps designed for theatre, because they are of the order 2900–3000 K with an appropriately longer life, ranging in size from 500–2000 W.

The American National Standards Institute (ANSI) have a different coding system, being three letters arranged in alphabetical order. The cross reference table gives the equivalent types in both systems and can be used not only as a substitute guide, but also to help the user to find alternative lamps of different wattage and voltage for his luminaire. To do this, identify the lamp base and the Light Centre Length (LCL) and look for alternative lamps that have the same; but care must be taken not to exceed the maximum rated wattage of the luminaire as this will cause the lamp to overheat and shorten its life and can damage the housing and present a safety hazard. It is also extremely important that lamps designated as having 'pinch protection' should only be used in luminaires designed for them. (See Pinch protected lamps – Section 2)

The tables have been collated from many different manufacturers' catalogues so it is not an easy task to select one catalogue and expect to find that it provides information on all types of lamps, but a good wholesaler should have the required information, if you supply him with the code and the voltage required. When ordering lamps for Europe, be careful to specify 230 V or 240 V because if 230 V lamps are used at 240 V, the life will be reduced to only 60% of the manufacturers' stated life.

In the tables that follow the lamps' light centre lengths are given in millimetres, life is given in hours and the colour temperature is in Kelvin degrees.

1 Single ended tungsten halogen incandescent lamps

	European code (LIF)	USA code (ANSI)	Volts	Colour temp.	Life	LCL	Base
250 W	–	DYG	30	3400	15	36.0	GY 9.5
300 W	CP-81	FKW	120	3200	150	46.5	GY 9.5
	CP-81	FSL	230	3200	150	46.5	GY 9.5
	CP-81	FSK	240	3200	150	46.5	GY 9.5
	M-38	–	230/240	2900	2000	46.5	GY 9.5
500 W	T-25		230/240	3000	300	46.5	GY 9.5
	T-18	FRF	120	3050	400	46.5	GY 9.5
	T-18	GCV	230	3050	400	46.5	GY 9.5
	T-18	GCW	240	3050	400	46.5	GY 9.5
	CP-82	FRG	120	3200	150	46.5	GY 9.5
	CP-82	FRH	230	3200	150	46.5	GY 9.5
	CP-82	FRJ	240	3200	150	46.5	GY 9.5
	M-40	–	230/240	2900	2000	46.5	GY 9.5
	T-1	DNW	240	2900	200	55.5	P28s
	T-17	FKF	230/240	2950	750	55.5	P28s
	T-17	BTL	120	2950	750	55.5	P28s
	T-28	–	230/240	3000	300	55.5	P28s
	T-24	BTL	120	2950	750	55.5	P28s
	–	BTM	120	3200	150	55.5	P28s
	–	EHC	120	3200	300	60.5	G 9.5
	–	EHD	120	2900	2000	60.5	G 9.5
	–	EGN	120	3200	150	63.5	G 22
	–	EGE	120	2900	2000	88.9	P28s
575 W	HX600	FLK	115	3200	300	60.5	G 9.5
	HX601	FLK/LL	115	3000	1500	60.5	G 9.5
	6989P	GLC	115	3200	400	60.5	G 9.5
	6989P	GLA	115	3100	1500	60.5	G 9.5
600 W	–	DYS	120	3200	75	36.0	GY 9.5
	–	FMB	120	3050	2000	51.0	GY 9.5
	HX602	GKV	230/240	3100	300	60.5	GY 9.5
	6986P	–	230	3200	400	60.5	GY 9.5
	6986P	GKV	240	3200	400	60.5	GY 9.5
	6991P	–	230	3100	1500	60.5	GY 9.5
	6991P	GLB	240	3100	1500	60.5	GY 9.5
650 W	–	DYR	230/240	3200	50	36.0	GY 9.5
	–	DYS	120	3200	75	36.0	GY 9.5
		EKD	120	3400	25	36.0	GY 9.5
	T-26	FRE	120	3050	400	46.5	GY 9.5
	T-26	GCT	230	3050	400	46.5	GY 9.5
	T-26	GCS	240	3050	400	46.5	GY 9.5
	CP-89	FRK	120	3200	200	46.5	GY 9.5
	CP-89	FRL	230	3200	150	46.5	GY 9.5
	CP-89	FRM	240	3200	150	46.5	GY 9.5
	T-12/T21	–	230/240	3000	750	55.0	GX 9.5
	CP-23/CP-67	–	120	3200	100	55.0	GX 9.5
	CP-23/CP-67	FVD	230/240	3200	100	55.0	GX 9.5
	T-13	FKA	120	3000	750	55.5	P28s
	T-13	FKB	230/240	3000	750	55.5	P28s
	CP-51/CP-69	FKL	120	3200	100	55.5	P28s

Single ended tungsten halogen incandescent lamps – continued

	European code (LIF)	USA code (ANSI)	Volts	Colour temp.	Life	LCL	Base
	CP-51/CP-69	FKM	230/240	3200	100	55.5	P28s
	CP-49	–	230/240	3200	50	55.5	P28s
	–	FKR	230/240	3100	300	60.5	G 9.5
	–	FKV	120	3150	300	60.5	G 9.5
	CP-39/CP-68	FKG	120	3200	100	63.5	G22
	CP-39/CP-68	FKH	230/240	3200	100	63.5	G22
	–	DTA	120	3200	300	87.0	P40s
750 W	–	BTN	120	3000	750	55.5	P28s
	–	BTP	120	3200	200	55.5	P28s
	–	EHF	120	3200	300	60.5	G 9.5
	–	EHG	120	3000	2000	60.5	G 9.5
	–	EGR	120	3200	200	63.5	G22
	–	EGG	120	2900	2000	88.9	P28s
900 W	–	BVA	120	3200	75	44.5	GY 9.5
	–	DZJ	230/240	3200	75	44.5	GY 9.5
1000 W	CP-98	–	230/240	3200	125	46.0	GY 9.5
	T-11	–	120	3050	750	55.0	GX 9.5
	T-11	–	230/240	3050	750	55.0	GX 9.5
	T-19	FWP	230	3050	750	55.0	GX 9.5
	T-19	FWR	230/240	3050	750	55.0	GX 9.5
	CP-24	–	120	3200	200	55.0	GX 9.5
	CP-24	–	230/240	3200	200	55.0	GX 9.5
	CP-70	FVA	230	3200	200	55.0	GX 9.5
	CP-70	FVB	240	3200	200	55.0	GX 9.5
	T-14/T20	–	120	3050	750	55.5	P28s
	T-14/T20	FKD	230/240	3050	750	55.5	P28s
	CP-52	FKN	230/240	3200	200	55.5	P28s
	–	BTR	120	3200	250	55.5	P28s
	CP-77	FEL	120	3200	300	60.5	G 9.5
	CP-77	FEP	230/240	3200	300	60.5	G 9.5
	–	FCV	120	3200	300	60.5	G 9.5
	T-30	–	230/240	3000	750	63.5	G22
	CP-40/CP-71	FKJ	230/240	3200	200	63.5	G22
	–	EGT	120	3200	250	63.5	G22
	T-16	–	230/240	3050	750	87.0	P40s
	T-15/T23	FKE	230/240	3050	750	88.9	P28s
	–	EGJ	120	3200	500	88.9	P28s
	–	EWE	230/240	3200	250	88.9	P28s
	–	BVT	120	3050	500	100.0	P40s
	–	BVV	120	3200	250	100.0	P40s
	–	CYV	120	3200	250	127.0	G 38
	CP-106	–	230/240	3200	400	127	G38
	–	DSE	120	3200	500	N/A	E40s
1200 W	T-31	–	230/240	3050	400	63.5	G22
	CP-93	–	120	3200	200	63.5	G22
	CP-93	–	230/240	3200	200	63.5	G22
	T-29	–	120	3050	400	67.0	GX 9.5
	T-29	FWS	230	3050	400	67.0	GX 9.5
	T-29	FWT	240	3050	400	67.0	GX 9.5

Single ended tungsten halogen incandescent lamps – continued

	European code (LIF)	USA code (ANSI)	Volts	Colour temp.	Life	LCL	Base
	CP-90	–	120	3200	200	67.0	GX 9.5
	CP-90	–	230/240	3200	200	67.0	GX 9.5
1500 W	–	DTA	120	3200	300	87.0	P40s
	–	CWZ	120	3200	300	100.0	P40s
	–	CXZ	120	3200	300	127.0	G 38
	–	DSF	120	3200	750	241.0	E40s
1900 W (2 filaments: 1250 W + 650 W)							
	CP-105	–	230/240	3050	250	143.0	GX38q
2000 W	CP-43/CP-72	–	120	3200	400	70.0	GY 16
	CP-43/CP-72	FTM	230	3200	400	70.0	GY 16
	CP-43/CP-72	FTL	240	3200	400	70.0	GY 16
	CP-79	–	120/230/240	3200	350	70.0	GY 16
	CP-75	–	230/240	3200	400	75.0	G 22
	CP-53/CP-74	–	120	3200	400	87.0	P40s
	CP-53/CP-74	–	230/240	3200	400	87.0	P40s
	CP-28	–	230/240	3200	300	87.0	P40s
	CP-92	–	120	3200	400	90.0	G 22
	CP-92	–	230/240	3200	400	90.0	G 22
	–	BVW	120	3200	400	100.0	P40s
	CP-41/CP-73	FKK	230/240	3200	400	127.0	G 38
	–	CYX	120	3200	400	127.0	G 38
	CP-34	–	230/240	3200	300	127.0	G 38
	–	BWA	120	3200	500	127.0	G 38
	–	FWG	120	3200	500	128.0	E40s
	CP-59/CP-76	–	230/240	3200	300	133.0	E40s
	–	BWF	120	3200	400	133.0	E40s
	–	FWH	120	3200	500	171.0	E40s
2500 W	CP-91	–	120	3200	400	90.0	G22
	CP-91	–	230/240	3200	400	90.0	G22
	CP-94	–	230/240	3200	400	127.0	G 38
2500 W (2 filaments, each 1250 W)							
	CP-30	–	230/240	3200	300	143.0	GX 38q
3000 W	HX-48	–	120	3200	400	127.0	G38
	HX-48	–	230/240	3200	400	127.0	G38
3500 W	CP-107	–	230/240	3200	400	165.0	G38
3750 W (2 filaments: 2500 W + 1250 W)							
	CP-58	–	230/240	3200	300	143.0	GX 38q
5000 W (2 filaments, each 2500 W)							
	CP-32	–	230/240	3200	300	143.0	GX 38q
5000 W	CP-29/CP-85	–	230/240	3200	500	165.0	G 38
	CP-29/CP-85	DPY	120	3200	500	165.0	G 38
	CP-46	–	230/240	3200	400	165.0	G 38
	CP-46	ECN	120	3200	400	165.0	G 38

Single ended tungsten halogen incandescent lamps – continued

	European code (LIF)	USA code (ANSI)	Volts	Colour temp.	Life	LCL	Base
10 000 W	CP-80	–	230/240	3200	400	254.0	G 38
	CP-80	EBA	120	3200	400	254.0	G 38
	CP-83	–	230/240	3200	500	254.0	G 38
	CP-83	DTY	120	3200	500	254.0	G 38
20 000 W	CP-27	–	230/240	3200	500	420	G 38
	CP-99	BCM	230/240	3200	350	354	G 38

2 Special 'pinch protected' tungsten halogen lamps

The lamp manufacturers state that 'pinch protected' lamps should only be used in dedicated 'pinch protected' luminaires and under *no* circumstances should they be used in existing standard luminaires. This is because 'pinch protected' lamps have either a shorter 'light centre length' than normal or a higher wattage for the same LCL to enable manufacturers to design smaller luminaires. If used in standard luminaires over-heating of the lamp and/or housing could result, e.g. fitting a 'pinch protected' 2 kW lamp with a G 22 base into a standard 1 kW Fresnel which has the same base and the same LCL. The pinch temperature of a standard tungsten halogen lamp is typically 400°C, whereas 'pinch protected' lamps can work at temperatures up to 500°C.

Wattage	Ref. no	Volts	Col. temp	Life	LCL	Base
1000	6995 IBP	120/230/240	3200	250	46.5	GY 9.5
1200	6980 Z	80	3300	250	63.5	G 22 (see note)
2000	6994 MBP	120/230/240	3200	500	63.5	G 22
5000	6963 NBP	120/230/240	3200	525	127.0	G 38

Note: Especially developed for high output luminaires.

3 Double ended tungsten halogen incandescent linear lamps

	European code (LIF)	USA code (ANSI)	Volts	Colour temp.	Life	Length	End caps
250 W	P1/8	–	30	3400	12	78.0	R7s
300 W	–	EHM	120	2950	2000	78.0	R7s
400 W	–	EHR	120	2900	2000	78.0	R7s
420 W	–	FFM	120	3200	100	78.0	R7s
500 W	P2/30	FDF	120	3200	400	118.0	R7s
	K1	–	230/240	2900	2000	118.0	R7s
	–	FCL	120	3000	2000	118.0	R7s

Double ended tungsten halogen incandescent linear lamps – continued

	European code (LIF)	USA code (ANSI)	Volts	Colour temp.	Life	Length	End caps
625 W	P2/10	–	230/240	3200	200	189.0	R7s
	P2/10	–	120	3200	200	189.0	R7s
	P2/15	–	230/240	3400	75	189.0	R7s
650 W	P2/6	FAD	120	3200	100	78.0	R7s
	–	DWY	120	3400	25	78.0	R7s
750 W	–	EJG	120	3200	400	78.0	R7s
800 W	P2/13	DXX	230/240	3200	75	78.0	R7s
	P2/11	EME	230/240	3200	150	118.0	R7s
1000 W	–	DXW	120	3200	150	93.0	R7s
	P2/35	–	230/240	3200	150	93.0	R7s
	P2/28	FCM	120	3200	300	118.0	R7s
	P2/28	–	230/240	3200	300	118.0	R7s
	P2/29	FHM	120	3200	300	118.0	R7s
	P2/20	–	230/240	3200	300	118.0	R7s
	K4	–	230/240	3000	2000	118.0	R7s
	–	FFT	120	3200	500	167.0	R7s
	P2/7	EKM	230/240	3200	200	189.0	R7s
1250 W	P2/12	–	230/240	3200	200	189.0	R7s
1500 W	–	FDB	120	3200	400	167.0	R7s
2000 W	P2/27	FEX	230/240	3200	300	143.0	R7s
	–	FEY	120	3200	300	143.0	R7s

4   *PAR sealed beam incandescent tungsten halogen lamps*

	Wattage	LIF	ANSI	Volts	Col. temp	Life	Beam angle (°)	Base
PAR 36	650	–	FCX	120	3200	100	40 × 30	Ferrule cap
	650	–	DWE	120	3200	100	40 × 30	Screw terminal
	650	–	FBO	120	3400	30	25 × 15	Screw terminal
	650	–	FBE	120	5000	35	25 × 15	Screw terminal
PAR 64	500	CP-86	–	230/240	3200	300	10 × 7	GX16d
	500	CP-87	–	230/240	3200	300	11 × 9	GX16d
	500	CP-88	–	230/240	3200	300	21 × 10	GX16d
	1000	–	FFN	120	3200	800	10 × 7	GX16d
	1000	CP-60	EXC	230/240	3200	300	12 × 6	GX16d
	1000	–	FFP	120	3200	800	13 × 10	GX16d
	1000	CP-61	EXD	230/240	3200	300	13 × 10	GX16d
	1000	–	FFR	120	3200	800	25 × 14	GX16d
	1000	CP-62	EXE	230/240	3200	300	25 × 14	GX16d
	1000	–	FFS	120	3200	800	70 × 70	GX16d
	1000	CP-95	EXG	230/240	3200	300	70 × 70	GX16d

Discharge Lamps

CAUTION: When selecting an alternative discharge lamp consult the luminaire/ballast manufacturer or his representative for a suitable replacement. Lamps of the same rating may have different operating characteristics or may be 'hot restrike' (*instant restart*) which require higher ignition voltages.

1 *Double ended linear discharge lamps*

Wattage	Code	Lamp volts	Correlated colour (K)	Life (Hrs)	Maximum length (mm)	End Caps
HMI (OSRAM) hot restrike						
200	HMI 200 W	80	6000	300	75	X515
575	HMI 575 W/GS	95	6000	750	135	SFc10
1200	HMI 1200 W/GS	100	6000	750	230	SFc15.5
2500	HMI 2500 W/GS	115	6000	500	355	SFa21
2500	HMI 2500 W/S	115	6000	500	210	SFa21
4000	HMI 4000 W	200	6000	500	405	SFa21
6000	HMI 6000 W	123	6000	500	450	S25.5
12 000	HMI 12000 W	224	6000	500	470	S25.5
12 000	HMI 12000 W/GS	160	6000	500	470	S30
18 000	HMI 18000 W	225	6000	250	500	S30
HTI (Osram) hot restrike						
300	HTI 300 W/DE	100	6500	600	92	SFc10.4
MSI (Philips) hot restrike						
200	MSI 200 W	80	5600	300	75	X515
575	MSI 575 W	95	5600	750	145	SFc10.4
1200	MSI 1200 W	100	5600	750	230	SFc15.5.6
2500	MSI 2500 W	115	5600	500	355	SFa21.12
4000	MSI 4000 W	200	6000	500	405	SFa21.12
6000	MSI 6000 W	123	6000	350	450	S25 5×60
12 000	MSI 12000 W	225	6000	250	470	S25 5×60

2 *Single ended linear discharge lamps*

Wattage	Code	Lamp volts	Correlated colour (K)	Life (Hrs)	Light centre length (mm)	Base
HMI (Osram) hot restrike						
125	HMI 123 W	80	6000	150	26.7	Special
200	HMI 200 W/SE	70	6000	200	39.0	GZY 9.5
270	HMI 250 W/SE	50	6000	250	35.0	FaX 1.5
400	HMI 400 W/SE	67	6000	650	60.0	GZZ 9.5
575	HMI 575 W/SE	95	6000	750	70.0	G22
1200	HMI 1200 W/SE	100	6000	750	107.0	G38
2500	HMI 2500 W/SE	115	6000	500	127.0	G38
4000	HMI 4000 W/SE	200	6000	500	142.0	G38

Single ended linear discharge lamps – continued

Wattage	Code	Lamp volts	Correlated colour (K)	Life (Hrs)	Light centre length (mm)	Base
HTI (Osram) not instant restart						
150	HTI 150 W	90	6500	750	30	GY 9.5
HTI (Osram) hot restrike						
270	HTI 250 W/SE	45	4600	250	35	FaX 1.5
400	HTI 400 W/SE	55	4800	250	35	FaX 1.5
600	HTI 600 W/SE	95	5300	300	35	FaX 1.5
1200	HTI 1200 W/SE	100	6000	600	59	GY 22
2500	HTI 2500 W/SE	115	6000	600	85	G22
HSR (Osram) not instant restart						
400	HSR 400 W	67	5600	650	62	GX 9.5
700	HSR 700 W	72	6000	1000	75	G22
MSR (Philips) not instant restart						
400	MSR 400	70	5900	1000	62	GX 9.5
575	MSR 575/2	97	7200	1000	65	GX 9.5
700	MSR 700/2	72	7200	1000	75	G22 X42
1200	MSR 1200	100	5900	800	85	G22/30X53
1200	MSR 1200/2	100	7200	800	85	G22
MSR/SA (Philips) not instant restart						
400	MSR 400 SA	54	5600	750	36.5	GY 9.5
700	MSR 700 SA	70	5600	500	39	GY 9.5
1200	MSR 1200 SA	100	5600	750	59	GY 22
MSR/HR (Philips) hot restrike						
125	MSR 125 HR	80	6000	200	39	GZX 9.5
200	MSR 200 HR	70	6000	200	39	GZX 9.5
400	MSR 400 HR	70	6000	750	60	GZZ 9.5
575	MSR 575 HR	97	6000	1000	70	G22
1200	MSR 1200 HR	100	6000	1000	107	G38
2500	MSR 2500 HR	115	6000	500	127	G38
4000	MSR 4000 HR	200	6000	500	142	G38
6000	MSR 6000 HR	125	6000	300	210	GY38
MSD (Philips) not instant restart						
200	MSD 200	70	6000	2000	55	GY 9.5
200	MSD 200/2	70	6700	750	55	GY 9.5
250	MSD 250	94	6700	750	55	GY 9.5
250	MSD 250/2	94	8500	750	55	GY 9.5
575	MSD 575	97	6000	750	65	GX 9.5
700	MSD 700	72	6000	3000	85	G22
1200	MSD 1200	100	6000	750	85	G22
CSI (GE) not instant restart						
400	CSI.990201	100	4000	500	25.5	Special pin
1000	CSI.990221	77	4000	500	63.5	G22
CID (GE) hot restrike						
200	CID.990211	70	5500	150	36.5	Special pin
575	CID.990415	95	5500	500	52.0	G22

Single ended linear discharge lamps – continued

Wattage	Code	Lamp volts	Correlated colour (K)	Life (Hrs)	Light centre length (mm)	Base
1000	CID.990222	77	5500	500	63.5	G22
2500	CID.990431	100	5500	350	127.0	G38

3   PAR sealed beam discharge lamps

Wattage	Code	Lamp volts	Correlated colour (K)	Life (hrs)	PAR (1/8" units)	Base
CSI (*GE*) not instant restart						
1000	CSI 991222	77	3800	3500	64	G38
CSI (*GE*) hot restrike						
1000	CSI 991422/HR	77	3800	3500	64	G38
CID (*GE*) not instant restart						
1000	CID.991225	77	5500	1500	64	G38
CID (*GE*) hot restrike						
1000	CID.991425/HR	77	5500	1000	64	G38
1200	CID.991435/HR	100	5500	1000	64	G38

4   Special application discharge lamps

Wattage	Code	Lamp volts	Correlated colour (K)	Life (hrs)	Light centre length (mm)	Base
CDM (*Philips*) *Single ended* not instant restart						
70	CDM-T 70W/830	70	3000	6000	56	G12
70	CDM-T 70W/942	70	4200	6000	56	G12
150	CDM-T 150W/830	82	3000	6000	56	G12
150	CDM-SA/T 150/942	82	4200	6000	56	G12
CDM (*PHILIPS*) *Double ended* not instant restart						
70	CDM-TD 70W/830	70	3000	6000	57.1	RX7s
150	CDM-TD 150W/830	82	3000	6000	66.0	RX7s

Appendix IV
Luminaire performances

All beam sizes are given for the 50% beam angle light output figures.

Discharge sources (Fresnel lens)

Distance (m)	Spot Intensity (lux)	Beam size (m)	Flood Intensity (lux)	Beam size (m)
200 W				
4	5156	1.27	859	4.16
6	2291	1.90	381	6.24
8	1289	2.53	214	8.33
575 W				
4	12500	0.70	1250	4.00
6	5555	1.05	556	6.00
8	3125	1.40	313	8.00
10	2000	1.75	200	10.00
1.2 kW				
6	10278	1.16	1944	6.11
8	5781	1.54	1094	8.15
10	3700	1.93	700	10.20
12	2570	2.31	486	12.23
14	1888	2.70	357	14.27
16	1445	3.08	273	16.30
2.5 kW				
8	17187	1.19	1562	10.00
10	11000	1.49	1000	12.50
12	7638	1.78	694	15.00
14	5612	2.08	510	17.50
16	4297	2.38	390	20.00
18	3395	2.68	309	22.50
20	2750	2.97	250	25.00
4 kW				
10	30000	1.57	2000	9.97
14	15306	2.20	1020	14.00
18	9260	2.83	617	18.00
22	6198	3.46	413	21.94

Discharge sources (Fresnel lens) – *continued*

Distance (m)	Spot Intensity (lux)	Beam size (m)	Flood Intensity (lux)	Beam size (m)
26	4438	4.09	296	25.93
30	3333	4.72	222	29.91
6 kW				
14	24 439	1.84	1531	12.47
18	14 784	2.36	926	16.03
22	9897	2.88	620	19.60
26	7086	3.41	444	23.15
30	5322	3.93	333	26.71
34	4144	4.46	260	30.28
12 kW				
18	30 864	1.82	1543	18.74
22	20 661	2.23	1033	22.90
26	14 793	2.63	740	27.07
30	11 111	3.04	556	31.23
34	8650	3.44	433	35.40
38	6925	3.85	346	39.56
42	5669	4.26	283	43.73
18 kW				
20	24 500	2.97	1625	21.27
24	17 013	3.57	1128	25.50
28	12 500	4.16	829	29.77
32	9570	4.76	635	34.02
36	7561	5.35	501	38.28
40	6125	5.95	406	42.54
44	5061	6.54	336	46.79

Discharge sources (PAR)

	Intensity (lux)			
Distance (m)	Spot	Narrow flood	Flood	Super wide flood
1.2 kW PAR				
10	25 000	7250	2000	1100
15	11 111	3222	889	489
20	6250	1812	500	275
25	4000	1160	320	176
30	2777	806	222	122
2.5 kW PAR				
10	33 750	13 700	4500	2000
15	15 000	6088	2000	888
20	8438	3425	1125	500
25	5400	2192	720	320
30	3750	1522	500	222

Discharge sources (PAR) – *continued*

Distance (m)	Intensity (lux)			
	Spot	Narrow flood	Flood	Super wide flood
4 kW PAR				
10	45 000	16 200	6000	2500
15	20 000	7200	2667	1111
20	11 250	4050	1500	625
25	7200	2592	960	400
30	5000	1800	667	278
6 kW PAR				
10	71 750	35 700	12 200	6800
15	31 889	15 867	5422	3022
20	17 937	8925	3050	1700
25	11 480	5712	1952	1088
30	7972	3967	1356	756

Tungsten sources

Distance (m)	Spot Intensity (lux)	Beam size (m)	Flood Intensity (lux)	Beam size (m)
800 W Redhead				
4	2500	3.07	406	7.46
6	1111	4.60	180	11.19
8	625	6.15	102	14.90
2 kW Blonde				
4	13 500	1.63	1575	5.60
6	6000	2.44	700	8.40
8	3375	3.26	394	11.20
10	2160	4.07	252	14.00
12	1500	4.88	175	16.80

Distance (m)	Intensity (lux)		
	Narrow spot	Medium flood	Wide flood
575 W PAR			
6	4285	2516	1110
8	2410	1415	625
10	1542	906	400
12	1071	629	278

Tungsten sources – *continued*

Distance (m)	Intensity (lux)		
	Narrow spot	Spot	Wide flood
1 kW PAR			
8	5000	4218	1953
10	3200	2700	1250
12	2222	1875	868
14	1632	1378	638
16	1250	1055	488

Distance (m)	Spot Intensity (lux)	Beam size (m)	Flood Intensity (lux)	Beam size (m)
1 kW Fresnel				
4	4609	0.77	675	4.8
6	2048	1.16	300	7.2
8	1152	1.54	169	9.61
2 kW Fresnel				
4	11562	0.70	1462	4.53
6	5139	1.05	650	6.79
8	2891	1.40	366	9.05
10	1850	1.75	234	11.32
12	1284	2.10	163	13.58
5 kW Fresnel				
6	13889	1.31	2083	6.79
8	7812	1.75	1172	9.05
10	5000	2.20	750	11.32
12	3472	2.63	521	13.58
14	2551	3.07	383	15.80
10 kW Fresnel				
8	19531	1.40	2656	7.30
10	12500	1.75	1700	9.10
12	8680	2.10	1181	10.90
14	6378	2.45	867	12.80
16	4883	2.80	664	14.60
18	3858	3.15	524	16.40
20	3125	3.50	425	18.20

Softlights

Distance (m)	Intensity (lux)	Intensity (lux) (with eggcrate)
1.25 kW Softlight		
2	2700	2250
3	1200	1000
4	675	562

Softlights – *continued*

Distance (m)	Intensity (lux)	Intensity (lux) (with eggcrate)
2.5 kW Softlight		
4	1562	1234
6	694	548
8	391	309
5 kW Softlight		
6	1215	972
8	684	546
10	438	350

Projectors and follow spots

Distance (m)	Intensity (lux)	Beam size (m)
600 W Profile projector 19° Fixed		
10	1270	3.35
12	882	4.02
14	648	4.69
600 W Profile projector 36° Fixed		
6	1667	3.9
8	937	5.2
10	600	6.5

Distance (m)	Narrow Intensity (lux)	Beam size (m)	Wide Intensity (lux)	Beam size (m)
600 W Profile projector 15°/32° Zoom				
6	4278	1.58	2277	3.44
8	2406	2.10	1281	4.59
10	1540	2.63	820	5.74
12	1069	3.16	569	6.90
14	786	3.69	418	8.04
1200 W Profile projector 24°/40° Zoom				
6	3055	2.55	1667	4.37
8	1718	3.40	937	5.82
10	1100	4.25	600	7.28
1 kW Xenon follow spot 6°/15° Zoom				
32	4199	3.52	488	8.43
36	3318	3.96	386	9.48
40	2687	4.40	312	10.53
44	2221	4.84	258	11.59
48	1866	5.28	217	12.64

Fluorescent sources

Distance (m)	Intensity (lux)	Intensity (lux) (with eggcrate)
220 W Fill light		
3	585	503
4	329	283
5	211	182

Distance (m)	Intensity (lux)	Intensity (lux) (with eggcrate)	Intensity (lux) (with intensifier)
256 W Key light			
3	640	512	1152
4	360	288	648
5	230	184	414

Appendix V
Formulae and conversion tables

Most scientific measurements are made using the International System of Units (Systeme International d'Units) or SI for short.

The three basic units are the *metre*, *kilogram* and the *second*. From these are derived the whole range of units which cover the world of physics. For the ease of our readers we have picked out only those units which are applicable to the subject matter in this book.

Measurement of length

Basic unit: *metre* (m)
Other units:

centimetre (cm)	= one hundredth of a metre $(10^{-2}\,\text{m})$
millimetre (mm)	= one thousandth of a metre $(10^{-3}\,\text{m})$
nanometre(nm)	= one thousandth millionth of a metre $(10^{-9}\,\text{m})$

Measurement of area

Basic unit: *square metre* (m^2)
Other units:

square centimetre = one ten thousandth of a square metre $(10^{-4}\,\text{m}^2)$

Measurement of mass

Basic unit: *kilogram* (kg)
Other units:

gram (g)	= one thousandth of a kilogram $(10^{-3}\,\text{kg})$
tonne (t)	= one thousand kilograms $(10^{3}\,\text{kg})$

Measurement of force

Basic unit: *Newton* (N)
One Newton is the force required to impart an acceleration of $1\,\text{m/sec}^2$ to a mass of 1 kg.

Measurement of electric current

Basic unit: *ampere* (A)
Other units:
  milliampere   = one thousandth of an ampere (10^{-3} A)

Measurement of thermodynamic temperature

Basic unit: *kelvin* (K)
Note: The kelvin scale used the same interval of degrees as the Celsius scale. 'Absolute zero'
         on the kelvin scale is *minus* 273°C.
    Thus: $K = (°C) + 273$.

Measurement of light

	Physical units	Luminous units*
Total light output	Radiant flux (watts)	Luminous flux (lumens)
Light emitted in a specific (candelas) direction	Radiant intensity (watts per steradian)	Luminous intensity
Light emitted from a unit area in a specific direction	Radiance (watts/cm^2 per steradian)	Luminance (candelas/cm^2)
Light striking a unit area	Irradiance (watts/cm^2)	Illuminance (lumens/m^2 = lux)

* Note: Luminous units take into account the eyes' photopic response.

Electrical formulae

Ohms law states that the current (I) flowing in a circuit is directly proportional to the applied
voltage (V) and inversely proportional to the resistance (R), thus:

$$I = \frac{V}{R} \quad V = IR \quad \text{and} \quad R = \frac{V}{I}$$

Power (P) in the circuit is given by the product of voltage (V) and current (I). The unit of power is
the watt (W), thus:

$$P = V \times I \text{ watts}$$

alternatively as $V = IR$ therefore $P = I^2 R$ watts

as $I = \dfrac{V}{R}$ therefore $P = \dfrac{V^2}{R}$ watts

The above formulae are those used for direct current (d.c.) circuits.
    For alternating current (a.c.) circuits, the formulae only hold true when the circuit is purely
resistive. That is, the voltage and current are in phase with each other. If the circuit contains
inductance or capacitance the voltage and current will be out of phase to some degree.
    To allow for this discrepancy we have to modify the formulae as follows:
    In an a.c. circuit the ratio of applied voltage (V) divided by current (I) is called the imped-
ance (Z):

$$Z = \frac{V}{I}$$

The power is given by: $P = VI \cos \phi$ watts where ϕ is the phase difference between the current and supply voltage. *Cos ϕ is called the power factor (PF)*

The power factor is also given by:

$$\frac{\text{power in watts}}{\text{rms volts} \times \text{rms amperes}}$$

For most practical measurements:

$$PF = \frac{\text{kilowatts}}{\text{Kilovoltamperes}}$$

Electrical energy

This is the measurement of power used over a period of time.

Thus : Watts $\times$ seconds = watt-seconds or 'joules' (J)

$$1\,\text{kWh} = 1000 \times 3600 \text{ watt-seconds}$$

$$= 3\,600\,000\,\text{J}$$

For practical purposes the units most used are:

kilowatts $\times$ hours = kilowatt-hours (kWh)

Generally called a unit of electricity

(a) Single phase resistive current

Note: current *lags* applied voltage by $\frac{1}{4}$ cycle or 90°

(b) Single phase inductive circuit

Note: current *leads* applied voltage by $\frac{1}{4}$ cycle or 90°

(c) Single phase capacitive circuit

Figure AV.1 Single-phase sine wave

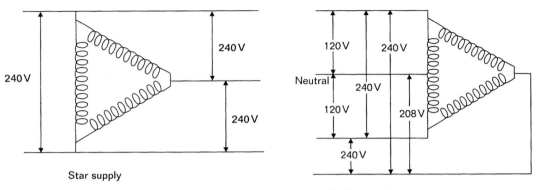

Star supply

Delta supply

Figure AV.2 Star and delta distribution

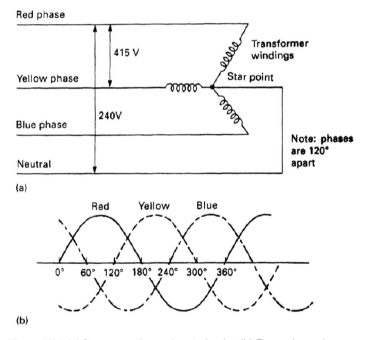

(a)

(b)

Figure AV.3 (a) Star connection and neutral point; (b) Three-phase sine wave

Conversion factors

Length
Inches × 25.4 = millimetres   Millimetres × 0.03937 = inches
Inches × 2.54 = centimetres   Centimetres × 0.3937 = inches
Feet × 0.3048 = metres   Metres × 3.281   = feet

Area
Sq. inches × 6.452 = sq. cms.   Sq. cms × 0.155   = sq. ins.
Sq. feet × 0.0929 = sq. metres   Sq. metres × 10.76 = sq. feet

Volume

Cubic ft. × 0.02832   = cubic metres
Cubic metres × 35.311 = cubic ft.

Mass

Pounds × 0.4536 = kilograms   kilograms × 2.205   = pounds
Tons × 1016   = kilograms   kilograms × 0.0009844 = tons
Tons × 0.9844   = tonnes   tonnes × 1.016   = tons

Pressure

1 Bar $= 100 \, kN/m^2$
1 Standard atmosphere $= 1.01325 \, bar = 101.325 \, kN/m^2$
1 lbf/in^2 $= 0.06895 \, bar = 6.895 \, kN/m^2$
1 Standard atmosphere $= 14.69 \, lbf/in^2$

Further reading

A–Z of Lighting Terms, Brian Fitt, Focal Press, 1999.

IEE Wiring Regulations, British Standards Institution.

BS 7909 (Code of Practice for Temporary Electrical Supply), British Standard Institution, 1998.

Control Systems for Live Entertainment, John Huntington, Focal Press, 2000.

Light and Colour, R. Daniel Overheim, David L. Wagner, John Wiley & Sons, 1982.

Light, Michael Freeman, Collins, 1990.

Light, Michael I. Sobell, University of Chicago Press, 1987.

Low Voltage Directive (73/23/EEC), European Community Publication, C199, July 1994.

Multiskilling for Television Production, Peter Ward, Alan Bermingham, Chris Wherry, Focal Press, 2000.

The EMC Directive (89/336/EEC), European Community Publication, L139, May 1989.

The Focal Encyclopaedia of Photography, Richard Zakia, Leslie Stroebel, Focal Press, 1995.

The Gaffers' Handbook, Harry C. Box (edited by Brian Fitt), Focal Press, 1998.

The Reproduction of Colour in Photography, Printing and Television, RWG Hunt, Fountain Press, 1988.

The Technique of Lighting for Film and Television, Gerald Millerson, Focal Press, 1991.

Index

9 780240 516516